Changing Employment Relations

Changing Employment Relations

BEHAVIORAL AND SOCIAL PERSPECTIVES

Edited by Lois E. Tetrick and Julian Barling

AMERICAN PSYCHOLOGICAL ASSOCIATION
WASHINGTON, DC

Published by the
American Psychological Association
750 First Street, NE
Washington, DC 20002

Copies may be ordered from
APA Order Department
P.O. Box 2710
Hyattsville, MD 20784

In the UK and Europe, copies may be ordered from
American Psychological Association
3 Henrietta Street
Covent Garden, London
WC2E 8LU England

Typeset in Minion by University Graphics, Inc., York, PA

Printer: Data Reproductions Corp., Rochester Hills, MI
Cover Designer: Berg Design, Albany, NY

Technical/Production Editor: Kathryn M. Lynch

Library of Congress Cataloging-in-Publication Data
Changing employment relations : behavioral and social perspectives /
    edited by Lois E. Tetrick, Julian Barling.
        p.   cm.
    Based on a conference sponsored by the Science Directorate of the
    American Psychological Association . . . [et al.].
    Includes bibliographical references and index.
    ISBN 1-55798-315-1
    1. Psychology, Industrial—Congress.   2. Work environment—
Congresses.   3. Industrial relations—Congresses.   4. Trade-unions—
Congresses.   5. Quality of work life—Congresses.   I. Tetrick,
Lois E.   II. Barling, Julian.
    HF5548.8.C354   1995
    331'.011—dc20   95-20863
                                                                                         CIP

British Library Cataloguing-in-Publication Data
A CIP record is available from the British Library.

Printed in the United States of America
First edition

APA Science Volumes

Taste, Experience, and Feeding: Development and Learning

Temperament: Individual Differences at the Interface of Biology and Behavior

Through the Looking Glass: Issues of Psychological Well-Being in Captive Nonhuman Primates

APA expects to publish volumes on the following conference topics:

Attribution Processes, Person Perception and Social Interaction: The Legacy of Ned Jones

Changing Ecological Approaches to Development: Organism–Environment Mutualities

Children Exposed to Family Violence

Conceptual Structure and Processes: Emergence, Discovery, and Change

Converging Operations in the Study of Visual Selective Attention

Genetic, Ethological and Evolutionary Perspectives on Human Development

Global Prospects for Education: Development, Culture, and Schooling

Maintaining and Promoting Integrity in Behavioral Science Research

Marital and Family Therapy Outcome and Process Research

Measuring Changes in Patients Following Psychological and Pharmacological Interventions

Psychophysiological Study of Attention

Stereotypes: Brain–Behavior Relationships

Work Team Dynamics and Productivity in the Context of Diversity

As part of its continuing and expanding commitment to enhance the dissemination of scientific psychological knowledge, the Science Directorate of the APA established a Scientific Conferences Program. A series of volumes resulting from these conferences is produced jointly by the Science Directorate and the Office of Communications. A call for proposals is issued twice annually by the Scientific Directorate, which, collaboratively with the APA Board of Scientific Affairs, evaluates the proposals and selects several conferences for funding. This important effort has resulted in an exceptional series of meetings and scholarly volumes, each of which has contributed to the dissemination of research and dialogue in these topical areas.

The APA Science Directorate's conferences funding program has supported 39 conferences since its inception in 1988. To date, 26 volumes resulting from conferences have been published.

WILLIAM C. HOWELL, PhD
Executive Director

VIRGINIA E. HOLT
Assistant Executive Director

Contents

Contributors

Jane E. Adams-Roy, Queen's University, Kingston, Ontario, Canada
Kristina Ahlén, The Swedish Institute for Work Life Research, Stockholm, Sweden
Sheldon Alexander, Wayne State University
Kathleen Barker, Bard College
Julian Barling, Queen's University, Kingston, Ontario, Canada
Anthony E. Carroll, Saint Mary's University, Halifax, Nova Scotia, Canada
Victor M. Catano, Saint Mary's University, Halifax, Nova Scotia, Canada
Paul F. Clark, Pennsylvania State University
Greg K. Cole, Saint Mary's University, Halifax, Nova Scotia, Canada
Cary L. Cooper, University of Manchester, Manchester, England
Annelies Daalder, University of Amsterdam, Amsterdam, The Netherlands
Clive J. A. Fullagar, Kansas State University
Daniel G. Gallagher, James Madison University
Michael E. Gordon, Rutgers—The State University of New Jersey
Sjoerd Goslinga, Free University, Amsterdam, The Netherlands
Mary Ann Hannigan, Wayne State University
Jean Hartley, University of London, London, England
Norman Hebert, Nova Scotia Government Employees Union, Dartmouth, Nova Scotia, Canada
C. Gail Hepburn, Queen's University, Kingston, Ontario, Canada
E. Kevin Kelloway, University of Guelph, Guelph, Ontario, Canada
Malgorzata A. Knap, Queen's University, Kingston, Ontario, Canada
Catherine A. Loughlin, Queen's University, Kingston, Ontario, Canada
Judi McLean Parks, University of Minnesota
Lucy A. Newton, Berry College
Sandra L. Robinson, New York University
Lynn M. Shore, Georgia State University

Robert R. Sinclair, Wayne State University

Anders Sjöberg, The Swedish Instititute for Work Life Research, Stockholm, Sweden

Valerie J. Sutherland, The Centre for Business Psychology, a joint venture between the Manchester School of Management and Coopers & Lybrand, U.M.I.S.T., Manchester, England

Magnus Sverke, The Swedish Institute for Work Life Research, Stockholm, Sweden

Lois E. Tetrick, Wayne State University

Gerrita van der Veen, Free University, Amsterdam, The Netherlands

Acknowledgments

A book such as this would not be possible without the contributions of the authors as well as a number of other individuals and organizations. First, directly or indirectly, all of the participants of the conference on which this book is based provided stimulating discussions that helped to frame the issues addressed in the chapters. Second, the multiple sponsors of the conference were key in making the conference and this resulting book happen. These sponsors were the Science Directorate of the American Psychological Association; the College of Labor, Urban, and Metropolitan Affairs at Wayne State University; the Departments of Psychology at Wayne State University and Queen's University; and the George Meany Center for Labor Studies.

Introduction

Part of the relatively short history of industrial and organizational psychology has been the story of change—more specifically, the story of how organizations and their employees have to respond and react to social changes. Almost without fail, these changes have been described as "profound" or accorded similar loftiness. Today's business climate is no exception. Firms are being faced with increased globalization of industry, and many organizations and employees throughout the world face similar changes in the employment relationship. For example, many organizations are increasing their use of contingent workers and reducing their long-term commitment to employees. At the same time, employees are finding their jobs have fundamentally changed, with increased emphasis on team structures, employee involvement, and empowerment initiatives.

This book examines the changes in the employment relationship from a behavioral and social sciences perspective, including theoretical and empirical works from the United States, Canada, the United Kingdom, Sweden, and The Netherlands. Although each chapter focuses on issues primarily from a single country, the commonalities concerning the increased use of contingent workers, the changing terms of the psychological contract of employees with their employers, and declining union representation are striking. Part One, Understanding the Nature of Change, focuses on understanding the nature of the changes that are occurring in employment relations, the effects of these changes, and the implications of these changes for future psychological research. Given the situation as described in Part One, Part Two, Meeting the Challenges of Change, addresses the challenges for organizations in managing these changes to achieve productivity and ensure the well-being of employees. The major focus of the chapters in this part of the book is on adapting to these changes primarily in union environments.

In Part One the nature of global changes in employment relations is described. Hartley (chapter 1) sets the stage by presenting a discussion of changes in the economic, political, and social spheres that are leading to changes in production processes, organizational structure and climate, job design, employee characteristics and attitudes, employment conditions, and the home–work interface. One aspect of the changing employment relationship, part-time employment, discussed by Hartley, is further explored by Barker (chapter 2). As both of these chapters indicate, the trend toward short-term, tenuous employment relationships is common throughout North America as well as in European countries with advanced industrial economies. Barker further discusses the implications of workplace divisions based on employment status (contingent or peripheral workers versus permanent or core employees). She suggests several avenues for future research that will allow us to better understand the ways moral exclusion may be associated with various forms of contingent employment in such areas as health and safety risks, social distancing, denigration, muzzled protest, and the accumulation of deficit.

The shift in attachment or commitment suggested by both Hartley and Barker is further explored by Alexander, Sinclair, and Tetrick (chapter 3). Viewing the employment relationship as an exchange relationship with mutual obligations occurring on the part of both the employer and the employee, Alexander et al. draw on organizational justice theory to explain individuals' attachment to their employers and extend this theoretical perspective to the relationship between employees and their unions. They further suggest that both employer and union strategies can affect justice perceptions that define and maintain the employment relationship.

Another common concern about the employment relationship is the notion of mutual obligations between the employer and employee. Earlier chapters have suggested that there have been fundamental shifts of employers away from such obligations as job security, commitment, and loyalty to the individual employee. To the extent that these changes are enacted unilaterally by the employer, employees may sense that their psychological contract with the organization has been violated. Robinson (chapter 4) presents data examining the consequences of perceived violations in the psychological contract. As is consistent with the chapter by Alexander et al., she suggests that organizations need to attend to the employees' perceived obligations within the employment relationship and that they can attempt to strategically manage these obligations to minimize the negative ramifications of violations of the psychological contract.

Change is generally recognized to be a potential source of stress and is alluded to in the first four chapters. Sutherland and Cooper (chapter 5) specifically address the consequences of changing employment relations and work conditions and subsequent stress among blue-collar workers. One approach that has been suggested to alleviate much of this stress is empowerment. Sutherland and Cooper provide a discussion of some of the pitfalls of empowerment initiatives that may actually result in increased stress rather than resulting in increased control and reduction of stress.

One issue raised by Sutherland and Cooper (and authors of earlier chapters as well) is the issue of occupational safety and health. The next two chapters in the book empirically address occupational health and safety issues. Adams-Roy, Knap, and Barling (chapter 6) suggest that potential managers are being inadequately trained in safety and health issues at the very time when such issues may be critical, given the trend toward increased contingent work and decreased emphasis on training in general. Loughlin, Hepburn, and Barling (chapter 7) demonstrate that future managers' attitudes toward occupational health and safety can be modified. Therefore, because occupational safety and health is a continuing, if not growing, concern, these two chapters suggest potential interventions in organizations.

One generally agreed on aspect of the employment contract is the provision of fringe benefits by employers. The present employment climate suggests two contradictory trends: increases in the provision of certain benefits to attract and retain employees and the reduction of certain benefits to reduce labor costs. Sinclair, Hannigan, and Tetrick (chapter 8), drawing on social exchange theory, present empirical evidence as to the role of benefit coverage and individuals' attitudes toward their employers.

In addition, in unionized work environments, the union may be viewed as being responsible for obtaining and preserving benefits for the membership; therefore, Sinclair et al. also examine the relation between benefit coverage and attitudes toward the union.

In Part Two, it is demonstrated that the changing employment relationship, although having an impact on employers and employees, also has potential impact on the organizations that represent workers (e.g., labor unions), including union members' attitudes toward their unions and participation in union activities. With the decline in unionization in the United States and some European countries, unions have become increasingly concerned with developing and maintaining their members' commitment as well as their own perceived legitimacy. The next three chapters in the book present theoretical and empirical evidence on the relationship between union instrumentality, perceived legitimacy, and union participation. On the basis of their analysis of U.S. union members, Shore and Newton (chapter 9) examine the relations between alienation from the union, perceived union instrumentality, loyalty to the union, and participation in union activities. Ahlén (chapter 10) and Sverke and Sjöberg (chapter 11) also examine the relationship between union instrumentality and participation among Swedish union members. Ahlén's analysis draws on union members' political efficacy experiences and their perceptions of union legitimacy, whereas Sverke and Sjöberg draw on instrumentality and value congruence to predict union membership behaviors and participation. Although they differ in theoretical orientation and focus on different countries, these chapters, taken together, suggest several common themes. First, unions as organizations are experiencing changes and are being affected by the changing employment relationships experienced by their members. Second, union members' attitudes are influenced by their perceptions of their relations with their union and the union's performance in representing their interests. Finally, participation in union activities and membership behaviors are, at least in part, a function of members' attitudes and attachments with the union itself.

Three additional chapters examine the issue of union participation in The Netherlands and Canada. Daalder (chapter 12) poses a parallel issue to the use of contingent and part-time workers in organizations by examining union participation among women and part-time workers in The Netherlands. Van der Veen and Goslinga (chapter 13), also using a Dutch sample, examine the predictability of participation in an industrial action (e.g., strike, work stoppage, and demonstration). Whereas the data presented in both of these chapters are correlational, Catano, Cole, and Hebert (chapter 14) describe a quasi-experiment that demonstrates that union commitment can be developed through a theoretically based intervention. Taken together, these three chapters suggest theoretical and empirical results from which labor organizations can develop strategies to influence members' attitudes and participation.

The chapters described so far have examined union participation from various theoretical perspectives, but one dissimilarity is evident. There does not appear to be a generally consistent and accepted definition of union participation. Fullagar, McLean Parks, Clark, and Gallagher (chapter 15) and Kelloway, Catano, and Carroll (chapter 16) raise the question as to what is meant by union participation and take a look at measurement issues surrounding union participation. Empirical evidence is presented in both chapters to test whether union participation should be conceptualized as a unidimensional, hierarchical concept or as a multidimensional construct possibly reflecting the multiple facets of union citizenship behavior. It is clear that further theoretical and empirical work is needed to resolve this debate.

Finally, we conclude the book with Gordon, Barling, and Tetrick's chapter outlining some remaining challenges to understanding the impact of the changing employment environment on employing organizations, employees, and unions (chapter 17). In a book such as this, it is impossible to present all of the factors that necessitate these changes. What is encouraging is that there appear to be several common themes across disciplines, theoretical perspectives, and countries. All of the authors have made suggestions for areas of future research. It is our hope that this collection will stimulate interesting and relevant research on the changing employment relationship and its consequences for organizations and employees. Such examination will provide useful answers to the challenges facing employers, employees, and trade unions.

PART ONE

Understanding the Nature of Change

Challenge and Change in Employment Relations: Issues for Psychology, Trade Unions, and Managers

Jean Hartley

Major shifts in the economic, political, and social spheres are having profound implications for employment and employment relations. These transformational changes require psychologists to reflect on and possibly refocus their research agendas to take into greater account the impact of change, uncertainty, and insecurity. The first section of this chapter examines changes in Western industrialized societies (especially the United Kingdom) that are leading to changes in production, work organizations, jobs, job-holders, employment conditions, and the home–work interface. The second section examines in more detail the consequences of these profound changes for the theory and practice of employment relations, arguing that psychologists have a great deal to offer in understanding the extent and stability of current changes in employment relations and in contributing to the understanding of employees' experiences of uncertainty. Throughout, I emphasize major points using examples from my current research in the banking industry in the United Kingdom to represent the kinds of research questions that might be fruitfully explored by psychologists in the field. This research helps to illustrate some opportunities for psychological contributions to the understanding of growing forms of employment and new types of employee.

CHANGES IN THE ECONOMIC, POLITICAL, AND SOCIAL SPHERES

There have been major changes and upheavals in the economic, political, and social context of organizations and of employment over the last decade. Some might say that these changes have been evident for a longer period, with a long trend of deindustrialization among Western industrialized societies such as the United States and the United Kingdom (e.g., Blackaby, 1979) and the increasing impact of free market societies. However, there appears to be an increasing scale, scope, and pace of change that has important implications for employment and for employment relations. How far should our theories of organizational psychology adapt to reflect these upheavals, which include increasing levels of uncertainty for organizations and for individuals? How do we incorporate the processes of change, complexity, and uncertainty into our theories of behavior in organizations? This represents a major challenge for organizational psychologists and may require new theories and approaches to thinking about behavior in the context of change and uncertainty.

This is not the place to fully develop the theoretical bases of these economic, political, and social changes. Here, I draw on the work of Benington and Taylor (1993) and other commentators to sketch some of the key changes that are having a profound effect on employment. These trends are drawn from an analysis of the United Kingdom, but there are some similarities with other Western industrialized countries such as the United States and Canada.

The Economic Context

A key change over the last decade has been the global restructuring of production. With the internationalization of capital has come a further reorganization of production. There is a debate among economists and sociologists as to how far industrialized economies are moving from a Fordist to a post-Fordist system of production. Clegg (1990) described the Fordist labor process as "semi-automatic assembly line production on the Detroit model" (p. 177). The Fordist process of production is based on mass production of standardized products for mass markets. The labor process is intensive and highly mechanized, with an organizational structure and culture that are hierarchical and control centered. Post-Fordist production (and consumption) is based on flexible, small-batch production, customized for particular markets. It requires a different organizational logic and possibly different employment relations.

Another development that is having, and will continue to have, a major impact on employment and employment relations is the internationalization of trade and the regrouping and new development of trading blocs. The integration of the European market is a significant economic development that is likely to have major impacts, through restructuring, on the number, type, and location of jobs (see Baine, Benington, & Russell, 1992; Ceccini, 1988). The impact on growth, stability, and change of the North American Free Trade Agreement, the Asian–Pacific Economic Cooperation forum, and General Agreement on Tariffs and Trade, now subsumed by the World Trade Organization, also promises to be significant. Some consequences of these organizations and agreements could be less predictability in world markets, more uncertain trading, and the strong likelihood of production overcapacity, leading to mergers of organizations and increasing concentration of economic activity and power.

Boom, slump, and recession face most industrialized societies, with, in the United Kingdom, two major periods of recession in the last 15 years. Recession has meant the closure of businesses, the loss of jobs, and increasing insecurity for many who survive downsizing and change (Hartley, Jacobson, Klandermans, & van Vuuren, 1991; Turner, 1995). Economists are saying that the peaks and troughs of economic activity are becoming less predictable.

Economic changes have contributed to changes in the structure of employment, which have been documented in detail by economists and sociologists (see, e.g., Gallie, Marsh, & Vogler, 1994; Millward, Stevens, Smart, & Hawes, 1992). These changes reflect both the differential impact of economic changes on industrial sectors and groups of employees and also organizational attempts to develop greater flexibility.

There has been a shift of jobs from manufacturing to the service sector (i.e., the decline of manufacturing, especially "smokestack" industries, and the growth of jobs in the service sector). Over the 10-year period prior to 1988, manufacturing in the United Kingdom went from 31% to 23% of jobs in the economy, and the downward trend is continuing. There have also been changes in the composition of the workforce, with a loss of full-time jobs traditionally undertaken by men (in the United Kingdom, around 0.3 million between 1984 and 1994) and an increase in full-time jobs taken by women (0.7 million new jobs in the same period) as indicated in the Labour Force Survey (1995). Part-time employment is the fastest growing sector of employment. In the United Kingdom, employees working part-time rose from 15.5% of the workforce in 1971 to 26% in 1991, and the Institute for Employment Research estimated that the trend will continue to 32.3% by the year 2001 (Trade Union of Congress [TUC], 1994). Some employers now talk of "key-time" rather than part-time working to signify the importance of such employment to their businesses. Part-time employment has risen significantly more for women than for men. Whereas women constitute 87% of the part-time workforce, the number of part-time jobs taken by men is increasing (Labour Force Survey, in press). The trend for both full- and part-time jobs is predicted to continue so that it is probably only a matter of time before more women are employed than men. Related to this is the trend toward part-time jobs, most of which are still undertaken by women. These changes have major implications for managers, for trade unions, and for employment relations because the typical worker is increasingly more likely to be a woman working part-time in a bank or in catering than it is to be a man working full-time in a car factory. The membership opportunities, but also challenges, for trade unions lie in attracting such workers—who are not, by tradition, trade union joiners—into the union.

Unemployment also has been at a high level in the United Kingdom for more than a decade (despite 29 changes in the definition of unemployment [Fryer, 1995], which means that official figures are underestimates of the underlying levels of unemployment). Official unemployment now stands at just under 10% (Central Statistical Office, 1995). It is not just the level but the length of unemployment that is of concern: In 1979, 25% of the unemployed had been in that state for more than a year, but the figure had risen to 41% in 1988. The restructuring referred to earlier suggests that job losses and unemployment will continue at high levels in the United Kingdom and in many other industrialized countries.

Furthermore, there is a dramatic increase in insecure and temporary employment, brought about partly by the casualization of employment (i.e., employees being hired on more casual, temporary, and ad hoc contracts) and also because of the economic uncertainties faced by work organizations (see also Barker, chapter 2, this volume). There were 157,000 temporary employees in the United Kingdom in 1994, which represented a 10% increase over the previous year (Labour Force Survey, 1995). For example, a recent survey in the United Kingdom found that 44% of employees were "very" or "fairly" concerned about losing their job in the next 12 months (Industrial Relations Services Employment Trends, 1993). Job insecurity is a matter of increasing concern for employees as organizations become leaner and strive for greater competitiveness (Hartley et al., 1991). Insecurity can arise through organizational difficulties in survival, but it can also arise because of technological and other organizational changes. Temporary employment has increased largely because of the casualization of the labor market, with an increase in employees on fixed-term contracts, an increase in those working on a self-employed basis, and the contracting-out of many services in both the private and public sectors. There has been discussion of the notion of the core and periphery workforces (e.g., Millward et al., 1992), the externalization of work (e.g., Pfeffer & Baron, 1988), and the shamrock organization (Handy, 1985), which has three "leaves": permanent core employees, a set of subcontractors, and a group of part-time and temporary workers (this last is currently the fastest growing area of employment). These illustrate the trend toward a peripheral workforce who may be poorly paid and on fixed-term, temporary, or even "on call" employment. Part-time workers still constitute a major part of those in insecure employment (Baine et al., 1992). In the United Kingdom the casualization of employment has been supported by legislation removing barriers to the free market, including the abolition of wages councils and the removal of many employment rights of protection against unfair dismissal.

The Political Context

In the United Kingdom in particular, but also in many European countries, there has been a dominance of New Right ideologies for the last decade and a half. New Right politicians, who have been in control of national government in the United Kingdom for some time, value the private market above all other organizational relationships and have been antagonistic to what they see as impediments to the operation of those markets. The emphasis is on the rights of the individual rather than the rights or responsibilities of the collective. In the United Kingdom, the aim has also been to centralize power at the national government level and to "roll back" the state from other areas of the economy.

Related to the dominance of such ideologies is the privatization and the marketization of the public sector. In the United Kingdom, major public corporations concerned with steel, coal, rail, and telecommunications have been or are due to be sold off to the private sector. A similar shift is happening in many other European countries. Such trends toward privatization are also evident in Canada and the United States. This may cause considerable employment uncertainty in parts of the public sector, such as local government, health, and the civil service, where the future of jobs is unknown, or where market forces push down wages, make some jobs redundant, and casualize others.

Importantly, there has also been a series of attacks on both trade unions and the professions, reducing their power, scope, and legitimacy through legislation (Crouch, 1995; Dickens & Hall, 1995; Millward et al., 1992). In the United Kingdom, legislation has made trade union organization more difficult and trade union action problematic and liable to severe financial penalties (e.g., Lewis & Simpson, 1982). The professions (trade unions by another name in some ways) have also been undermined by the UK government, intent on removing what they perceive as barriers to the free workings of the market (e.g., Young, 1989). The consequences of legislative change for trade unions have been very severe in the

United Kingdom. Trade union membership has declined dramatically (Waddington, 1992).

Overall, the political developments over the 1980s and early 1990s have not been favorable to trade unions, especially in the United Kingdom. The Social Chapter of the Treaty of Maastrict of the European Union, aimed at providing employee rights to information, health and safety, and occupational benefits, has not been endorsed by the UK government.

The Social Context

Europe is also experiencing deep demographic change: notably the aging of the population. (This is also occurring in North America.) The proportion of people aged over 65 across the European Union countries is predicted to rise dramatically between 1985 and 2025 (Baine et al., 1992). The worker-to-pensioner ratio in the United Kingdom is set to fall by 35% between 2000 and 2030 (Baine et al., 1992). A rapidly aging population structure and a decrease in the proportion of wage-earners to dependents means that there will be a smaller workforce providing for an elderly population, with a consequent shift in services, in organizational markets, and in jobs.

We have also been witnessing, over a long period of time, changes in the nuclear family and in household composition. There are changes in the patterns of parenting, with a doubling of the number of lone parents between 1973 and 1989 (Employment Department, 1993). One in five families is now headed by a single parent (*Social Trends*, 1993). There are also more reconstituted families, with step-relations in the household. There are more (and a growing proportion of) single-person households, not all of whom are pensioners (Baine et al., 1992). The changes in the nuclear family and parenting have considerable implications for our assumptions about who is in paid employment and under what pressures and motivations. This could have profound consequences for employment relations, raising issues of equality and the home–work interface that have not been widely considered previously.

In the United Kingdom, we have also witnessed the development of polarization and poverty on a scale not seen since before the Second World

War (Benington & Taylor, 1993). Those who are employed have become wealthier (on average) over the last 15 years, whereas those outside or on the edge of employment have had reductions in incomes and living standards. The number of children living in poverty has tripled in Britain in the last 15 years, leaving Britain the European Union nation with the third highest rate of child poverty (Benington & Taylor, 1993). Poverty overall in Britain (i.e., including unemployed and older people) is only surpassed by Portugal of the European Union countries (Benington & Taylor, 1993). One of the consequences of polarization and poverty in the United Kingdom is that the impact of losing or leaving employment is now much more severe than it was previously.

Overall, the changes in the economic, political, and social contexts represent an increase in the scale, scope, and pace of change that organizations and individuals are having to deal with. Of course, change and uncertainty have always existed in organizations and in employment, but I would like to suggest that the scale, scope, and pace of change is now such that it represents a quantum shift in the experience of change. The economic context in particular indicates that uncertainty and change are likely to continue, with major impacts on individuals in employment, on employee–organization linkages, and on the management of organizations.

The Psychological Context

Many research questions become apparent as one considers the effect of these rapid changes. How do the uncertainties of the marketplace affect the well-being of families? As the workforce ages, are fewer chances for advancement available to younger workers? How will jobs, services, and taxation shift to meet the needs of elderly individuals? How do changes in family structure affect employment relations? For example, is there a difference in union joining among single parents and families in which there is a female head of household? To what extent does the desire for family flexibility and maintenance of family structures contribute to the increase in the number of part-time workers?

On the organizational level, how would a shift to post-Fordist production affect employment relations for employers and employees more accustomed to the Fordist system? How do mergers and downsizing affect worker morale and union joining and participation? How do affected companies restructure themselves and their internal systems to maximize production and minimize adjustment problems for employees? How do blue-collar workers adapt to the decline in manufacturing and assembly-line work? What types of retraining would be most effective for this group? How well could former manufacturing workers adapt to careers in the growing service sector?

In the public sector, as governments move to privatize some of their work, how are public employees affected? When public service sector jobs, once thought to be more stable and secure than those in the private sector, are eliminated, how do employees adapt? How do the newly privatized organizations restructure themselves to become more financially competitive?

One side effect of economic uncertainty appears to be an increase in the use of part-time staff as a mechanism for controlling costs. How does the trend toward part-time work affect an employee's ability to negotiate for equitable work terms? Psychologists could examine whether, and how, institutions are changing to accommodate part-time workers or whether unions must respond to the unmet needs of this growing population. The ramifications of the shift to part-time work pose many worthwhile research questions as one of many changes that have an impact on work organizations, on employment, and on employment relations.

AN EMPIRICAL EXAMPLE OF CHANGES IN THE BANKING INDUSTRY IN THE UNITED KINGDOM

My own ongoing work may illustrate some of the opportunities for psychologists in this area. To determine how part-time work affects union joining and participation, I initiated a study in which I chose to focus on a group of employees in a white-collar service area, the banking industry, with a relatively high level of part-time jobs and in an industry that is undergoing considerable change and restructuring, including job losses in some areas and growth in others. The finance industry also has the fastest growth in part-time employment (TUC, 1994). The target group of employees is those for whom trade union membership, although accepted in the industry, is not an automatic activity. If trade unions are to recruit, they will need to recruit among such employees. If managers wish to develop policies relating to trade union recognition for employees, this may increasingly be a significant group. This research examines the attitudes toward trade unions among part-time employees in the United Kingdom. The study began as a small project concerned with the impact of changes in employment relations but has grown through strong interest from both employers and the trade union involved. In particular, the focus of this research concerned social influences within the workplace on the decision to join a union or not join. Empirically, there is still relatively little research on trade union joining and membership in the United Kingdom (but see Guest & Dewe, 1988; Hartley, 1992b).

Theoretically, the issue of union joining and membership is valuable for several reasons. There is a need to develop theory that is process oriented, which means theorizing union joining and membership as a process of socialization in the workplace (while accepting external predisposing influences such as family and education). There is a need to recognize the importance of social factors within and outside of the workplace in the joining decision: for example, the influence of social identities about being a union member or not, and of being a member of a group separate from management (what is often called "them and us" identity), as well as the social influences of management and colleague approval. The inclusion of social factors in the modeling of union joining might help to modify the overly individualistic and rational decision-making theories of union joining that currently exist.

In the research overall, social influences are conceived in terms of four factors: family background; workplace social identity (both union identity and employee identity, although only the second is reported in this chapter); social networks in the workplace; and social approval from managers and colleagues. This chapter reports only on family background and employee identity; the other measures of social influence are reported elsewhere (Hartley, in press). The research here also examines differences between union members and nonmembers rather than within-group differences based on (for union members) degree of involvement or level of union commitment, which are reported elsewhere (Hartley, in press).

The overall model of union membership being used in this research is indicated in Figure 1, although, as stated above, not all features of this model are being reported in this chapter. In this chapter, I examine differences between union and nonunion members among the full- and key-time (part-time) employees in terms of demographic variables, job and organization attitudes, family background and social identity ("them and us"), and union beliefs about the instrumentality and autocracy of trade unions in general.

Respondents and Setting

The results reported here relate to a bank chosen for research purposes because in its back office function of check processing, it employs large numbers of part-time (or key-time) staff. (The full research study includes a finance house as an additional study site.) A full 79% of the bank's check-processing staff work key-time at seven sites across England in clerical, data inputting, and other computer-related functions. The average length of working week for the key-time employee is 16 hours. Two thirds of the key-time staff work only in the evenings, between 4 p.m. and midnight, which is when each center is busiest, working against tight deadlines to prepare checks for clearing with other banks the following day in London. Each center is a "greenfield" (totally newly built) site, with most key-time staff recruited for the new operations, and some full-time staff coming from other operations within the bank. Although in some respects this organization represents the newer forms of employment (women working part-time in a service industry and operating under flexible hours for the benefit of the employer), in its organization of production it is highly Taylorist: There is a strict division of labor with clear rules about procedures, detailed supervision, and a mass-production activity. The only difference from a traditional Fordist organization is the flat hierarchy—only three

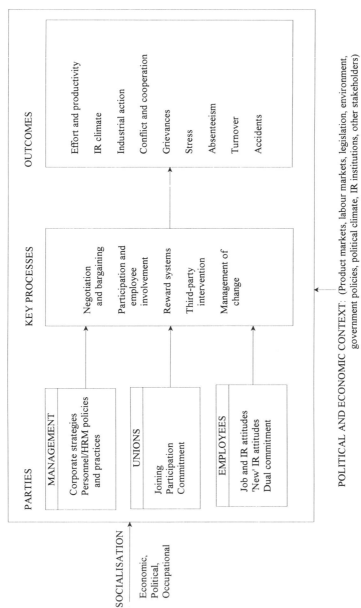

ORGANISATION

PARTIES | KEY PROCESSES | OUTCOMES

MANAGEMENT
Corporate strategies
Personnel/HRM policies and practices

UNIONS
Joining
Participation
Commitment

EMPLOYEES
Job and IR attitudes
'New' IR attitudes
Dual commitment

Negotiation and bargaining

Participation and employee involvement

Reward systems

Third-party intervention

Management of change

Effort and productivity

IR climate

Industrial action

Conflict and cooperation

Grievances

Stress

Absenteeism

Turnover

Accidents

SOCIALISATION
Economic,
Political,
Occupational

POLITICAL AND ECONOMIC CONTEXT: (Product markets, labour markets, legislation, environment, government policies, political climate, IR institutions, other stakeholders)

Figure 1

Model of union joining used in this research. HRM = human resource management; IR = industrial relations.

levels of management (although much control can be exercised through information technology, which provides details of each employee's productivity and error rates by the hour).

Measurement of Variables Related to Union Membership

There is little research from a psychological perspective on the impact of employment category (full-time vs. part-time) on union joining and membership (Barling, Fullagar, & Kelloway, 1992, cited two papers, one of which concerned male part-timers; although see also Daalder, chapter 12, this volume). It is known from analysis of aggregate union membership figures that part-timers are much less likely than full-timers to join a union in the United Kingdom (e.g., Green, 1990), but some of this effect is due to structural factors such as opportunities to work in locations where unions exist. Are there differences in attitudes, intentions, or social influences on joining that are related to employment category? Do key-timers differ from full-timers in their motivations for joining or not joining?

To assess these questions, a survey was distributed to a 40% sample of the bank's staff. The survey consisted of a 140-item questionnaire (slightly fewer questions for nonmembers), mainly consisting of 5-point Likert scales, using both established and original scales to measure job satisfaction, organizational commitment, attitudes toward and trust in management, union identity, "them and us" identity, views of trade unions in general and in this workplace, union commitment, and reasons for joining or not joining the trade union, participation levels, and attitudes. A total of 662 employees below the manager level in seven check processing centers in England received the survey. Staff were given time during work to complete the questionnaire, which they were told was a study of attitudes toward employment relations in the 1990s by a university researcher. Both the trade union and the company agreed to the distribution of the questionnaire. In addition, 30 interviews were conducted with both full-time and key-time staff in three of the centers. Staff returned 587 usable questionnaires, for a response rate of 88.7%. The sample closely matched the population in terms of gender (men constituted only 13% of the workforce) and employment status (full- or key-time), with 79% of the popu-

lation being key-time (part-time) workers. Details of the research measures are available on request from the author.

Results and Discussion

An important question is whether key-timers have a similar propensity to join the union compared with full-timers. The results show that the proportions of key-time employees in the union are similar regardless of gender and that the same is true of the proportions of full-time employees: Twenty-seven percent of female key-timers and 22% of male key-timers are in the union, whereas for full-timers the figures are considerably higher, with 74% of women and 72% of men being members of the union. The results are therefore highly significant by employment category but not by gender.

This result confirms other research into trade union membership and attitudes (e.g., Deshpande & Fiorito, 1989; Green, 1992; Kochan, 1979), also reported by Barling et al. (1992): that gender is not a predictor variable of trade union attitudes or of intention to join the union. As Barling et al. noted, "[membership] differences are more likely a function of the unequal distribution of males and females within different jobs in the workplace, and the considerable challenges in organizing part-time, temporary, 'female' jobs" (1992, p. 34). This suggests that the shift in the economy from "male" to "female" jobs may be less important than the shift from full- to part-time jobs. However, further research would be needed to be certain of this. On the issue of gender, I also note Barling et al.'s (1992) concern that gender differences may emerge in different areas of trade union activity such as participation (although, again, how much is due to structural employment and domestic position rather than motivation and attitudes is unclear).

Given the low level of unionization among key-time employees and the much higher level for full-timers, in any analysis of the processes that encourage or discourage union membership it seems wise to treat these two groups as separate. Therefore, some analyses based on differences between union members and nonmembers were conducted for key-time employees separately from full-time employees. The comparisons are based

on the model introduced earlier (see Figure 1). Analyses reported here are based solely on responses from women, that they constitute the large majority of the sample (87%) and that this avoids any possible confounding effects of gender in these bivariate analyses.

The results are reported in Table 1. Looking first at the key-time group, there are a number of demographic variables that distinguish union members from nonmembers. The union members are more likely to be in an older age category and to have worked for the bank longer (this may reflect earlier employment in a full-time capacity in the bank in other operations), and they are also less likely to have a significant economic role in their household (less likely to be a sole earner rather than a main, joint, or contributory earner). Having children to care for has no effect on their union membership, although there is some restriction of range because most key-timers have children and, as found in the interviews, that is an important reason for their working key-time, especially in evening-based employment. Job grade is also not important as a predictor of union membership (although most key-timers are clustered in the lower grades, and so again there is some restriction of range).

The demographic results for women working full-time show some differences in predictors of union membership. Here, job grade is significant, with those in higher grades more likely to be members (a finding supported by other research; see, e.g., Barling et al., 1992). The finding about economic role is similar to the finding for key-timers, but no other demographic predictors are significant. In fact, there are few demographic differences among women working full-time that relate to union membership, unlike among key-timers. Future exploration of the data might examine whether the key-timers group contains different subgroups according to whether the employee is a career returner or a woman who has taken little or no time away from employment.

The results in relation to social influence in the workplace at this stage are available only for family background and for social identity. Key-timers, whether union member or nonmember, report no difference in their perceptions of the union interest level of each parent (on a 5-point scale ranging from *not a union member* to *committed member*). The questions about

Table 1

Results of Analyses Comparing Union Members and Nonmembers Among Women Working Key-Time and Women Working Full-Time

Variable	Women working key-time	Women working full-time
Demographic		
Age	Union members older	*ns*
Grade	*ns*	Union members higher grade
Length of service	Union members longer service	*ns*
Economic role	Union members less likely to be sole earner in household	Union members less likely to be sole earner in household
Children	*ns*	*ns*
Social influences		
Family background	*ns*	Union members more likely to report union-active father
	Union members more likely to have another member in household	Union members more likely to have another member in household
Social identity	Union members stronger sense of "them and us"	*ns*
	Union members stronger sense of union as a group	*ns*
Job attitudes		
Job satisfaction	Union members less satisfied	*ns*
Career	*ns*	*ns*
Organization attitudes		
Management relations	Union members less positive about management group skills	*ns*
Trust in management	Union members less trusting	Union members less trusting
Company commitment	*ns*	*ns*

Table 1 (cont.)

Results of Analyses Comparing Union Members and Nonmembers Among Women
Working Key-Time and Women Working Full-Time

Variable	Women working key-time	Women working full-time
Union beliefs		
Instrumentality of union	Union members see union as instrumental in achieving benefits	Union members see union as instrumental in achieving benefits
Big labor image	Union members less concerned about image	Union members less concerned about image

NOTE: *ns* means nonsignificant on statistical tests (*t* test and chi-square as appropriate). Full details available from author.

social identity are revealing: Key-time union members report a stronger sense of "them and us" compared with key-time nonmembers. However, this difference did not occur for full-timers, where "them and us" identity does not distinguish union members and nonmembers. Social identity issues in the workplace do not have such an impact for full-time employees.

On job and organization attitudes, union members among the key-timers are less job satisfied (both on the total measure and on a number of its facets) than their nonunion counterparts. However, as has been noted (Hartley, 1992b), although this may predict union membership, it does not in itself provide a satisfactory explanation for joining a union. Key-timer union members are also less trusting of management, both in its abilities and in its intentions. They are also less complimentary about the skills of their managers in interpersonal relations. Interestingly, there are no differences in the level of commitment to the company between key-time union members and nonmembers. As an aside, the results also indicated that key-timers in general are not less committed than full-timers in general to the company.

By contrast, there are few differences on job and organization attitudes between union members and nonmembers among the full-time employees. Only the variable of trust in management shows union members to be less trusting. Clearly, job and organization attitudes play a potentially larger role in the making of union members among key-timers than they do among full-timers in this organization.

The results on union attitudes show that union members in both employment categories see unions as having a positive role to play in bringing about benefits and managing change. Also, union members are less likely to see unions as autocratic.

Although these are only preliminary results, they do suggest that the examination of differences between key- and full-time employees is worth pursuing, although differences based on gender are unlikely to be important. There are more, and different, predictors of union membership among key-time staff than there are among full-time staff. There are indications, from the data reported here, of greater dissatisfaction on a number of variables among the key-time union members as compared with the full-time union members, and the reasons for this need to be examined further.

PSYCHOLOGICAL CONTRIBUTIONS TO THE UNDERSTANDING OF EMPLOYMENT RELATIONS

A number of commentators have described some of the profound consequences of change for employment relations in Western nations over the last decade (e.g., Hartley & Stephenson, 1992; Kochan, Katz, & McKersie, 1986; Millward et al., 1992). These include a decline in trade union membership; the narrowing sphere of influence of trade unions at the workplace, organization, and national levels; the advent of human resource management; the increase in nonunion companies in industrialized countries; the increased interest in the production and personnel techniques and ideas of large Japanese companies; the move to create greater flexibility in the workforce; the promotion of individualism; and a reduction in major forms of industrial conflict, especially strikes. However, although these changes have been described by industrial relations writers, and to a lesser extent, psychologists, I argue that the changes have been insufficiently set in the context that maps out the consequences for individuals, for organizations, and for employment relations.

For example, in my ongoing study discussed here, there were more and different predictors of union membership among part-time workers when compared with full-time workers (see Table 1). This phenomenon implies that only by taking context into account can unions, employers, and psychologists recognize and respond to such differences.

The decline of trade union membership and activity across the United Kingdom, the decline of collective bargaining, and the apparent reduction in conflict might lead us to the conclusion that employment relations are of little relevance to the modern, competitive organization and that the study of employment relations is anachronistic or obsolete. I believe this would be a mistaken view both because of the quality of the evidence and because of the way the subject of employment relations is defined (Hartley, 1992a). Psychologists have a great deal to offer here. The time has never been richer to conduct research with trade unions and on employee–organization linkages. There are great challenges for researchers and practitioners in the field. There has been a burgeoning of interest from psychologists, despite the apparent difficulties of the area (see Barling et al., 1992; Gordon & Nurick, 1981; Hartley & Kelly, 1986).

The idea that employment relations is dead—or dying—does not take into account the existing evidence or the pressing need to interpret the changes we have already witnessed. There are different views about both the extent and the stability of the changes in employment relations. Our theories about what has happened so far will affect our theories about the increasing pace and scope of change and uncertainty on future employment relations. There is no doubt that there is enormous change taking place in employment relations, but the questions we are left with are how permanent are the changes and also what is replacing traditional industrial relations. Psychology has a contribution to make to assessing the scope and especially the degree of permanence of changes in relations between employees and management. As some of the psychological research on the "new industrial relations" points out (e.g., Guest, 1989; Kelly & Kelly,

1991), we need to assess how far some of the changes (such as reduced levels of major conflict) or claimed improved relations at greenfield sites are due to compliance or to commitment. In other words, are the apparently improved relations between employees and managers due to pragmatic recognition of the changed balance of power? Or are there genuine changes in attitudes and motivation as a result of better management styles and practices? Any assessment of the stability or longevity of change requires the evaluation of the extent to which attitudes, beliefs, and values have changed on the part of managers and of employees—and a theoretical explanation of why those changes have occurred. Kelly and Kelly (1991) suggested that theories of intergroup behavior, including contact theory, realistic conflict theory, and self-perception theory, may be relevant here.

As another example, psychology might also be deployed in assessing the extent to which the high productivity, company commitment, and improved industrial relations behavior reported on many greenfield sites are due to stable or temporary change. Is the effect of the Hawthorne kind? That is, is the impact due to the high initial interest from managers and commentators rather than the effect of the changes per se? Will we see a decline in production and industrial relations when such plants are well established (as, in fact, Kochan and Verma have suggested, as reported in Kochan et al., 1986)? Psychology can also contribute to understanding the kinds of relations that are replacing or supplementing, in some quarters, traditional collective bargaining and other industrial relations practices. Psychology is a key discipline in the theory and practice of human resource management, for example.

The field of employment relations is much broader than has traditionally been defined by industrial relations scholars of the institutional school (e.g., Dunlop, 1958; Flanders, 1965). It would be a severe mistake to see the field as limited by the boundaries of collective bargaining, strikes, and workplace trade union militancy. Whereas in the 1950s collective bargaining was seen as a great social invention able to institutionalize industrial conflict (e.g., Dubin, 1954; Kornhauser, Dubin, & Ross, 1954), in more recent years it has become the prerogative of a smaller and smaller group of employees in industrialized societies. Collective bargaining can be seen

as largely a phenomenon of Fordist or highly bureaucratized organizations, covering large workplaces, often in manufacturing or in large-scale
service organizations, where male manual workers worked full-time and
continuously for their working lives. Although such employment relations
continue to be highly important, they no longer represent the heartlands
of the employment experience for many. We need employment relations
theories that cover the part-time waitress, the student working in a bar on
an occasional basis, and the staff who work in supermarkets, leisure parks,
and gas stations. In the words of Keenoy (1985), everyone who is in employment has got an industrial relation.

Mapping the Field of the Psychology of Employment Relations

The broader picture can be encompassed with a definition of the field as
"the processes of control over work relations" (Hyman, 1975, p. 31). Hartley and Kelly (1986) noted that

> more and more industrial relations as a field of study is coming to
> recognise that there are individual as well as collective aspects in the
> control of the employment relationship. . . . Control may be exer-
> cised by various individuals and parties using a variety of techniques
> and tactics. (p. 162)

As I have argued elsewhere (Hartley, 1992a), this does not imply that psychology can address issues only at the individual level. Indeed, the field of
the psychology of employment relations may be criticized for being insufficiently social and collective in its orientation. The point is that employment relations can be seen as both formal and informal processes in
employment; as concerned with individuals, groups, and organizations;
and as increasingly about motivation and influence as well as control.

My attempt to map the field of employment relations is provided in
Figure 2. This outlines where psychology has and could contribute to the
field of employment relations. It is not intended to be definitive but to
show areas of current and potential enquiry. The focus is on behavior and
social processes within the organization, because this is the locale of most

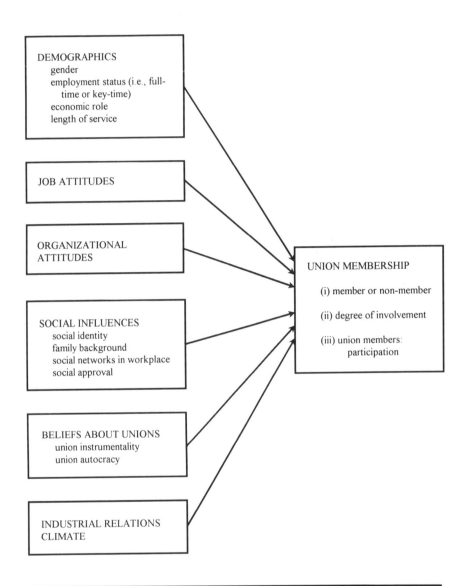

Figure 2

The field of the psychology of employment relations. From "The Psychology of Industrial Relations," by J. F. Hartley, in C. L. Cooper and I. T. Robertson (Eds.), *International Review of Industrial and Organizational Psychology* (pp. 201–243). Copyright 1992 by John Wiley and Sons. Reprinted with permission.

work by psychologists (although the field should not be theoretically limited by this empirical fact). In terms of theory, the central concerns are with the processes of conflict and cooperation, and the mixed motives of accommodation and of competition that lie behind the interdependence and power relations between the parties. The parties themselves (employees and employees' organizations, managers and their organizations, and the state, although the last is not directly represented in the figure) are also of considerable interest.

Figure 2 also indicates the role of the environment, in terms of the economic, political, and social context that has been discussed in this chapter. The scale, scope, and pace of change in the environment means that the context is significant for psychological research into employment relations. We are experiencing changes in forms of organization, changes in the type of employee (increasing numbers of women entering the labor force, increasing proportions of unemployed men), changes in employment conditions (more casualized and peripheral working, more part-time work), and changes in the home–work interface (more employed women carrying responsibility for families while being heads of households). These changes will have important consequences for our research agenda for the future: a stronger interest in new forms of employment and new types of employee. This, of course, includes the study of part-time (key-time) employees and other types of contingent workers, because of the burgeoning of this type of employment in Western industrialized societies, as well as a greater consideration of the impact of job insecurity on employees' feelings and behaviors at work, including interactions between managers and employees (both may be experiencing insecurity).

The changes in the economic, political, and social contexts also have major implications for managers and for trade unions. Employers and managers have to develop policies and practices that take into account the changing capacities, needs, and demands of the workforce and that take into account the rising insecurity and changing psychological contracts. If employees have to become more flexible for the firm to remain competitive, then what are the consequences for the levels of commitment and investment made by employees in their organization? For trade unions also, the changes in employment and employees means they will no longer be able to rely on traditional joining and participation behaviors of full-time workers in large factories and offices. What are the consequences for trade unions and for managers of having more flexible but also less stable workforces? The model of union membership and participation that I used in my study is a graphic example of the numerous variables affecting membership that are vulnerable to contextual change (see Figure 1).

How will power relations between employees, trade unions (where they exist), and managers be changed by uncertainty about the future? Some earlier research I have conducted suggests that the consequences of insecurity are not straightforward in their impact on employment relations: Employees may feel more insecure and less powerful, but managers may also feel a loss of power through being in thrall to the market and competitive pressures (Hartley et al., 1991). My research also has suggested that it is the job, not the job holder, that is likely to be a significant source of the differences between groups. All of these elements underline the necessity for psychologists to undertake research that is structurally grounded and that takes organizational and wider contexts into account before drawing conclusions about personal aptitude, preference, or ability. In addition, as change and uncertainty continue apace, researcher involvement with practitioners in working to understand change may also lead to more collaborative methodologies than psychologists have traditionally used.

CONCLUSION

In this chapter I argue that changes in the economic, political, and social spheres are having, and will continue to have, major impacts on employment and for employment relations. The scale, scope, and pace of change are such that they represent a quantum leap in the amount of change with which people and organizations are having to deal. We are witnessing major changes in organizations, in types of job and job conditions, in types of job-holder, and in types of relations between home and work. Changes especially in the economic sphere suggest that organizations and employees will be living with much higher levels of uncertainty than in the past.

This is likely to have major implications for employment relations, only some of which are we starting to realize.

Already, employment relations have been transformed in many Western industrialized countries over the last decade and a half. Trade union power, influence, and activity have declined—in some countries dramatically—industrial action and militancy on a large scale have declined, and collective bargaining is no longer such a central institution providing benefits for employees. Instead, we have witnessed the development of more individualized forms of management influence and control. Further changes may be anticipated as organizations, employees, and their representatives attempt to cope with continuing changes, less stable workforces, and increasing insecurity over jobs and employment.

These changes present challenges and opportunity for researchers, for trade unions, and for managers, although some of the changes may not be comfortable, desired, or desirable. As psychologists, we have a role to play in mapping, understanding, and theorizing about the change processes and about the impact of uncertainty on organizations, employee–organization linkages, and individual well-being.

REFERENCES

Baine, S., Benington, J., & Russell, J. (1992). *Changing Europe.* London: National Council for Voluntary Organizations.

Barling, J., Fullagar, C., & Kelloway, E. (1992). *The union and its members.* New York: Oxford University Press.

Benington, J., & Taylor, M. (1993). Changes and challenges facing the UK welfare state in the Europe of the 1990s. *Policy and politics, 21*, 121–134.

Blackaby, F. (1979). *Deindustrialisation.* London: Heinemann.

Ceccini, P. (1988). *1992: The benefits of a single market.* Aldershot, England: Wildwood House.

Central Statistical Office. (1995). *Monthly digest of statistics* (Vol. 595, p. 31). London: Her Majesty's Stationery Office.

Clegg, S. (1990). *Modern organizations.* Newbury Park, CA: Sage.

Crouch (1995). The state: Economic management or incomes policy. In P. K. Edwards (Ed.), *Industrial relations: Theory and practice in Britain* (p. 229). Oxford, England: Basil Blackwell.

Deshpande, S. P., & Fiorito, J. (1989). Specific and general beliefs in union voting models. *Academy of Management Journal, 32,* 883–897.

Dickens, L., & Hall, M. (1995). The state: Labour law and industrial relations. In P. K. Edwards (Ed.), *Industrial relations: Theory and practice in Britain* (p. 255). Oxford, England: Basil Blackwell.

Dubin, R. (1954). Constructive aspects of industrial conflict. In A. Kornhauser, R. Dubin, & A. Ross (Eds.), *Industrial conflict.* New York: McGraw-Hill.

Dunlop, J. (1958). *Industrial relations systems.* New York: Holt, Rinehart & Winston.

Employment Department. (1993, August). Families, work and the use of childcare. *Employment Gazette,* pp. 361–369.

Flanders, A. (1965). *Industrial relations: What is wrong with the system?* London: Faber.

Fryer, D. (1995). The bereft agency? *The Psychologist, 8,* 265.

Gallie, D., Marsh, C., & Vogler, C. (1994). *Employment and unemployment.* London: Oxford University Press.

Gordon, M. E., & Nurick, A. J. (1981). Psychological approaches to the study of unions and union–management relations. *Psychological Bulletin, 90,* 293–306.

Green, F. (1990). Trade union availability and trade union membership in Britain. *Manchester School of Economic and Social Studies, 58,* 378–394.

Green, F. (1992). Recent trends in British trade union density. *British Journal of Industrial Relations, 30,* 445–458.

Guest, D. E. (1989). Human resource management: Its implications for industrial relations and trade unions. In J. Storey (Ed.), *New perspectives on human resource management* (pp. 41–55). London: Routledge & Kegan Paul.

Guest, D. E., & Dewe, P. (1988). Why do workers belong to a trade union? A social psychological study in the UK electronics industry. *British Journal of Industrial Relations, 26,* 178–194.

Handy, C. (1985). *The future of work.* Oxford, England: Basil Blackwell.

Hartley, J. F. (1992a). The psychology of industrial relations. In C. L. Cooper & L. Robertson (Eds.), *International review of industrial and organizational psychology* (Vol. 7, pp. 201–243). New York: Wiley.

Hartley, J. F. (1992b). Trade union membership and joining. In J. F. Hartley & G. M. Stephenson (Eds.), *Employment relations: The psychology of influence and control at work* (pp. 163–183). Oxford, England: Basil Blackwell.

Hartley, J. F. (in press). Ideology and trade union participation in the UK. In P. Pasture (Ed.), *The lost perspective? Trade unions and ideology in Europe*. Aldershot, England: Avebury.

Hartley, J. F., Jacobson, D., Klandermans, B., & van Vuuren, T. (1991). *Job insecurity: Coping with jobs at risk*. Newbury Park, CA: Sage.

Hartley, J. F., & Kelly, J. E. (1986). Psychology and industrial relations: From conflict to co-operation? *Journal of Occupational Psychology, 59*, 161–176.

Hartley, J. F., & Stephenson, G. M. (1992). Introduction: The psychology of employment relations. In J. F. Hartley & G. M. Stephenson (Eds.), *Employment relations: The psychology of influence and control at work* (pp. 1–16). Oxford, England: Basil Blackwell.

Hyman, R. (1975). *Industrial relations: A Marxist introduction*. London: Macmillan.

Industrial Relations Services Employment Trends. (1993, May). Fear of redundancy. *Industrial Relations Review and Report, 541*, 7.

Keenoy, T. (1985). *Invitation to industrial relations*. Oxford, England: Basil Blackwell.

Kelly, J. E., & Kelly, C. (1991). "Them and us": Social psychology and "the new industrial relations." *British Journal of Industrial Relations, 29*, 25–48.

Kochan, T. (1979). How American workers view labor unions. *Monthly Labor Review, 102*, 23–31.

Kochan, T., Katz, H., & McKersie, R. (1986). *The transformation of American industrial relations*. New York: Basic Books.

Kornhauser, A., Dubin, R., & Ross, A. (Eds.). (1954). *Industrial conflict*. New York: McGraw-Hill.

Labour Force Survey. (1995). *Quarterly Bulletin, 11*, 24.

Labour Force Survey. (in press). *Quarterly Bulletin*.

Lewis, R., & Simpson, B. (1982). Disorganising industrial relations: An analysis of Sections 2–4 and 10–14 of the Employment Act 1982. *Industrial Law Journal, 11*, 227–244.

Millward, N., Stevens, M., Smart, D., & Hawes, W. (1992). *Workplace industrial relations in transition*. Aldershot, England: Dartmouth.

Pfeffer, J., & Baron, J. (1988). Taking the workers out: Recent trends in the structuring of employment. In B. M. Staw & L. L. Cummings (Eds.), *Research in organizational behavior* (Vol. 10, pp. 257–303). Greenwich, CT: JAI Press.

Social trends. (1993). London: Her Majesty's Stationery Office.

Trade Union of Congress. (1994). *Part-time work in Britain: Analysis of trends in part time work and the characteristics of part-time workers in 1994*. London: Author.

Turner, R. (1995). *The British economy in transition*. London: Routledge & Kegan Paul.

Waddington, J. (1992). Trade union membership in Britain, 1980–1987: Unemployment and restructuring. *British Journal of Industrial Relations, 30*, 287–324.

Young, H. (1989). *One of us*. London: Macmillan.

2

Contingent Work: Research Issues and the Lens of Moral Exclusion

Kathleen Barker

What was once thought to be a minor leak from the pool of full-time and full-year jobs has become, if not a flood, at least a steady stream. That steady stream is currently termed *contingent employment.* Contingent workers—independent contractors and some part-time workers; migrant, seasonal, leased, and temporary workers; and certain homeworkers—have long been a fixture of the workplace (Morse, 1969). What is noteworthy is that short-term and tenuous arrangements between the employer and the worker have recently spread throughout North America as well as European countries with advanced industrial economies (Gustavsen, 1986; Prieto & Martin, 1990).

The purpose of this chapter is to review the key research developments and critical issues in the study of contingent work, with special attention to the contingent workers of higher education. I also briefly address the metatheoretical construct of moral exclusion (Opotow, 1990). The lens of moral exclusion permits the viewer to focus on individuals and groups who are socially constructed as invisible, for example, the "invisible faculty" of higher education (Gappa & Leslie, 1993). A brief presentation of research on the contingent workers of the academy is provided along with goals for future research.

CONTINGENT WORK

During the past 20 years, multiple features of the workplace have changed, and one of the more significant alterations has been the rise and deployment of a flexible workforce. For example, Spalter-Roth and Hartmann (1992) found that less than 50% of all workers in the United States were employed full-time and full-year for the same employer in 1987. Many individuals were packaging various jobs together to make a living wage, whereas others were self-employed or working in a series of jobs across the year. Independent contractors, including some homeworkers, migrant and seasonal workers, individuals working part-time on an involuntary basis, and temporary workers hired directly or through the temporary help service industry, currently constitute what has come to be termed the *contingent workforce*. Multiple job holders are also sometimes included in this definition (Spalter-Roth & Hartmann, 1992; cf. Nardone, 1993). Increasingly in both North America and certain advanced industrial economies in Europe (Gustavsen, 1986; Warme, Lundy, & Lundy, 1992), individuals working in other than full-time or permanent positions have been referred to as the "just-in-time workforce" (Plewes, 1988), or "peripheral" (Morse, 1969), "disposable" (Pollack & Bernstein, 1985), and "contingent" (A. Freedman, 1986) workers. As late as 1987, one could argue that such jobs were always part and parcel of workplace identities and were in the personal history, if not the résumé, of many citizens. Such jobs have long been a fixture of the workplace in the United States (Morse, 1969). However, the emergence of global economies, corporate restructuring, worldwide immigration, and the conversion of the U.S. manufacturing economy to a service one have all been associated with the increase in short-term or uncertain arrangements between employer and employee (Coates, 1988; McKay, 1988).

The number of contingent workers in the United States has been estimated to range from 29.9 million to 36.6 million, or 25% to 30% of the workforce (Belous, 1989; cf. Polivka & Nardone, 1989). Almost half of all jobs created during the 1980s were part-time and temporary jobs, many in the service economy (Tilly, 1990). Of the 16 million new jobs created in the United States between 1979 and 1989, nearly a quarter were part-time, and 40% of these part-time jobs were involuntary (Appelbaum, 1992). Involuntary part-time work, jobs held by individuals who would rather work full-time, accounts for most of the growth in part-time employment (Tilly, 1990). In 1992, one third of all individuals working part-time were doing so on an involuntary basis (U.S. Department of Labor, 1993a, 1993b). Since 1982, temporary employment has grown 10 times faster than overall employment (Hiatt & Rhinehart, 1993). Temporary workers may work full-time, part-time, part-year, or intermittently, and this category also includes employees who are "leased" to employers. Temporary workers are disproportionately White and minority women and minority men (Lapidus, 1989). Finally, certain contractual arrangements may qualify as contingent work. For example, some independent contractors may have contractual arrangements with only one firm. Some employers may use such arrangements to avoid conferring employee status and the benefits (company benefits and Social Security contributions) associated with employee status (U.S. General Accounting Office, 1991).

Contingent work, especially involuntary contingent work, has expanded. The reasons for employers' inclination to increase contingent work include the following:

1. Contingent workers earn less. It is estimated that part-time professionals earn on average $8.30 per hour compared with full-time peer earnings of $14.80. Part-time clericals average $5.70 per hour compared with an average of $8.80 per hour for their full-time counterparts (Belous, 1989; cf. Blank, 1990). Of the 5 million Americans paid at or below the minimum wage in 1987, 44% were women working part-time (Levitan & Conway, 1992). Most part-time jobs continue to be low wage and low skill positions (Tilly, 1992).

2. Contingent workers provide firms with flexibility. Between 1979 and 1989, Fortune 500 companies shed one quarter of their workforce (New Ways to Work, 1992). Whether restraining expansion or recovering from downsizing, many firms may hire specialists for short-term projects. Part-time and temporary employees meet these demands, so that these firms work much the same as firms that developed a "just-in-time-inventory" (Plewes, 1988).

3. Contingent workers receive minimal investment. Training and career advancement are typically absent in contingent employment (M. Freedman, 1988). Regardless of occupational level, individuals working part-time report exclusion on the job, ranging from organizational to interpersonal and skill-enhancement opportunities (Barker, 1993). Company-sponsored benefits, such as health insurance and pension coverage, are provided, respectively, to 22% and 26% of those working part-time (Rebitzer & Lowell, 1991).

4. Contingent work may be used to eliminate (Axelrod, 1987) or avoid unionization (Appelbaum & Gregory, 1988; Carré, duRivage, & Tilly, 1995; Nine to Five, National Association of Working Women, 1986;) and health and safety regulations (Rebitzer, 1995).

RESEARCH THEMES AND KEY DEVELOPMENTS
Defining the Issues: Early Conferences

Three conferences on contingent work represent the range and progression of themes and questions on this topic. At the first conference it was proposed that there were four basic changes in traditional employment that were associated with contingent work (Christensen & Murphree, 1988). The first was a shift in the notion of *time;* that is, how long and when people work. A second shift concerned the assumption of *permanency;* that is, employees can now be hired for a limited amount of time or on a contractual basis with no promise of future employment. Third, it was noted that contingent work may be part of a trend in which the site or *location* of work is becoming more fluid. Conference papers demonstrated that scholars were concerned with the possibility that an increasingly smaller group of core or permanent employees would exist alongside an increasingly larger outer circle composed of contingent workers with fewer worker protections, privileges, and perquisites of employment (U.S. Department of Labor, Women's Bureau, 1988). It was therefore reasoned that the fourth major shift associated with contingent work concerned the *social* contract. The social contract refers to federal laws that guarantee certain protections (workers' compensation, overtime compensation for nonexempt employees, unemployment, equal opportunity, occupational safety and health regulations) as well as local social contracts (e.g., formal contracts with employer or union) and implied and psychological contracts premised on norms or traditions (cf. Robinson, chapter 4, this volume).

One year later, a Cornell conference explored union strategies to keep pace with the development of part-time and temporary work. At the third conference on part-time and contingent work, held in 1991 at the Economic Policy Institute, contingent work was recognized as a key way that companies shifted the burden of risk and uncertainty onto employees. Although there is nothing inherently wrong with flexible arrangements, the social impact of contingent work—the erosion of health insurance, pension adequacy, and skills training for part-time and contingent workers—was viewed as a complex phenomenon that required extensive research (Appelbaum, 1992; duRivage, 1992a).

Early Stages of Research

Despite these conferences and the research conducted to date, contingent work is relatively unexplored and is rarely integrated within theory and research on the work place. Reasons for this are considered below.

The first reason may have to do with the way contingent work has taken root in academia itself. From the early 1970s, when higher education experienced major financial crises, there has been an increase in the number of contingent workers in higher education: adjunct instructors (Gappa & Leslie, 1993).

Of 885,796 faculty and instructional staff, 291,427 or 32.9%, are working part-time (U.S. Department of Education, 1994). Male faculty constitute 67.2% of full-time faculty. Women constitute 45.3% of part-time faculty. Of those working part-time, 23.8% are teaching without faculty status, compared with 3% of those working full-time. Even if public 2-year, public liberal arts, private 2-year, and religious and other specialized institutions (except medical) are eliminated from the analysis, part-time faculty account for approximately 25% of faculty and instructional staff (see Table 1; U.S. Department of Education, 1994).

Table 1	
Symptoms of Moral Exclusion	
Exclusion specific processes (Unlikely in everyday life)	Ordinary processes (Frequently occur in everyday life)
Biased evaluation of group	Groupthink
Derogation	Transcendent ideologies
Dehumanization	Deindividuation
Fear of contamination	Moral engulfment
Expanding the target	Psychological distance
Accelerating the pace of harm doing	Condescension
Open approval of destructive behavior	Technical orientation
Reducing moral standards	Double standards
Blaming the victim	Unflattering comparisons
Self-righteous comparisons	Euphemisms
Desecration	Displacing responsibility
	Diffusing responsibility
	Concealing the effects of harmful behavior
	Glorifying violence
	Normalizing violence
	Temporal containment of harm doing

NOTE: From "Moral Exclusion and Injustice: An Introduction," by S. Opotow, 1990, *Journal of Social Issues*, 46(1), pp. 10–11. Copyright 1990 by *Journal of Social Issues*. Adapted with permission.

It would take almost 10 years for academe's innovations with contingent work to take a toehold in corporate and government human resource operations. Although some part-time and temporary faculty are topic experts who prefer flexibility in the form of temporary arrangements and some are supplementing retirement benefits or nonacademic full-time earnings (Gappa & Leslie, 1993), many are involuntarily employed on an as-needed basis and are multiple job holders (dubbed "subway dons" or "freeway fliers"), traveling from campus to campus to make a living wage (Abel, 1984).

Given that these faculty arrangements occur in an academic setting, one would expect to find that adjunct employees had been the focus of more than a few empirical studies. Such is not the case. In fact,

> there is little basic scholarship on [contingent] faculty. . . . While numerous articles and reports have appeared in the journals and the ERIC system, most are based on experiences of individuals or single institutions. Some present highly subjective polemical arguments. (Gappa & Leslie, 1993, p. 4)

Contingent work, for some researchers and faculty, is a sensitive issue because it is a *local* issue. The discomfort of faculty or researchers in conducting research on contingent work may be due, in part, to their own disparate privileges. As in other settings (Ouchi, 1981), the contingent workers of the academy cushion full-time faculty from unpredictable financial hardships: Faculty numbers contract and expand, but a core of tenured and tenure-track faculty retain their valued positions and perks (Gappa & Leslie, 1993, p. 279). Not only does the predicament of adjunct faculty seem unfair, but their conditions of employment may also feel irreconcilable at the local level.

The second reason concerns the restructuring of the workplace that coincided with increased worker demands for flexibility (Christensen & Murphree, 1988). Flexibility was considered, at first, to be the hallmark of contingent arrangements, and employee demands for this characteristic were seen as the reason for its rise. This interpretative model of contingent work is considered below.

Yet another reason for the paucity of research on contingent work concerns the fact that until the late 1980s, many researchers thought that contingent work was a cyclic reaction to economic stress: a slow but reversible leak of jobs from the full-time, full-year community of jobs. We now know this has not occurred. Segmentation theory (Gordon, Edwards, & Reich, 1982) analyzed successive stages of economic stress in the United States from the colonial period onward. In each period, severe economic upheavals have been resolved through a novel, transformative shift in institutional structures (e.g., the emergence of wage labor and corporate monopolies) that subsequently affected the individual, the group, and organizations and laws (e.g., antitrust laws, immigration policies, and the rise of unions). Such a shift began to coalesce in the late 1980s. Economic stress has led to experimentation in the workplace with workplace "attachments," and these new conditional relationships are becoming increasingly institutionalized and substituted for older workplace attachments.

Finally, and perhaps most importantly, there has been no consensus regarding the definition of contingent work, either statistically or conceptually (Barker & Christensen, 1995). For example, some researchers include all independent contractors in their estimates of contingent workers. Others reason that this would mean the inclusion of affluent members of society, such as physicians, in the final estimate (Polivka & Nardone, 1989). One working definition states that a set of characteristics such as variable hours and job insecurity must be present to designate the job as contingent (Polivka & Nardone, 1989). In an effort to make contingent work coherent, Polivka and Nardone (1989) offered the following definition: "any job in which an individual does not have an explicit or implicit contract for long-term employment *or* [italics added] one in which the minimum hours worked can vary in a nonsystematic manner" (p. 11). However, some workers may be working in either full-or part-time jobs that are premised on high turnover. Such jobs are not solely or even primarily structured around their work schedules or attachments as much as they are based on the ability of the employer to keep wages low and internal labor markets flat through the lack of promotion and salary increases. In the definition and enumeration of contingent workers, researchers are concerned that the murky area of part-time employment will contain many jobs that will fall outside the definition of contingent work (duRivage, personal communication, May 1994). In addition, the issue of multiple job holders remains ambiguous.

Work attachments, traditionally designated in stable relational terms (full-time, part-time, employed, unemployed) coexist with a new set of workplace relationships. As of this writing, the Bureau of Labor Statistics has designed a supplement to the Current Population Survey that was implemented in January 1995. This survey will be the first major effort of the U.S. Department of Labor to conceptually and statistically define contingent work and enumerate workers.

Epistemological Issues and Research Models

From a social psychological perspective, the act of defining contingent work is directly linked with its designation as a "social problem." The definition of a social problem is a political, historical, and sociological event, and therefore an epistemological one (Unger, 1986). The definition itself may or may not become an epistemological force as it reframes the questions that need to be asked and the potential solutions. Contingent work is no exception. Its definition and mediation of expanding and contracting individual outcomes within society are not bereft of either controversy or conflict. For example, some economists may argue that felt job insecurity is too vague, subjective, or challenging to measure. Organizational or social psychologists would argue that job insecurity may be problematic to some degree but not unsolvable or inconsequential to the issue of definition. Fischoff (1990) ruminated that the analyses of economists may not "ring true" (p. 651) to psychologists' norms and tastes, and this may also be true of the definition of contingent work. There is an urgent need for more cross-disciplinary scholarship and debate on the definition of contingent work, including whether the term itself obfuscates more than clarifies workplace phenomena.

A second consideration in the definition of a social problem could be characterized as the tension between the individual level of focus and the environmental level of focus (Caplan & Nelson, 1973). The level of focus inevitably leads to questions concerning the locus of explanation (Mednick, 1989), and this is true with contingent work. Is contingent work profit-driven, an employer necessity, or fueled by individuals' role requirements or preferences? Each locus of explanation for the phenomenon emphasizes and deemphasizes competing explanations in the attempt to define the social problem and its causes and solutions.

The first model attends to organizational profit strategies, but I term it the *expense model*. In this model, there is a focus on employers' profit-incentive strategies coupled with a critical analysis of the disadvantages of such arrangements for workers. This model does not assume that all contingent arrangements are bad. However, authors writing from this perspective deconstruct accounts that single-sidedly praise the advantages of contingent arrangements. For example,

> business often casts part-time employment as an accommodation of workers' desire for flexibility. Terms such as "mothers' hours" and "after-school work" reflect this representation of short schedules. While many employees clearly prefer the flexibility offered by part-time work, employers frequently reap the lion's share of the benefit. (Levitan & Conway, 1992, p. 50)

The expense model is buttressed by the growing evidence that a need for flexibility does not account for the growth in jobs that are less than full-time or permanent; rather, employers have specifically created such jobs in order to create a less attached workforce that is part-time (Tilly, 1992) and temporary (Golden & Appelbaum, 1992; Hartmann & Lapidus, 1989). Employee hardships are salient in this model. Martella (1992), summarizing her research on temporary agencies and temporary workers in Philadelphia, noted that

> temporary work is characterized by ambiguous employment relationships. Many temps dislike the incongruity between their formal employer (the temporary service) and their day-to-day supervisors and co-workers (at the client companies). Temporary workers note that the services fail to uphold their responsibilities as employers, even though they expect temps to behave as loyal employees. Long-term temps ... resent the lack of benefits. .... The employment benefits offered by temporary services serve more as a public relations tool than comprehensive protection. (p. 144)

Within this model, issues concerning injustice from the worker's perspective clearly predominate.

The second model I term the *flexibility model* for employers or employees. Research in this area focuses on contingent work as either (a) solving the human resource problems associated with cost and production flexibility or (b) providing for worker demands for flexibility (mostly for mothers).

The assumption that contingent workers are or can be cost-saving has received some recent preliminary attention. Many employers have used part-time and contingent work to reduce the costs of wages and benefits in order to maintain flexibility and competitiveness (Golden & Appelbaum, 1992). Contingent work arrangements and part-time work may provide both employer and employee with needed flexibility. However, recent research indicates that the deployment of human resources in such arrangements is at best a "mixed blessing" as wages and productivity "have followed each other in a downward spiral" (Tilly, 1992, p. 16):

> Employers who hire secondary part-timers unquestionably gain lower hourly wage and benefit costs. However they also find higher turnover, lower productivity, and less employee reliability. These disadvantages emerge not because all part-time workers are inherently bad workers, but because secondary part-time employment often attracts less productive and less committed workers . . . and encourages more casual attitudes toward work. (Tilly, 1992, p. 34)

According to Nollen (1993), a number of critical issues are raised for managers in the use of contingent workers: Is contingent labor cost effective? Can flexibility be found among core employees? And how can contingent labor be made equitable for workers? Nollen is not convinced that contingent workers are the ideal solution to workforce flexibility. In concluding a case study of three companies, he noted that contingent workers are probably going to be less productive than core employees but also that most new workers need some training on the job over and above prior experience in order to be productive. The more training costs, the more profitable it is to keep workers on the job. According to Nollen (1993),

> this leads to a fundamental dilemma. In many cases, contingent workers must stay on the job a reasonable length of time to be cost effective. Yet contingent workers by definition have no attachment

to the company and are not expected to stay on the job a long time. (p. 8)

The second component of the flexibility model considers the positive components of contingent work, notably flexibility, for working mothers and others. Part-time work schedules and role responsibilities are prominent in this model (e.g. Schwartz, 1989), but the attendant risks are not, such as reduced contributions to a pension plan. Workers, including contingent workers, are not a homogenous mass. Some women complacently accept part-time employment without health benefits because they receive spousal benefits (Christensen, 1989), whereas other workers are forced to opt for "inflexibility" due to the penalties associated with "flexibility" (Allen, 1989). Involuntary part-time workers such as female workers who are unmarried or heads of households struggle with the absence of benefits (Kahne, 1992).

A substantial challenge to the flexibility perspective concerns (a) the issue of women working involuntarily in contingent jobs because they cannot afford full-time day care and (b) the differential experience of older contingent workers. Younger and affluent women may report a preference for part-time arrangements that permit a braiding of work and family concerns that are specific to particular life stages. Alternatively, older Americans, especially women, may resort to contingent work as a hedge against financial and social disintegration (Christensen, 1990). A significant contribution, however, of the flexibility model is that it focuses on potential solutions for work–family issues through contingent arrangements. A future research question concerns the degree to which jobs can be restructured to harmonize with the responsibilities associated with changes in the life span development of both men and women. Those conducting research from the flexibility perspective provide subtle shading to the polarization evident in the broader context of research on contingent work. For the very reasons that companies use contingent arrangements, however, contingent workers report strains associated with possessing only a slender filament of attachment in their employment relationships. Although all families experience financial stress and difficulty in scheduling child care and making family-related plans at one time or another, Christensen (1995) reported that these problems are exacerbated in a context of unstable employment relationships.

To conclude, the changing landscape of work mandates that researchers be aware of which model they are assuming in their approach to studying contingent work. Furthermore, it will be increasingly necessary to capture data, not from the frozen forms of employment categories that emerged after World War II, but from new, many times overlapping categories that have emerged with posteconomic restructuring (e.g., mergers, acquisitions, and downsizing) and that increasingly characterize the current workplace. As findings regarding contingent work emerge, researchers should be alert to differences in the definition of contingent work and the implicit models of research.

MORAL EXCLUSION AND SOCIAL PSYCHOLOGICAL IMPLICATIONS OF CONTINGENT WORK

The emergence of contingent work has resulted in a new set of workplace divisions in which workers are designated as being contingent or permanent and the workplace is composed of groups of workers who are core employees or peripheral workers. Yet just as conditions for full-time, permanent employees vary, so are there differences among contingent workers based on occupation, industry, and whether the firm itself is a core firm or a peripheral firm in its industry and the economy (Appelbaum, 1992). For many institutions or firms, current economic conditions serve as an incentive to use contingent workers. Economic recovery has not mandated the rehiring of permanent workers; rather, temporary workers and overtime pay are used to avoid a permanent attachment to workers (Collins, 1994). Therefore, contingent work is a major innovation that has been accompanied by a transformation in how owners and managers think about their workforce in making their staffing decisions (Barker & Christensen, 1995). That cognitive leap is the partial eclipse of an older workplace paradigm, one in which the employee was an investment and was a member of one's community, maybe even one's moral community. In its place a new paradigm has emerged: one of cost analysis.[1] It is a *cost* framework in which the worker is a commodity rather than an investment. The worker is viewed as fungible, expendable, and if needed, disposable. What is now happening in many firms is that two frameworks of meaning are coexisting within the same site (Barker & Christensen, 1995; Christensen, 1995). One framework, that of being *valued,* exists for a core group of employees, and a second framework, that of being a *cost,* exists for increasing numbers of contract, temporary, and involuntary part-time workers, some of whom retain some employee rights under federal law, others of whom do not (Christensen, 1995). I propose that the concept of moral exclusion is implicated in a *cost* view of employees and that the concept provides a useful framework in which the social construction of privileges, entitlements, and penalties of being a contingent worker can be understood. The *lens of moral exclusion* refers to understanding how moral exclusion functions. When considering contingent work with this understanding, one can see its otherwise invisible aspects.

The literature on the justice implications of the scope of moral and community and moral exclusion is found in the writings of Deutsch (1985), Opotow (1990), and Staub (1987). First coined by Staub (1987), *moral exclusion* is said to occur "when individuals or groups are perceived as *outside the boundary in which moral values, rules, and considerations of fairness apply* . . . they are perceived as nonentities, expendable" (Opotow, 1990, p. 1). Opotow (1990) noted that instances of "moral exclusion occur when we fail to recognize and deal with undeserved suffering and deprivation. . . . In this case harm doing results from unconcern or unawareness of others' needs or entitlements to basic resources, such as housing, health services, respect, and fair treatment" (p. 2). From the literature

---

[1]Historically, the investment strategy was rarely applied to women and minorities (Morse, 1969), and the sexual division of labor is distinct from what I call the division by workforce. Although the sexual division of labor was intractable and penalized working women and their families, the division occasionally protected women. For example, during the Depression era, women were harangued for taking "jobs from men," but their low wages made them appealing in many instances (Kessler-Harris, 1982, pp. 262–264). It is as yet difficult to imagine when and how a cost framework would protect employees in a parallel fashion today.

on harm doing, Opotow extracted a series of more than two dozen symptoms that operationally define moral exclusion for empirical research. Opotow also noted that the list is not exhaustive but may provide researchers with a conceptual umbrella for the study of moral exclusion. These symptoms are listed in Table 1, and further detail is found in Opotow's (1990) study. The lens of moral exclusion provides an organizing framework within which research on contingent workers can be explored. A discussion of health and safety issues will be followed by an examination of case study material that conceptualizes contingent work within a particular context, academe. Case study material is organized by a number of organizational and social themes that include skill development, stigma and identity, declining beliefs in meritocracy, the accumulation of deficits, and muzzled protest.

Health and Safety

Many current laws and policies, frozen in the standards or expectations of the past, are based on older notions of the workplace and worker protections. A variety of emerging employment relationships, such as joint employment between a contracting employer and a providing agency or company, are not adequately addressed by current labor law and policy (duRivage, 1992b). For example, to avoid liability for accidents, employers will avoid appearing as if they supervise or control contract workers. The appearance of such control extends to worker training (Rebitzer, 1995), with serious implications for worker health and safety (Wells, Kochan, & Smith, 1991). Unions are prevented from organizing contingent workers because, as in the case of independent contractors, the employer is regarded as "neutral" and "insulated from collective economic actions such as picketing or striking in the event of a labor dispute" (Carré et al., 1995, p. 319). Exclusion from the moral community is often premised on the use or creation of stigmatizing characteristics (Opotow, 1990). Such exclusion is hinted at in the following description: "Contract employees were generally treated as a separate and distinct workforce . . . contract work forces dressed differently [and] used separate entrances" (Wells et al., 1991, p. 96).

Such daily distinctions may be harmless on the surface. Alternatively, such distinctions may suggest a system of exclusionary practices that foster multiple forms of citizenship within the organization.

In the petrochemical industry, contract workers were preferred because they were not provided with health benefits (Wells et al., 1991). They also were given more dangerous work even though they were not as experienced as direct hires or core employees. There was a lapse of supervision of contract workers that resulted in more accidents for contract workers than core workers. Attorneys had advised many of the companies to avoid a joint relationship, such as training or supervision, with the contract employees (Kochan, Wells, & Smith, 1992) because the National Labor Relations Board has typically failed to recognize joint employer liability (Carré et al., 1995).

When the nonemployee status of the high-risk worker results in exclusion from plant safety training programs—programs that are required for regular employees—a pernicious form of moral exclusion could be said to have occurred. In fact, in the petrochemical industry one third to one half of such workers are not included in plant worker safety programs (Kochan et al., 1992).

If the psychological notion of justice refers to the boundaries of community (Deutsch, 1985), then organizational "flexibility" suggests a one-way permeable membrane through which individuals pass to the margins, to the corners, or out of an organization.[2] The passing of individuals to the margins of the organization in the Phillips 66 example exemplifies notions of organizational competitiveness based on a disposable worker, not a trained worker. As Kochan et al. (1992) noted, there is an asynchrony between the rhetoric of national policy and the adequacy of programs for developing a knowledgeable workforce. For organizational researchers, there is a need to consider when and how exclusionary practices are based on the rhetoric of competitiveness but are premised on the flexibility of a disposable, contingent workforce.

---

[2]Alternatively, flexibility may represent some bending of human resources without breaking human resources (Christensen, 1989).

Interpersonal, Organizational, and Skills Issues

In a study of 326 women working full-and part-time in male-dominated (e.g., law) and female-dominated (e.g., nursing) professions, as well as in traditional occupations (e.g., clerical), reports of part-time workers indicated that they were organizationally and interpersonally excluded and disadvantaged in skill opportunities when compared with the reports of their full-time peers (Barker, 1993). Part-time workers reported being more vulnerable to layoffs and being perceived as less committed to their organization by colleagues and supervisors than full-time workers, but there were no differences between the career goals of full-time and part-time working women. If workers in these "good" part-time jobs (Tilly, 1990) report such psychological reactions, what about workers who are even more tenuously attached? Research is needed that examines the range, nature, and long-term implications of exclusion on the job for other contingent workers.

Interviews with contingent workers in the academy yield some preliminary evidence. Both individual and group interviews were conducted with adjunct instructors. Interviews were conducted with instructors who had averaged 3 years of teaching experience in higher education and instructors who had completed all but the dissertation for the doctoral degree (ABD) or possessed their doctoral degree and had an average of 9 years of teaching experience. One limitation of the data is that less experienced instructors were voluntarily employed in contingent arrangements, whereas those who had completed or nearly completed doctoral requirements were seeking full-time academic work and therefore were involuntarily working in such arrangements. Finally, although it is not appropriate to generalize from case study data, the interview data provide interesting glimpses into the nature and terms of exclusion for the contingent workers of academe.

Generally, adjuncts reported discouragement and disappointment (Barker, 1994). Many said they were made to feel like second-class citizens compared with tenured or tenure-track faculty. This feeling is rooted in the invisibility afforded to many adjuncts (Gappa & Leslie, 1993) and is a symptom of exclusion. Active exclusionary devices were the typical lack of office space, mailboxes, and support staff. However, invisibility may shade into denigration in some instances. One instructor reported attending departmental parties (always invited by posted notices, not by personal invitation), but reported being repeatedly ignored by department faculty. Yet the contingent workers of the academy are not always invisible. An ABD in psychology at an urban public university made this point:

> When they want something from you, it changes. All of a sudden, for just a couple moments, they [the department chair] are actually talking to you like a colleague. "Will you teach the drug course?" "Can you make it more of a health psych course than a biopsych course?". . . At my school they don't tell you when they are going to evaluate your class. So, this department chair, who I helped out [by teaching the course], sent the most hostile evaluator in the department who of course [also] happened to be a physiological psychologist . . . and this woman hated the syllabus. After that class, I sat outside the chair's office until he would see me . . . Then I made this decision. (Sharon P., now retraining in clinical psychology)

Resentment and bitterness is not how all adjuncts expressed their feelings about their jobs and work conditions. Many were simply frustrated, others were resigned, but a few were deeply disappointed by their university employment.

In general, graduate students reported feeling censored in their concerns about a livelihood. Older ABDs and PhDs talked about denial as an everyday form of coping with the lack of jobs in their fields, and this denial about the lack of academic openings was clearly something that they had in common with their own teachers and supervisors:

> The first class I ever took in graduate school, I remember [that] the first professor in my first class said: "We're not here to think about jobs or money . . . we are here to [discuss] literature."

Interestingly, one adjunct reported that it was routine for her professors to apologize for not retiring, and in two cases the professors were near 70.

Subordination, Identity, and Stigma

One of the more riveting statements by an adjunct points to more than social distance and denigration. The following statement was made by a White adjunct with 11 years' experience. What the adjunct is observing is that working as an adjunct acquires a stigma, a racelike quality in a racist society, that permanently changes the identity of the worker to others: "Working as an adjunct is like becoming a Black. You cannot become 'White' again." Although institutions erect conditional or contingent relationships with workers, they still provide a filter through which identity is valued or stigmatized.

Contingent work fractures the assumptions many individuals brought with them into the academy. Instructors reported that it was a common practice to be asked to teach courses that ended up not being offered. Many of the adjuncts interviewed taught at schools that did not provide a formal employment contract until after the first or second week of school, so that if there were not enough attendees, the course was "bumped" and the contingent worker was without a class, work, and earnings.

Accumulating Deficits

Older adjuncts reported receiving two messages: that teaching the "general" courses was good but also that an attitude existed that anything taught by adjuncts was less than adequate:

> It's a course taught by an adjunct. How good can an adjunct be? . . . Or they ask you, "what can you teach that's basic." . . . I'd kill to teach something slightly more specific than everything! . . . Gee, what happens if I find that, that mythical full-time job, and they suddenly ask me to teach something specific, and I'm going . . . can I do that, can I remember anything beyond Beethoven was a composer in this century? I'm going, yeah. Can I be more specific than to say, "Yes, he wrote nine symphonies?" . . . There's this real fear that someone's gonna ask me a real tough question, faculty to faculty, job interview or something, and I'm just gonna go, I have to go home and look it up. There's this feeling that, yeah, I've been do-

ing this for 10 years. . . . I've paid my dues with my PhD, when do
I get to use it? (Fiona, ABD, Music)

Working as an adjunct may give the individual needed teaching experiences and help in professionally socializing the individual. Research is needed, however, that specifies the impact of the cost framework over time. For example, as workers are enveloped within this framework, are they (a) valued for their skills and readiness to apply these on short notice, or are they also (b) devalued because their merit has a planned obsolescence? In addition, is it the transience or migration from campus to campus ("subway dons," "freeway fliers") that contributes to devaluation? When and how does this help to create a perceptual set that contingent workers, in a *cost* framework, are more disposable than the permanent employees, in a *value* framework, with whom they work or are supervised?

Another area of needed research concerns the findings regarding exclusion in skill enhancement opportunities (Barker, 1993), a finding that echoes the work of Kochan and colleagues. The comments from the ABD in music are suggestive regarding the long-term consequences of contingent work. For example, consider how beliefs and expectations of permanent medical personnel in a hospital are organized around the issue of training on new medical equipment. If, for example, a contingent nurse is consistently passed over when training on the new equipment is conducted, over time that individual could be considered to be *accumulating deficits* of contingency, just as the comments of the ABD in music suggest.

Declining Meritocracy: Changes in Entitlement

Perhaps the most interesting shift that was observed was based on time spent in a contingent job and concerned the belief in meritocracy. Employment as a contingent worker, especially for knowledge workers, may foster particular achievement-related contradictions that are rooted in occupational socialization and the stated mission of the collegium. For another, contingent work also may result in a decline in the belief in meritocracy, a belief system that is the glue of many forms of institutional life. In fact, contingent work may be the solvent that dissolves older forms of workplace privilege.

There are few beliefs as strongly supportive of the American Dream as the belief in meritocracy. *Meritocracy* was a term introduced by Michael Young (1958) in the book *The Rise of Meritocracy* and signified a system thought to advance merit (intelligence plus effort) in education as a basis of individual achievement. More recently the term has assumed greater meaning in the sense that all job-holders attain their jobs on the basis of merit alone. No matter where one is in the hierarchy of the labor market, a component of meritocracy predicates one's current position on past performance. Therefore, the cult of meritocracy predicts that social mobility is not selectively attained due to structural factors, but individually deserved through personal merit (Scruton, 1982, p. 297).

Although it is beyond the scope of this chapter, a comparison of two separate groups of adjunct instructors indicated that the ideology of meritocracy has a limited shelf life. Although second- and third-year graduate assistants were not naive about the limited job prospects in academia, none challenged departments' actions and goals in supplying individuals with doctorates to a job market that was nonexistent for many. These younger students were not naive, but they were qualitatively more upbeat about their future than the adjunct ABDs or PhDs who were feeling stuck in contingent jobs. Those who felt stuck reported a sense of loss, but not because of any individual errors they had made in their careers. They did not believe that colleagues who did obtain full-time work were more able or capable. One adjunct discussed this in the context of a department in which department retirements resulted not in a national search but in adjunct appointments at a much smaller fraction of the retiree's remuneration.[3] Perceptions of the legitimacy of their graduate school training and faculty were greatly undermined as instructors focused on whether their generation of scholars was getting a fair deal. Those with the most experience in the academy reported a sense of dwindling legitimacy of their own role in the academy, accompanied by a negative interpretation of their

---

[3]Many people do not know what adjuncts earn. In New York City, the range of pay is fairly wide, but generally low. At the School of Social Work at New York University, adjuncts are paid $1,400 as of 1992 for teaching a graduate course in research methods. At City University of New York, individuals without a doctorate were paid $2,000 per undergraduate course as of spring 1994. With a doctorate, individuals earn slightly less than $2,500.

role in maintaining the status and well-being of full-time faculty members.

Muzzled Protest

Summarizing the social psychological literature on entitlement, Major (1993) commented that a sense of entitlement is "experienced as a moral imperative or right . . . derived from a complex interplay of comparison standards and justifications and is shaped by what we want or value" (p. 143). When entitlement is violated the individual is supposed to experience disappointment, sadness, or frustration (Major, 1993). The motivational qualities of entitlement should also lead that person to seek change. The contingent workers of the academy, however, do not universally seek change, as is clearly seen in their lack of union membership or representation and the fact that many stay but do not seek change. Many participants in the research believed they could not engage openly in a politics of resistance. Like temporary workers in clerical industries (Tucker, 1993), they mostly reported discouragement and disappointment in their workplace, and when they did try to engage the system, it was at the level of nonconfrontational tactics, such as gossip or exit. Unlike the temporary workers in clerical jobs, however, the PhD and doctoral candidate have been professionally socialized. It is argued that one aspect of professional socialization is to learn to mute or muzzle protest concerning injustice so as to gain a footing in the profession.

After 9 years of teaching at least two courses each semester, recruiting majors, attending department meetings, and organizing department festivities, one adjunct was "let go" during a phone call from the new chair:

> I felt like I had a job, a poor paying job, but I loved my work, my students. . . . I was devastated by the politics [when] I was told that I wasn't needed. The new chair hated my teaching mentor. (Marsha, 14 years in a doctoral program, ABD, and working full-time as a secretary).

Marsha's involvement in department and teaching activities may have violated what I term the adjunct's "invisibility law," and this may have, in part, led to her forced exit. As she explained to me, she felt that teaching required a commitment and she honored that by her activities in the department. Herein is the asynchrony between the professional in a contingent job and the employer: The chair had a "new" tradition and procedure on her side as she easily detached Marsha from the department through a process known as nonrenewal. "In the department store as in the university, part-timers are cheaper and certainly more easily dismissed" (Warme & Lundy, 1988, p. 202).

Many adjuncts commented on their uneasiness with the power relations of their department. One adjunct felt it was impossible to counter unfairness at the interpersonal or organizational level and that organizing a union or coalition was "a waste of time." The same person later commented on the politics of course scheduling. In his department, some adjuncts were given coveted classes and time slots, and he was one of this "loyal" group. "Troublemakers" were given the very worst meeting times on a "take it or leave it" basis. Almost all of the older adjunct instructors approved of union organization but claimed that the current union, which also represented full-time faculty, did not actively recruit adjuncts. The implications for academic freedom need to be followed-up.

The Teacher of the Year at one college clearly violated the invisibility law. Following his award, he was officially told of his nonrenewal so late that course assignments for the following semester were already assigned at other schools. Students protested to the administration and department. The adjunct left the school for another contingent academic position.

Labor laws that do not recognize the new worker–employer relationships could be said to muzzle resistance and protest at the collective level. Examples of moral exclusion include the outlawing of public-sector unions in a number of states (Virginia, Texas, and Missouri) and the misclassification of contract workers who work for the state literally as employees, not contractors (Carré et al., 1995). Researchers have noted that a dual framework of value and cost may ultimately disempower those academics who have benefited from the use of contingent workers to preserve their own positions (Warme & Lundy, 1988).

FUTURE DIRECTIONS FOR RESEARCH ON CONTINGENT WORK

The national financial conditions of the last few years provided an economic petri dish that resulted in a new set of workplace relationships that are conditional in nature. This chapter has discussed ways in which the lens of moral exclusion reveals penalties that may be associated with various forms of contingent employment: health and safety risks, social distancing, denigration, muzzled protest, and the accumulation of deficit, to name a few.

The psychological, as opposed to economic, face of contingent work requires amplification through research and theory. One avenue of research would be further development and utilization of the reciprocal constructs of privilege and exclusion. We need to critically examine some of the cultural assumptions that have an impact on our research questions. If we are successful in doing so, we will not only conduct better research with wider policy payoffs, but we will also unlock systems of privilege and stimulate citizen discourse. Here, the work of Kochan and colleagues is especially relevant not only for its findings, but also for methods that contextualize the workplace from a variety of viewpoints. Adler (1994) has suggested that current models of organizational socialization, commitment, and culture may have limited utility for organizations redefined by the rise of contingent work.

Another avenue of future research concerns human resources decision-making. Analysis of the efficacy of contingent staffing, as suggested by Nollen and Tilly, is also needed. Another area is the long-term effects of working contingently that have only been hinted at in research. The supposed "choice" to work contingently should not shroud issues that have significant human costs associated with them. Over and beyond race, gender, and disability, when and how does contingent work result in accumulative disadvantage for citizens such as elderly individuals, who, after a lifetime of contingent work, may be without pensions, life insurance, and other benefits upon retirement (cf. Christensen, 1990)? Finally, we also need an analysis of the sociolegal frameworks that have served as a brake or facilitator in the emergence of the contingent workforce. In this regard, the analysis by Gonos (1993) of the legal dimensions underlying employment affiliation and the emergence of triangular employment relationships is an excellent starting point.

Contemporary contingent employment provides opportunities to explore the lamina of privilege and distinctions accorded to certain workers over others, a layered citizenship within settings.[4] One outcome of systematic layered citizenship is the stifling of protest at the individual (Tucker, 1993) and collective levels. Speaking on the issue of social justice and processes of exclusion, one social psychologist commented that whenever issues of merit, tradition, and choice infiltrate discourse, such concepts are used to legitimate and gloss over the exclusion of some in protection of others not excluded (Fine, 1990). The future of research on contingent work will not only result in the much needed study of the experiences of contingent workers; it will also lead to greater understanding of academe's own layers of privilege based on the use of contingent educators.

REFERENCES

Abel, E. K. (1984). *Terminal degrees: The job crisis in higher education.* New York: Praeger.

Adler, S. (1994, July). *The Protean worker: Implications for organizational theory and practice.* Paper presented at the meeting of the International Association of Applied Psychology, Madrid, Spain.

Allen, S. (1989). Flexibility and working time: A gendered approach. In J. Agassi & S. Haycock (Eds.), *The redesign of working time: Promise or threat?* Berlin: Edition Sigma.

Appelbaum, E. (1992). Structural change and the growth of part-time and temporary employment. In V. L. duRivage (Ed.), *New policies for the part-time and contingent workforce* (pp. 1–14). Armonk, NY: Sharpe.

Appelbaum, E., & Gregory, J. (1988). Union responses to contingent work: Are win–win outcomes possible? In *Flexible workstyles: A look at contingent la-*

---

[4]I am indebted to Michelle Fine for reading an earlier draft and suggesting this term based on the construct of moral exclusion (Opotow, 1990).

bor (pp. 69–75). Washington, DC: U.S. Department of Labor, Women's Bureau.

Axelrod, J. (1987). Who's the boss? Employee leasing and the joint employer relationship. *The Labor Lawyer, 3*, 853–872.

Barker, K (1993). Changing assumptions and contingent solutions: The costs and benefits of women working full and part-time. *Sex Roles, 28*, 47–71.

Barker, K. (1994, August). *Contingent workers in higher education: Adjunct professors and their psychological responses to invisibility.* Paper presented at the 102nd Annual Convention of the American Psychological Association, Los Angeles.

Barker, K., & Christensen, K. (1995). *From entitlement to privilege.* Unpublished manuscript.

Belous, R. S. (1989). *The contingent economy: The growth of the temporary, part-time and subcontracted workforce.* Washington, DC: National Planning Association.

Blank, R. M. (1990). Are part-time jobs bad jobs? In G. Burtless (Ed.), *A future of lousy jobs: The changing structure of U.S. wages.* Washington, DC: Brookings Institution.

Caplan, N., & Nelson, S. D. (1973). On being useful: The nature and consequences of psychological research on social problems. *American Psychologist, 28*, 199–211.

Carré, F. J., duRivage, V. L., & Tilly, C. (1995). Representing the part-time and contingent workforce: Challenges for unions and public policy. In L. G. Flood (Ed.), *Unions and public policy.* Westport, CT: Greenwood Press.

Christensen, K. (1989). *Flexible staffing and scheduling in U.S. corporations* (Res. Bulletin No. 240). New York: Conference Board.

Christensen, K. (1990). Bridges over troubled water: How older workers view the labor market. In P. Doeringer (Ed.), *Bridges to retirement: Trends in the labor market for older workers* (pp. 175–207). Ithaca, NY: ILR Cornell.

Christensen, K. (1995). *Contingent work arrangements in family-sensitive corporations.* Boston: Boston University, The Work and Family Institute.

Christensen, K., & Murphree, M. (1988). Introduction to conference proceedings. In K. Christensen & M. Murphree (Eds.), *Flexible workstyles: A look at contingent labor* (pp. 1–4). Washington, DC: U.S. Department of Labor, Women's Bureau.

Coates, V. T. (1988). Office automation technology and contingent work modes. In K. Christensen & M. Murphree (Eds.), *Flexible workstyles: A look at contingent labor* (pp. 29–33). Washington, DC: U.S. Department of Labor, Women's Bureau.

Collins, S. (1994, July 4). The new migrant workers. *U.S. News and World Report*, pp. 51–55

Deutsch, M. (1985). *Distributive justice: A social psychological perspective*. New Haven, CT: Yale University Press.

duRivage, V. L. (1992a). New policies for the contingent workforce. In *New ways to work: New policies for part-time and contingent workers. Summary of a conference on the changing workforce* (pp. 12–18). San Francisco: Author.

duRivage, V. L. (1992b). *New policies for the part-time and contingent workforce*. In V. L. duRivage (Ed.), *New policies for the part-time and contingent workforce* (pp. 89–121). Armonk, NY: Sharpe.

Fine, M. (1990). "The public" in public schools: The social construction/constriction of moral communities. *Journal of Social Issues, 46*(1), 107–119.

Fischoff, B. (1990). Psychology and public policy: Tool or toolmaker? *American Psychologist, 45*, 647–653.

Freedman, A. (1986, January). Jobs: Insecurity at all levels. *Across the Board*, pp. 4–5.

Freedman, M. (1988). Shifts in labor market structure and patterns of occupational training. In K. Christensen & M. Murphree (Eds.), *Flexible workstyles: A look at contingent labor* (pp. 65–68). Washington, DC: U.S. Department of Labor, Women's Bureau.

Gappa, J. M., & Leslie, D. W. (1993). *The invisible faculty: Improving the status of part-timers in higher education*. San Francisco: Jossey-Bass.

Golden, L., & Appelbaum, E. (1992). What is driving the boom in temporary employment? *American Journal of Economics and Sociology, 51*, 473–492.

Gonos, G. (1993, March). *Temporary work and the growth of atypical employment*. Paper presented at the meeting of the Eastern Sociological Society, Boston.

Gordon, D. M., Edwards, R., & Reich, M. (1982). *Segmented work, divided workers: The historical transformation of labor in the United States*. Cambridge, England: Cambridge University Press.

Gustavsen, B. (1986). Evolving patterns of enterprise organization: The move toward greater flexibility. *International Labour Review, 125*, 367–382.

Hartmann, H., & Lapidus, J. (1989). *Temporary work*. Washington, DC: Institute for Women's Policy Research.

Hiatt, J. P., & Rhinehart, L. (1993, August 12). The growing contingent workforce: A challenge for the future. *Daily Labor Report, 154*, E1–E6.

Kahne, H. (1992). Part-time work: A hope and a peril. In B. D. Warme, K. Lundy, &

L. A. Lundy (Eds.), *Working part-time: Risks and opportunities* (pp. 295–309). New York: Praeger.

Kessler-Harris, A. (1982). *Out to work: A history of wage-earning women in the United States.* New York: Oxford University Press.

Kochan, T. A., Wells, J. C., & Smith, M. (1992, Summer). Consequences of a failed IR system: Contract workers in the petrochemical industry. *Sloan Management Review*, pp. 79–89.

Lapidus, J. (1989). *The temporary help industry and the operation of the labor market.* Unpublished doctoral dissertation, University of Massachusetts at Amherst.

Levitan, S. A.., & Conway, E. (1992). Part-timers: Living on half rations. In B. D. Warme, K. Lundy, & L. A. Lundy (Eds.), *Working part-time: Risks and opportunities* (pp. 217–228). New York: Praeger.

Major, B. (1993). Gender, entitlement, and the distribution of family labor. *Journal of Social Issues, 49*(3), 141–160.

Martella, M. (1992). *The rhetoric and realities of contingent work: The case of women in clerical temporary work.* Unpublished doctoral dissertation, Temple University, Philadelphia.

McKay, R. V. (1988). International competition: Its impact on employment. In K. Christensen & M. Murphee (Eds.), *Flexible workstyles: A look at contingent labor* (pp. 23–28). Washington, DC: U.S. Department of Labor, Women's Bureau.

Mednick, M. T. (1989). On the politics of psychological constructs: Stop the bandwagon, I want to get off. *American Psychologist, 44*, 1118–1123.

Morse, D. (1969). *The peripheral worker.* New York: Columbia University Press.

Nardone, T. (1993, August). Contingent workers: Characteristics and trends. In K. Barker (Chair), *Contingent employment: Empirical perspectives.* Symposium conducted at the annual meeting of the Academy of Management, Atlanta.

New Ways to Work. (1992). *New policies for part-time and contingent workers.* San Francisco: Author.

Nine to Five, National Association of Working Women. (1986). *Working at the margins: Part-time and temporary workers in the United States.* Cleveland, OH: Author.

Nollen, S. (1993). *Exploding the myth: Is contingent labor cost-effective?* San Francisco: New Ways to Work.

Opotow, S. (1990). Moral exclusion and injustice: An introduction. *Journal of Social Issues, 46*(1), 1–20.

Ouchi, W. G. (1981). *Theory Z: How American business can meet the Japanese challenge.* Reading, MA: Addison-Wesley.

Plewes, T. J. (1988). Understanding the data on part-time and temporary employment. In K. Christensen & M. Murphee (Eds.), *Flexible workstyles: A look at contingent labor* (pp. 9–13). Washington, DC: U.S. Department of Labor, Women's Bureau.

Polivka, A. E., & Nardone, T. (1989, December). On the definition of "contingent work." *Monthly Labor Review,* pp. 9–16.

Pollack, M. A., & Bernstein, A. (1985, April 1). Part-time workers: Rising numbers, rising discord. *Business Week,* 62–63.

Prieto, J. M., & Martin, J. (1990). New forms of work organisation. *Irish Journal of Psychology, 11,* 170–185.

Rebitzer, J., & Lowell, T. (1991). A model of dual labor markets when product demand is uncertain. *Quarterly Journal of Economics, 106,* 1373–1383.

Rebitzer, J. B. (1995). Job safety and contract workers in the petrochemical industry. *Industrial Relations, 34,* 40–57.

Schwartz, F. N. (1989). Management women and the new facts of life. *Harvard Business Review, 110,* 65–76.

Scruton, R. (1982). *A dictionary of political thought.* New York: Hill & Wang.

Spalter-Roth, R., & Hartmann, H. (1992). *Exploring the characteristics of self-employment and part-time work among women.* Washington, DC: Institute for Women's Policy Research.

Staub, E. (1987, August). *Moral exclusion and extreme destructiveness: Personal goal theory, differential evaluation, moral equilibration and steps along the continuum of destruction.* Paper presented at the 95th Annual Convention of the American Psychological Association, New York.

Tilly, C. (1990, March). Reasons for the continuing growth of part-time employment. *Monthly Labor Review,* pp. 10–18.

Tilly, C. (1992). Short hours, short shrift: Causes and consequences of part-time work. In V. L. duRivage (Ed.), *New policies for part-time and contingent workers* (pp. 15–44). Armonk, NY: Sharpe.

Tucker, J. (1993). Everyday forms of employee resistance. *Sociological Forum, 8,* 25–45.

Unger, R. K. (1986). Looking toward the future by looking at the past: Social activism and social history. *Journal of Social Issues, 42*(1), 215–227.

U.S. Department of Education. (1994). *Faculty and instructional staff: Who are they and what do they do?* (Rep. No. 94-346). Washington, DC: U.S. Department of Education, National Center for Education Statistics.

U.S. Department of Labor. (1993a, January). *Employment and earnings.* Washington, DC: U.S. Department of Labor, Bureau of Labor Statistics.

U.S. Department of Labor. (1993b, August). *Handbook of labor statistics.* Washington, DC: U.S. Department of Labor, Bureau of Labor Statistics.

U.S. Department of Labor, Women's Bureau. (1988). *Flexible workstyles: A look at contingent labor.* Washington, DC: Author.

U.S. General Accounting Office. (1991, March). *Workers at risk* (GAO Rep. No. HRD-91–56). Washington, DC: Author.

Warme, B., & Lundy, K. (1988). Erosion of an ideal: The 'presence' of part-time faculty. *Studies in Higher Education, 13,* 202–213.

Warme, B. D., Lundy, K. L. P, & Lundy, L. A. (1992). Introduction. In B. D. Warme, K. L. P. Lundy, & L. A. Lundy (Eds.), *Working part-time: Risks and opportunities* (pp. 1–17). New York: Praeger.

Wells, J. C., Kochan, T. A., & Smith, M. (1991). *Managing workplace safety and health: The case of contract labor in the U.S. petrochemical industry.* Beaumont, TX: Lamar University, John Gray Institute.

Young, M. D. (1958). *The rise of meritocracy, 1870–2033: The new elite of our social revolution.* New York: Random House.

3

The Role of Organizational Justice in Defining and Maintaining the Employment Relationship

Sheldon Alexander, Robert R. Sinclair, and Lois E. Tetrick

It is clear that many major changes have occurred in the work environment, as indicated in other chapters in this volume. It seems to be the consensus of many that further changes will occur (Commission on the Future of Worker–Management Relations, 1994). The question appears not to be how to stop or reverse these changes, but how these changes are best managed from a societal, organizational, and individual perspective. Change has been acknowledged to have an impact on individuals' attitudes and behaviors. Although changes within the work environment can result in ambiguity, stress, and resistance to change, alterations in the employment relationship need not be universally negative.

The employment relationship has been viewed as an exchange relationship with mutual obligations occurring on the part of both the employer and the employee. These perceived obligations have been termed the *psychological contract* by Rousseau and her colleagues, and violations of the psychological contract result in reduced trust, commitment, and citizenship behaviors (Rousseau, 1989). It is proposed here that an individual's relationship with the union also can be construed as an exchange relationship with a resulting psychological contract, that is, perceived mutual obligations between the union member and the union.

When environmental factors result in a perceived change in the obligations of the parties involved in the psychological contract, it has been suggested that both the outcomes and the means of achieving changes to the obligations of the parties are of critical importance (Shore & Tetrick, 1994). The concepts of justice and fairness appear central to our understanding of the impact of changing employment relationships. In this chapter we briefly review the historical development and key constructs in organizational justice theory, present relevant empirical research on workplace issues affecting the employee–employer relationship, and extend this literature to the employee–union relationship. Figure 1 is a schematic representation of the role of justice perceptions in defining and maintaining the employment relationship.

HISTORICAL DEVELOPMENT AND KEY CONSTRUCTS

The study of the impact of justice and injustice in group and organizational settings has grown rapidly in the past decade. This has been true particularly for studies of justice in the workplace (see Cropanzano, 1993; Greenberg, 1990; Sheppard, Lewicki, & Minton, 1992). Several aspects of organizational justice have been identified. The major categories, as discussed below, are distributive, procedural, interactional, interpersonal, retributive, and systemic justice.

Distributive Justice

The first type of justice examined in the psychological and organizational literature was distributive justice (Homans, 1961), which deals with the allocation or distribution of rewards or resources to people. The focus is on the perception of the fairness of the outcomes received by an individual (i.e., the person gets the outcome he or she deserves). Homans's (1961) distributive justice rule proposed that the reward/cost ratio of Person A should be equal to the reward/cost ratio of Person B (a comparison other, or referent); or the profit/investment ratios of the two parties should be equal. In 1965, Adams extended these ideas into a detailed theory of in-

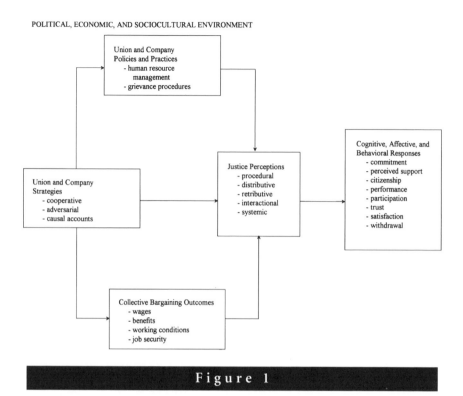

POLITICAL, ECONOMIC, AND SOCIOCULTURAL ENVIRONMENT

Figure 1

Schematic representation of the role of justice perceptions under changing employment relationships.

equity, which provided the major impetus to justice research in organizational settings.

Adams's (1965) theory stated that perceived fairness would occur only if the perceiver's outcomes/inputs ratio was seen as being equal to the outcomes/inputs ratio of a comparison other. Psychological inequity occurs if the ratios are perceived as being unequal. Inequity leads to emotional distress, which leads to attempts to reduce the inequity or restore equity. Adams presented a detailed list of the behavioral and psychological methods people use to try to restore equity. This was followed by a virtual explosion of equity research using social and organizational contexts.

Much of the research yielded results consistent with equity theory (see Mowday, 1983). Underpaid workers reduced their inputs, and the overpaid increased their inputs.

Although equity theory had heuristic value, challenges developed from at least three different directions. Early criticisms focused on the experimental procedures used by Adams (1965) and others. More compelling challenges to equity theory were raised in conceptual analyses of justice and distributive behavior (e.g., Deutsch, 1975; Leventhal, 1976). Critics argued that equity theory presented a limited view of the nature of distributive justice. People may use a number of distributive justice rules in determining whether outcomes are fair or unfair, such as equality, need, seniority, or reciprocity. Deutsch (1975) argued that the particular norm a person uses is determined by the type of situation and the underlying goals and values the person applies to that situation. Deutsch suggested that such distributive justice rules as equality of allocation to all recipients, or of allocation to the recipients in greatest need, would sometimes be judged fairer than allocations according to the equity rule. Later, in a series of experiments with groups working on a wide range of tasks, Deutsch found that subjects often preferred the equality rule and were more productive on some tasks when rewards were distributed equally rather than equitably (Deutsch, 1985). In other studies, Tornblum and Jonsson (1985) provided cross-cultural evidence for the equality norm. In a major theoretical reanalysis of justice, Leventhal (1980) argued that people use different distributive justice rules in different situations and often use a combination of justice rules in any given situation.

A third challenge to equity theory proposed that perceptions of injustice encompass more than whether one receives the outcome one deserves. Conceptions of fairness involve other types of justice in addition to distributive justice, and these other justice dimensions may be more important in determining a person's behavior. Additional concepts such as procedural justice (Thibaut & Walker, 1975), interactional justice (Bies & Moag, 1986), interpersonal justice (Tyler & Bies, 1990), retributive justice (Hogan & Emler, 1981), and systemic justice (Sheppard et al., 1992) were introduced. The past decade of research and theory development has seen a major shift from equity and distributive justice to the study of these newer justice topics.

Procedural Justice

The concept of procedural justice was introduced by Thibaut and Walker (1975), who argued that it was independent of the perceived fairness of outcomes. In a series of experiments using courtroom and conflict settings, they demonstrated that perceptions of the fairness of the processes leading up to decisions had their own unique effects on peoples' attitudes and behavior. They argued that the key factor in judgments of procedural justice was process control—the degree to which disputants felt they could influence the process leading to a decision made by a third party. The procedural justice concept had a liberating effect on students of justice and soon began to be applied to other social and organizational contexts (e.g., Alexander & Ruderman, 1987; Tyler & Caine, 1981).

In regard to procedural justice theory, there were two key developments in the 1980s. Leventhal (1980) suggested that judgments of procedural fairness were much more complex than the Thibaut and Walker (1975) process control model. Leventhal proposed that there were at least six different procedural justice rules that people use in making judgments of fairness: (a) consistency over time and persons; (b) bias suppression, or the absence of personal self-interest by the allocator; (c) accuracy, in that the decision was based on accurate information; (d) correctability, allowing for the modification of decisions; (e) representativeness of the concerns of all recipient groups; and (f) ethicality based on prevailing moral or ethical standards. Violation by a decision maker of one or more of these rules leads to perceptions of procedural injustice (Leventhal, 1980). Furthermore, Leventhal believed that these rules might be used either singly or in various combinations, that different situations might call forth different rules, and that each rule might exert different weight in different circumstances.

More recently, the development of the group value model by Lind and Tyler (1988) has begun to influence the study of procedural justice in organizational settings. The process control theory of Thibaut and Walker

(1975) suggested that procedural justice was valued because the recipient felt it increased the likelihood of receiving a fair outcome. Lind and Tyler referred to this as the "self-interest model." In contrast, the group value model says that procedural justice is important because it has value-expressive or relational significance (Tyler & Lind, 1992). People identify with groups and value their long-term relationships with authorities, groups, and organizations. Being treated with fair procedures is an indicator that one is valued by the group or authority figure. Unfair procedures have a powerful effect because they threaten one's self-esteem, indicate that one is not valued as a person, and suggest that the decision maker regards that person as an inferior human being. Tyler (1989) proposed that three key processes influence these procedural justice judgments: (a) neutrality of the procedures, (b) trust in the decision maker, and (c) indicators of the recipient's social standing, such as being treated with respect by others. Empirical support has been obtained in recent studies (Tyler, 1989, 1990).

Because much of the work on procedural justice has emphasized the processes that precede decision making or the allocation of an outcome, it is very important to point out that postdecisional processes can also affect perceptions of procedural justice and the consequences of those perceptions. Alexander and Ruderman (1987) found that appeal procedure fairness was an important component of overall perceptions of procedural justice. The pioneering work of Bies and his colleagues has shown that the accounts or explanations given after unfavorable outcomes influence employees' procedural justice perceptions and their subsequent behavior (Bies & Shapiro, 1987).

Interactional Justice

Growing out of the work on procedural justice has been an interest in interactional justice (Bies & Moag, 1986). The distinction here is between the formal rules and procedures and the actual implementation of those procedures. Interactional justice refers to one's perception of the actual treatment from others as procedures are carried out. This concept has led to important research, exemplified by the work of Bies and his colleagues on social accounts and explanations of decisions made by the decision maker (e.g., Bies & Shapiro, 1987). The presence of accounts or excuses for unfavorable decisions reduced recipients' perceptions of injustice and negative evaluations of the decision maker.

There has been some controversy over whether interactional justice is yet another type of justice or is another aspect of the broader phenomenon of procedural justice. Greenberg (1990) argued that although interactional factors are important, they do not define a new type of justice. Rather, they identify some interpersonal aspects of procedural justice. This view is consistent with the group value model of procedural justice, which emphasizes trust, standing, respect, and relationships (Lind & Tyler, 1988; Tyler & Lind, 1992). A rapprochement on this issue may be emerging. Tyler and Bies (1990) jointly published an analysis of the *interpersonal* aspects of procedural justice, suggesting that procedural justice consists of both the formal procedures and the proper interpersonal enactment of those procedures. Tyler and Bies believed there are several norms involved in this interpersonal aspect of procedural justice, including (a) adequately considering employees' viewpoints, (b) suppressing personal biases, (c) applying decision-making criteria consistently across employees, (d) providing timely feedback to employees after a decision, and (e) providing an explanation for the decision (Tyler & Bies, 1990).

More recently, Greenberg (1993a) offered a new model of organizational justice. In this model he suggested that different social or interactional aspects of justice may be elements of either procedural justice or distributive justice. Greenberg used the term *informational justice* to describe the social aspects of procedural justice and the term *interpersonal justice* to describe the social aspects of distributive justice. Whatever the ultimate resolution of these differing views, the introduction of the concept of interactional justice by Bies has had the positive effect of highlighting interpersonal factors influencing fairness judgments.

Retributive Justice

The issue of retributive justice, the perceived fairness of punishment, has received less attention in the organizational literature than the work on procedural and distributive justice, which focused primarily on reward allocations. Hogan and Emler (1981) presented a theoretical discussion of retributive justice and its importance. They argued that retributive justice is more basic than distributive justice and lamented the lack of research on it: "Retributive justice is more salient than distributive justice in most people's ordinary social expectations . . . the process of retribution is older, more primitive, more universal, and socially more significant [than allocating and exchanging benefits on a just basis]" (Hogan & Emler 1981, p. 131). More recently, McLean Parks and Kidder (1994) presented a model integrating the notions of psychological contracts, retributive justice, and anti-role behaviors in organizations. Although the use of punishment in organizations is fairly common (Arvey & Jones, 1985), the study of retributive justice is scarce. However, a number of recent articles suggest this may be changing (e.g., Alexander & Oliansky, 1994; Ball, Trevino, & Sims, 1993; Trevino, 1992).

Systemic Justice

The concept of systemic justice was introduced by Sheppard, Lewicki, and Minton (1992). They proposed that people make judgments of fairness at three different levels. The first level involves outcome justice (distributive justice); the second involves procedural justice; and the third level is systemic justice, the fairness of the system within which the outcomes and the procedures were generated. The distinction Sheppard et al. made is an important one. It is similar to the contrast made by Brickman, Folger, Goode, and Schul (1981) in their discussion of microjustice versus macrojustice. Outcomes judged to be fair at the individual level may lead to unfair consequences at the broader organizational or societal levels. Or, employees may regard the specific outcome rules or procedural rules used as fair but feel certain additional justice rules must apply at the system level to avoid injustice. This concept of levels of justice also raises the issue of justice at various levels within an organization (dyad, work group, department, plant, company) and the need to determine whether different justice rules operate at different organizational levels.

The term *systemic justice* also was used by Greenberg (1993a) as one of four classes of justice in his model of organizational justice; the other three classes are *informational, configural,* and *interpersonal* justice. For Greenberg, systemic justice referred to "the variety of procedural justice that is accomplished via structural means. This is the class of justice that was originally studied by procedural justice scholars" (1993a, pp. 83–84). Thus, Greenberg treated systemic justice more narrowly than did Sheppard et al. (1992).

JUSTICE AND THE EMPLOYER–EMPLOYEE RELATIONSHIP

The review just provided of the various types or levels of organizational justice indicates the relevance of justice concepts to workplace issues and to employer–employee relationships. In this section, we briefly review the justice literature as it has examined changes in the employment relationship, including pay and compensation systems; changes to working conditions through drug testing, smoking bans, and related issues; and the impact of layoffs on victims and survivors. We also discuss implementation and participation in employee involvement programs, conflict and dispute resolution, and reactions toward the employer and agents of the employer as a result of perceived justice or injustice.

Pay and Compensation Systems

Some of the earliest empirical work on the psychology of justice dealt with the perceived fairness of pay and compensation (Patchen, 1961), and early discussions of equity focused on pay (Adams, 1965; Homans, 1961). Equity theory strongly influenced subsequent pay satisfaction research (Heneman, 1985). More recent research has confirmed that the perceived distributive fairness of pay relates strongly to measures of satisfaction with one's pay, even more than does the actual amount of pay (Folger & Konovsky, 1989). That reactions to pay were influenced by perceived outcome fairness was not surprising. However, evidence that procedural factors influenced pay reactions attracted notice and continues to be of interest. For example, in an early procedural justice experiment, Folger (1977) found that "voice" led participants to react more favorably to pay inequities than did a mute condition. This phenomenon came to be labeled the "fair process effect" (Greenberg & Folger, 1983). The same outcome is perceived as fairer if the procedures are fair. More recent work has dealt with issues influenced by some of the major changes occurring in American industry, such as pay freezes and pay cuts. Schaubroeck, May, and Brown (1994) found that perceived procedural fairness had a mitigating effect on reactions to a long-term pay freeze, even when the procedural justice treatment was introduced a year after the pay freeze began. In research on pay cuts, Greenberg (1993b) found that employee theft increased and that both procedural and distributive justice manipulations could mitigate these negative effects.

Drug Testing, Smoking Bans, and Related Issues

Increasingly, health-related issues that at one time would have been regarded as personal or private matters have come to be thought of as workplace problems that must be dealt with by management because of their presumed effects on productivity or coworkers. Increasing attention is being paid to alcohol use, drug use, smoking, overeating, and so forth. The growth in employee assistance programs may be related to concerns about the deleterious effects on the organization of such personal habits. We raise these matters here because research is beginning to suggest that the effectiveness of organizational interventions may be strongly influenced by justice phenomena and the fairness perceptions of employees.

Konovsky and Cropanzano (1991) examined the influence of perceived procedural and distributive fairness of a drug testing program on employees' turnover intentions, job satisfaction, organizational commitment, trust in management, and performance appraisals. Justice perceptions did predict these criterion measures, and outcome fairness added no unique variance once procedural justice factors had been accounted for. Tepper (1994) found that employees of companies with drug testing programs were more likely to focus on procedural justice issues, whereas employees of companies without drug testing programs focused on the distributive justice of drug testing programs. Thus, different justice rules were used by employees facing different situations. Greenberg (1994) studied employee acceptance of a corporate smoking ban. He found that the greater the perceived fairness of the smoking ban, the greater the acceptance. The effects of the fairness manipulations were strongest for heavy smokers. The results of these studies strongly suggest that fairness perceptions can play a significant role in influencing employee reactions to a company's health-related intervention or behavioral control programs.

Layoffs and Reactions of Victims and Survivors

Major downsizing, restructuring, layoffs, and job loss in the past decade have been noted in many studies of organizational behavior and the workplace (e.g., Leana & Ivancevich, 1987). Studies of reactions of layoff victims and layoff survivors increasingly have identified justice and fairness concerns as significant factors influencing postlayoff responses. Receiving less attention has been the question of reactions toward the former employer. What about resentment, which in its most extreme manifestation can lead to violence toward the former employer? Although such research is difficult to carry out, focusing on justice issues may provide useful insights.

Increasingly, attention also is being paid to reactions of employees who remain in the organization following layoffs (e.g., Brockner, Grover, Reed, DeWitt, & O'Malley, 1987). The evidence indicates that there are changes in organizational commitment, job satisfaction, and turnover intentions and that the perceived fairness of the layoffs may be a key determinant of survivor reactions (Brockner, DeWitt, Grover, & Reed, 1990; Davy, Kinicki, & Scheck, 1991). Procedural justice appears to be especially important in mediating reactions of survivors toward their jobs and their employers (Davy et al., 1991). The influence of unfair procedures on the reactions of both victims and survivors appears to be greatest when outcome negativity is high for victims (Konovsky & Brockner, 1993).

Employee Involvement, Participation, Quality of Work Life and Related Issues

Following the classic study by Coch and French (1948) of worker participation in decision making, this issue has been examined extensively by students of industrial relations and organizational behavior. In a recent review of the literature, Leana and Florkowski (1992) pointed out that the relatively new term *employee involvement* deals with an old, and often studied, idea that increased worker participation will lead to positive outcomes (e.g., less turnover, resistance to change, and alienation; enhanced productivity, product quality, employee attitudes, and motivation; and better relations with management). This topic has been examined under a variety of labels such as quality of work life, quality circles, workplace democracy, participative management, autonomous work groups, gainsharing, and so forth.

Our interest lies in the connection between justice theories and employee involvement processes. It is suggested that key elements of procedural justice (process control, Thibaut & Walker, 1975; voice, Folger, 1977; worker participation, Alexander & Ruderman, 1987; standing, Tyler, 1989) are significantly related to employee involvement issues. Discussion of possible relationships between procedural justice and participatory decision making was initiated by Greenberg and Folger (1983).

Conflict and Dispute Resolution

The classic theory of procedural justice was developed by Thibaut and Walker (1975) within a dispute resolution framework. Much supportive research using courtroom or legal settings followed (e.g., Lind, Kurtz, Musante, Walker, & Thibaut, 1980). This work was soon extended to the issue of disputes in work and organizational settings, with procedural justice being the focus of attention (e.g., Lewicki & Sheppard, 1985). Karambayya and Brett (1989) examined managerial third-party dispute resolution behavior. Mediational styles of dispute resolution were judged to be procedurally fairer than other styles and to lead to fairer outcomes. More recently, Shapiro (1993) made a detailed analysis of procedural justice and its importance for dispute management. Here, we wish only to provide a reminder of the obvious: Disputes are a significant feature of changing employment relations and of union–management relationships. An examination of justice issues (especially procedural justice) holds promise of developing new insights into such industrial relations problems.

Reactions Toward Supervisors, Management, and the Employing Organization

Some of the earliest, strongest, and most frequently replicated findings on the effects of organizational justice involve workers' reactions toward immediate supervisors, upper management, and the total organization. Justice perceptions have consistently had a major influence on satisfaction with one's supervisor, trust in one's supervisor, trust in top management, organizational commitment, and organizational citizenship (Alexander & Ruderman, 1987; Folger & Konovsky, 1989; Moorman, Niehoff, & Organ, 1993). However, procedural justice has been found to be an especially important determinant of such organizational attitudes as well as attitudes and behavior toward authority (Alexander & Ruderman, 1987; Moorman et al., 1993; Lind & Tyler, 1988; Tyler & Lind, 1992).

ORGANIZATIONAL JUSTICE AND LABOR UNIONS

Although the literature cited above strongly indicates the importance of justice and fairness in the employment relationship, much of the research and theory has had a limited view of the actual structure that exists in many work environments. The organizational justice literature tends to focus almost exclusively on the employer–employee relationship to the exclusion of considerations of union representation. We suggest below that union mechanisms can affect perceptions of justice between the union and the employer, the employer–employee relationship, and within the union itself.

Brett (1980) pointed out that an individual's initial interest in unionization is related to unmet expectations (as part of one's psychological contract) about fair wages and fair working conditions. In reality, perceived organization injustice plays a central role in both initial union organizing campaigns and the ongoing employment relationship between union member and employer as well as in the relationship between union member and union. J. J. Lawler (1986) pointed out that although psychological research on union certification elections frequently assumes a rational decision-making process in which potential members weigh the benefits against the costs of membership, such research does not consider the role of organizing tactics by the union and antiunion tactics by the employer. The employer makes efforts to convince the individual that the workplace is currently just, and the union attempts to convince employees that the union is the only means through which workplace injustice can be addressed (cf. Brett, 1980; Gordon & Fryxell, 1993). Thus, unionization has the potential to turn the workplace into an interest battleground as both employer and union make efforts to shape workers, perceptions to suit their own ends (see Sheppard et al., 1992). Our contention is that this process extends beyond the certification campaign to the ongoing employment relationship. Whether the result of deliberate strategic attempts to influence individuals' perceptions or unintended consequences of union or management practices, company and union policies and practices will influence individuals' perceptions of the fairness of both the company and the union.

Union Mechanisms That Affect Justice

Barling, Fullagar, and Kelloway (1992) listed wages, fringe benefits, job security, and working conditions as the "bread and butter" issues for unions. Justice concerns play a role in unions' efforts in each of these areas. Compensation packages (wages and benefits) are generally better in unionized settings (when compared with nonunionized individuals in similar classes of jobs). Unions tend to negotiate uniform wages for a given job classification; fight against piece-rate and merit pay (performance-based) reward systems; and bargain based on the needs of senior and less mobile (in terms of employment) employees rather than the conditions of the local labor market. Barling et al. (1992) pointed out three ways in which these tendencies influence equity or distributive justice issues related to compensation: (a) They equate outcomes received by individuals; (b) they influence the weighting schemes that individuals use for inputs by clarifying what inputs are used for compensation decisions; and (c) they influence the individual's choice of referent for equity perceptions (it becomes individuals in the same bargaining unit or grade; see Ambrose, Harland, & Kulik, 1991, for discussion of the role of social referents in justice perceptions). Unions also affect justice related to job security through formal procedures for layoff and termination (Barling et al., 1992).

Perhaps more psychologically interesting for justice researchers are the effects of unions on working conditions and the general psychological climate of the workplace. Unions increase awareness of job-related hazards and negotiate higher wage rates for hazardous jobs (Kochan, 1980). Furthermore, one of the general functions of unions is to protect employees from arbitrary treatment by management (Gordon & Fryxell, 1993; Sheppard et al., 1992). Unions reduce arbitrariness by (a) defining the limits of managerial authority, (b) the process of collective bargaining, and (c) ensuring that employees have the right to grieve abuses of authority under the resulting contract (Sheppard et al., 1992).

Unions also enhance justice by providing employees with voice mechanisms in the workplace. Sheppard et al. (1992) suggested that voice mechanisms ensure employees of fair treatment, provide a context for the appeal of unfair treatment through grievances, improve the effectiveness of the organization over time, and sustain employee loyalty and commitment. In unionized settings voice methods include the grievance system, employee assistance programs, newsletters, and union committees and meetings (Sheppard et al., 1992). Sheppard et al. (1992) pointed out that a lack of voice systems probably contributed to the birth of the labor movement—they suggested that any system that stays unfair long enough will either fail completely or become subject to external procedural controls (such as unions). Hoerr (1991) suggested two alternatives to unions relative to workplace fairness: governmental intervention and fairness-related human resources programs (i.e., quality circles). However, Hoerr (1991) also pointed out that (a) "laws tend to work best where unions are present to ensure that the laws are enforced" (p. 32), (b) vast sets of governmental rules are likely to be more inflexible than unions ever were, (c) "HR [human resources] programs to ensure fairness often break down . . . where they are needed most—in situations of severe conflict" (p. 32), and (d) "neither [alternative] provides workers with an independent source of power in the organization" (Weiler, 1990, in Hoerr, 1991, p. 32).

The labor movement also has motivated managers in nonunionized settings to pay more attention to fairness concerns in their attempts to avoid unionization (E. E. Lawler & Mohrman, 1987). This concern may or may not be genuine as managers often report being more interested in appearing fair than in actually being fair (Greenberg, 1988). Furthermore, it is sometimes argued that company-implemented employee-voice or involvement programs such as participatory management systems are used as devices to actually enhance management control over workers (Parker, 1991). It seems clear that justice considerations are a fundamental component of employees' desires for union representation as well as efforts by management to keep unions out of their workplace.

Union Effects on the Employer–Employee Relationship

When a collective bargaining agreement is in place, justice concerns remain an important influence on union members' perceptions of their employer. Mellor (1990) found that in union locals where the rate of membership loss had been the greatest, the rank and file were more likely to attribute strikes to unfair management practices than members in union locals in which membership had suffered smaller declines. In work sites where membership declines were smaller, members were more likely to acknowledge that the blame for strikes was shared by both sides.

Unions affect the employment relationship by placing emphasis on different rules of justice than those that might be used in nonunion settings. James (1993) noted that internal workplace culture/climate (i.e., individualism vs. collectivism) affects choice of justice rules. Bierhoff, Buck, and Klein (1986) showed that equity principles are salient when individual differences are emphasized, whereas equality principles are salient when workers emphasize solidarity. Distributive justice is maximized when the justice principle used matches the situation. Labor unions' emphasis on collectivism and solidarity has the practical effect that unions bargain for seniority rules, against two-tiered pay systems, and for increased control over task assignments and job definitions.

Although relatively little psychological research exists regarding labor unions' influence on members' perceptions of their employer, the causal-accounts literature in the field of justice has much to offer, particularly for the strategic view of union–management relations. Bies and Shapiro (1987) described causal accounts as "explanations regarding a person's responsibility for his or her actions" (p. 201). Causal accounts are an important aspect of procedural justice in organizational decisions and have been shown to have effects on justice that are distinct from formal procedures (Bies & Shapiro, 1987). If fairness is a central concern relative to labor–management relations, then causal accounts for actions become important, particularly when the organization is viewed as an interest battleground (Sheppard et al., 1992) or when the outcome of interest is unfavorable (Tyler & Bies, 1990). Mellor (1992) applied Bies's (Bies & Moag, 1986) work on interactional justice to layoffs, pointing out that both the company and the union may try to convince the membership that the other is to blame. Tyler and McGaw (1986) noted that leaders often attempt to convince the public that procedures that produce unfair outcomes are actually fair—they strive for the appearance of fairness. In building support for a strike or to win a certification election, union leaders may focus on the faults of management. One aspect of the union's message is likely to be their causal account for past actions by management (e.g., management laid off workers so they could keep their expensive bonus packages). Management is likely to offer a completely different causal account for the same action (e.g., "We had to lay off workers to ensure the long-term viability of the organization"). The union's membership (or potential members) must make decisions about the believability of the accounts of one side or the other.

Most research on causal accounts has not focused directly on labor–management relations. Schaubroeck et al. (1994) found that the explanation given for a pay freeze reduced the effects of the pay freeze on individuals' justice perceptions and intentions to leave, satisfaction, and commitment. Bies, Shapiro, and Cummings (1988) found that the effect of a causal account on procedural justice depends on the reasoning supporting the claim as well as the sincerity of the individual offering the account. Although direct empirical evidence is lacking, the causal-accounts literature suggests a theoretical basis for our linkage between J. J. Lawler's (1986) strategic view of labor-organizing campaigns and our notion that individuals' perceptions of ongoing union and management policies and practices are linked to their resultant attitudes and behavior through their perceptions of workplace justice. Individuals' perceptions of the reasons underlying various management and union activities play an important role in their resultant attitudes and behaviors.

Eisenberger, Huntington, Hutchison, and Sowa (1986) used social exchange theory to suggest that individuals form broad perceptions of their employing organization's commitment to them as individuals, which they termed *perceived organizational support.* Thus, commitment to the employment relationship is a two-way street. Although a connection between organizational support and perceptions of organizational justice seems logical, to our knowledge no research has examined this issue in the workplace directly. However, this view is consistent with research supporting the group value model of procedural justice (Tyler & Lind, 1992). One study examined the impact of unionization on perceived organizational support as well as the effect of unionization on the relationship between benefit programs and individuals' perceptions of organizational support. Sinclair, Hannigan, and Tetrick (1994) found that union membership accounted for unique variance (beyond age, gender, and income as well as individuals' benefit coverage and beliefs about the types of benefits employers should offer) in perceived organizational support but did not interact with level of benefit coverage in prediction of perceived organizational support.

Justice and Intraunion Issues

Justice concerns also play a critical role in union members' attitudes and behaviors toward their union. Gordon and Fryxell (1993) pointed out that the National Labor Relations Board is concerned primarily with principles of procedural justice. Unions are bound by the Duty of Fair Representation "to represent all members of the bargaining unit without hostile discrimination, fairly, impartially, and in good faith" (Gordon & Fryxell, 1993, p. 235). Thus, whereas management must at least appear to be fair, unions are legally required to do so. In the day-to-day functioning of the union, the grievance system represents the principle means through which workplace justice is maintained (Gordon & Fryxell, 1993).

Feuille and Delaney (1992) attempted to analyze complaints and grievance procedures in nonunion settings and compare them with union settings. In their review of the recent research literature, they found that an organizational justice perspective, with particular attention to procedural justice, provides a promising approach to better understanding these issues. Furthermore, labor relations research suggests that (a) the procedural justice of a grievance system is more important than the system's distributive justice (e.g., Klaas, 1989); (b) union stewards are more concerned than managers with procedural and distributive justice issues relative to grievance resolution (Martin & Cusella, 1986); and (c) the union's image is more dependent on the grievance system than is management's, especially concerning union commitment (Clark & Gallagher, 1989; Eaton, Gordon, & O'Keefe, 1992). Supportive data also are provided by Fryxell and Gordon (1989), who found that procedural justice accounted for more variance than distributive justice in prediction of members' satisfaction with the union (although distributive justice was also related to satisfaction with the union), satisfaction with the grievance system, and satisfaction with management. Procedural justice also accounted for more variance than workplace justice or job satisfaction in prediction of satisfaction with the union. Gordon and Fryxell (1993) provided several useful suggestions for future research on grievances and concluded that "a union's relations with its constituents is tied more closely to the procedural and distributive justice afforded by its representation in the grievance system than by any other type of benefit provided in the collective bargaining agreement" (p. 251).

Justice issues have been studied relative to other union attitudes such as union commitment. Mellor (1992) found that belief in management's causal account for a layoff moderated the relationship between layoff severity (percentage of workforce laid off) and willingness to work for the union. Willingness to work for the union increased when belief in the account was low and decreased when belief in the account was high. Johnson, Tetrick, and Johnson (1992) found that distributive justice was negatively related to participation and willingness to work for the union. Distributive justice also was related to satisfaction, expectations of the union and the local, and steward and supervisor support. Sinclair, Alexander, and Tetrick (1994) found that organizational justice was negatively related to willingness to work for the union after income, job type, and union instrumentality were controlled for.

Social exchange theory may also play a part in the findings that voluntariness of union membership has been shown to play a role in justice perceptions. Tyler (1986) suggested that procedural justice issues are more important when membership in an institution is imposed as compared with freely chosen membership in institutions. Conlon and Gallagher (1987) pointed out that voluntariness of union membership is an important issue in union commitment and presented empirical evidence showing different patterns of relations among company and union commitment as well as intrinsic and extrinsic job satisfaction for union members, individuals who have never been union members, and those who have left the union. Fryxell and Gordon (1989) found that procedural justice was more highly correlated with satisfaction with the union and management when membership in the union was imposed. They concluded that procedures that are viewed as just will be more closely linked to satisfaction in imposed relationships because they enhance predictability and control in individuals' perceptions of the employment relationship.

Barling et al. (1992) pointed out that organizational behavior in unionized settings is politicized. For instance, grievances are rarely resolved simply on the merit of each individual case—rather the union may "horse-trade" grievances with management as part of the collective bargaining process (Gordon & Fryxell, 1993). The political nature of labor–management relations and organizational behavior provides an opportunity to connect labor–management relations with justice-related research in political participation.

Tyler and McGaw (1986) pointed out that political inaction under a condition of distributive unfairness may be accounted for by considering the procedural aspects of decision making. If individuals believe that fair procedures were followed, then they are less likely to take action to rectify distributive unfairness. Tyler and McGaw also argued that research shows that this effect is more common when the object of evaluation is a system rather than an individual. Political actions, then, are based more on systemic justice. Extending this argument to unionization decisions or union participation, one would expect that more macro- or systemic-level fairness assessments such as judgments of the fairness of organizational procedures would be expected to predict union activity more than one individual's treatment by another individual. If the individual believes that the employer is generally fair, then one would expect that individual to be less active in a union. Furthermore, Greenberg (1988) showed that individuals will cognitively distort small injustices so they appear to be just. The centrality of procedural justice to evaluations of a union has been echoed by Leung, Chui, and Au (1993), who concluded from their review of the literature that procedural variables have a stronger impact on variables related to institutions or authorities and distributive variables have greater effects on variables related to specific outcomes such as pay satisfaction. Their analysis suggests that distributive justice may be more important in members' evaluations of outcomes that the union has secured from collective bargaining, whereas procedural justice may be more important in union members' evaluations of their union and its leadership.

Discussion

From this review of the literature on organizational justice and its extension to unionized work environments, it becomes clear that justice and injustice research can broaden our understanding of the impact of the changing employment relationship at the individual, organizational, and even societal levels. First, it must be recognized that the development, maintenance, and modification of employment relationships take place in a political, social, and economic environment. This may be the most global form of systemic justice.

Justice perceptions are formed and modified in the context of a strategic environment in which unions and companies seek to explain organizational events in ways that will favor either or both companies and unions. The strategies of unions and companies can influence individual perceptions of justice in one of two ways. The first is direct, through each side's causal accounts for organizational events (e.g., layoffs, mergers, changes in resource allocations). Characteristics of these explanations (such as the believability of the message) influence individuals' perceptions of organizational justice on a number of levels as well as perceived justice within the union.

The second way that strategies influence justice perceptions is indirect, through the influence of strategies on union and company policies and practices and collective bargaining outcomes. As long as policies are set and collective bargaining is conducted in terms of the strategies of both parties, the resulting influence on justice may be intended or unintended. For instance, a union may bargain against two-tier pay systems in part to increase pay equity. Conversely, horse-trading grievances as part of contract negotiations may reduce perceptions of justice on the part of those individuals who filed the grievances if they feel that their grievances were not resolved to their satisfaction. Finally, the existing theoretical and empirical literature supports our contention that justice influences individuals' cognitive, affective, and behavioral responses (e.g., Sheppard et al., 1992). This literature suggests that it is not only what changes are implemented but also the processes by which the changes are implemented—that is, procedural and interactional justice—that have an impact on employees' responses to changes in the employment relationship. Therefore, the justice literature may serve as a guide for understanding the effects of strategic initiatives of both employers and unions in shaping employment relationships.

REFERENCES

Adams, J. S. (1965). Inequity in social exchange. *Advances in Experimental Social Psychology, 2*, 267–299.

Alexander, S., & Oliansky, M. (1994, August). *Organizational effects of the procedural and distributive justice of workplace punishment.* Paper presented at the 102nd Annual Convention of the American Psychological Association, Los Angeles.

Alexander, S., & Ruderman, M. (1987). The role of procedural and distributive justice in organizational behavior. *Social Justice Research, 1*, 177–198.

Ambrose, M. L., Harland, L. K., & Kulik, C. T. (1991). Influence of social comparisons on perceptions of organizational fairness. *Journal of Applied Psychology, 76*, 239–246.

Arvey, R. D., & Jones, A. P. (1985). The use of discipline in organizational settings: A framework for future research. In L. L. Cummings & B. M. Staw (Eds.), *Research in organizational behavior* (Vol. 7, pp. 367–408). Greenwich, CT: JAI Press.

Ball, G. A., Trevino, L. K., & Sims, H. P. (1993). Justice and organizational punishment: Attitudinal outcomes of disciplinary events. *Social Justice Research, 6,* 39–67.

Barling, J., Fullagar, C., & Kelloway, E. K. (1992). *The union and its members: A psychological approach.* New York: Oxford University Press.

Bierhoff, H. W., Buck, E., & Klein, R. (1986). Social context and perceived justice. In H. W. Bierhoff, R. L. Cohen, & J. Greenberg (Eds.), *Justice in social relations* (pp. 165–185). New York: Plenum Press.

Bies, R. J., & Moag, J. S. (1986). Interactional justice: Communication criteria of fairness. In R. J. Lewicki, B. H. Sheppard, & M. H. Bazerman (Eds.), *Research on negotiation in organizations* (Vol. 1, 43–55). Greenwich, CT: JAI Press.

Bies, R. J., & Shapiro, D. L. (1987). Interactional fairness judgments: The influence of causal accounts. *Social Justice Research, 1,* 199–218.

Bies, R. J., Shapiro, D. L., & Cummings, L. L. (1988). Causal accounts and managing organizational conflict: Is it enough to say it's not my fault? *Communication Research, 15,* 381–399.

Brett, J. M. (1980, Spring). Why employees want unions. *Organizational Dynamics,* pp. 47–59.

Brickman, P., Folger, R., Goode, E., & Schul, Y. (1981). Microjustice and macrojustice. In M. J. Lerner & S. C. Lerner (Eds.), *The justice motive in social behavior: Adapting to times of scarcity and change* (pp. 173–202). New York: Plenum Press.

Brockner, J., DeWitt, R., Grover, S., & Reed, T. (1990). When it is especially important to explain why: Factors affecting the relationship between mangers' explanations of a layoff and survivors' reactions to the layoff. *Journal of Experimental Social Psychology, 26,* 389–407.

Brockner, J., Grover, S., Reed, T., DeWitt, R., & O'Malley, M. (1987). Survivors reactions to layoffs: We get by with a little help for our friends. *Administrative Science Quarterly, 32,* 526–541.

Clark, P. F., & Gallagher, D. G. (1989). Building member commitment to the union: The role of the grievance procedure. *Work Place Topics, 1*(2), 16–21.

Coch, L., & French, J. R. P. (1948). Overcoming resistance to change. *Human Relations, 1,* 512–532.

Commission on the Future of Worker–Management Relations. (1994). *Fact finding report*. Washington, DC: U.S. Department of Labor.

Conlon, E. J., & Gallagher, D. G. (1987). Commitment to employer and union: Effects of membership status. *Academy of Management Journal, 30*, 151–162.

Cropanzano, R. (1993). *Justice in the workplace: Approaching fairness in human resource management*. Hillsdale, NJ: Erlbaum.

Davy, J. A., Kinicki, A. J., & Scheck, C. L. (1991). Developing and testing a model of survivor responses to layoffs. *Journal of Vocational Behavior, 38*, 302–317.

Deutsch, M. (1975). Equity, equality, and need: What determines which value will be used as the basis of distributive justice? *Journal of Social Issues, 31*, 137–149.

Deutsch, M. (1985). *Distributive justice: A social psychological perspective*. New Haven, CT: Yale University Press.

Eaton, A. E., Gordon, M. E., & O'Keefe, J. H. (1992). The impact of quality of work life programs and grievance system effectiveness on union commitment. *Industrial and Labor Relations Review, 45*, 591–604.

Eisenberger, R., Huntington, R. Hutchison, S., & Sowa, D. (1986). Perceived organizational support. *Journal of Applied Psychology, 71*, 500–507.

Feuille, P., & Delaney, J. T. (1992). The individual pursuit of organizational justice: Grievance procedures in nonunion workplaces. In G. R. Ferris & K. M. Rowland (Eds.), *Research in personnel and human resources management* (Vol. 10, pp. 187–232). Greenwich, CT: JAI Press.

Folger, R. (1977). Distributive and procedural justice: Combined impact of "voice" and improvement on experienced inequity. *Journal of Personality and Social Psychology, 35*, 108–119.

Folger, R., & Konovsky, M. (1989). Effects of procedural and distributive justice on reactions to pay raise decisions. *Academy of Management Journal, 32*, 115–130.

Fryxell, G. E., & Gordon, M. E. (1989). Workplace justice and job satisfaction as predictors of satisfaction with union and with management. *Academy of Management Journal, 32*, 851–866.

Gordon, M. E., & Fryxell, G. E. (1993). The role of interpersonal justice in organizational grievance systems. In R. Cropanzano (Ed.), *Justice in the workplace: Approaching fairness in human resource management* (pp. 231–255). Hillsdale, NJ: Earlbaum.

Greenberg, J. (1988). Cultivating an image of justice: Looking fair on the job. *Academy of Management Executive, 2*(2), 155–157.

Greenberg, J. (1990). Organizational justice: Yesterday, today and tomorrow. *Journal of Management, 16,* 399–432.

Greenberg, J. (1993a). The social side of fairness: Interpersonal and informational classes of organizational justice. In R. Cropanzano (Ed.), *Justice in the workplace: Approaching fairness in human resource management* (pp. 79–103). Hillsdale, NJ: Erlbaum.

Greenberg, J. (1993b). Stealing in the name of justice: Informational and interpersonal moderators of theft reactions to underpayment inequity. *Organizational Behavior and Human Decision Processes, 54,* 81–103.

Greenberg, J. (1994). Using socially fair treatment to promote acceptance of a work site smoking ban. *Journal of Applied Psychology, 79,* 288–297.

Greenberg, J., & Folger, R. (1983). Procedural justice, participation, and the fair process effect in groups and organizations. In P. B. Paulus (Ed.), *Basic group processes* (pp. 235–256). New York: Springer-Verlag.

Heneman, H. G., III. (1985). Pay satisfaction. In G. R. Ferris & K. M. Rowland (Eds.), *Research in personnel and human resources management* (Vol. 3, pp. 115–139). Greenwich, CT: JAI Press.

Hoerr, J. (1991, May–June). What should unions do? *Harvard Business Review,* pp. 30–45.

Hogan, R., & Emler, N. P. (1981). Retributive justice. In M. J. Lerner & S. C. Lerner (Eds.), *The justice motive in social behavior* (pp. 125–143). New York: Plenum Press.

Homans, G. C. (1961). *Social behavior: Its elementary forms.* New York: Harcourt, Brace.

James, K. (1993). The social context of organizational justice: Cultural, intergroup, and structural effects on justice behaviors and perceptions. In R. Cropanzano (Ed.), *Justice in the workplace: Approaching fairness in human resource management* (pp. 21–49). Hillsdale, NJ: Erlbaum.

Johnson, W. R., Tetrick, L. E., & Johnson, G. J. (1992, May). *A model of union participation in the United States: A comparison of two disparate locals.* Paper presented at the Seventh Annual Conference of the Society for Industrial and Organizational Psychology, Montreal, Ontario, Canada.

Karambayya, R., & Brett, J. M. (1989). Managers handling disputes: Third-party roles and perceptions of fairness. *Academy of Management Journal, 32,* 687–704.

Klaas, B. S. (1989). Managerial decision making about employee grievances: The impact of the grievant's work history. *Personnel Psychology, 42,* 53–68.

Kochan, T. A. (1980). *Collective bargaining and industrial relations.* Homewood, IL: Irwin.

Konovsky, M. A., & Brockner, J. (1993). Managing victim and survivor layoff reactions: A procedural justice perspective. In R. Cropanzano (Ed.), *Justice in the workplace: Approaching fairness in human resource management* (pp. 133–153). Hillsdale, NJ: Erlbaum.

Konovsky, M., & Cropanzano, R. (1991). Perceived fairness of employee drug testing as a predictor of employee attitudes and job performance. *Journal of Applied Psychology, 76,* 698–707.

Lawler, E. E., III., & Mohrman, S. A. (1987). Unions and the new management. *Academy of Management Executive, 1*(3), 293–300.

Lawler, J. J. (1986). Union growth and decline: The impact of employer and union tactics. *Journal of Occupational Psychology, 59,* 217–230.

Leana, C. R., & Ivancevich, J. M. (1987). Involuntary job loss: Institutional interventions and a research agenda. *Academy of Management Review, 12,* 301–312.

Leana, C. R., & Florkowski, G. W. (1992). Employee involvement programs: Integrating psychological theory and management practice. In G. R. Ferris & K. M. Rowland (Eds.), *Research in personnel and human resources management* (Vol. 10, pp. 233–270). Greenwich, CT: JAI Press.

Leung, K., Chui, W. H., & Au, Y. F. (1993). Sympathy and support for industrial actions: A justice analysis. *Journal of Applied Psychology, 78,* 781–787.

Leventhal, G. S. (1976). The distribution of rewards and resources in groups and organizations. *Advances in Experimental Social Psychology 9,* 91–131.

Leventhal, G. S. (1980). What should be done with equity theory? New approaches to the study of fairness in social relationships. In K. Gergen, M. Greenberg, & R. Willis (Eds.), *Social exchange: Advances in theory and research* (pp. 27–55). New York: Plenum Press.

Lewicki, R. J., & Sheppard, B. H. (1985). Choosing how to intervene: Factors affecting the use of process and outcome control in third party dispute resolution. *Journal of Occupational Behavior, 6,* 49–64.

Lind, E. A., Kurtz, S., Musante, T., Walker, L., & Thibaut, J. W. (1980). Procedure and outcome effects on reactions to adjudicated resolution of conflicts of interest. *Journal of Personality and Social Psychology, 39,* 643–653.

Lind, E. A., & Tyler, T. R. (1988). *The social psychology of procedural justice.* New York: Plenum Press.

Martin, E. A., & Cusella, L. P. (1986). Persuading the adjudicator: Conflict tactics in the grievance procedure. In M. L. McLaughlin (Ed.), *Communication yearbook 9* (pp. 533–552). Beverly Hills, CA: Sage.

McLean Parks, J., & Kidder, D. L. (1994). "Till death do us part . . .": Changing work relationships. In C. L. Cooper & D. M. Rousseau (Eds.), *Trends in organizational behavior* (Vol. 1, pp. 110–136). New York: Wiley.

Mellor, S. (1990). The relationship between membership decline and union commitment: A field study of local unions in crisis. *Journal of Applied Psychology, 75*, 258–267.

Mellor, S. (1992). The influence of layoff severity on post layoff union commitment among survivors: The moderating effect of the perceived legitimacy of a layoff account. *Personnel Psychology, 45*, 579–600.

Moorman, R. H., Niehoff, B. P., & Organ, D. W. (1993). Treating employees fairly and organizational citizenship behavior: Sorting the effects of job satisfaction, organizational commitment, and procedural justice. *Employee Rights and Responsibilities Journal, 6*, 209–225.

Mowday, R. T. (1983). Equity theory predictions of behavior in organizations. In R. M. Steers & L. W. Porter (Eds.), *Motivation and work behavior* (3rd ed., pp. 91–113). New York: McGraw-Hill.

Parker, M. (1991). Participation or control? *ACADEME, 77*, 44–48.

Patchen, M. (1961). *The choice of wage comparisons.* Englewood Cliffs, NJ: Prentice Hall.

Rousseau, D. M. (1989). Psychological and implied contracts in organizations. *Employee Responsibilities and Rights Journal, 2*, 121–139.

Schaubroeck, J., May, D. R., & Brown, F. W. (1994). Procedural justice explanations and employee reactions to economic hardship: A field experiment. *Journal of Applied Psychology, 79*, 455–460.

Shapiro, D. L. (1993). Reconciling theoretical differences among procedural justice researchers by re-evaluating what it means to have one's views "considered": Implications for third-party managers. In R. Cropanzano (Ed.), *Justice in the workplace: Approaching fairness in human resource management* (pp. 51–78). Hillsdale, NJ: Erlbaum.

Sheppard, B. H., Lewicki, R. J., & Minton, J. W. (1992). *Organizational justice: The search for fairness in the workplace.* Lexington, MA: Lexington Books.

Shore, L. M., & Tetrick, L. E. (1994). The psychological contract as an explanatory framework in the employment relationship. In C. L. Cooper & D. M. Rousseau (Eds.), *Trends in organizational behavior* (Vol. 1, pp. 91–109). New York: Wiley.

Sinclair, R. R., Alexander, S., & Tetrick, L. E. (1994, April). *Organizational justice, union instrumentality, and company and union commitment.* Paper presented at the Ninth Annual Conference of the Society for Industrial and Organizational Psychology, Nashville, TN.

Sinclair, R. R., Hannigan, M. A., & Tetrick, L. E. (1994, May). *Sources of social exchange asymmetry between unions and companies: Relations between benefit coverage and individuals' attitudes toward company and union.* Paper presented at the American Psychological Association conference on the Psychology of Industrial Relations Under Changing Employment Relationships: An International Perspective, Detroit, MI.

Tepper, B. J. (1994). Investigation of general and program-specific attitudes toward corporate drug-testing policies. *Journal of Applied Psychology, 79,* 392–401.

Thibaut, J. W., & Walker, L. (1975). *Procedural justice: A psychological analysis.* Hillsdale, NJ: Erlbaum.

Tornblum, K. Y., & Jonsson, D. R. (1985). Subrules of the equality and contribution principles: Their perceived fairness in distribution and retribution. *Social Psychology Quarterly, 48,* 249–261.

Trevino, L. K. (1992). The social effects of punishment in organizations: A justice perspective. *Academy of Management Review, 17,* 647–676.

Tyler, T. R. (1986). When does procedural justice matter in organizational settings? In R. J. Lewicki, B. H. Sheppard, & M. H. Bazerman (Eds.), *Research on negotiation in organizations* (Vol. 1, pp. 7–23). Greenwich, CT: JAI Press.

Tyler, T. R. (1989). The psychology of procedural justice: A test of the group value model. *Journal of Personality and Social Psychology, 57,* 830–838.

Tyler, T. R. (1990). *Why people obey the law: Procedural justice, legitimacy, and compliance.* New Haven, CT: Yale University Press.

Tyler, T. R., & Bies, R. (1990). Interpersonal aspects of procedural justice. In J. S. Carroll (Ed.), *Applied social psychology and organizational settings* (pp. 77–98). Hillsdale, NJ: Erlbaum.

Tyler, T. R., & Caine, A. (1981). The role of distributional and procedural fairness in the endorsement of formal leaders. *Journal of Personality and Social Psychology, 41,* 642–655.

Tyler, T. R., & Lind, E. A. (1992). A relational model of authority in groups. *Advances in Experimental Social Psychology, 25,* 115–191.

Tyler, T. R., & McGaw, K. M. (1986). Ideology and the interpretation of personal experience: Procedural justice and political quiescence. *Journal of Social Issues, 42,* 115–128.

4

Violation of Psychological Contracts: Impact on Employee Attitudes

Sandra L. Robinson

Contemporary employment relationships are in transition. The demise of employee loyalty and the need for employees to take care of themselves are touted as a sign of the times (Hirsch, 1989). An important aspect of employment relationships is the psychological contracts that permeate them (Rousseau, 1989). As beliefs in reciprocal and promised obligations between employee and employer, psychological contracts can, when violated, generate mistrust, dissatisfaction, and possibly the dissolution of the relationship itself (Argyris, 1960; Rousseau, 1989). The purpose of this study was to examine the impact of psychological contract violation on employees' subsequent attitudes.

PSYCHOLOGICAL CONTRACTS AND EMPLOYMENT RELATIONSHIPS

Contracts are at the foundation of employment relationships (Barnard, 1938), establishing the inducements and contributions basic to membership in organizations. Whether written or unwritten, contracts are promises to provide something in exchange for something else (Farnsworth, 1982). Rousseau (1989) distinguished between three types of contracts within organizations: formal contracts, implied contracts, and psychological contracts. Formal contracts are written agreements and are thus easy to identify. Implied contracts, on the other hand, are unwritten agreements that arise from repeated interactions between two parties. For example, if an employer always pays for overtime hours, an implied contract is likely to arise that such payment will continue to occur in the future, even if there is no formal policy or written agreement in this regard. The terms of an implied contract are less easy to identify than the terms of a formal contract and can be inferred only by observing the relationship and the patterned actions of the parties to the agreement.

A psychological contract is conceptually distinct from both a formal and an implied contract. A psychological contract is an individual's *beliefs about* the terms and conditions of an agreement to which that individual is party. Beliefs regarding the mutual employment obligations between an employee and an employer constitute a psychological contract with respect to the employee–employer relationship (Rousseau, 1989; Rousseau & Parks, 1993). These beliefs may or may not be shared by the other party to the agreement. Indeed, for a variety of reasons, parties to a contract may have very different perceptions of its terms (Rousseau, 1989). This perceptual, individual nature of psychological contracts is their defining attribute, making them distinct from both formal contracts and implied contracts (Weick, 1981).

EXECUTION OF THE PSYCHOLOGICAL CONTRACT

Over the course of the employment relationship, parties engage in reciprocal exchanges in accordance with each party's psychological contract. According to Parks (1992), contract parties may fulfill the contract in varying degrees: (a) comply with the contract and fulfill its terms; (b) go beyond the terms of the contract, honoring its intent rather than the letter of the contract; or (c) violate or breach the terms of the agreement. Maintenance of the employment relationship requires that each party engage in actions that fulfill or exceed the obligations they have promised to the other. Employees attempt to fulfill their part of the contract and look to the organization to fulfill its contractual obligations (Shore & Tetrick, 1994).

Various organizational events and circumstances may create changes in the employment relationship that, in turn, increase the likelihood that one party will violate the psychological contract of the other; that is, one party will fail to comply with some of the terms of the other party's psychological contract (Robinson & Rousseau, 1994; Rousseau, 1990). As the trends toward globalization, restructuring, and strong international competition continue, organizations are increasingly pressured to make rapid changes and accommodations to new and often unforeseen circumstances (Tsui, Porter, Pearce, & Tripoli, 1990). For these reasons, it is becoming increasingly necessary for organizations to manage, renegotiate, and, in some cases, violate the employment contracts they have established with their employees. Organizations undergoing change will often be either unable or unwilling to fulfill the promised contractual terms they have made to each employee (Hirsch, 1991; Tichy, 1983). As Robinson and Rousseau (1994) found, almost 55% of employees believed their employment contract had been violated by their employer in the past 2 years. At a minimum, we need to understand the implications of these organizational changes with respect to the potential costs associated with violating employees' contracts. The focus of this study was on the impact of psychological contract violation by the employer on employees' subsequent attitudes toward the organization.

THE IMPACT OF PSYCHOLOGICAL CONTRACT VIOLATION

Psychological contract violation is said to occur when one party perceives the other to have failed to comply with some of the terms of their psychological contract (Rousseau, 1989). When psychological contract violation occurs it produces a specific form of distributive injustice that may have unique and intense attitudinal, behavioral, and emotional reactions for the parties involved (Rousseau, 1989; Rousseau & Parks, 1993). These reactions emanate, in part, from the violated party's not receiving earned contributions from the employer. From the employee's perspective, the employee has fulfilled his or her side of the bargain and the employer has failed to reciprocate. The reactions that follow from psychological contract violation are similar to the reactions that follow from unmet expectations (Wanous, 1977) or from perceptions of inequity (Adams, 1965).

The intense reactions following psychological contract violation also emanate from receiving treatment that is inconsistent with standards of law, good faith dealing, contracts, and general standards of right and wrong—treatment that violates the "correctness standard" as discussed by Sheppard, Lewicki, and Minton (1992). When promises and considerations have been exchanged in the context of a relationship, violation goes far beyond the sense of inequity or unmet expectations of specific rewards or benefits to also include more general beliefs about respect for persons, codes of conduct, and other patterns of behavior associated with relationships involving trust (Rousseau, 1989). For example, an employee who receives lower wages than he or she had expected or had hoped to earn might feel dissatisfied or inequitably treated, but an employee who was promised a raise for hard work and fails to get it after working hard is likely to feel wronged and betrayed. Inequity can be remedied, but psychological contract violation, which causes lower trust and a sense of betrayal, cannot be so easily repaired. In summary, it is posited that the impact of psychological contract violation on employees' attitudes toward the organization will be stronger than the impact of mere unmet expectations on those attitudes.

In this chapter I discuss some specific predictions about the effects of psychological contract violation on employee attitudes. Specifically, it is posited that the experience of violation will lead to significant negative changes in important organizationally directed attitudes; that is, violation will lead to a decrease in the employee's level of trust in the organization, satisfaction with the organization, and commitment to the organization.

Trust

Underlying a psychological contract is trust, developed from a belief that contributions will be reciprocated and that a relationship exists where actions of one party are bound to those of another. Trust, based on confidence in the faith, goodwill, or moral integrity of another, is essential for stable social relationships (Blau, 1964).

Trust is tied to past or expected exchange (Haas, 1981; Osgood, 1966; Zand, 1972), in that it developed from repeated cycles of reciprocity between two parties (Zucker, 1986). In the context of the employment relationship, the longer the relationship endures with repeated exchange, the more the employee and employer come to believe that such action will continue into the future, and the more trust develops between the two parties (Axelrod, 1984; Blau, 1964; Boss, 1978; Jennings, 1971; Zand, 1972).

Exchange develops trust, but it can also destroy it. Failure to fulfill promised obligations decreases trust in the reneging party. The violation subjects the relationship to a form of trauma in which the factors that led to the emergence of a relationship, such as trust and good faith, are undermined.

Hypothesis 1: Violation of employees' psychological contracts by their employers decreases employees' trust in their employers.

Satisfaction

Psychological contract violation will also reduce employees' satisfaction with both the job and the organization itself. First, violation produces a discrepancy between what was expected and what was received—a major source of dissatisfaction (e.g., Wanous, 1973). Second, what the employer promised but failed to provide may often be those aspects of one's work that are important sources for work satisfaction. Motivation to perform, and obtain satisfaction from, one's job may be reduced when the employee can no longer rely on the promised inducements associated with performance (Porter & Lawler, 1968).

Hypothesis 2: Violation of employees' psychological contracts by their employers decreases employees' satisfaction.

Commitment

Commitment has often been conceptualized in an exchange framework, whereby performance and loyalty are offered in return for material benefits and rewards (e.g., Angle & Perry, 1983; Becker, 1960). From this calculative perspective, it can be argued that violation will decrease organizational commitment because it decreases the employee's belief that the employer will fulfill future promises and contributions. Commitment has also been conceptualized from an affective perspective, focusing on employees' sense of attachment, identification, or affiliation with the organization (e.g., Mowday, Steers, & Porter, 1979; Porter, Steers, Mowday, & Boulian, 1974). From this perspective, it can be argued that psychological contract violation may decrease employee commitment because it signals to employees that the firm may not value their contributions or care about their well-being (Eisenberger, Huntington, Hutchison, & Sowa, 1986). As such, employees may, in turn, reduce their emotional attachments to the organization.

Hypothesis 3: Violation of employees' psychological contracts by their employers decreases employees' commitment to the organization.

Psychological contracts refer to perceptions of the mutual obligations in employment relationships (Robinson, Kraatz, & Rousseau, 1994; Rousseau, 1989). These contracts serve to maintain and build the employment relationship. As employment relationships change, so must the psychological contracts within them. In some cases, these contracts are renegotiated; in other cases these contracts are breached or violated. This study examined the impact of psychological contract violation by testing these three hypotheses. More specifically, this study explored how employees' attitudes toward the organization would be affected when their employers reneged on the employment agreement. Data were collected by surveying 126 employees over a 30-month period: after they had negotiated and accepted an offer of employment, 18 months on the job, and 30 months on the job. It was found that psychological contract violation at 18 months on the job was negatively related to employees' trust of their employer, satisfaction, and commitment to the organization after 30 months on the job.

METHOD

Participants

Participants of this study were 126 alumni of a midwestern graduate business school. Thirty-four percent were women. On completion of the study, the average age of the participants was 30 years ($SD = 2.01$) and the mean number of years of full-time work experience was 6.29 years ($SD = 1.78$). Average salaries were $69,200, ranging from $25,000 to $160,000. The respondents worked in a wide variety of industries: consulting (23.5%), food and kindred products (17.5%), chemicals and allied products (13.7%), financial services (18.6%), machinery (5.5%), electronic equipment (3.3%), transportation equipment (3.3%), wholesale and retail trade (2.7%), petroleum and energy products (2.7%), and others (9.2%).

Procedure

Participants were surveyed three times over the course of a 30-month period. The first survey (Time 1) was given to 264 graduates of a master's of business administration (MBA) program who had recently accepted a job offer. They had the opportunity to win a cash prize in return for their participation. Two hundred eighteen graduates responded, resulting in a response rate of 83%. The second survey (Time 2) was mailed 18 months later to the 218 participants of the first survey. Participants were asked to mail the completed surveys directly back to the researcher in provided self-addressed stamped envelopes. Two weeks after the surveys were mailed, a follow-up letter was sent. Four weeks after the surveys were mailed, handwritten notes encouraging participation were sent. A total of 184 completed surveys were returned and 6 were returned undelivered due to changes in addresses (a response rate of 87%). The third survey (Time 3) was mailed 12 months after the second survey to the 184 remaining participants. Again, a follow-up reminder was sent 2 weeks after the survey was mailed and handwritten notes encouraging participation were sent 4 weeks later. In total, 164 respondents returned completed useable surveys and 4 were returned undelivered due to changes in addresses. The response rate on the third survey was 91%.

Given that the hypotheses in this study involved assessing employees' attitudes over a 30-month period, those respondents who had changed employers between the three surveys ($n = 38$) were not included in the analyses. Hence, the sample size was 126.

Independent Variables

This study investigated the impact of psychological contract violation on employees' subsequent attitudes toward the employment relationship. Therefore, perceived psychological contract violation measured at Time 2 was used to predict subsequent trust in one's employer, satisfaction, and commitment measured at Time 3.

Psychological contract violation. Psychological contract violation was assessed at Time 2 by asking participants about the degree to which their employers had fulfilled a variety of promised obligations. Participants were provided with the following list of seven obligations: promotion and advancement, high pay, pay based on current level of performance, training, long-term job security, career development, and sufficient power and responsibility. These obligations are from Rousseau's (1990) measure of psychological contracts, which has been used in several previous studies (Robinson et al., 1994; Robinson & Rousseau, 1994; Rousseau, 1990). Based on interviews with human resource managers from 13 engineering, accounting, and manufacturing firms, Rousseau identified these as the most common promises made during recruitment to MBA graduates.

Participants were asked to indicate the degree to which their employer had fulfilled each of the seven obligations. They used a scale ranging from 1 to 5 (*not at all fulfilled* to *very well fulfilled*). These ratings were reverse-scored and aggregated to provide a measure of psychological contract violation. Coefficient alpha for this measure was .85.

Trust. Trust in one's employer was measured at Time 1 as a control variable and at Time 3 as a dependent variable on a scale developed by Robinson and Rousseau (1994). The scale included seven items reflecting the dimensions of trust identified by Gabarro and Athos (1976). Sample items include "In general, I believe my employer's motives and intentions are good" and "My employer is not always honest and truthful." Participants used a 5-point scale. Coefficient alpha for the Time 1 measure was .82; for Time 3 it was .87.

Satisfaction. Satisfaction was assessed at Time 1 as a control variable using Kunin's (1955) Faces Scale, which is composed of a series of faces with a range of expressions. Participants are asked to indicate which face best describes how they feel about their job in general. Satisfaction as a dependent variable was assessed at Time 3 using the Faces Scale along with two other satisfaction items: "Working for this organization is very satisfying for me" and "I am satisfied with my job." Participants used a 5-point scale to indicate the extent to which they agreed with each statement. These three satisfaction items were aggregated. Coefficient alpha for this measure was .94.

Commitment. Commitment was assessed at Time 3 using the short form of Porter and Smith's (1970) measure of organizational commitment. Participants read nine statements and, using a 5-point scale, they indicated the extent to which they agreed with each statement. Sample items include "I talk up this organization as a great organization to work for" and "I really care about the fate of this organization." Coefficient alpha for this scale was .84.

Control Variables

The observed relationships between psychological contract violation and subsequent employee attitudes could be attributed to (a) disgruntled employees not obtaining desired perks such as promotions and pay increases or (b) unmet expectations, employees not getting what they had hoped or expected to obtain (independent of any violation of initial promises or obligations made on the part of the employer). To control for these possibilities, the number of pay increases, number of promotions, and unmet expectations were also assessed.

Promotions. Participants were asked at Time 3 how many promotions, if any, they had received since joining their firm.

Pay increases. At Time 3 participants were asked to indicate the number of pay increases, if any, they had received since joining their firm.

Unmet expectations. At Time 1 and Time 3, participants were asked how much they expected each of seven items would be present in their work situation (these seven items were the same as the obligations used in the violation measure—promotion and advancement, high pay, pay based on your current level of performance, training, long-term job security, career development, and sufficient power and responsibility). Participants used a 0 to 100 scale, with anchors *This characteristic is/will be completely absent from my organization* to *The greatest possible amount of this characteristic is/will be found in my organization.* Coefficient alpha of this measure at Time 1 was .74; for Time 3 it was .77, therefore expectations at each time period were aggregated. Differences between the amounts indicated at Time 3 and the amounts indicated at Time 1 were used as an index of the extent to which initial expectations were not met.

RESULTS

Table 1 reports the means and standard deviations of each of the measures used in the study, as well as their zero-order intercorrelations. Psychological contract violation was moderate, given that the mean was 2.52 ($SD = 0.76$) within a possible range of 1 to 5. Psychological contract violation measured at Time 2 was found to be related to employee attitudes measured at Time 3: trust in one's employer ($r = -.39$, $p < .01$); satisfaction ($r = -.44$, $p < .01$); and commitment ($r = -.54$, $p < .01$).

To test the hypotheses, hierarchical regressions were performed. In the first step, each dependent variable was regressed only on the control variables. In the second step, psychological contract violation was added to the equation. The results of these regression equations are presented in Table 2.

Hypothesis 1, predicting that employers' violation of the psychological contract would be negatively related to employee trust, was supported. After controlling for number of promotions received, number of pay increases received, trust at Time 1, and unmet expectations, violation of the psychological contract at Time 2 was found to be negatively related to trust

Table 1

Descriptive Statistics and Intercorrelations of All Variables

Variable	M	SD	1	2	3	4	5	6	7	8
1. Trust, Time 1	4.11	0.57	—							
2. Trust, Time 3	3.40	0.84	.34**	—						
3. Satisfaction, Time 1	4.54	0.65	.47**	.31**	—					
4. Satisfaction, Time 3	4.01	1.25	.14	.55**	.19*	—				
5. Commitment, Time 3	3.32	0.71	.25**	.69**	.17	.78**	—			
6. Psychological contract violation	2.52	0.76	-.20*	-.39**	-.19*	-.44**	-.54**	—		
7. Number of promotions	1.04	0.72	.08	.01	.02	.16	.08	-.06	—	
8. Number of pay increases	2.37	0.80	.02	.08	.09	.13	.06	-.07	.25**	—
9. Unmet expectations	10.40	16.69	.11	-.30**	.11	-.32**	-.35**	.29**	-.07	-.26**

*p < .05. **p < .01.

Table 2

Results of Hierarchical Regression Analyses

Variable	Trust (Time 3)		Satisfaction (Time 3)		Commitment (Time 3)	
	Step 1	Step 2	Step 1	Step 2	Step 1	Step 2
Trust, Time 1	.34***	.29***				
Satisfaction, Time 1			.23***	.15		
Promotions	−.03	−.04	.14	.12	.06	.04
Pay increases	.00	.00	.02	.01	−.04	−.04
Unmet expectations	−.31***	−.24**	−.32***	−.22**	−.33***	−.20***
Psychological contract violation		−.25***		−.33***		−.47***
F	6.04***	6.69***	5.72***	8.07***	4.78***	13.45***
R^2	.17	.23	.16	.26	.11	.32

NOTE: Entries represent standardized beta coefficients.
*$p < .05$. **$p < .01$. ***$p < .001$.

in one's employer at Time 3 ($\beta = -.24$), $F(5, 114) = 6.69$, $p = .001$, $R^2 = .23$.

Hypothesis 2 predicted that violation would be negatively related to employee satisfaction. This hypothesis was also supported. After controlling for number of promotions received, number of pay increases received, satisfaction at Time 1, and unmet expectations, violation of the psychological contract at Time 2 was found to be negatively related to satisfaction at Time 3 ($\beta = -.33$), $F(3, 115) = 8.07$, $p = .001$, $R^2 = .26$.

Hypothesis 3, predicting that violation would be negatively related to employee commitment, was also supported. After controlling for number of promotions received, number of pay increases received, and unmet expectations, violation of the psychological contract at Time 2 was found to be negatively related to commitment at Time 3 ($\beta = -.47$), $F(3, 115) = 13.45$, $p = .001$, $R^2 = .32$.

DISCUSSION

These findings demonstrate that when employees believe their employer has breached or violated their psychological contract, employees, in turn, reduce their trust in their employer as well as their satisfaction with and commitment to the organization. Psychological contracts, involve elements of trust, a sense of relationship, and a belief in the existence of a promise of future benefits. When the contract is reneged on by the employer, it invokes feelings, of mistrust and betrayal. These feelings, in turn, alter an employees' otherwise positive attitudes toward the relationship and the organization itself.

When organizational conditions change, employees may not get what they wanted or expected from the employment relationship. Not surprisingly, employee trust, satisfaction, and commitment are reduced when valued goods are not received or when expectations are not met (Wanous, 1977). However, it is the failure to receive *what was promised* from one's employer, not just what one expected or hoped for, that has the greatest impact on subsequent employee attitudes toward the employment relationship. As this study demonstrates, the impact of psychological contract violation exceeds the effects produced by mere unmet expectations or inequity, because the variation coefficient is significant even when the unmet expectation variable is in the equation. Promises that are reneged on have a unique and acute impact above and beyond the impact of the employee not obtaining desired goods or tangible assets from the employment relationship.

These results speak only to the impact of violation on changes in employees' attitudes. However, these changes in attitudes can have significant implications for organizational effectiveness. For example, trust is crucial to organizational effectiveness (Golembiewski & McConkie, 1975). Trust has a "spiral reinforcement" quality such that a decline in trust often leads to further decline in trust. A lack of trust is associated with a decrease in the quality of communication (O'Reilly & Roberts, 1976), cooperation (Deutsch, 1973), effective problem solving (Boss, 1978), and performance (Zand, 1972). Similarly, a decline in satisfaction is associated with a decline in organizational citizenship behavior (Bateman & Organ, 1983; Organ & Konovsky, 1989), extrarole performance that is important to organizational survival (Barnard, 1938; Katz, 1964; Katz & Kahn, 1978). A loss of commitment has also been associated with a decline in prosocial organizational behavior (O'Reilly & Chatman, 1986), absenteeism (Clegg, 1983; Cotton & Tuttle, 1986), and turnover (Cohen, 1993). In summary, the results of this study, combined with previous research on these attitudes, suggest that organizations may incur significant costs as a result of reneging on their employees' psychological contracts.

The findings presented here suggest that employers should attempt to understand how employees perceive the obligations within the employment relationship and, more important, employers should attempt to manage those obligations. The current trend toward restructuring, downsizing, and other organizational changes increases the likelihood that organizations may inadvertently or purposely violate their employees' psychological contracts. At a minimum, organizations must at least be cognizant of the potential costs that may be incurred as a result of such violation. In the event of changes in the employment relationship, organizations should perhaps seek to renegotiate the psychological contract and establish new terms that reflect the new organizational conditions, rather than ignore or violate the terms of the current agreement. Such efforts may lessen the affective reactions associated with psychological contract violation.

Limitations

This study may be limited to the extent that it examined the impact of violation on a distinct employee population; namely, graduates of a prestigious MBA program. It could be posited that this group of employees is more prone to violation given the overzealous efforts of recruiters to attract candidates of this caliber. Similarly, one might expect that the reaction of these employees to psychological contract violation is stronger given that they may have chosen their current employer over many others on the basis of promises that were subsequently violated. Employees with fewer employment options may feel less betrayed when their employer breaches the employment agreement. However, we would expect that most employees, not only MBA graduates, would experience similar changes in attitudes following psychological contract breach. Future research should explore this possibility by looking at the occurrence and impact of violation on employees of various occupations, across both union and nonunion settings.

Another possible limitation of this study is that all of the variables were assessed using self-report. Nevertheless, given that this study was interested in employee attitudes and psychological contract violation, which by definition are perceptual in nature, the use of self-reports was appropriate. Furthermore, the typical problem of common-method bias associated with self-reports was largely reduced in this study given that the independent and dependent variables were assessed 12 months apart.

Future Directions

A number of future research directions can be suggested from these results. First, as previously mentioned, it would be worthwhile to replicate this study using different employee populations in both union and nonunion settings. Second, future research should explore potential moderating variables of the relationships found in this study. For example, it may be the case that the impact of violation on subsequent attitudes can be mitigated by using social accounts or other interactional forms of justice (Bies & Moag, 1986). The employer may renege on the employees' psychological contract, but the loss of trust, satisfaction, and commitment may be reduced if the employer offers a valid explanation for why the breach was necessary or unavoidable. Third, future research should examine the antecedents of psychological contract violation. This chapter posited that violation is more likely to occur during times of organizational change. However, this was not empirically explored. Organizational change, organizational performance, and a host of other organizational-level, employee-level, and relationship-level factors may affect the occurrence of psychological contract violation. Given the apparent negative ramifications of psychological contract violation, it would be worthwhile to understand under what circumstances violation is most likely to occur.

REFERENCES

Adams, J. S. (1965). Inequity in social exchange. *Advances in Experimental Social Psychology, 2,* 267–299.

Angle, H. L., & Perry, J. L. (1983). Organizational commitment: Individual and organizational influences. *Work and Occupation, 10,* 123–146.

Argyris, C. (1960). *Understanding organizational behavior.* Homewood, IL: Dorsey.

Axelrod, R. (1984). *The evolution of cooperation.* New York: Basic Books.

Barnard, C. (1938). *The functions of the executive.* Cambridge, MA: Harvard University Press.

Bateman, T. S., & Organ, D. W. (1983). Job satisfaction and the good soldier: The relationship between affect and employee citizenship. *Academy of Management Journal, 26,* 587–595.

Becker, H. S. (1960). Notes on the concept of commitment. *American Journal of Sociology, 66,* 32–40.

Bies, R. J., & Moag, J. S. (1986). Interactional justice: Communication criteria of fairness. In R. J. Lewicki, B. H. Sheppard, & M. H. Bazerman (Eds.), *Research on negotiations in organizations* (Vol. 1, pp. 43–55). Greenwich, CT: JAI Press.

Blau, P. M. (1964). *Exchange and power in social life.* New York: Wiley.

Boss, R. W. (1978). Trust and managerial problem solving revisited. *Group and Organizational Studies, 3,* 331–342.

Clegg, C. W. (1983). Psychology of employee lateness, absence, and turnover: A methodological critique and an empirical study. *Journal of Applied Psychology, 68,* 88–101.

Cohen, A. (1993). Organizational commitment and turnover: A meta-analysis. *Academy of Management Journal, 36,* 1140–1157.

Cotton, J. L., & Tuttle, J. M. (1986). Employee turnover: A meta-analysis and review with implications for research. *Academy of Management Review, 11,* 55–70.

Deutsch, M. (1973). *The resolution of conflict.* New Haven, CT: Yale University Press.

Eisenberger, R., Huntington, R., Hutchison, S., & Sowa, D. (1986). Perceived organizational support. *Journal of Applied Psychology, 71,* 500–507.

Farnsworth, E. (1982). *Contracts.* Boston: Little, Brown.

Gabarro, J. J., & Athos, J. (1976). *Interpersonal relations and communications.* Englewood Cliffs, NJ: Prentice Hall.

Golembiewski, R. T., & McConkie, M. L. (1975). The centrality of interpersonal trust in group processes. In C. L. Cooper (Ed.), *Theories of group processes*. New York: Wiley.

Haas, D. (1981). Trust and symbolic exchange. *Social Psychology Quarterly, 44*, 3–13.

Hirsch, P. (1989). *Pack your own parachute*. Reading, MA: Addison-Wesley.

Hirsch, P. (1991). *Undoing the managerial revolution? Needed research on the decline of middle management and internal labor markets.* Unpublished manuscript, Northwestern University, Evanston, IL.

Jennings, E. (1971). *Routes to the executive suite.* New York: McGraw-Hill.

Katz, D. (1964). The motivational basis of organizational behavior. *Behavioral Science, 9*, 131–146.

Katz, D., & Kahn, R. L. (1978). *The social psychology of organizations.* New York: Wiley.

Kunin, T. (1955). The construction of a new type of attitude measure. *Personnel Psychology, 8*, 143–145.

Mowday, R. T., Steers, R. M., & Porter, L. W. (1979). The measurement of organizational commitment. *Journal of Vocational Behavior, 14*, 224–247.

O'Reilly, C. A., III, & Chatman, J. (1986). Organizational commitment and psychological attachment: The effects of compliance, identification, and internalization on pro-social behavior. *Journal of Applied Psychology, 71*, 492–499.

O'Reilly, C., & Roberts, K. (1976). Relationships among components of credibility and communication behaviors in work units. *Journal of Applied Psychology, 61*, 99–102.

Organ, D. W., & Konovsky, M. (1989). Cognitive versus affective determinants of organizational citizenship behavior. *Journal of Applied Psychology, 74*, 157–164.

Osgood, C. (1966). *Perspective of foreign policy.* Palo Alto, CA: Pacific Books.

Parks, J. M. (1992, May). *The role of incomplete contracts and their governance in delinquency, in-role, and extra-role behaviors.* Paper presented at the meeting of the Society for Industrial and Organizational Psychology, Montreal, Ontario, Canada.

Porter, L. W., & Lawler, E. E. (1968). *Managerial attitudes and performance.* Homewood, IL: Irwin.

Porter, L. W., & Smith, F. L. (1970). *The etiology of organizational commitment.* Unpublished manuscript, University of California, Irvine.

Porter, L. W., Steers, R. M., Mowday, R. T., & Boulian, P. V. (1974). Organizational commitment, job satisfaction, and turnover among psychiatric technicians. *Journal of Applied Psychology, 59*, 603–609.

Robinson, S., Kraatz, M., & Rousseau, D. (1994). Changing obligations and the psychological contract: A longitudinal study. *Academy of Management Journal, 37*, 137–152.

Robinson, S., & Rousseau, D. (1994). Violating the psychological contract: Not the exception but the norm. *Journal of Organizational Behavior, 15*, 245–259.

Rousseau, D. (1989). Psychological and implied contracts in organizations. *Employee Responsibilities and Rights Journal, 2*, 121–139.

Rousseau, D. (1990). New hire perceptions of their own and their employer's obligations: A study of psychological contracts. *Journal of Organizational Behavior, 11*, 389–400.

Rousseau, D., & Parks, J. (1993). The contracts of individuals and organizations. In L. L. Cummings & B. M. Staw (Eds.), *Research in organizational behavior* (Vol. 15, pp. 1–47). Greenwich, CT: JAI Press.

Sheppard, B. H., Lewicki, R. J., & Minton, J. W. (1992). *Organizational justice.* Lexington, MA: Lexington Books.

Shore, L. M., & Tetrick, L. E. (1994). The psychological contract as an explanatory framework in the employment relationship. In C. L. Cooper & D. M. Rousseau (Eds.), *Trends in organizational behavior* (Vol. 1, pp. 91–109). New York: Wiley.

Tichy, N. (1983). *Managing strategic change.* New York: Wiley.

Tsui, A., Porter, L., Pearce, J., & Tripoli, A. (1990, August). *Employee–organization relationships: An inducement-contribution conceptualization.* Paper presented at the meeting of the Academy of Management, Miami, FL.

Wanous, J. P. (1973). Effects of a realistic job preview on job acceptance, job attitudes, and job survival. *Journal of Applied Psychology, 58*, 327–332.

Wanous, J. P. (1977). Organizational entry: Newcomers moving from outside to inside. *Psychological Bulletin, 84*, 601–618.

Weick, K. (1981). *The social psychology of organizing.* Reading, MA: Addison-Wesley.

Zand, D. E. (1972). Trust and managerial problem solving. *Administrative Science Quarterly, 17*, 229–239.

Zucker, L. (1986). Production of trust: Institutional sources of economic structure, 1840–1920. In L. L. Cummings & B. M. Staw (Eds.), *Research in organizational behavior* (Vol. 8, pp. 53–111). Greenwich, CT: JAI Press.

5

Out of the Frying Pan Into the Fire: Managing Blue-Collar Stress at Work

Valerie J. Sutherland and Cary L. Cooper

Decades of workplace research since the early 1900s have demonstrated that physical and psychosocial factors contribute to a wide range of health disorders among blue-collar workers. Indeed, it appears that stress and strain are inescapable facets of contemporary blue-collar work. Stress is triggered in the working environment by both tangible, physical factors such as climatic, chemical, biological, and radiological hazards and intangible psychosocial hazards such as aspects of work organization, job content, and management methods (Health and Safety Executive [HSE], 1993). These stress-inducing factors can impair health, well-being, and quality of life in complex, interactive ways.

In this chapter we review some of the major stressors among blue-collar workers and consider the extent to which changes in employment relations and work conditions have resolved the problems of stress for this occupational group. The sources of stress analyzed here include the organizational structure and climate (including lack of participation and job control), work load, hours of work, shift work, new technology, and exposure to risk and hazard. Included is a discussion of "empowerment" as an initiative that aims to increase the level of job control among blue-collar workers.

ORGANIZATIONAL STRUCTURE AND CLIMATE

Landy and Trumbo (1980) stated that organizational climate consists of four factors: autonomy, structure, reward, and consideration orientation. The organization is perceived to have a personality to the extent that these factors are present in the way the organization treats its members. Lack of participation in the decision-making process, lack of effective consultation and communication, unjustified restrictions on behavior, the practice of business politics, and the absence of a sense of belonging are the key sources of stress associated with being in an organization (Cooper, Cooper, & Eakes, 1988). Lack of opportunity to participate in the decision-making process is associated with negative mood and negative behavioral responses such as escapist drinking and heavy cigarette smoking. Increased opportunity to participate in decision making results in improved performance, lower staff turnover, and improved levels of mental and physical well-being (Margolis, Kroes, & Quinn, 1974). As more and more organizations realize that their employees can be a critical source of competitive advantage, the significance of worker participation is beginning to be acknowledged.

Apathy is a significant factor in the cause of accidents, and so participation and worker involvement are also important factors in safety performance among blue-collar workers. Indeed, a significant reduction in accidents was observed among blue-collar workers in a continuous process production plant following the introduction of a behavior-based approached to accident reduction that directly involved shop-floor personnel in the identification and self-monitoring of safety behavior (Sutherland, Makin, Phillips, & Cooper, 1993). This program provided the workforce with control over their own safety behavior at work and acknowledged that job control is an important factor in the understanding of response to stress at work.

Although it is acknowledged that a wide variety of stress factors are potentially harmful (HSE, 1993), recent research evidence points to lack of control at work as a predictor of a number of adverse and costly outcomes for the individual, the organization, and society. By the nature of the role and task, determined by the organizational structure of the work environment, blue-collar workers tend to have low jurisdiction over their jobs. As part of a complex, highly organized process that is often remote from the final product, the blue-collar worker is active for only one third or one half of the 24-hour day. Therefore, a sophisticated process of coordination by management is deemed vital to the success of capital-intensive industry. Thus, the blue-collar worker tends to be regarded as a small cog in the machinery who is controlled rather than in control.

Control, however, is not a simple concept. To understand control, one must also understand such issues as expectations of control and self-selection into a controlling work environment. A lack of control in the workplace also results in exposure to other stressors, for example, the inability to escape boredom, poorly ventilated conditions, and noise during a 12-hour shift except in monitored, formalized work breaks (Fisher, 1985). Because of these confounding issues, it is difficult to establish causation and the impact of lack of control at work among blue-collar workers. Nevertheless, there is moderate support for the notion that a variety of deleterious outcomes are associated with lack of control at work. Shouksmith (1990) reviewed studies that examined discretionary latitude and control over work pace and speed and concluded that the amount of control a worker has over job activities seems to relate to levels of personal satisfaction and adjustment. More specifically, Landsbergis, Schnall, Deitz, and Friedman (1992) tested Karasek's (1979) job demand–control model and found that when demographic variables were controlled for, the individuals in the "strain" jobs (high control, low decision latitude, low autonomy) had the highest levels of job dissatisfaction, and low social support in the workplace significantly exacerbated this condition. Low levels of demand and high decision-making latitude in a job (i.e., the "relaxed" condition described by Karasek) were associated with the lowest level of job dissatisfaction and trait anxiety. Workers in the "active" jobs (high work demands, high level of control) reported the highest levels of job involvement but were also likely to manifest Type A behavior characteristics. Because both job involvement and a need for control in the work environment are desired states for Type A individuals, this finding appears to reinforce Fisher's (1985) concerns about control expectations and self-selection into a job.

Kawakami, Haratani, and Takashi (1992) attempted to overcome some of the criticism of cross-sectional investigations by conducting a 3-year prospective study of male blue-collar workers in Japan. This team of researchers discovered that a lack of control over work pace and poor human relations at work were significantly associated with symptoms of depression. In the United States, a survey conducted by Northwestern National Life Assurance Company (Froiland, 1993) concluded that job stress is generally the consequence of a high level of job demand and little control over one's work. In fact, levels of job demand at work continue to rise as the size of the blue-collar workforce shrinks, requiring individuals to work harder, and for longer, during overtime working. The situation is made worse by the need to take responsibility for the tasks of coworkers who are absent from work due to sickness, holiday entitlement, and training activities. Harrell (1990) suggested that lack of control in the work place also has implications for safety at work in terms of accidental injury and risk perception. Harrell found that autonomy and freedom were identified as the stronger predictors of perceived risk, compared with task repetitiveness and the pace of work.

Overall, the evidence suggests that a perceived lack of control at work is a stress-inducing factor, and varying attempts to remedy this negative situation are documented. However, if members of the blue-collar workforce are to be provided with more opportunities to participate and take greater control over production, quality, and safety, it is not unreasonable to assume that they will demand a greater reward for these efforts. If organizations do not share gains with the workforce, it is likely that stress levels will increase. Research suggests that the obstacle of employee skepticism that improved productivity, performance, and quality will result in better competitive advantage to the organization can be overcome if the changes in the style of working practices are accompanied by a new pay policy. Lowman (1993) stated that organizations must be more flexible and think beyond tried and true pay practices to produce reward systems with variable features and options. Indeed, Levine (1990) supported this view by stating the four characteristics of a firm's industrial relations system that are necessary for employee support of participation: (a) some form of profit sharing or gain sharing, (b) job security, (c) measures to build up group cohesiveness, and (d) guaranteed individual rights. However, it is still necessary to establish the degree to which the new styles of working for blue-collar workers actually have an impact on the stress associated with work load, and the issues of job demands and work load are considered in the following sections.

Work Load

Having too much to do (quantitative overload) or work that is too difficult (qualitative overload) are forms of stress in the work environment. Various symptoms and behavioral malfunctions are associated with the experience of job overload, although the stress associated with work load is complex. French and Caplan (1973) suggested that quantitative and qualitative load produces many different symptoms in addition to psychological and physical strain; these include job dissatisfaction, job tension, lowered self-esteem, threat, embarrassment, high cholesterol levels, increased heart rate, increased skin resistance, and more cigarette smoking. Although most of us readily agree that having too much to do at work causes tension and strain that manifests itself in a wide variety of symptoms, it must also be acknowledged that work underload is a potentially damaging stress factor in the workplace. If the employee does not have enough work to do, he or she may become bored, and this also occurs when the task itself does not use the skills or potential of the worker. Therefore, in a job underload state, either quantitative or qualitative, the workforce is likely to be apathetic and bored, levels of motivation are probably low, and high levels of absenteeism are the costly consequences suffered by industry.

Quantitative Overload

Both physical and mental job overload are potent stressors at work. Having to work under time pressures in order to meet deadlines is an independent source of stress, and studies show that stress levels increase as difficult deadlines draw near. There is also a relationship between objective, quantitative overload and cigarette smoking, a risk factor in coronary heart disease and cancer (French & Caplan, 1970). Linked to the concept of overload is the issue of "work pace." Rate of working has been shown to be a significant factor in blue-collar ill-health, especially when the worker is not able to control the pace. In a national survey in the United States, Margolis et al. (1974) found that quantitative overload was significantly related to a number of symptoms or indicators of stress, including poor motivation, low self-esteem, absenteeism, escapist drinking, and an absence of making suggestions to employers.

Qualitative Overload

This occurs when the individual does not feel capable of performing the given task or duties, perhaps because of inadequate training to do the job. There is evidence that qualitative overload as a source of stress is strongly related to perceived low levels of self-esteem. In fact, this form of overload can occur when a worker is promoted to a supervisory position on the grounds of superior work performance, but the lack of experience or training in the supervision of others, or work delegation, can result in considerable strain and pressure for the individual and the subordinates involved.

Quantitative Underload

Boredom in the daily work routine as a result of too little to do may be regarded as quantitative underload, which can result in inattentiveness. This is potentially hazardous if the employee fails to respond appropriately in an emergency. Lack of stimulation may be potentially more damaging during a night shift when employees could be having difficulty adjusting to the changes in sleep patterns but do not have enough work to keep them alert (Poulton, 1978). Boredom was identified as a significant source of stress among crane operators (Cooper & Kelly, 1984), and boredom and lack of challenge were found to be significant predictors of raised levels of anxiety, depression, and reported job dissatisfaction. Because long periods of inactivity are in the nature of the job, job redesign would be necessary to alleviate this problem. Job overload or underload may result from the irregular flow of work that is not under the control of the worker. This is not restricted to paced assembly lines, because many outdoor occupations are paced by climatic conditions. Pace may therefore vary from complete shutdown to hectic as workers try to keep to contract deadlines in unpredictable conditions. In addition to financial gain, the promise of the next contract may depend on successful completion of the current job. Thus, the workforce is exposed to strain and pressure that they cannot control or change.

Qualitative Underload

Qualitative underload may be as damaging as overload in that an individual is not given the opportunity to use acquired skills or to develop full potential ability. As with quantitative underload, boredom and shifts or lapses in attention may have serious consequences. Underload due to lack of stimulation leads to low morale and poor motivation to work. The individual feels that he or she is not getting anywhere and is powerless to show perceived and actual skills and talent. Udris (cited in International Labor Office [ILO], 1986) suggested that qualitative overload was associated with dissatisfaction, tension, and low self-esteem, whereas qualitative underload was linked to dissatisfaction, depression, irritation, and psychosomatic complaints.

The effects of underload are aggravated by a lack of control over the work situation. Paced assembly lines are often characterized as unstimulating work environments, where the pace may be high (quantitative overload), but the nature of the task itself could be classified as a qualitative underload. Benyon and Blackburn (1972) reported the feelings of tension resulting from boredom among workers on a packing-line system, because their work provided no sense of achievement or satisfaction. The job stress associated with factory work that is passive and has low skill demands, lack of variety, repetitiveness, and low decision latitude can also spill over

115

into leisure time and negatively affect life outside of work. New technology and the increasing automation of industry can reduce the quantitative overload condition, but it produces jobs that are highly repetitive, dull, and monotonous, and this is detrimental to physical and mental well-being. Opportunities for increased participation in decision making and job control could therefore help to alleviate the stress associated with qualitative underload, but would increase the burdens of responsibility on to the workforce.

Hours of Work

Flexibility continues to be one of the most widely discussed issues in labor market studies (Watson, 1994). Conditions of employment that offer more flexible ways of working may help to balance the stress associated with work load and be more cost-effective for the organization. Thus, the employer may be able to offer relative job security in return for greater flexibility over the timing of hours worked. In some instances, family-friendly working practices such as job sharing, home working, voluntarily reduced working week, and term-time working might be available. In the UK a proportion of the workforce in craft and plant and machine operative occupations work a compressed workweek (11% and 8% of these groups, respectively, are contracted on either a 9-day fortnight or a 4.5-day week; Watson, 1994). Although some of these arrangements are facilitated by bargaining for shorter hours, certain firms have adopted the compressed week by the introduction of 12-hour shift working, instead of five shifts of approximately 8 hours' duration. This might seem attractive to the employee who qualifies for a 3- or 4-day work break under this arrangement; however, the pattern might be deleterious, in terms of load, if the job requires heavy physical activity or concentration for a 12-hour work period. Indeed, employees working this type of shift pattern also complain about the long period of inactivity during the time-off period. Clearly, this is an area that requires further investigation. Also, in practice, it is observed that these schemes may not be available to all personnel in the organization, thereby creating stress due to the perceived inequality of the system or the denial of choice for certain workers. In fact, recent surveys suggest that an increased number of workers are employed in jobs that offer no alternative to continuous shift working.

Shift Work

Because we are increasingly becoming a 24-hour society, the need to work shifts is now a common occupational stress factor. In order to maximize the usage of expensive capital equipment and plant many organizations operate a 24-hour business, which means that a considerable proportion of the workforce have jobs requiring them to work in shifts, some of which involve working staggered hours. In the UK it is estimated that 21% of men and 14.4% of women are engaged in shift working. In some occupations it is higher; for example, 34% of plant and machine operatives work a shift system (Watson, 1994). Despite considerable research efforts, it is not possible to make generalizations regarding which shift system is best, but it is clear that shift work represents a major source of stress for many workers (Monk & Tepas, 1985). Shift workers complain more frequently of fatigue and gastrointestinal troubles than day workers, and the impact of shift working on eating habits may be responsible. Influences are both biological and emotional, due to circadian rhythm disruption, temperature fluctuation, and adrenaline excretion rhythms. Shift work affects blood temperature, metabolic rate, blood sugar levels, mental efficiency, and work motivation. Three factors need to be optimized for successful coping with shift work: sleep, social and family life, and circadian rhythms. These factors are interrelated, so that a problem with one can negate the positive effects of success achieved in the others. Ultimately, roster designs should aim to maximize the positive effects and minimize the negative impact of shift work on health and social life caused by the disruption to circadian rhythms. Research evidence suggests that certain individuals with steeper adrenaline curves than normal are those who tolerate shift work best; that is, those with a pattern of very high adrenaline levels during the day and very low levels at night. The steeper rhythm is less vulnerable to distortion, and the rationale is that nonadaptation is better than partial adaptation. Although some people may be physiologically better suited to shift work, many blue-collar workers have no choice. Therefore, it is suggested that rapidly rotating shift systems with few night shifts in succession may be best because this causes less circadian rhythm disruption.

Disturbance of nocturnal sleep leads to daytime fatigue and sleepiness, which impairs motivation and vigilance, thus affecting safety at work. Lavie, Kremerman, and Wiel (1982) found that industrial workers who complained about their sleep had significantly more work accidents, repeated work accidents, and significantly more sick days per work accident. Furthermore, complaint of daytime sleepiness was related to multiple work accidents independent of age and physical effort required at work. Although it must be acknowledged that observed daytime sleepiness can be symptomatic of narcolepsy or breathing disorders, this behavior may also be a response to stress associated with reduced mental well-being (including symptoms of depression and somatic anxiety). Individuals forced to work night shifts or early morning shifts suffer from sleep disturbance in that the quantity and quality of their sleep differs as a consequence of shift working. Daytime sleep is both more fragile and unstable than nocturnal sleep. However, the night-shift worker may be able to take catnaps to catch up on sleep loss, thus reducing the sleep debt that accumulates (it is suggested that over a 7-day period, the employee could effectively lose the equivalent of at least 1 night's sleep). This source of stress for shift workers may exacerbate other stress factors in the work environment; for example, irritability with other employees and intolerance of the physical conditions at work. Although there are obvious problems associated with the need to work shifts on a regular basis, employees who habitually work long hours may experience considerable strain or pressure at work, especially when they are also required to cope with the introduction of new technology in the workplace.

New Technology

Technological advancement and automation have removed some of the tangible, physical strains from blue-collar employment, but they have also changed the nature of the job. Thus, one source of stress has perhaps been replaced with another, resulting in a lack of stimulation, underutilization of skills, and boredom that characterizes many blue-collar occupations. It also means that in rapidly changing work environments, skills may quickly become obsolete. The need to constantly become familiar with new equipment and systems may pose a threat to the individual. Unless adequate training is provided, potentially stressful situations may develop when new technology is introduced into the workplace and the individual feels unable to do the given task.

Changes introduced by automation and computerization demand flexibility, an ability to alter former practices, and ability to reorient and adapt. Older, established staff may find it a strain to make such dramatic changes, and these feelings of pressure may be exacerbated when they see the younger generation of workers, educated to higher standards and familiar with computers, quickly grasping the new ways of working. We try to protect ourselves against the unknown and so tend to resist change in the work environment. New and unfamiliar work patterns cause worry and anxiety and pose a threat to our perception of autonomy and self-control. The individual may also experience a threat to job security if the introduction of new technology accompanies a reduction in staffing requirements in the organization. The employee often faces an extended period of time at work in the knowledge that he or she may ultimately become redundant when the automation or computerization process has become established. This time of uncertainty is very stressful. Threat of job loss is a potent source of stress associated with several serious health problems, including ulcers, colitis, and alopecia and increased muscular and emotional complaints. The morale and motivation of the workforce is affected, with subsequent negative impact on productivity and efficiency.

Indirectly, fear of job loss and insecurity in times of high unemployment adversely affect both the individual and the organization. A keen, competitive job market may threaten the quality of peer relationships at a time when social support is of particular importance. The stress associated with feelings of insecurity may otherwise be reduced by the buffering effect of good supportive relationships at work, and this may be broken down if the workforce perceives that competition is necessary to retain one's job. Other individuals may stay in a job that is disliked or unsuitable because no alternative for change exists.

In a recessionary climate the organization faces a considerable challenge in developing a dedicated workforce. The loss of employment security may be expected to affect an employee's performance and sense of loyalty, and a lack of commitment to the organization is an obvious potential consequence. Because it is acknowledged that committed employees are more productive and creative and make a greater contribution, it is important for the organization to decide if a layoff is really necessary. As the real costs of layoff and rehire are understood, some organizations are finding innovative approaches to downsizing and reducing the stress of job insecurity on staff. For example, Robinson and Druker (1991) described the response to downsizing by the State of Maine, which was required to cut $15 million from the personnel budget, potentially resulting in 600–700 layoffs. By high-level, informal labor–management communication, the agreement between union and the administration was reached outside the context of formal collective bargaining negotiations. The savings were made through five options: voluntary reduced workweek, flexible position staffing, time off without pay, position leave, and sabbatical leave. Faltermayer (1992) suggested other alternatives to layoffs, including curbing of new hiring when jobs become vacant, reducing pay, paring contingent workers, encouraging early retirement, and keeping the workforce lean in prosperous times. Clearly, these solutions are not without stress for the workforce, but they might be preferred to unemployment.

Exposure to Danger and Hazard

Risk and hazard associated with danger in certain occupations may be a source of stress. Blue-collar workers in the United States rated health and safety hazards as a highly significant source of job discontent (Wallick, 1972). Many occupational groups are identified as high risk in terms of physical danger, but it is possible that a continued emphasis on the need for safety in a hazardous environment might be the greater source of stress. It is suggested that it is human nature to avoid thinking about danger or death in a hazardous or risky environment and that it is necessary to block out some of the realities the worker must otherwise continually face. Various studies indicate that some workers do perceive risks and hazards associated with the job as a source of stress. Casters in the steel industry and crane operators acknowledged the dangers of the job (Cooper & Kelly, 1984; Kelly & Cooper, 1981), and awareness of danger and the consequences of making a mistake were significant predictors of depression and anxiety among crane operators. In a Norwegian study, 36% of offshore platform personnel felt unsafe about helicopter transport; 34% felt unsafe about evacuation facilities, and 24% were concerned about the risk of fire and explosion (Hellesøy, 1985).

Risk of exposure to certain chemicals is frequently reported as one of the most harmful perceived stressors among blue-collar workers (ILO, 1986). This risk includes the possible inhalation of vapors and dust and exposure to chemicals that are irritants to the skin. Adequate protective clothing is vital, but training and education are equally important in reducing the stress associated with working in a potentially hazardous environment. The perceived adequacy of medical facilities and the ability to cope with an emergency situation mitigate the potentially stressful, risky situation. The risks and dangers associated with many occupations cannot be changed, but the perception of risk can be reduced by training and education (to ensure rational and logical reasoning about the risks involved). This is very important, because anxious and obsessional employees are less motivated to work, tend to have low morale, and may be more vulnerable to accidents (Sutherland & Cooper, 1991). In the long term, they may also suffer some of the consequences of stress-related illness, including heart disease and ulcers.

It is suggested that as new employment relationships, such as temporary and contract employment, start to appear, the stresses and strains of the workplace may become more acute for certain occupational groups. For example, in the petrochemical industry the use of contract employees continues to be a widespread practice, offering the industry the labor flexibility needed in meeting seasonal and market demands for gas and oil products. However, researchers suggest that this creates stress that can have potentially severe adverse effects on workplace safety (Kochan, Smith, Wells, & Rebitzer, 1994). Indeed, for a variety of reasons, contract workers in the offshore oil and gas industries are usually reported as having a greater incidence of injuries than the oil company personnel (although this finding was not established by the current authors in a study of personnel working in the United Kingdom sector of the North Sea; Sutherland & Cooper, 1991). However, it was observed that the perceived inequity of status of employment was acknowledged by both contractor and oil company personnel working offshore and was believed to be detrimental to working relationships, safety, and performance in this unique environment (Sutherland & Cooper, 1991).

Several authors have voiced concerns about the increased use of contingency workers in blue-collar occupations, where core, contractual, and flexible employees carry out the same duties but receive quite different rewards and benefits. A recent survey in the United States found that 44% of organizations from the Fortune 500 companies were relying more on contingent workers than they did 5 years ago. Indeed, today, the largest U.S. employer is a staffing firm (Payne & Baigts, 1994). These new employment relations require the employees to be more self-reliant and active in determining their own future. Thus, they must become more independent as they define their own needs and take responsibility for meeting them. This would seem to be desirable outcome for an organization seeking to employ individuals who are willing to take more responsibility in the workplace but could be disadvantageous in that the contract status personnel may not be as committed to the goals of the organization as the core workers. Clearly, we need to learn more about these patterns of employment relations and the implications for the mode of working that incorporates employee empowerment, self-direction, and leaderless groups.

CHANGING BLUE-COLLAR EMPLOYMENT RELATIONS AND WORK CONDITIONS TO REDUCE STRESS: HAS THE PROBLEM BEEN SOLVED?

Considerable technological advancement, automation, and stricter legislation and controls have been introduced to alleviate or remove many of the tangible, physical hazards of the blue-collar workplace. But it is clear that not all sources of stress can be eliminated or minimized in the blue-collar working environment, and some of the changes in employment relations and work conditions that have been introduced have spawned other stress-inducing factors.

Programs of job enlargement, job enrichment, job rotation, increased participation in decision making, and shared ownership have been introduced to alleviate some of the blue-collar stressor problems described above, but these have created separate problems and different sources of stress in the work environment. For example, job enlargement, job enrichment, and job rotation can result in both qualitative and quantitative overload and role conflict; and increased participation in decision making can result in disruption to interpersonal and social relationships, role ambiguity, and status incongruence in the workplace. Kalimo (1987) suggested that aggravated monotony may have been the price to pay for the newly invented methods of scientific management introduced during the period of industrialization. Many blue-collar workers have exchanged their physical strains for mental burdens as they have become more distanced from direct contact with the product itself and now engage in the passive business of machine monitoring, which requires constant attention and where failure or breakdown is associated with high demand. Indeed, as already noted, capital-intensive industry has created the need for shift working, which is associated with both emotional and biological load. Many of the changes introduced to alleviate the physical stress and strain of the workplace have resulted in the fragmentation of work, increased psychological load, and a perceived lack of control among blue-collar workers.

Increased awareness and understanding of this unsatisfactory work environment, which deprived the blue-collar workers of "well-rounded involvement and wholesome challenge" (Shostak, 1985), vital for the maintenance of physical and psychological well-being, has resulted in various attempts to increase the amount of control among blue-collar workers through empowerment of the workforce.

What Is Empowerment?

Empowerment is a strategy that seeks to increase job control among blue-collar workers by giving them responsibility for, for example, improving quality, managing their own safety and health, and making judgments about production levels and staffing. The theory is that workers themselves are in the best position to improve their performance and that self-management offers job satisfaction. In simple dictionary terminology the verb *empower* means "to enable." In practice, this should allow individuals in a firm to have more autonomy in decision making. However, managers have tended to regard empowerment simply as delegation of authority and resource sharing rather than as enabling and have thereby created stress for the blue-collar workforce exposed to this new way of working (Conger & Kanungo, 1988).

The rise of the movement toward an empowered workforce stems from the demise of some large Western organizations during the 1970s, which prompted the adoption of more team-focused management practices from Japan. Empowerment has become a management vogue of the 1990s, and a literature review indicates the popularity of this relatively new approach to human resource management: Twenty-five finalists of Industry Week's 1993 America's Best Plants competition reported that they put major emphasis on employee empowerment and the use of work teams (Sheridan, 1994).

It is acknowledged that many production environments now require control to be devolved to as low a level as possible, so shop-floor workers are given both the authority and the capability to manage the production process. Lawler (1992) described this as the "high involvement approach," and it demands a highly flexible and multiskilled workforce. Empowerment means the reduction of role stress by increasing participation in decision making and increasing job and work-schedule autonomy by job re-design. In practice it uses problem-solving groups to address stress-inducing factors in the workplace. Typically, the positive effects are in terms of employee attitudinal and behavioral outcomes, which might include reductions in role conflict and role ambiguity and an increase in perceived influence, which in turn have a positive impact on reported job satisfaction and cause a decrease in intention to quit the company. Furthermore, it is suggested that organizational effectiveness is enhanced by the sharing of power with subordinates.

Although evidence exists to support the effectiveness of these interventions (Burke, 1993), some researchers fear that when they are packaged together as an empowerment initiative, certain stress-inducing circumstances may arise. The first issue concerns the concept of organizational power and the second issue is related to the operationalization of empowerment through team working; that is, the use of semiautonomous work groups. Ultimately, however, empowerment also changes the nature of the organizational culture, and that can be stressful. These issues are considered in the following sections.

Many organizations have effected structural change (i.e., delayering) that was intended to give power to the shop-floor personnel through responsibility but has failed to make significant changes to actual behaviors (Werner, 1992). Some of the blame for failure is due to the reluctance of the shrinking number of personnel in management and supervisory jobs to change their traditional role of "controller" to that of "visionary." When accompanied by the sense of learned helplessness of a workforce traditionally dependent on their superiors, the status quo is likely to remain or to get worse because the supervisory and management resources are too stretched and are unable to cope with the new situation. In fact, Werner (1992) commented, "Flattening has erroneously been wielded as a tool when it is in fact a by-product of empowerment" (p. 55). Indeed, the lack of supervisory and management presence from the shop floor is probably exacerbated because of the need to spend a considerable amount of time in the team meetings that characterize empowerment initiatives.

Typically, empowerment tends to be operationalized through the mechanism of shop-floor teams, often referred to as semiautonomous work groups (SAWGs; also known as *quality circles* and *focus groups*). The literature highlights the importance of a variety of factors as contributors to success in the SAWG, including control, self-efficacy, self-esteem, job satisfaction, communication, commitment, involvement, and trust. Clearly, the need for adequate training must extend beyond the task and role demands of the individual and should include teamwork training. Landes (1994) warned that "empowered people start wielding authority with the same disregard for cooperation and teamwork that the empowerment movement is intended to eradicate" (p. 118). He suggested that people need to be equipped with knowledge, skills, and tools in order to be effective, cooperative team workers, rather than self-empowered individuals.

Although the use of team working has intuitive appeal, it should also be recognized that teams can undermine strong leadership by diluting, retarding, and complicating organizational decision making, thus creating frustrations and problematic interpersonal relationships in the workplace. Good teamwork skills and clearly defined parameters of the decisions that the team can make will help to avoid or alleviate this potential problem. An American Gallup survey (Williams, 1993) indicated that shop-floor employees are more likely to receive training as part of a team than as individuals: 8 out of 10 full-time workers reported some kind of work-team activity and 84% were involved in more than one team. However, one third of respondents said their involvement with teams was not part of their normal work and was an additional duty. Thus, the empowerment initiative that demands teamwork is likely to add to the workload demands of blue-collar workers. Alternatively, these activities might take the individual away from the shop floor, adding to the burdens of the employees left behind to stand in for their absent coworkers. This is a crucial factor in both safety and production performance, in circumstances where the workforce has already been downsized to minimal requirement as part of the business rationalization program that tends to precede an empowerment initiative. Again, however, it seems that management still tends to impose control on the SAWG and maintain strict boundaries on autonomy, and lack of trust appears to be a crucial factor.

Not surprisingly, empowerment needs a certain organizational culture in which to flourish and will also have an impact on the culture of an organization, thus, increasing the stress potential for both blue- and white-collar workers.

Culture Change: A Potential Stress Inducer

A workforce acclimatized to a dependency culture, typically found in blue-collar work environments (where workers are always told what to do and do not have to make decisions for themselves), cannot move easily or rapidly to mutual dependence (that is, control shared by mutual agreement), or to an interdependence culture (characterized by flexibility, interchange of activities, joint decision making, and sharing of control), which is vital for the success of an empowerment initiative. If management attempts to give up control too quickly, or the employees try to escape from being controlled when the authority figure will not give up control, the workforce is likely to become counterdependent (Cox & Makin, 1994). In this situation the workforce will probably fight back with acts of rebellion (e.g., wildcat strikes, overtime ban, work to rule). Cox and Makin suggested that a safe way of moving from dependence is to negotiate handing over more and more control until equal sharing is achieved. Because it is difficult to judge the rate at which change can best be made, and managers seem to want to initiate such changes as soon as the decision from the top is decreed, it is not surprising that the handing of control to the workforce, as an empowerment initiative, causes stress, fails, or is rife with problems.

McGrath (1994) suggested that it is necessary to overcome a state of learned helplessness and low self-esteem before employees are able to exercise their new power and authority. Problems occur because the changes in policy and practices that result from the empowerment initiative are not really understood. Therefore, more attention to communication of the message is required. McGrath also believed that a lack of training for the new role and task is a reason for the failure of empowerment as a means of giving more control in the workplace. Thus, the outcome is stress inducing rather than stress reducing.

Coping With High Work Load Demands by Increasing Job Control

It is suggested that the job demand–control model proposed by Karasek (1979) appeals to the economists and decision makers in an organization because it suggests that workers exposed to high levels of demand (i.e., load) are more able to cope with this source of stress if they also perceive they have a high degree of decision-making latitude and autonomy in the job. Therefore, empowerment and high involvement is likely to continue to be of interest in the current economic and market conditions. However, for a variety of reasons, stress reduction cannot automatically be assumed as a consequence of empowerment.

As mentioned earlier, the dictionary defines *empowerment* as "to authorize or enable," but often responsibility is given without the power necessary to effect the desired action. Employees are therefore likely to become frustrated if they perceive that they do not have any real power. Successful empowerment also requires managers to behave honestly, with more openness and with integrity. These changes and the altered nature of the relationship between shop floor and management (particularly supervisors and middle managers) require careful consideration and understanding in order to avoid the potential stressors that exist. Empowerment can be successful only if the workers are given the training and the authority they need to manage their own jobs. A committed workforce needs to be coached instead of managed. The essential ingredient for this is trust, but changing employment relations and work conditions do not automatically bring trust.

CONCLUSION

Changing employment relations and work conditions in order to improve the quality of working life and reduce stress among blue-collar workers has been a prime concern for researchers and industry in the past decade. In this chapter we have discussed some of the major stressors that have a deleterious impact on the health, well-being, and happiness of blue-collar workers. Although much has been done to reduce or eliminate stress at work, many of the options available, such as job rotation, job sharing, and job enrichment, bring different pressures. In fact, many of the changes have simply not provided the stress-free work environment expected because they have spawned yet other sources of stress that need to be addressed.

There is a tendency to view such changes as a set of techniques, often owned by management, rather than paying sufficient attention to the nature of the change or the processes that underlie the construct. By seeking to provide blue-collar staff with more control at work through the mechanism of empowerment it is likely that practitioners have alienated both management and the shop-floor workforce because of a limited understanding of the concept. As Werner (1992) commented, "You can take the boy out of the procedural straightjacket, but you cannot easily take the procedural straightjacket out of the boy" (p. 58).

Haste for change, lack of attention to reward systems, inequality of power, mistrust, and a lack of skills to cope with these new ways of working will compound the likelihood of failure and resistance to change in the employment conditions of blue-collar workers. Change must extend to include both management and leadership style and the culture and climate of the organization. As Einstein observed, "If you take one atom out of a molecule to study it, you very quickly find that it is hitched to the whole universe."

REFERENCES

Benyon, H., & Blackburn, R. M. (1972). *Perception of work: Variations within a factory.* Cambridge, England: Cambridge University Press.

Burke, R. J. (1993). Organizational level interventions to reduce occupation stress. *Work & Stress, 7*(1), 77–87.

Conger, J. A., & Kanungo, R. N. (1988). The empowerment process: Integrating theory and practice. *Academy of Management Review, 13,* 471–382.

Cooper, C. L., Cooper, R. D., & Eakes, L. H. (1988). *Living with stress.* Harmonsworth, Middlesex, England: Penguin Health.

Cooper, C. L., & Kelly, M. (1984). Stress among crane operators. *Journal of Occupational Medicine, 26,* 575–578.

Cox, C., & Makin, P. (1994). Overcoming dependence with contingency contracting. *Leadership and Organization Development Journal, 15*(5), 21–26.

Faltermayer, E. (1992). Is this layoff necessary? *Fortune, 125*(11), 71–86.

Fisher, S. (1985). Control and blue collar work. In C. L. Cooper & M. J. Smith (Eds.), *Job stress and blue collar work* (pp. 19–50). New York: Wiley.

French, J. R. P., & Caplan, R. D. (1970). Psychosocial factors in coronary heart disease. *Industrial Medicine, 39,* 383–397.

French, J. R. P., & Caplan, R. D. (1973). Organizational stress and individual strain. In A. J. Marrow (Ed.), *The failure of success* (pp. 30–66). New York: Amacon.

Froiland, P. (1993). What cures job stress? *Training, 30*(12), 32–36.

Harrell, A. W. (1990). Perceived risk of occupational injury: Control over pace of work and blue collar versus white collar work. *Perceptual and Motor Skills, 70*(3, Pt. 2), 1351–1359.

Health and Safety Executive. (1993). *Stress research and stress management: Putting theory to work* (Contract Research Rep. No. 61).

Hellesøy, O. H. (Ed.). (1985). *Work environment Stratfjord field.* Bergen, Norway: Universitetforlaget.

International Labor Office. (1986). *Psychological factors at work: Recognition and control* (Report of the Joint ILO/WHO Committee on Occupational Health, Ninth Session, 1984). Geneva: Author.

Kalimo, R. (1987). Psychosocial factors and workers' health: An overview. In R. Kalimo, M. A. El-Batawi, & C. L. Cooper (Eds.), *Psychosocial factors at work and their relation to health* (pp. 3–18). Geneva: World Health Organization.

Karasek, R. (1979). Job demands, job decision latitude and mental strain: Implications for job re-design. *Administrative Science Quarterly, 24,* 285–309.

Kawakami, N., Haratani, N., & Takashi, A. S. (1992). Effects of perceived job stress on depressive symptoms in blue collar workers of an electrical factory in Japan. *Scandinavian Journal of Work, Environment, & Health, 18*(3), 195–200.

Kelly, M., & Cooper, C. L. (1981). Stress among blue collar workers: A case study of the steel industry. *Employee Relations, 3*(2), 6–9.

Kochan, T. A., Smith, M., Wells, J. C., & Rebitzer, J. B. (1994). Human resource strategies and contingent workers: The case of safety and health in the petrochemical industry. *Human Resource Management, 33*(1), 55–77.

Landes, L. (1994). The myth and misdirection of employee empowerment. *Training, 31*(3), 116–118.

Landy, F. J., & Trumbo, D. A. (1980). *Psychology of work behavior.* Homewood, IL: Dorsey.

Landsbergis, P. A., Schnall, P. L., Deitz, D., & Friedman, R. (1992). The patterning of psychological attributes and distress by "job strain" and social support in a sample of working men. *Journal of Behavioral Medicine, 15,* 379–405.

Lavie, P., Kremerman, S., & Wiel, M. (1982). Sleep disorders and safety at work in industry workers. *Personality and Individual Differences, 6,* 305–311.

Lawler, E. E. (1992). *The ultimate advantage: Creating the high involvement organization.* San Francisco: Jossey-Bass.

Levine, D. I. (1990). Participation, productivity and the firm's environment. *California Management Review, 32*(4), 86–100.

Lowman, D. L. (1993). "New pay": Compensation for people, not jobs. *Employment Relations Today, 20*(1), 37–45.

Margolis, B., Kroes, W., & Quinn, R. (1974). Job stress: An unlisted occupational hazard. *Journal of Occupational Medicine, 1*(16), 659–661.

McGrath, R., Jr. (1994). Organizationally induced helplessness: The antithesis of empowerment. *Quality Progress, 27*(4), 89–92.

Monk, T. M., & Tepas, D. I. (1985). Shift work. In C. L. Cooper & M. J. Smith (Eds.), *Job stress and blue collar work* (pp. 65–84). New York: Wiley.

Payne, P. P., & Baigts, G. S. (1994). Getting to the core. *Business Mexico, 4*(4), 46–48.

Poulton, E. C. (1978). Blue collar stressors. In C. L. Cooper & R. Payne (Eds.), *Stress at work* (pp. 51–81). New York: Wiley.

Robinson, B., & Druker, M. (1991). Innovative approaches to downsizing: The experience in Maine. *Employment Relations Today, 18*(1), 79–87.

Sheridan, J. H. (1994). How do you stack up? *Industry Week, 243*(4), 53–56.

Shostak, A. B. (1985). Blue-collar alienation. In C. L. Cooper & M. J. Smith (Eds.), *Job stress and blue collar work* (pp. 7–18). New York: Wiley.

Shouksmith, G. (1990). Job control, paced tasks and discretion. *Perceptual and Motor Skills, 71,* 409–410.

Sutherland, V. J., & Cooper, C. L. (1991). *Stress and accidents in the offshore oil and gas industry.* Houston, TX: Gulf.

Sutherland, V. J., Makin, P., Phillips, R., & Cooper, D. (1993). An attitude problem. *Occupational Safety & Health, 23*(7), 44–47.

Wallick, F. (1972). *The American worker: An endangered species.* New York: Ballantine Books.

Watson, G. (1994, July). The flexible workforce and patterns of working hours in the UK. *Employment Gazette*, pp. 239–247.

Werner, M. (1992). The great paradox: Responsibility without empowerment. *Business Horizons, 35*, 55–58.

Williams, K. (1993). Employee teams increase quality and productivity. *Management Accounting, 75*(3), 19.

6

Commitment to Occupational Health and Safety in Management Training

Jane E. Adams-Roy, Malgorzata A. Knap, and
Julian Barling

Over the last 3 years, more than 1.75 million employees were injured on the job in Canada. Furthermore, as startling as this situation may seem, this figure is derived from Statistics Canada, which counts only those injuries that (a) were reported to workers' compensation boards and commissions and (b) necessitated the employee taking time off from work to recover. If injuries that do not necessitate taking time off from work are included, the number of injuries doubles. In addition, there are undoubtedly a significantly greater number of injuries that occur but are not reported at all due to circumstances such as lack of knowledge on the part of employees concerning workers' compensation procedures (Statistics Canada, 1992).

In the United States, the picture is just as grim. More than 200,000 men and women have died on the job in the last 20 years (Kinney, 1990). Despite federal intervention in the United States through the formation of the Occupational Health and Safety Administration, some sectors of the economy have actually experienced declines in workplace safety

Portions of this research were supported by a grant from the Social Sciences and Humanities Research Council of Canada.

(Waldman, de la Peña, Springen, Howard, & Smith, 1989). Joseph Kinney, Director of the United States National Safe Workplace Institute, contends that employers were outraged when Bill S.2154 was introduced in 1990. It stated that flagrant violations of health and safety that resulted in serious bodily injury or even death to employees would be punishable by prison terms of up to 5 years for injury and 10 years for death.

OCCUPATIONAL HEALTH AND SAFETY ISSUES

Occupational health and safety issues have increasingly received greater attention in both the media and the workplace over the last several years. Waldman et al. (1989) stated that workers listed occupational safety as their primary job-related concern, ahead of salary, benefits, and day care, and trade unions have long pushed for the removal of safety hazards from the workplace (Fisher & Fletcher, 1989). Although the workers themselves may believe that occupational safety is the major priority, there is a prevailing opinion that management does not share this concern. A commonly held belief is that despite the suffering and potential long-term effects of injuries on the workers themselves, as well as the financial cost and loss of productivity borne by the organization, employers and managers still do not regard occupational health and safety as a serious or significant issue.

Bill Sells, a senior executive who worked for 30 years in the asbestos industry, stated that middle and lower level managers at Johns-Manville continued to endanger the health of both workers and customers even after senior management had recognized the critical health and safety implications of the industry. He stated that denial of health and safety issues became part of the corporate culture and that this blunder eventually not only cost thousands of lives, but also destroyed an entire industry (Sells, 1994).

In a review of companies with varying accident rates, Zohar (1980) found that successful safety programs existed in those organizations that had a strong management commitment to safety. The involvement of senior management in safety activities was conspicuously absent in high accident companies but present in those with low accident rates. Furthermore, those companies exhibiting relatively low accident rates had recognized that safety was an integral part of production systems and incorporated safety into company meetings and production scheduling. Zohar (1980) concluded that only a genuine change in management attitudes and increased commitment would improve the safety level in industrial organizations because it was the organizational climate that most influenced workers' behaviors. Management attitudes toward safety and its relevance to general production processes created a climate that guided and directed work behaviors.

Thus, although increased legislation concerning occupational health and safety and the technological advances that have been made toward improving the safety of workers are necessary, it can be argued that they are not sufficient, because the role of managers in creating a workplace climate that emphasizes the importance of occupational health and safety is critical (Zohar, 1980). Instead, what is also required is an active commitment on the part of management to occupational health and safety. The question motivating the present study was the extent to which any such commitment to occupational health and safety is likely to occur. The specific purpose of this study was to investigate whether individuals currently enrolled in university-level management training programs would demonstrate this commitment. Do these future managers, who will ultimately be responsible for enforcing workplace health and safety standards, consider occupational health and safety to be a significant issue?

To assess this, the current research addressed several questions. First, in free recall, would respondents—all of whom were future managers—consider occupational health and safety an issue of which managers are cognizant? Second, when compared with other issues managers encounter on a daily basis, how important would they consider occupational health and safety? Third, what importance is placed on occupational health and safety in current university education programs? Last, what is the current knowledge among future managers of health and safety issues that would affect the performance of their duties?

METHOD

Participants

A total of 92 volunteer respondents from two different universities were sampled. Three surveys were discarded because of incomplete data, leaving 89 usable surveys.

Group 1 consisted of 32 master's of business administration (MBA) students from an eastern Canadian university. The mean age of this sample was 34 years. The second and third groups consisted of 57 participants from a large central Canadian university. Group 2 consisted of 38 students from the first year of an executive MBA program, and Group 3 consisted of 19 individuals enrolled in their second year of the same executive MBA program. Their mean ages were 33 and 38 years, respectively.

Ninety percent of the total sample stated they had previously been employed in a full-time capacity. The mean number of years of employment was 11.5.

Measures

Respondents were asked first to state, in a free-recall situation, five issues they believed were important for managers to be aware of for effective performance as managers. They were then asked to rank order a specific list of nine issues, based on the same criterion, with occupational health and safety included as one of the issues. These nine issues were compiled from suggestions of students currently completing an MBA program and one professor teaching in the program not associated with the current research. Respondents were also provided with the identical list of issues and asked to rank order them based on the importance they had received in their management education. In this way, inferences could be made about the extent to which future managers are being prepared to accept their responsibilities for overseeing workplace health and safety. Finally, to assess their knowledge of occupational health and safety, they responded to 10 questions about occupational health and safety legislation in their jurisdiction that directly affected their managerial activities.[1]

Procedure

Students were asked at the beginning of a class if they would be willing to participate in a study on management education. Volunteer respondents were then given a letter explaining the study. If they agreed to participate, they received each of the four parts of the questionnaire separately so that the "free-recall" questions could not be biased if respondents chose to examine the whole questionnaire. Because of this, they were asked to affix any four digit number they could recall (e.g., the last four digits of their student number or phone number) on the top of each page so that the four pages could be collated. This was possible in all cases.

RESULTS

When the respondents were asked to list spontaneously five issues of importance, there was no mention of occupational health and safety (or any relevant synonyms) as an issue for effective management by any of the respondents (see Table 1). One respondent did list "health," but it was not clear whether the respondent meant personal health or occupational health and safety, and there was no way of ascertaining this post hoc.

Respondents then received a second page asking them to rank order a list of issues that were listed for them. As can be seen from Figure 1, respondents ranked occupational health and safety last in terms of its perceived importance.

The next page that was distributed asked the respondents to rank order the importance each of the 10 areas had received in their graduate management education. As can be seen from Figure 2, occupational health and safety was perceived to have received the least attention in their graduate education.

---

[1]Because these items are specific to the occupational health and safety legislation currently in place in the specific jurisdiction, their applicability across context and time is limited. The items can be obtained from Julian Barling, School of Business, Queen's University, Kingston, Ontario K7L 3N6 Canada.

Table 1

Responses (Summed) to Question, "Please List Five Areas or Issues Which You Feel Are Important for Managers to Be Aware of for Their Effective Performance as Managers"

Area/issue listed	Total
Dealing with subordinates/human resources	165
Leadership style/personal characteristics	64
Financial/accounting/economics	56
Goal-setting/strategy/policy	41
International business/trade	29
Miscellaneous (law, environment, networking)	18
Administration/operations	16
Marketing/sales	15
Communication systems	13
Technological advancement	10
Customer service	4
Health	1
Total	431

NOTE: Total number of possible responses is 445, but some respondents listed less than the 5 allowed.

Finally, participants were asked to answer 10 questions about occupational health and safety legislation specific to their provincial jurisdiction. All 10 questions specifically focused on occupational health and safety issues that would affect their daily performance as managers. Scores ranged between 0 and 10, and the mean score for the entire group was 4.38.

DISCUSSION

In general, the results of this survey indicated that students currently enrolled in graduate-level management education programs do not consider occupational health and safety to be a significant issue for day-to-day management and that occupational health and safety is not covered in detail in

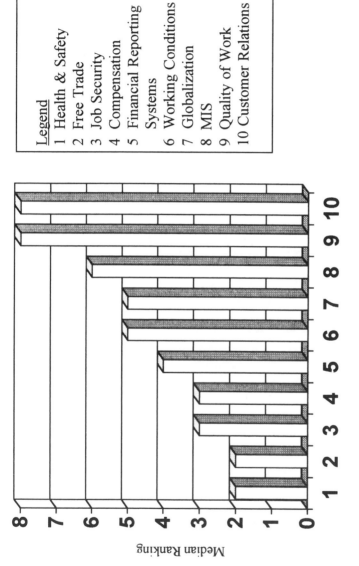

Perceived importance for management

Figure 1

Median ranking for the question, "Please rank order the following ten questions in order of how important you feel they are for management in general." MIS = management information systems.

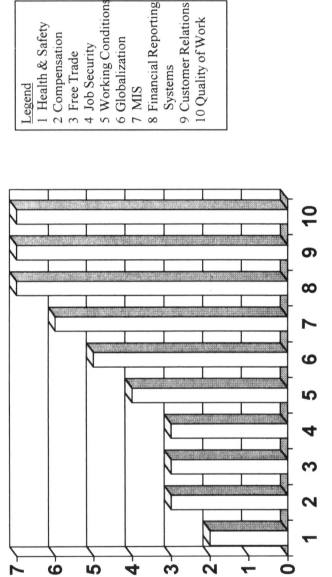

Legend
1 Health & Safety
2 Compensation
3 Free Trade
4 Job Security
5 Working Conditions
6 Globalization
7 MIS
8 Financial Reporting Systems
9 Customer Relations
10 Quality of Work

Attention received during university education

Figure 2

Median ranking for the question, "Please rank order the following ten questions in order of the importance they have been given in your university education." MIS = management information systems.

their education. Not only did they fail to list health and safety as a significant management issue in the free-recall portion of the questionnaire, they also rated it as of least importance when it was listed with other relevant management issues. Not surprisingly, therefore, they also do not possess a significant knowledge about occupational health and safety, as demonstrated by their overall score on the knowledge portion of the survey.

This pattern of findings, although unsettling in light of the fact that current workplace accident statistics suggest that occupational health and safety issues should be at the forefront of responsible management practices, is hardly surprising given that respondents stated that health and safety had received comparatively little attention in their graduate management education. This could also be a factor in their rating occupational health and safety as relatively unimportant, as students may be justified in inferring that issues not covered in such courses are of relatively less importance for management. Stated somewhat differently, if potential managers are not taught that occupational health and safety is important, it is difficult for them to think and act otherwise.

However, notwithstanding the lack of emphasis on occupational health and safety in respondents' education, equally disturbing is the fact that 90% of the respondents stated they had previously held full-time jobs. Furthermore, the mean length of time in such employment was 11.5 years, and 71% stated that this employment had been in managerial positions. Thus, although the lack of managerial education is a part of the problem, it cannot be wholly responsible. Clearly, despite ongoing and widespread attempts to introduce legislation and the emphasis placed on this issue by employees, management personnel consider occupational health and safety to be of little importance (Sells, 1994). This conclusion is supported by Fisher and Fletcher's (1989) findings. In a questionnaire given to managers, supervisors, and workers at five companies in South Africa, significant deficiencies were found in the level of safety knowledge of all respondents, including management and safety representatives. Intriguingly, four of the five companies from Fisher and Fletcher's (1989) study had achieved "five-star safety ratings" (the highest attainable) assigned by the National Occupational Safety Association.

In assessing the external validity of the current findings, one empirical question that remains is whether the results obtained in the present study are specific to the two universities studied. Stated somewhat differently, perhaps these two universities are unique in their failure to education students about occupational health and safety. We argue that this is not the case: Pakalnis (1994) surveyed 42 schools of business (or commerce) in Canada, asking about the extent to which occupational health and safety is included in their curricula at the graduate and undergraduate level. He showed that such programs uniformly place very little emphasis on occupational health and safety education.

In conclusion, current accident statistics unquestionably demonstrate that managers need to be aware of occupational health and safety issues, from both a human safety and a productivity perspective, and the results of this study (and that of Pakalnis, 1994) point to the need for management training programs to reexamine their present curricula. Educating potential managers is a necessary first step in addressing the problem, particularly because the promotion of a climate of safety is critical in achieving a safe workplace, and the role of managers on this process is crucial (Zohar, 1980). A change in the occupational health and safety climate is even more crucial with the changing employment conditions. Early indications suggest that with the trend toward contingent work, less emphasis is being placed on training in general, and health and safety training in particular, for full-time and contingent workers. This may be associated with increased health and safety risks (Kochan, Smith, Wells, & Rebitzer, 1994).

REFERENCES

Fisher, J., & Fletcher, P. (1989). Who knows about safety law? *South African Journal of Labour Relations, 11*, 33–44.

Fussell, P. (1983). *Class: A guide through the American status system.* New York: Simon & Schuster.

Kinney, J. (1990, September 10). Why did Paul die? *Newsweek,* p. 11.

Kochan, T. A., Smith, M., Wells, J. C., & Rebitzer, J. B. (1994). Human resource strategies and contingent workers: The case of safety and health in the petrochemical industry. *Human Resource Management, 33*, 55–77.

Pakalnis, V. (1994). *Occupational health and safety: A blind spot in teaching at Canadian Schools of Business.* Unpublished manuscript, School of Business, Queen's University, Kingston, Ontario, Canada.

Sells, B. (1994, March–April). What asbestos taught me about managing risk. *Harvard Business Review*, pp. 76–90.

Statistics Canada. (1992). *Work injuries 1989–1991* (Catalogue #72–208). Ottawa, Canada: Author.

Waldman, S., de la Peña, N., Springen, K., Howard, J., & Smith, V. (1989, December 11). Danger on the job. *Newsweek*, pp. 42–46.

Zohar, D. (1980). Safety climate in industrial organizations: Theoretical and applied implications. *Journal of Applied Psychology, 65*, 92–106.

7

Changing Future Managers' Attitudes Toward Occupational Health and Safety

Catherine A. Loughlin, C. Gail Hepburn, and
Julian Barling

Every year 100,000 workers are killed or die of work-related accidents or diseases; 400,000 are disabled; and 6 million are hurt at work in the United States (e.g., Fussell, 1983). A U.S. worker is five times more likely to die than a Swedish worker and three times more likely to die than a Japanese worker (Kinney, 1990). In Canada each year, there are approximately five disabling injuries for every 100 employees on the job (Werther, Davis, Schwind, & Das, 1990). This issue is not new, and workers and labor organizers have long regarded occupational health and safety as a primary workplace issue, if not the primary issue they face at work. Recently, concern with workplace health and safety issues seems even more justified given current employment changes in both the public and private sectors in North America. The replacement of long-term, full-time employees with temporary, part-time, or contracted employees has been found to influence workplace health and safety in unanticipated and serious ways. For example, in a study of contingent/contract workers in the petro-

Portions of this research were supported by a grant from the Social Sciences and Humanities Research Council of Canada and by a doctoral fellowship from the Social Sciences and Humanities Research Council of Canada.

chemical industry in the United States, changes in the flow of communication on the job between full-time and contract employees (as well as a deficit in contractor's safety training) were found to be responsible for serious health and safety consequences (Kochan, Smith, Wells, & Rebitzer, 1994). Thus, more than ever, it is necessary for management to recognize that occupational health and safety is a legitimate area of concern on the job (whether dealing with full-time workers, contingent workers, or the interaction between the two).

In response to concerns about the unacceptable rates of death and injury on the job (as well as changes in workplace legislation and legal liability), North American management has recently been forced to address this issue. Consequently, during the last decade workplace health and safety has received greater attention. The "careless worker" model, which assumes that workplace accidents occur because workers fail to be cautious or to protect themselves, is no longer appropriate. Instead, it is increasingly being recognized that employers and employees must cooperate and share the responsibility for workplace health and safety (Werther et al., 1990).

In general, management tends to view occupational health and safety as a "technical and independent aspect of the production process, detached from other management operations" (Zohar, 1980, p. 101). Thus, management's focus has typically been on technological procedures (i.e., safety systems) or legal concerns (i.e., financial liability). This narrow focus is unlikely to lead to meaningful change in workplace health and safety. In contrast, what is necessary is for occupational health and safety to be perceived as falling within the managerial domain along with other normal functions (e.g., financial restraint or attention to human resources; Sells, 1994). A brief discussion of management's role in achieving workplace health and safety illustrates why this is so important.

MANAGEMENT'S ROLE IN WORKPLACE HEALTH AND SAFETY

An organization's health and safety climate helps determine the safety of that work environment (Miner, 1992). Employees are well aware of the norms concerning appropriate workplace health and safety behavior (e.g., employees share common perceptions of the safety climate in their company). Furthermore, workers' perceptions of management's attitudes about safety are critical in determining the level of this climate (e.g., Sagan, 1993). Safety programs work best where the climate is positive, and the level of this climate is correlated with the effectiveness of safety programs as judged by safety inspectors (Zohar, 1980).

If the health and safety climate in a company is not positive among top management, workers are unlikely to create such a climate on their own. Organizational leaders must place a high priority on safety, because unless they are willing to devote considerable financial resources to safety, accidents will continue to occur (Sagan, 1993). In addition, clear communication of the importance that a company's leadership places on health and safety is necessary to ensure that all organizational members share a common vision of the company's priorities (Sagan, 1993).

Unfortunately, management often does not attend to workplace health and safety issues until a safety concern has taken on primary importance for the company's subsistence (e.g., black lung disease among coal mining firms, Miner, 1992; or asbestos poisoning among building materials manufacturers, Sells, 1994). For example, in his article about the asbestos industry, Sells (1994) blamed management for their failure to be accountable in terms of workplace safety. He stated that "what took thousands of lives and killed an industry was management's failure to insist on its own responsibilities" (Sells, 1994, p. 76). If an organization's culture encourages denial concerning workplace safety, problems get buried and people continue to get hurt or die on the job (Sells, 1994). There are recent powerful reminders of what can happen when a commitment to safety is lacking among management, and the film *Death on the Job* reveals many instances of preventable workplace deaths.

In 1980, Zohar concluded that "a genuine change in management attitudes and increased commitment" to safety would be necessary if the level of safety in industrial organizations was ever to improve (p. 101). However, a recent study done by Adams-Roy, Knap, and Barling (chapter 6, this volume) provides sufficient reason to question whether any changes have occurred in management attitudes over the past decade. These researchers found that students currently enrolled in management training programs (i.e., master's of business administration students in Canada) simply do not possess knowledge about workplace health and safety issues, nor do they consider occupational health and safety as a significant issue for management. It would appear that such a change has simply not occurred, nor is it being encouraged in current management education programs. Likewise, in interviewing faculty associated with human resources in 47 schools of business in Canada, Pakalnis (1994) found that there is very little attention given to occupational health and safety in regular human resources curricula.

It is critical that management become aware of the issues involved in occupational health and safety and of their role in determining the safety climate of an organization. In addition, they must receive sufficient knowledge concerning the management of workplace health and safety issues in their education and training programs.

THE PRESENT RESEARCH

This research focused on the attitudes of future managers currently engaged in university education and on whether their attitudes toward management's role in occupational health and safety can be altered. Educators have the attention of these students. Unless occupational health and safety is given a higher priority in management education, while students are learning and forming their attitudes, we are unlikely to see positive changes in management's workplace health and safety attitudes and behavior. However, because they do not consider occupational health and safety as a significant issue for management (Adams-Roy et al., chapter 6, this volume), it is first necessary to arouse the attention of these students in order to elevate their interest in this topic.

We tested whether the attention of future managers could be gained using an in-class video presentation (i.e., could the single viewing of a film affect their attitudes toward management's role in workplace health and safety). The film *Death on the Job* documents the way decisions made by management in many U.S. companies can result in preventable workplace deaths if not enough care and attention is given to the safety and welfare of the workers. This movie powerfully depicts how workers' deaths are a direct result of decisions made by management in the fishing, construction (tunneling), and petrochemical industries. For example, the health and safety consequences of fewer people doing more work, the hiring of contract workers, and the pressure to produce regardless of safety are highlighted (Kochan et al., 1994). If the intervention is successful, after viewing this movie students' awareness of workplace health and safety issues and management's responsibility in this area should increase. In addition, they should be more receptive to learning about this topic.

WHY SHOULD A MOVIE AFFECT ATTITUDES?

In political communication studies the docudrama hypothesis states that docudrama (a combination of melodramatic fiction and news documentary) has a forceful effect on viewers' images of social and political events. Public views of both prior and current history are apparently shaped by these dramas. That is, viewers think that they are seeing a recreation of genuine events, and this frames their memory of the past (Adams et al., 1985).

Adams et al. (1985) conducted the first large-scale field study on the effects of a motion picture (either docudrama or pure fiction) on the political and social attitudes of adults. They tested whether the viewing of a movie released just prior to the 1984 U.S. presidential campaign (*The Right Stuff;* a docudrama about the 1963 astronaut John Glenn, who was then a political candidate) could affect people's attitudes toward Glenn as a presidential candidate. The findings demonstrated that those watching the movie did view Glenn significantly more favorably as a presidential contender than those who had not seen the film. Thus, the notion that viewing a movie could change attitudes had been confirmed.

Bateman, Sakano, and Fujita (1992) illustrated the power of this medium using the film *Roger and Me.* This film depicts the aftermath of the closing of General Motors' plants in Flint, Michigan. The town of Flint and the 30,000 people who lost their jobs are portrayed as the victims of a disloyal corporation (headed by Roger Smith, General Motors' chief executive officer). American business is the clear villain in this picture, and both a U.S. and a Japanese sample experienced more negative attitudes toward U.S. business after viewing this film. In 1985, Adams et al. had demonstrated that viewing a film could affect viewers' political attitudes. Bateman et al. (1992) now demonstrated that a movie could also influence work-related attitudes.

Thus, the first goal of our study was to determine whether viewing a film (*Death on the Job*) could affect future managers' attitudes toward the way U.S. and Canadian management make decisions concerning workplace health and safety issues. Because people tend to respond favorably to a fact-based message even when it is obviously biased (i.e., intended to change one's perceptions, cognitions, and behavior; Jowett & O'Donnell, 1986), it was anticipated that even a single viewing of *Death on the Job* would affect viewer's attitudes toward management and toward occupational health and safety. It may also influence their tendency to view health and safety as within the realm of a managers' responsibility.

Viewing *Death on the Job* may also make students more sympathetic toward workers in labor–management disputes over health and safety issues. Thus, the second goal of this study was to determine whether participants' likelihood of siding with labor in both Canada and the United States would increase significantly after viewing this film.

The third objective was to determine whether any attitude change would be stable over time. In the Adams et al. (1985) study, approximately the same proportion of people declared that the film had influenced their opinion of John Glenn 2 to 3 weeks after watching it as immediately after viewing the film. Thus, we tested whether the same would hold true for the effects of any changes in attitudes toward management based on viewing the film *Death on the Job*. If any changes were indeed stable, opportunities for management education would be enhanced.

The final goal of this research was to identify whether attitudes toward U.S. and Canadian managers would differ. Although the actual incidents in the movie involved a U.S. company, because of the similarity and proximity between these countries, students may simply evaluate these countries in the same way. In this case Canada's ratings are likely to fall along with those of the United States after students view the film. In contrast, it is also possible that because Canada is typically viewed as more socialist, unionized, and worker friendly, there may be a tendency to think that occupational health and safety is better managed in Canada than in the United States. In this case U.S. management is likely to be viewed more negatively than Canadian management to begin with. Furthermore, attitudes toward Canadian business may actually become even more positive after viewing this film as a result of the comparison to the United States. This prediction is based on Bateman et al.'s (1992) finding that Japanese participants rated Japanese business more positively after viewing *Roger and Me* (supposedly in contrast to what they had just seen as the situation in the United States). Thus, attitudes toward U.S. business and Canadian business were measured separately and compared in order to test these two possible outcomes.

METHOD

Participants

In light of the focal role of management in forming the health and safety climate in an organization, we were interested in measuring the attitudes of future managers. Thus, we first sampled Canadian undergraduate business students (age range = 17–23 years) and other university students in an introductory organizational behavior course (age range = 18–22 years). Students registered in these classes were asked to complete questionnaires regarding their attitudes toward U.S. and Canadian management (i.e., in terms of occupational health and safety).

Materials

Movie. Death on the Job (DiPersio & Guttentag, 1991) documents the way negligent management decisions can result in preventable workplace deaths and injuries. Workplace accidents in three industries (fishing, construction, and petrochemical) are considered in this film (six major workplace accidents in total): (a) The 1990 sinking of the *Aleutian Enterprise* (an Arctic Alaska Company factory trawler) is depicted, in which the overloading of the boat with fish and the failure to fix a broken safety alarm cost 9 workers their lives. (b) The 1988 S.A. Healy Company's tunneling disaster in Milwaukee is covered, in which the threat of deadly methane gas was ignored by management until the failure to provide spark-proof equipment interacted with the methane to cause an explosion killing 3 workers. (The company was later charged with two counts of reckless homicide.) (c) Four incidents in the petrochemical industry in Texas are highlighted. In 1987, some of the Marathon plant's safety systems were disengaged in order to speed up the "turnaround procedure" (in which the plant is off-line), causing hydrochloric gas to be spread for miles. In August 1989, an explosion at Phillips Petroleum killed 2 workers and injured several others. Then, in October, a massive explosion in the same plant killed 23 people and injured another 232 (caused by outside contract workers who were brought in to clear a clogged reactor line). Finally, in 1990 an explosion of a waste-water tank at the Arco Chemical plant killed 17 workers. In every case, the primary issue was the same: the rush to get "on-line," the failure to fix current systems, or the by-passing of safety systems. For example, in the Phillips explosion, company employees had refused to work on the clogged line due to safety risks, as a result of which management hired contract workers who would do the job and not ask questions. In a 2-year period, 500 people were injured in these petrochemical plants in Texas, and 50 workers lost their lives. Needless to say, this movie portrays management in a negative manner and clearly sympathizes with the workers.

Questionnaire. Sixteen items were adapted from the materials developed by Bateman et al. (1992) to measure attitudes toward management on a 7-point scale (1 = *strongly disagree*, 7 = *strongly agree*). These questions measured the level of respect that students had for management in major corporations (e.g., "Almost all of the people running major corporations are responsible people who know what they are doing"; "It seems to me that most corporate executives are unethical"). More specific questions concerning the integrity of managers with respect to health and safety issues in the workplace were also included (e.g., "Most top business leaders are devoted to the health and welfare of their employees"; "Management takes workers' health and safety into account when making decisions about the bottom line"; "Management fully informs employees about health and safety risks at work"). The tendency to sympathize with workers in health and safety disputes was also measured on a 7-point scale, using a single item ("In worker/management disputes concerning health and safety I usually sympathize with the workers"). For these measures the questionnaire had columns in which respondents indicated the degree to which they agreed with each statement for each country (one for Canada and one for the United States). The questionnaire took about 5 minutes to complete.

Procedure

Study 1: Attitude change. Students in the first group (experimental group; $n = 50$) were pretested, saw the film, and were then given a posttest (an intact class was used during a 1.5-hour class period). To control for the fact that exposure to the items might cause students to think about these issues or change their opinions of management, a nonexperimental control group ($n = 42$) was also tested. They were given the pretest at the beginning of a class unrelated to health and safety, and at the end of the class (1.5 hours later) they received the posttest. In a later class (after both of these tests were completed) this group viewed the film as a class exercise.

Study 2: Stability of attitude change. To test whether the effects of any changes in attitudes toward management were stable, students in a third group ($n = 29$) viewed the film and completed a posttest (again after a 1.5-hour class period). Then, after a 2-week period, they completed the same questionnaire at the beginning of a class unrelated to occupational health and safety. In the final group students' attitudes at all three time periods were measured (i.e., before viewing the film, after viewing the film, and then again 2 weeks later). Thus, in Group 4 ($n = 26$) students were pretested, saw the film, and were then given the posttest (during a 1.5-hour class period). Following a 2-week period the same respondents were given a delayed posttest at the beginning of a class unrelated to occupational health and safety.

RESULTS

Analyses of covariance (with pretest scores used as covariates to adjust for initial differences) were used to test for any differences in posttest performance in Groups 2 and 3. Attitudes toward Canadian and U.S. management, as well as their likelihood of siding with labor in Canada and the United States, were compared. A repeated measures analysis of variance (ANOVA) was used in the fourth group. This group allowed us to test whether students' attitudes after 2 weeks were different from their original attitudes before the movie (i.e., we could compare students' attitudes at all three time periods: before viewing the film, after viewing the film, and then again 2 weeks later).

Study 1: Attitude Change

In terms of attitudes toward Canadian management, the experimental group's posttest scores were significantly lower than the control group's posttest scores, $F(2, 88) = 60.85$, $p < .01$. The adjusted means (after controlling for any pretest differences) were 3.25 and 3.99, respectively. Attitudes toward U.S. management followed the same pattern. The experimental group's posttest scores were significantly lower than the control group's posttest scores, $F(2, 88) = 62.64$, $p < .01$. The adjusted means (after controlling for any pretest differences) were 3.01 for the experimental group and 3.83 for the control group. Thus, attitudes toward both Canadian and U.S. management were significantly more negative among students who had viewed the film than among those who had not viewed it. (For all unadjusted means and standard deviations in Studies 1 and 2 concerning attitudes toward both Canadian and U.S. management, see Table 1.)

In terms of the likelihood of siding with labor in Canadian labor–management disputes, posttest scores of the experimental group were significantly higher than those of the control group, $F(2, 88) = 8.04$, $p < .01$.

Table 1

Studies 1 and 2: Unadjusted Means and Standard Deviations for Attitudes Toward Canadian and U.S. Management

Measure	Canada		United States	
	M	SD	M	SD
Study 1				
Group 1 (experimental)				
Pre	3.93	0.56	3.72	0.56
Post	3.22	0.66	2.98	0.66
Group 2 (control)				
Pre	4.00	0.60	3.78	0.68
Post	4.02	0.62	3.85	0.67
Study 2				
Group 3				
Post	3.46	0.60	3.20	0.69
Delay	3.75	0.54	3.59	0.50
Group 4				
Pre	3.61	0.64	3.40	0.63
Post	2.77	0.74	2.30	0.78
Delay	2.91	0.94	2.56	0.90

The adjusted means (after controlling for any pretest differences) were 5.02 for the experimental group and 4.32 for the control group. Attitudes toward siding with labor in U.S. labor–management disputes were not significantly different from each other (although differences were in the same direction). Thus, only concerning labor–management disputes in Canada were students who had viewed the film significantly more likely to believe that they would side with labor in labor–management disputes than those who had not viewed the movie. (For all unadjusted means and standard deviations in Studies 1 and 2 concerning this measure, see Table 2.)

Finally, in the experimental group, participants' attitudes toward U.S. management were significantly more negative than their attitudes toward

| | Table 2 | | | |

Studies 1 and 2: Unadjusted Means and Standard Deviations for Likelihood of Siding With Labor in Labor–Management Disputes

	Canada		United States	
Measure	*M*	*SD*	*M*	*SD*
Study 1				
Group 1 (experimental)				
Pre	4.22	1.31	4.33	1.21
Post	4.94	1.27	4.96	1.30
Group 2 (control)				
Pre	4.57	1.50	4.48	1.52
Post	4.43	1.53	4.63	1.43
Study 2				
Group 3				
Post	5.46	1.43	5.50	1.43
Delay	4.75	1.48	4.75	1.48
Group 4				
Pre	4.64	1.97	4.64	2.01
Post	6.05	1.25	6.00	1.27
Delay	5.41	2.02	5.59	1.82

Canadian management on both the pretests, $t(44) = -5.46, p < .001$, and posttests, $t(44) = -4.02, p < .001$. Participants in the control group also had significantly more negative attitudes toward U.S. management than Canadian management on both the pretest, $t(39) = -4.94, p < .001$, and posttest, $t(39) = -5.12, p < .001$, measures.

Study 2: Stability of Attitude Change

Questionnaires completed 2 weeks following the posttest showed significantly more positive attitudes toward Canadian and U.S. management, $t(27) = -2.41, p < .05$, and $t(27) = -3.08, p < .01$, respectively. In this study the likelihood of siding with labor in Canada and the United States significantly decreased during the 2-week delay, $t(27) = 2.10$, $p < .05$, and $t(27) = 2.21$, $p < .05$, respectively. As in the two previous studies, participants continued to report significantly more negative attitudes toward U.S. management than Canadian management on both measures, $t(27) = -6.79$, $p < .001$, and $t(27) = -3.56$, $p < .001$, respectively (see Table 1 for means).

Initially, these results seemed to suggest that students' attitudes were reverting to their pre-viewing levels (i.e., their attitudes toward management's behavior concerning occupational health and safety became more positive as time passed since viewing the film). However, because there was no pretest, we had no way of knowing whether students' attitudes after 2 weeks were still different from their original attitudes before the movie (i.e., they could be recovering somewhat while still being significantly different from what they were to begin with). For this reason, we tested the fourth group.

A repeated measures ANOVA revealed significant main effects for both time, $F(2, 42) = 22.53$, $p < .001$, and country, $F(1, 21) = 12.73$, $p < .01$. The interaction was not significant, $F(2, 42) = 1.76$, $p > .05$. Consequently, because there was no significant interaction (indicating that the effects for time were the same for attitudes toward both U.S. and Canadian management), from this point on we discuss the combined means for these groups.

Planned comparisons revealed that both posttest attitudes toward management and delayed measure attitudes were significantly more negative than pretest attitude scores, $t(42) = 4.48$, $p < .001$, and $t(42) = 3.55$, $p < .001$, respectively. Interestingly, and in contrast to the previous study, the posttest scores and the delay measure scores did not differ, $t(42) = 0.94$, $p > .05$. In addition, the likelihood of siding with labor in Canada and the United States significantly increased after viewing the film, $t(42) = 2.59$, $p < .05$, and although it decreased slightly after 2 weeks' time, this reduction was not significantly different from the posttest scores. However, with this reduction in the tendency to side with labor, the level of this effect after 2 weeks' time now failed to be significantly different from the original pretest level.

DISCUSSION

In Study 1 we tested whether the film *Death on the Job* was capable of changing future managers' attitudes toward the way U.S. and Canadian management make decisions concerning workplace health and safety issues. This study demonstrated that students who viewed the film significantly changed their attitudes toward management: Their attitudes became more negative toward both U.S. and Canadian management. Students not viewing the film experienced no significant attitude change. In addition, students who viewed the film had an increase in their likelihood of siding with labor in both Canadian and U.S. labor management disputes. However, only attitudes toward siding with labor in Canadian labor–management disputes were significantly different after viewing the film. Although for the United States, differences were in the same direction (the adjusted means—controlling for any pretest differences—were 5.00 for the experimental group and 4.58 for the control group), they fell short of significance.

In Study 2 we measured students' attitudes toward management at all three time periods (i.e., before viewing the film, immediately after viewing it, and 2 weeks later). In this case we found that attitudes remained stable for the 2 weeks after viewing the film (i.e., there was no significant change between the posttest and 2-week delay measures). In addition, both the postviewing scores and the 2-week delay scores differed significantly from the pre-viewing scores. In terms of students' likelihood to support workers in labor–management disputes, students were significantly more likely to support labor after viewing the movie than they were before. These attitude changes also appear to be stable (i.e., this group showed no significant change between their posttest and delay scores).

Although the stability of this attitude change was demonstrated, it should be recalled that in the third group tested (i.e., students measured immediately after viewing the film and then again 2 weeks later), attitudes actually became significantly more positive over the 2-week period. In addition, they had also significantly decreased in their support for labor in labor–management disputes. Thus, it seemed as though attitudes toward management were gradually reversing over time. However, because we did not test the initial levels of these attitudes, we were unable to determine whether their attitudes were in fact returning to baseline levels. Given the results of the fourth group, it would now appear that although attitudes toward management do relapse somewhat over a short time period (e.g., a 2-week period), they may remain significantly different from initial attitudes (i.e., prior to viewing the film). Interestingly, our study also highlights the potential danger of taking a cross-sectional snapshot of individuals' attitudes without a consideration of changes in attitudes over time (i.e., the potential to misunderstand a phenomenon due to a restricted time range).

The final objective of this study was to identify whether attitudes toward U.S. and Canadian management would differ. In terms of United States–Canada differences, attitudes toward U.S. management were always significantly more negative than attitudes toward Canadian management. However, attitudes toward both U.S. management and Canadian management were affected in exactly the same ways by the film (i.e., students viewing the film evaluated both countries more negatively and continued to do so after 2 weeks' time, and those not viewing the movie did not change their attitudes).

There seemed to be a tendency for students to think that the health and safety situation was generally better in Canada than in the United States (i.e., U.S. management was viewed more negatively than Canadian management throughout). This may be because Canada is often viewed as more unionized and worker friendly, or because the participants were biased in favor of their own country. However, although the actual incidents in the movie were from the United States, there also appears to have been a tendency for perceptions of Canadian managers to fall after viewing the film. This may have occurred because of the similarity and proximity between these countries. Thus, although initially seen as discrepant in levels of occupational health and safety, both countries are negatively affected to an equivalent extent. Interestingly, these results do not support Bateman et al.'s (1992) finding that Japanese participants rated Japanese business more positively after viewing a movie negatively portraying the situation in the United States. Yet these differences would seem to be easily explained by the traditional relationships between Japan and the United States versus between Canada and the United States.

If attitudes toward management's role in occupational health and safety are affected by this film, we may be creating an audience more receptive to workplace health and safety education. The need for management commitment to occupational health and safety was outlined at the beginning of this chapter. Furthermore, to be more than an empty gesture, this responsibility must be sincere and proactive; "managers must go well beyond appearances, union demands, and the letter of the law. They must anticipate and lead the drive to head off environmental hazards and risks" (Sells, 1994, p. 77). If any positive changes are to be made in the area of workplace health and safety, company leaders must be committed to this goal. This will necessitate that managers design jobs with safety in mind, establish safety-training programs, give safety officials high status, and have executives on safety committees. Only organizations with management teams dedicated to these issues will be able to reduce workplace accidents (Werther et al., 1990). Through socialization and training, managers will need to develop a strong organizational culture emphasizing safety (Sagan, 1993). In short, administrators will have to convince employees that safety makes a difference (Miner, 1992). This type of commitment among managers may begin by gaining their interest while they are still students (as well as providing them with the tools to affect workplace health and safety in their training programs). Films such as *Death on the Job* may aid in this process.

Making students more receptive may be particularly critical in light of the fact that the legal system today holds management accountable for occupational safety and health: Since the mid-1970s the courts began applying a new "retroactive standard" in terms of health and safety. As Sells (1994) noted, management in the United States can be held responsible for what they should have known and acted on.

Management must take responsibility for health and safety through the entire stream of production from obtaining raw materials to discarding old products (Sells, 1994). This can be costly. However, as Sells cogently argued, the alternative can be even more costly. If students are to be trained to be effective managers, they must be aware of health and safety concerns in the workplace. In the years to come managers can no longer afford to be ignorant of these issues.

REFERENCES

Adams, W., Salzman, A., Vantine, W., Suelter, L., Baker, A., Bonvouloir, L., Brenner, B., Ely, M., Feldman, J., & Ziegler, R. (1985). The power of *The Right Stuff*: A quasi-experimental field test of the docudrama hypothesis. *Public Opinion Quarterly, 49*, 330–339.

Bateman, T. S., Sakano, T., & Fujita, M. (1992). Roger, me, and my attitude: Film propaganda and cynicism toward corporate leadership. *Journal of Applied Psychology, 77*, 768–771.

DiPersio, V., & Guttentag, W. (Producers and Directors). (1991). *Death on the job.* [film].

Fussell, P. (1983). *Class: A guide through the American status system.* New York: Simon & Schuster.

Jowett, G., & O'Donnell, D. (1986). *Propaganda and persuasion.* Newbury Park, CA: Sage.

Kinney, J. A. (1990, September 10). Why did Paul die? *Newsweek*, p. 11.

Kochan, T. A., Smith, M., Wells, J. C., & Rebitzer, J. B. (1994). Human resource strategies and contingent workers: The case of safety and health in the petrochemical industry. *Human Resource Management, 33*(1), 55–77.

Miner, J. B. (1992). *Industrial-organizational psychology.* New York: McGraw-Hill.

Pakalnis, V. (1994). *Management education for occupational health and safety.* Unpublished manuscript, Queen's University, School of Business, Kingston, Ontario, Canada.

Sagan, S. D. (1993). *The limits of safety: Organizations, accidents, and nuclear weapons.* Princeton, NJ: Princeton University Press.

Sells, B. (1994, March –April). What asbestos taught me about managing risk. *Harvard Business Review*, pp. 76–90.

Werther, W. B., Davis, K., Schwind, H. F., & Das, H. (1990). *Canadian human resource management* (3rd ed.). Toronto: McGraw-Hill Ryerson.

Zohar, D. (1980). Safety climate in industrial organizations: Theoretical and applied implications. *Journal of Applied Psychology, 65*, 96–102.

8

Benefit Coverage and Employee Attitudes: A Social Exchange Perspective

Robert R. Sinclair, Mary Ann Hannigan, and Lois E. Tetrick

Recent changes in the economic environment, combined with an increased sensitivity to the impact of psychological disorders and family functioning on employee attitudes and work behaviors, have influenced companies to reassess the role of human resource policies, such as benefits packages, in their overall strategic plans. Two contradictory trends have developed that highlight the complexities of human resource management's attempts to proactively influence organizational attitudes and behavior. First, to attract and retain high-quality employees in light of changing workforce demographic characteristics, employers are expanding the realm of benefit coverage to include more family-related benefits such as child care in addition to traditional benefits such as health care and retirement plans (Greenberger, Goldberg, Hamill, O'Neil, & Payne, 1989; Schiemann, 1987). Second, increased emphasis on leanness and reducing labor costs have spurred organizations to streamline benefits programs by cutting absolute levels of coverage (Balkin & Griffeth, 1993). Alternatively, they may have developed flexible benefit plans that allow employees some degree of choice among specific benefits so that they receive coverage that meets personal needs while reducing overall program costs (Barber, Dunham, & Formisano, 1992; Dreher, Ash, & Bretz, 1988). Building on previous research (Dreher et al., 1988; Williams, 1993), this chapter extends the literature on employee attitudes and benefits programs in two ways: (a) by examining the relationship between specific types of benefits (i.e., health and family benefits) and attitudinal outcomes and (b) by examining the impact of unionization on the relationship between benefit coverage and company-related attitudes as well as the relationship between benefit coverage and union commitment.

BENEFIT COVERAGE AND EMPLOYEE ATTITUDES TOWARD THE COMPANY

Dreher et al. (1988) noted that "compensation managers are ultimately interested in the affective and behavioral consequences associated with changes in benefit system components" (p. 251). The provision of benefits is a major component of the costs of human resource management and administration; therefore, one would expect to find a substantial literature on the effects of benefits programs on employee attitudes. Until recently, this has not been the case. Schiemann (1987) suggested that benefits programs can affect employee turnover, recruitment, and motivation as well as employee attitudes. However, most of the existing empirical research has focused on some aspect of satisfaction with benefits, typically as part of a larger study of compensation satisfaction (see Miceli & Lane, 1991, for a review).

We propose that social exchange theory (e.g., Blau, 1964) and organizational commitment (e.g., Mowday, Steers, & Porter, 1979) provide useful perspectives for understanding the impact of organizations' provision of benefits on individual's attitudes and behavior. From this perspective the relationship between an employee and the employing organization can be seen as involving an exchange of commitments—in which the quality of the exchange determines the future actions of both parties. The compensation package, including benefits, is a salient factor in this exchange. Eisenberger, Huntington, Hutchison, and Sowa (1986) have led the way in recognizing this exchange perspective with their proposal that commitment is a two-way street. Employees must first believe that the company values them as individuals, which they call "perceived organizational support," before they will reciprocate with commitment to the company, a sense of loyalty, and identification with the organization (Meyer & Allen, 1984). The provision of benefits that cover employees' physical well-being (health care benefits) and recognize the importance of the individual within a broader context than the work setting (family-oriented benefits such as parental leave and child-care support) are suggested as two categories of fringe benefits that contribute to the exchange relationship. Therefore, we hypothesized that both health care benefits and family-responsive benefits would be related to perceived organizational support, organizational commitment, and intentions to remain with the organization.

Meyer and Allen (1984; Allen & Meyer, 1990) distinguished between *affective* and *continuance* organizational commitment. Continuance organizational commitment occurs when an individual believes that greater costs are incurred by leaving the organization (e.g., loss of job tenure, costs associated with relocation, or loss of accrued pension benefits) than those incurred by remaining. Higher levels of benefit coverage would be expected to predict continuance commitment. This especially might be the case with health care coverage, which frequently precludes treatment for pre-existing conditions when one enters a new health care plan. A desirable benefits package would influence an individual's feeling of continuance commitment by creating a sense of being economically bound to the organization because the individual would have to forego the benefits package to move to a different organization. In contrast to continuance commitment, the term *affective commitment* refers to a sense of loyalty and identification with the organization's goals and values, a willingness to exert considerable effort on behalf of the organization, and a strong desire to remain a member of the organization (Allen & Meyer, 1990; Meyer & Allen, 1984; Mowday et al., 1979). To the extent that employees interpret the benefits provided by their employer as valuing them as individuals, we hypothesized that benefits packages would be related to affective commitment as well as continuance commitment and the intention to remain with the employer.

Kinicki, Carson, and Bohlander (1992) found that employee attitudes are influenced by employee's perceptions of their firm's commitment to human resource programs. Similarly, Koys (1991) found that employees' perceptions of the motives underlying human resource policies influence employee attitudes toward the company. If the employees believe that the policy was implemented simply to comply with existing legal requirements, its impact on their attitudes is likely to be minimal. However, human resource policies that are attributed to a fairness motive, rather than a legal compliance motive, are related to organizational commitment (Koys, 1991). Therefore, a benefit that an individual sees as something all employers should or do offer (e.g., vacation or health care benefits) may not influence perceptions of organizational support or commitment. On the other hand, benefits that are considered less commonplace and that are viewed as more discretionary are hypothesized to be more strongly related to perceived organizational support and commitment. Family-responsive benefits are less commonplace than health care benefits, being a relatively new phenomenon (Ferber, Farrell, & Allen, 1991), and have been found to be related to organizational commitment and other employee attitudes such as job satisfaction (Galinsky & Stein, 1990; Greenberger et al., 1989). Therefore, it would be expected that family-responsive benefits would signal a greater concern and commitment to employees on the part of the organization than health care benefits. Provision of these benefits would have a tendency to move the exchange relation from a more economic exchange to a more social exchange (Blau, 1964). Thus, provision of family-responsive benefits are hypothesized to be more strongly related to perceived organizational support and affective commitment than the provision of health care benefits.

Miceli and Lane (1991) developed an equity-based model of benefit satisfaction that has received partial support (Williams, 1993). Although Miceli and Lane explicitly stated that their model is not intended to be comprehensive, it makes a valuable contribution by pointing out that both the actual benefits received and beliefs about the kind and amount of benefits that should be received are potentially important determinants of relevant attitudes. Miceli and Lane did not specifically posit an interaction between benefit beliefs and actual benefits received; however, the results of Greenberger et al.'s study (1989) suggest that it may be the joint effect of the employer's providing certain benefits and belief in the importance of such benefits that actually relate to perceived organizational support and commitment. Therefore, based on this extension of Miceli and Lane's model, we hypothesized that there would be an interaction between benefit coverage and beliefs about whether employers, in general, should provide such benefits in predicting the relation with perceived organizational support, affective commitment, continuance commitment, and employees' intention to remain with their employers.

UNIONS AND BENEFITS PROGRAMS

Compensation, including fringe benefits, has been a central focus of traditional collective bargaining over the years (Barling, Fullagar, & Kelloway, 1992). However, very little empirical evidence exists to explain how the presence of a union influences attitudinal or behavioral outcomes associated with benefits programs. Given that one goal of most unions is to secure higher levels of financial outcomes for their members, the extent of benefits coverage secured by the union is expected to reflect union instrumentality, which is based on an economic exchange (Newton & Shore, 1992). However, as Sinclair and Tetrick (in press) and Shore, Tetrick, Sinclair, and Newton (1994) pointed out, winning benefits for the membership through collective bargaining could signal to the unions' members that the union values them as individuals. Therefore, one would expect benefit coverage to be related to union commitment.

Gordon, Philpot, Burt, Thompson, and Spiller (1980) described union commitment as consisting of (a) feelings of loyalty to the union, (b) a sense of responsibility to the union, (c) a willingness to exert effort on behalf of the union, and (d) a belief in the general principles of unionism. Although these dimensions have been found to be strongly related to each other, Tetrick (1993) suggested that the dimensions of union commitment should be considered separately in terms of their relation to other constructs. Some evidence for this was provided by Sinclair, Alexander, and Tetrick (1994), who found significant bivariate correlations between two forms of union instrumentality and union loyalty but not willingness to exert effort for the union. Therefore, if benefit coverage is viewed as contributing to union instrumentality, there may be differential relations with specific dimensions of union commitment. Also, as suggested above, with respect to benefit coverage and company commitment, we further hypothesized that beliefs about whether employers should provide these benefits are expected to moderate the relations between benefit coverage and union commitment.

The question arises whether union members attribute their benefits to the effort of the union, management, or both. Herrick (1990) suggested that if joint labor–management programs are to be successful, the credit for achievements needs to be equally shared by management and the union. In the case of fringe benefits, coverage is won or maintained during collective bargaining, but management typically administers the benefits. To the extent that union members attribute benefit coverage to the union, we hypothesized that the relation between benefit coverage and company attitudes (perceived organizational support, affective commitment, continuance commitment, and intention to remain) would be weaker for union members. To further support differences in the strength of relations between benefit coverage and company attitudes, one could argue that employees in nonunionized settings should have a stronger link between benefit coverage and company attitudes because there was no collective action prompting the company to offer the benefits, assuming that the benefit is not legally mandated. Therefore, the purpose of this study was to examine the relationship of both provision of and beliefs about benefits with individual's attitudes toward their company and union.

METHOD

Participants and Procedure

The sample for the present research consisted of residents of a Midwestern metropolitan area. A random digit dialing procedure was used to contact individuals to request their participation in the study. Telephone requests were made until 500 individuals agreed to fill out a survey that was subsequently mailed to their home. Of these 500, 298 (59.6%) returned usable surveys. Past benefits literature suggested that job type must be controlled for when examining benefits (Shapiro & Sherman, 1987). Furthermore, because unionization was a focus, it was deemed desirable to have equal numbers of union members and nonunion members in the analyses. Consequently, a subsample was drawn that consisted of 76 union members (85% of all union members in the total sample) and 76 nonunion members (36% of all nonunion members in the total sample), with equal proportions of union and nonunion members in each of five categories of jobs: professionals (38.2% of subsample), skilled labor (30.3%), service workers (15.8%), office/clerical workers (13.2%), and semiskilled laborers (2.6%). Thus, although differences in the proportion of individuals in one or another profession may bias the results in favor of professions with higher levels of representation, the bias should be similar for nonunionized and unionized individuals, making comparisons between them more tenable. Fifty-three percent of the sample were male, 86% were White, and 59% were married, with no significant differences on gender, race, and marital status between the unionized and nonunionized workers.

Measures

Benefit beliefs and coverage. Benefit beliefs were assessed by having respondents indicate how important they felt it was for employers to offer each of the individual benefits using a 6-point scale format (1 = *employers should not offer this benefit;* 6 = *employers should always offer this benefit*). Scales representing unit-weighted means of the items in each benefit category were then constructed. Internal consistency estimates of .84 and .87 (alphas) were obtained for family and health benefits, respectively. To index benefit coverage, respondents indicated whether their employer provided each of 16 benefits. Items were coded dichotomously (i.e., 1 = *offered by employer;* 0 = *not offered by employer*). The benefits came from two categories: family (10 items; e.g., paid maternal leave, child-care subsidies) and health (6 items; e.g., retiree health coverage, medical care). For each type of benefit, scales were formed by summing the items. Prior to summing, each benefit was assigned a weight based on the proportion of people in the entire sample that indicated that they did not have the benefit. Thus, greater weights were assigned to less common benefits, with the assumption that these benefits would have greater psychological impact on individuals' attitudes. Respondents were given a *don't know* option when indicating coverage on each benefit (this response was treated as missing data). The proportion of respondents indicating they did not know about individual benefits ranged from 3.3% for family medical coverage to 47.4% for adoption leave. This result clearly supports previous research (Dreher et al., 1988; Williams, 1993) indicating that employees are often poorly informed about their benefits package.

Organizational and union attitudes. Items from Meyer and Allen's (1984) Affective Commitment (eight items; $\alpha = .86$) and Continuance Commitment (six items; $\alpha = 72$) scales were used to measure organizational commitment. The 17-item short form ($\alpha = .95$) of the Survey of Perceived Organizational Support (Eisenberger et al., 1986) was used to tap organizational support perceptions. The short form was developed by retaining the items with the highest factor loadings from Eisenberger et al.'s original study. Five items ($\alpha = .74$) were written to reflect intentions to remain with the organization (e.g., "I think of quitting my job"). Union commitment was measured with three items from each of three dimensions of the union commitment scale developed by Gordon et al. (1980). The items tapped Union Loyalty ($\alpha = .77$), Willingness to Work for the Union ($\alpha = .70$), and Responsibility to the Union ($\alpha = .74$). The union commitment items selected for each dimension were the three items with the highest factor loadings (from Gordon et al., 1980) for each dimension assessed.

RESULTS

Descriptive statistics for all the variables are presented in Tables 1 and 2. Union members reported higher levels of health benefits coverage and continuance commitment as well as lower levels of organizational support but reported similar levels of beliefs concerning whether employers should provide health care and family-oriented benefits, affective commitment, and intention to remain with their employer. Furthermore, union members were older than the nonunion members and reported higher levels of personal income. Given these differences in background characteristics between the samples, age, personal income, and gender were included as control variables in all subsequent analyses.

The first three hypotheses concerned the relationship of benefit pro-

Table 1

Group Means, Standard Deviations, and Difference Tests

Variable	Union members		Nonunion members		
	M	SD	M	SD	t
Family benefits	0.97	1.04	0.88	1.10	0.34
Health benefits	1.33	0.50	0.79	0.63	5.14**
Family benefit beliefs	4.81	1.15	4.74	1.08	0.35
Health benefit beliefs	6.38	1.31	6.24	0.88	0.74
Affective commitment	3.03	0.82	3.29	0.85	−1.90
Continuance commitment	3.64	0.80	3.37	0.76	2.12*
Intention to remain	3.73	0.64	3.52	0.90	1.62
Organizational support	3.04	0.76	3.44	0.83	−3.05**
Age	41.95	9.69	36.50	12.04	3.07**
Personal income[a]	3.39	1.11	2.66	1.37	3.54**
Gender					
Male	55.3%		51.7%		0.48
Female	44.7%		48.3%		
Loyalty to the union	3.32	0.92	—	—	—
Responsibility to the union	3.71	0.72	—	—	—
Willingness to exert effort					
on union's behalf	3.19	0.93	—	—	—

[a]Income was indexed by asking respondents to indicate their income in the last year in $15,000 increments. Dash indicates data collected only on union members.
*$p < .05$. **$p < .01$.

Table 2

Separate Group Correlation Matrices and Combined Sample Reliability Estimates

Variable	1	2	3	4	5	6	7	8	9	10	11
1. Family benefits	—	.36*	.05	.15	.41**	.12	.23	.32*	-.09	.19	-.33*
2. Health benefits	.33*	—	-.08	.14	.01	.22	.30*	-.02	-.06	.27*	-.20
3. Family benefit beliefs	.50**	-.05	.84	.15	-.08	-.07	-.22*	-.26*	-.04	-.09	-.09
4. Health benefit beliefs	-.02	-.07	.41**	.87	.00	.14	.21*	.02	-.01	.10	.13
5. Affective company commitment	.32*	.07	-.06	-.26*	.86	.04	.56**	.73**	.21*	-.03	-.07
6. Continuance company commitment	.07	.09	-.05	.10	.07	.72	.20*	-.10	.09	-.06	.03
7. Intention to remain with company	.35*	.37**	-.11	-.04	.28**	.03	.74	.60**	.29**	.22*	-.07
8. Organizational support	.21	.08	-.06	-.28*	.70**	-.34**	.03	.95	.24*	.18	.00
9. Age	-.39*	.20	-.36**	-.12	.19	.03	.11	.00	—	.32**	.04
10. Personal income	.03	.58**	-.22*	-.32**	.09	.02	.29**	.00	.24*	—	.28**
11. Gender (1 = female)	.01	.26*	-.35**	.01	-.10	.06	.21*	-.11	-.07	.27*	—
12. Loyalty to the union	.14	.13	.11	-.19	.47**	-.13	.13	.32**	.24*	.22*	.06
13. Responsibility to the union	.12	-.06	.11	.12	.07	-.04	-.08	-.11	-.01	-.05	.05
14. Willingness to exert effort for the union	.07	.09	-.02	-.18	.38	-.13	.15	.17	.19	.06	.04

NOTE: Union members below diagonal; union commitment correlations for union members only. Pairwise deletion of missing cases, sample sizes for the correlations range from 27 to 69. Reliability estimates for the two groups combined are underlined on the diagonal.

*$p < .05$. **$p < .01$.

vision to perceived organizational support, affective and continuance organizational commitment, and intentions to remain with the organization. Specifically, health and family benefit provision was hypothesized to be positively related to perceived organizational support, affective and continuance organizational commitment, and intention to remain with the organization. Furthermore, we expected that provision of family-responsive benefits would be more strongly related to perceived organizational support and affective commitment than would health benefits. These hypotheses were tested using hierarchical multiple regression. For each dependent variable (support, affective and company commitment, and intentions to remain), age, gender, and income were entered on the first step and benefit provision was entered on the second step. Separate sets of analyses were conducted for each type of benefit. Results of these analyses are presented in Table 3.

Family benefit coverage accounted for a significant proportion of variance in affective commitment ($\Delta R^2 = .18$, $p < .05$), perceived organizational support ($\Delta R^2 = .09$, $p < .05$), and intention to remain with the organization ($\Delta R^2 = .08$, $p < .05$). Health benefits coverage accounted for significant proportions of variance in continuance commitment ($\Delta R^2 = .05$, $p < .05$) and intention to remain with the organization ($\Delta R^2 = .06$, $p < .05$). Some support was obtained for all of the first three hypotheses. Several significant relationships were obtained for both family and health benefits with the criterion variables (Hypothesis 1), relationships were demonstrated between benefit provision and both types of commitment (Hypothesis 2), and family benefit provision accounted for a significant proportion of variance in affective commitment and perceived organizational support, whereas health benefit provision did not (Hypothesis 3).

The fourth hypothesis was that beliefs about whether employers should provide specific benefits moderated the relations between benefit coverage and company attitudes. This hypothesis was tested by adding two additional steps to the regression equations constructed to address the first three hypotheses. Benefit beliefs was entered on the third step, and a term representing the interaction of benefit beliefs and benefit coverage was en-

Table 3

Prediction of Company Attitudes/Intentions From Background Characteristics,
Benefit Coverage, and Benefit Beliefs (ΔR^2)

Dependent variable	Step 1: background characteristic[a]	Step 2: benefit coverage	Step 3: benefit beliefs	Step 4: interaction term[b]	Final R^2
Family benefits					
Affective commitment	.03	.18**	.03	.05*	.29**
Continuance commitment	.01	.02	.00	.05*	.09
Perceived support	.01	.09**	.06*	.00	.16
Intention to remain	.10	.08**	.03	.07**	.27**
Health benefits					
Affective commitment	.03	.00	.02	.02	.08
Continuance commitment	.01	.05**	.01	.02	.09
Perceived support	.01	.02	.01	.00	.05
Intention to remain	.10**	.06**	.01	.21**	.37**

[a]Background characteristics are age, personal income, and gender. [b]Interaction refers to the Benefit Level × Union Membership Status interaction.
*$p < .10$. **$p < .05$.

tered on a fourth step. Results of these analyses are also presented in Table 3.

There was partial support for the hypothesized Benefit Belief × Benefit Coverage interaction in predicting company attitudes. The Family Benefit Beliefs × Family Benefit Coverage interaction was significant for predicting affective commitment ($\Delta R^2 = .05$, $p < .05$) and intention to remain with the organization ($\Delta R^2 = .07$, $p < .05$). The Health Benefit Beliefs × Health Benefit Coverage interaction was significant for intention to remain with the organization ($\Delta = .21$, $p < .05$; final $R^2 = .37$, $p < .05$). The Family Benefit Beliefs × Family Benefit Coverage interaction produced a significant change in the multiple correlation for prediction of continuance commitment ($\Delta R^2 = .05$, $p < .05$), but the multiple correlation for the equation after this step was not significant.

Using a procedure described by Aiken and West (1991), simple regression analyses were conducted to examine the nature of the interactions for the equations with significant interaction terms and a significant final multiple correlation. Although family benefit coverage was positively related to affective commitment, this relationship was slightly stronger for those with weaker family benefit beliefs ($\beta = 0.70$) than for those with stronger family benefit beliefs ($\beta = 0.62$). With respect to the interaction of family benefit coverage and beliefs in prediction of intention to remain with the organization, individuals with weaker family benefit beliefs had stronger intentions to remain in the company when benefit coverage was low. As their level of benefit coverage increased, intention to remain with the organization decreased slightly ($\beta = -0.12$). For individuals with stronger family benefit beliefs, intention to remain with the organization remained relatively constant at different levels of family benefit coverage ($\beta = 0.06$). The health benefit coverage relationship with intention to remain with the organization also is stronger for individuals with weaker health benefit beliefs ($\beta = 1.10$) when compared with individuals with stronger benefit beliefs ($\beta = 0.85$).

The fifth hypothesis was that benefit coverage would be related to union commitment, and we speculated that there may be different relationships between provision of specific types of benefits and specific dimensions of union commitment. Furthermore, we hypothesized that there would be an interaction between benefit coverage and beliefs relative to union commitment. Hierarchical moderated multiple regression was used to address these hypotheses. For each dimension of union commitment, age, gender, and income were entered as control variables on the first step, followed in successive steps by benefit coverage, benefit beliefs, and the Benefit Coverage × Belief interaction term. Separate analyses were conducted for each type of benefit.

Table 4 presents the results of the regression analyses predicting union commitment dimensions from the demographic variables, benefit coverage, benefit beliefs, and the Benefit Beliefs × Benefit Coverage interaction. Only two effects were significant. These were the Family Benefits Beliefs × Family Benefits Coverage interaction terms in predicting responsibility to

Table 4

Prediction of Union Commitment Dimensions From Background Characteristics, Benefit Coverage, and Benefit Beliefs (ΔR^2)

Dependent variable	Step 1: background characteristics[a]	Step 2: benefit coverage	Step 3: benefit beliefs	Step 4: interaction term[b]	Final R^2
Family benefits					
Loyalty to the union	.09	.05	.03	.07	.24
Responsibility to union	.01	.01	.05	.56**	.64**
Willingness to exert Effort for union	.04	.02	.00	.49**	.55**
Health benefits					
Loyalty to the union	.09	.00	.01	—	.10
Responsibility to union	.01	.00	.01	—	.02
Willingness to exert Effort for union	.04	.00	.03	—	.07

NOTE: Dash indicates that entry of this term exceeded tolerance limits for the equation; consequently change in multiple correlation associated with it could not be assessed.
[a]Background characteristics are age, personal income, and gender. [b]Interactions refers to the Benefit Level × Union Membership Status interaction.
*$p < .10$. **$p < .05$.

the union ($\Delta R^2 = .56$, $p < .05$; final $R^2 = .64$, $p < .05$) and willingness to exert effort for the union ($\Delta R^2 = .49$, $p < .05$; final $R^2 = .55$, $p < .05$). Colinearity problems prevented evaluation of the Health Benefit Beliefs × Health Benefit Coverage interaction. Because only 2 effects out of 24 evaluated (8%) approached the number that would be expected by chance alone, the size of the effects made them compelling enough to be discussed.

Examination of the nature of the interactions was conducted using the same simple regression procedure discussed above. The negative relation between family benefit coverage and responsibility to the union was stronger for individuals with weaker benefit beliefs ($\beta = -2.69$) as compared with individuals with relatively stronger benefit beliefs ($\beta = -1.80$). A similar pattern of relations was found for prediction of willingness to work for the union. A stronger negative relationship between benefit coverage and willingness to work for the union was obtained for individuals with weaker benefit beliefs ($\beta = -1.58$) than that obtained for individuals with stronger benefit beliefs ($\beta = -1.01$).

The final hypothesis was that the relations between benefit coverage and company attitudes would differ among union and nonunion employees. To test this hypothesis, moderated, hierarchical regression analysis was performed in which background characteristics were entered first to control for age, gender, and income effects. Then the specific class of benefits (either family benefits or health care benefits) was entered, followed by union membership, and finally the term representing the Benefit Coverage × Union Membership interaction. The results of these analyses are shown in Table 5.

None of the interactions were significant, providing no support for our hypotheses that union representation would weaken the relation between benefit coverage and company attitudes. However, for the family benefits equations, union membership accounted for a significant proportion of variance in affective commitment ($\Delta R^2 = .04$, $p < .10$; final $R^2 = .26$, $p < .05$) and perceived organizational support ($\Delta R^2 = .09$, $p < .05$; $R^2 = .18$, $p < .10$). For the health benefits equations, union membership accounted for significant proportions of variance in perceived organizational support ($\Delta R^2 = .06$, $p < .05$; final $R^2 = .09$, $p < .10$) and affective commitment ($\Delta R^2 = .03$, $p < .05$), although the final multiple correlation for the health benefits equation predicting affective commitment was not significant.

DISCUSSION

As part of the exchange relation between employees and their companies, it was hypothesized that fringe benefits foster perceptions of organizational support, affective commitment, continuance commitment, and the intention to remain with the employer. The results support our hypotheses that provision of benefits was related to attitudes toward and perceptions of the organization. Both family and health benefits were related to

Table 5

Regression Results Predicting Company Attitudes/Intentions From Background
Characteristics, Benefit Coverage, and Unionization (ΔR^2)

Dependent variable	Step 1: Background characteristics[a]	Step 2: Benefit coverage	Step 3: Union membership	Step 4: Interaction term[b]	Final R^2
Family benefits					
Affective commitment	.03	.18**	.04*	.00	.26**
Continuance commitment	.01	.02	.02	.00	.06
Perceived support	.01	.09**	.09**	.00	.18*
Intention to remain	.10*	.08**	.00	.00	.18*
Health benefits					
Affective commitment	.03	.00	.03*	.00	.07
Continuance commitment	.01	.05**	.01	.00	.07
Perceived support	.01	.02	.06**	.01	.09*
Intention to remain	.10**	.06**	.00	.00	.16**

[a]Background characteristics are age, personal income, and gender. [b]Interaction refers to the Benefit Level × Union Membership Status interaction.
*$p < .10$. **$p < .05$.

intention to remain with the organization. Further family benefits were related to perceived organizational support and affective commitment, and health benefits were related to continuance commitment. These findings illustrate the importance of looking at separate classes of benefits in organizational research. Family benefits are provided more at the organization's discretion than are health benefits; consequently, family benefits were related to positive attitudes toward the organization as well as to the sense that the organization values its individual employees. Health benefits, on the other hand, are less discretionary in the sense that employers are usually expected to provide them. Consequently, these benefits do not influence employees' perceptions that they are valued by the company or their affective commitment. However, employees of companies that provide health benefits perceive that greater costs would be incurred by leaving the organization and thus having to forego the benefits package; thus, their continuance commitment is higher.

The results also suggest that Miceli and Lane's (1991) model can be extended to predict other attitudes. Family benefits were related to affective commitment and perceived organizational support, and health benefits predicted continuance commitment. Both types of benefits predicted intention to remain with the organization. The results, taken as a whole, support the idea that both benefit beliefs and benefit coverage are important; their interaction rather than the unique effects of each accounts for much of the variance in certain attitudes or intentions. Future research should consider possible interactions between the demographic characteristics of employees and benefit level and beliefs. For instance, individuals with children may have stronger beliefs that organizations should provide some form of child-care assistance. Those with weaker beliefs are less likely to intend to remain, particularly at low levels of coverage. These individuals may see membership in the organization that provides these benefits as particularly desirable. Conversely, for the individual who expects these benefits, receiving them says nothing about the desirability of remaining a member of the organization.

Although benefit coverage was related to company attitudes, it was not related to union commitment. The significant Family Benefit Beliefs × Coverage interactions indicate that family benefit provision is related to union commitment for individuals with certain beliefs about benefits. Individuals who received high levels of family benefit coverage and who felt that organizations did not have to provide these benefits were less willing to work for the union and felt less responsibility toward the union than their counterparts who had stronger beliefs that organizations should provide family benefits.

These results suggest that unions need to develop an awareness of what specific benefits are important to their membership and make sure that their members are aware of the union's role in securing provision of specific employee benefits. These findings, coupled with the positive relationships between benefit provision and employees' attitudes toward their company, suggest that organizations are doing a better job of communicating their role in employees' benefit coverage than are unions. After benefits are secured (through the collective bargaining process), unions typically turn their attention to issues such as grievance resolution. Efforts by the union to communicate information about benefits to employees may help increase the strength of the relationship between benefit coverage and union commitment. Furthermore, we can speculate that the labor-relations climate of the organization may play a role in these findings (cf. Gordon & Ladd, 1990). In adversarial climates organizational or union strategies to influence perception of fringe benefits may increase commitment to one side at the expense of the other. In cooperative climates, shared credit for benefits may increase both company and union commitment. Further research on these issues would clearly be interesting and of practical value to both companies and unions.

Comparative studies of predictors of company and union commitment are of interest from a theoretical standpoint. Tetrick (1993) noted the asymmetries in the social exchange relations for individuals with their company and their union. That study provides evidence that one aspect of this asymmetry is the relationship of benefit provision to company but not union commitment. Little information exists on the extent to which union commitment and company commitment tap similar psychological constructs (indeed, it is frequently argued that they are very different). Loyalty to the union seems to most closely parallel affective company commitment; thus, direct comparisons between the two are informative. The other dimensions of union commitment are very different in nature from the company attitudes studied; thus these analyses allow one to draw only conclusions that certain union attitudes are related to benefit coverage in a manner that is different from the relationship between benefit coverage and certain company attitudes and intentions. Tests of asymmetries in social exchange may be confounded with differences in the nature of the union and company constructs being evaluated.

Our findings are consistent with Koys's (1991) notion that organizational commitment is influenced by human resource policies that are motivated by fairness rather than legal compliance. The amount of discretion the organization has in offering the benefit appears to be a key factor in determining whether its provision will be related to commitment. Comparisons of the effect of human resource policies such as benefits programs on perceptions of company support with their effect on perceptions of union support would provide an interesting next step to this line of research, particularly if this were coupled with evaluations of steward and supervisor support.

The data from this study do not support the hypothesized moderating effect of union membership on benefit coverage and company attitudes. None of the interaction terms representing the moderating effect of union membership on the relation between benefit coverage and attitudes or intentions were significant. Therefore, it appears that although the benefits were won as a result of collective bargaining, members do not discount the benefits provided by the company at least concerning the relations between provision of these benefits and perceived organizational support, affective commitment, continuance commitment, and intention to remain with the company. Union membership was related, however, to perceived organizational support and affective commitment even after controlling for age, gender, income, and benefit coverage, with union members expressing less commitment to them on the part of their companies and affective commitment.

Although our hypotheses concerning union membership were not supported, there were differences in the relations between each type of benefit coverage (family-oriented benefits and health care benefits) and company attitudes and intentions. This result confirms our expectation that different types of benefits influence different outcomes. Provision of family benefits influences individuals' affective commitment but not their continuance commitment. Furthermore, family benefits provision influences individuals' intentions to remain with the organization as well as their sense of the organization's commitment to them as individuals (perceived organizational support). Health care benefits, on the other hand, were related to intention to remain and continuance commitment, but not to affective commitment or support. This suggests that individuals are more likely to leave the organization if they do not have these more common benefits, but provision of these benefits is not related to positive feelings toward the organization or a sense of organizational support. Differing expectations about health and family benefits would explain the findings. Because health care benefits probably are expected by most individuals, their provision does not influence individuals' global feelings about their company or give them any indication of the company's commitment to them as individuals. Conversely, family benefits, which are much less common, may indicate to the individual that the organization is in fact committed to them. Given the social exchange basis of commitment, a relationship between family benefit provision and affective company commitment was hypothesized and supported.

Methodological Concerns and Limitations

This study has many of the limitations of survey research. The sample sizes of 76 each for the union and nonunion subgroups places limits on the power and stability of any statistical significance tests. More complex is the finding that large numbers of people indicated that they did not know whether they had certain benefits. Employees may be interested only in benefits that meet a personal need. For instance, the single woman with no dependents is likely to have limited cause to seek information about paternity leave. This, coupled with the often-cited weaknesses in companies' communication of their benefit plans to their employees (e.g., Dreher et al., 1988; Williams, 1993), makes a complete understanding of the psychological effects of benefits programs difficult. Further research is needed to clarify this issue. A third issue is that we addressed only whether the organization provided the benefit. Dreher et al. (1988) pointed out that factors such as the amount the employee contributes may play a role in their perceptions of benefits packages. Furthermore, individuals are often covered under a spouse's or other family member's benefit package; we would expect that their attitudes toward their company are not as strongly influenced by provision of benefits that they already have through another source.

SUMMARY AND CONCLUSION

This chapter reports the results of an investigation into the effects of benefits programs on individuals' attitudes toward their company and union. Miceli and Lane's (1991) model of benefit satisfaction is applied to the prediction of other attitudes and behavioral intentions. The model is extended by considering the interactive effects of benefit beliefs and benefit coverage on the outcome variables. The model is also extended by our finding that different classes of benefits have different psychological outcomes. Furthermore, benefits programs are identified as a source of social exchange asymmetry between union attitudes and company attitudes. Benefits programs influence members attitudes toward their company more than they influence union members' attitudes toward their union, although family benefits and family benefit beliefs together strongly influenced two union commitment dimensions. The second aspect of social exchange asymmetry studied was not supported. Although union members appear to differ in their attitude toward their company when compared with nonunion members, as a general rule union membership did not influence relations between benefit coverage and the attitudes or intentions studied.

REFERENCES

Aiken, L. S., & West, S. G. (1991). *Multiple regression: Testing and interpreting interactions.* Newbury Park, CA: Sage.

Allen, N. J., & Meyer, J. P. (1990). The measurement and antecedents of affective, continuance, and normative commitment to the organization. *Journal of Occupational Psychology, 63,* 1–18.

Balkin, D. B., & Griffeth, R. W. (1993). The determinants of employee benefits satisfaction. *Journal of Business and Psychology, 7,* 323–339.

Barber, A. E., Dunham, R. B., & Formisano, R. A. (1992). The impact of flexible benefits on employee satisfaction: A field study. *Personnel Psychology, 45,* 55–75.

Barling, J., Fullagar, C., & Kelloway, E. K. (1992). *The union & its members: A psychological approach.* New York: Oxford University Press.

Blau, P. M. (1964). *Exchange and power in social life.* New York: Wiley.

Dreher, G. F., Ash, R. A., & Bretz, R. D. (1988). Benefit coverage and employee cost: Critical factors in explaining compensation satisfaction. *Personnel Psychology, 41,* 237–254.

Eisenberger, R., Huntington, R., Hutchison, S., & Sowa, D. (1986). Perceived organizational support. *Journal of Applied Psychology, 71,* 500–507.

Ferber, M. A., Farrell, B., & Allen, A. (1991). New family-related benefits. In *Work and family: Policies for a changing work force* (pp. 114–154). Washington, DC: National Academy Press.

Galinsky, E., & Stein, P. J. (1990). The impact of human resource policies on employees. *Journal of Family Issues, 11,* 368–383.

Gordon, M. E., & Ladd, R. T. (1990). Dual allegiance: Renewal, reconsideration, and recantation. *Personnel Psychology, 43,* 37–69.

Gordon, M. E., Philpot, J. W., Burt, R., Thompson, C. A., & Spiller, W. E. (1980). Commitment to the union: Development of a measure and an examination of its correlates. *Journal of Applied Psychology, 65,* 479–499.

Greenberger, E., Goldberg, W. A., Hamill, S., O'Neil, R., & Payne, C. K. (1989). Contributions of a supportive work environment to parents well-being and orientation to work. *American Journal of Community Psychology, 17,* 755–783.

Herrick, N. (1990). *Joint management and employee participation: Labor and management at the crossroads.* San Francisco: Jossey-Bass.

Kinicki, A. J., Carson, K. P., & Bohlander, G. W. (1992). Relationship between an organization's actual human resource efforts and employee attitudes. *Group and Organization Management, 17,* 135–148.

Koys, D. J. (1991). Fairness, legal compliance, and organizational commitment. *Employee Rights and Responsibilities Journal, 4,* 283–291.

Meyer, J. P., & Allen, N. J. (1984). Testing the "side-bet theory" of organizational commitment: Some methodological considerations. *Journal of Applied Psychology, 69,* 372–378.

Miceli, M. P., & Lane, M. C. (1991). Antecedents of pay satisfaction: A review and extension. In K. M. Rowland & G. R. Ferris (Eds.), *Research in personnel and human resources management* (Vol. 9, pp. 235–309). Greenwich, CT: JAI Press.

Mowday, R. T., Steers, R. M., & Porter, L. W. (1979). The measurement of organizational commitment. *Journal of Vocational Behavior, 14,* 224–227.

Newton, L. A., & Shore, L. M. (1992). A model of union membership: Instrumentality, commitment, and opposition. *Academy of Management Review, 17,* 275–298.

Schiemann, W. A. (1987). The impact of corporate compensation and benefit policy on employee attitudes and behavior and corporate profitability. *Journal of Business and Psychology, 2,* 8–26.

Shapiro, K. P., & Sherman, J. A. (1987). Benefit plans designs. *Personnel Journal, 66,* 49–53.

Shore, L. M., Tetrick, L. E., Sinclair, R. R., & Newton, L. A. (1994). Validation of a measure of perceived union support. *Journal of Applied Psychology, 79,* 971–977.

Sinclair, R. R., Alexander, S., & Tetrick, L. E. (1994, April). *Organizational justice, union instrumentality, and company and union commitment.* Paper presented at the Ninth Annual Conference of the Society for Industrial and Organizational Psychology, Nashville, TN.

Sinclair, R. R., & Tetrick, L. E. (in press). Social exchange and union commitment: A comparison of union instrumentality and union support perceptions. *Journal of Organizational Behavior.*

Tetrick, L. E. (1993, June). *Developing and maintaining union commitment: A theoretical framework.* Paper presented at invited conference on union commitment, Amsterdam.

Williams, M. L. (1993, May). *Determinants of employee benefit level satisfaction.* Paper presented at the Eighth Annual Conference of the Society for Industrial and Organizational Psychology, San Francisco.

PART TWO

Meeting the Challenges of Change

9

Union–Member Relations: Loyalty, Instrumentality, and Alienation

Lynn M. Shore and Lucy A. Newton

Organizations in recent years have seen a shift in the way work is done and also in the manner in which workers are used as firms adjust to increased competitive pressures and internationalization. In a survey of U.S. manufacturing firms, Osterman (1994) found that about 35% of private-sector establishments with 50 or more employees have used some sort of innovative or flexible work system. These new systems include introduction of total quality management programs, increased usage of contingent workers, redesign of jobs, and formation of autonomous work teams. The employee–employer relationship has changed in many firms where these transformations have taken place (Belous, 1989), but little research has been conducted to study these changes.

It is likely that these organizational transformations will also have effects on unions and union members, although the nature of these potential effects is unclear at present. Although there are opportunities for unions in organizing contingent workers and becoming more involved in labor–management cooperative programs, there are also potential threats. The bargaining power of unions may be decreased by a loss of numbers of permanent or core employees or by changed work rules that infringe on unions' traditional power to bargain over wages and job classifications. These impending changes and possible threats make it more important than ever to fully understand the relationships that union members have with their unions, including members who view the union positively as well as those with more negative perceptions of the union.

Recent research has increasingly focused on reasons for union member attachment to unions (Newton & Shore, 1992), including studies examining member loyalty (Fullagar & Barling, 1989; Gordon, Philpot, Burt, Thompson, & Spiller, 1980; Tetrick, Thacker, & Fields, 1989) and instrumentality (DeCotiis & LeLouarn, 1981; Fullagar & Barling, 1989). Both union loyalty and union instrumentality represent positive attitudes toward unions by their members; there has been little discussion in the literature of members who are alienated or opposed to their unions (Newton & Shore, 1992). A similar trend has occurred in the union participation literature in that participation has been conceptualized as consisting of behaviors that are supportive of unions (e.g., attending meetings, serving as officers; Gordon et al., 1980; Kelloway & Barling, 1993; Leicht, 1989). As a result, little is known about members who have negative feelings about their union or behave in a manner that may be harmful to the union. Thus, the purpose of this study was to examine a broader array of attitudes and behaviors than has been included in prior research on relationships between unions and members, including both positive (loyalty, instrumentality) and negative (alienation) member attitudes as well as positive and negative forms of participation. More specifically, this study compared union loyalty, union instrumentality, and union alienation to determine whether they would differentially affect positive and negative forms of union participation.

UNION–MEMBER RELATIONS

Newton and Shore (1992) proposed that members may assess their relationship with the union based on two dimensions, ideological and instrumental. The *ideological dimension* is the value-based and affective orientation of members in relation to their union, whereas the *instrumental dimension is* the members' cognitive assessment of the costs and benefits associated with union representation. Both dimensions range from positive to negative.

According to Newton and Shore (1992), the ideological dimension consists of alienation on the negative end and of commitment or loyalty on the positive end. Alienation is based on an emotional detachment from the union as well as ideological opposition to the union, such that members high on alienation prefer not to be members of the union. Union loyalty (Gordon et al., 1980; Tetrick, Thacker, & Fields, 1989; Thacker, Fields, & Tetrick, 1989) reflects pride in being a union member and a realization of the benefits of membership in the union.

The instrumentality dimension also ranges from negative to positive. With positive instrumentality, workers feel bound to their unions because of the benefits associated with union representation. In contrast, workers high on negative instrumentality believe that the presence of the union harms the level and type of benefits received.

UNION PARTICIPATION

Many of the studies in the recent resurgence of interest in union participation have focused on participation as a global measure conceptualized exclusively as a positive outcome for the union (Gordon et al., 1980; Kelloway & Barling, 1993; Leicht, 1989). An underlying assumption of this research is that the more members participate in activities such as voting, meeting attendance, and serving in office, the stronger the union (Gallagher & Strauss, 1991). Most of these behaviors are high-visibility activities, which may be engaged in by only a small percentage of the membership. In addition, this stream of research has not included activities that may be detrimental to the union. Thus, this particular operationalization of union participation has limited the scope of research on the issue and has led to perhaps unnecessarily narrow conclusions about the nature of participation.

Another related issue is whether participation is a unidimensional or multidimensional construct. There are researchers on both sides of this issue, with McShane (1986), Klandermans (1986), and Cohen (1994) arguing for multidimensionality, whereas the majority have used a single comprehensive union participation measure (Anderson, 1979; Fullagar & Barling, 1989; Huszczo, 1983; Hagburg, 1966; Hoyman & Stallworth, 1987; Kelloway & Barling, 1993; Kuruvilla, Gallagher, Fiorito, & Wakabayashi, 1990; Leicht, 1989). We believe that a single comprehensive measure of union participation does not reflect the variety of behaviors members may engage in with regard to the union for a number of reasons. First, a number of writers have argued that a very small percentage of members are strongly emotionally involved in the union and concomitantly engage in the activities that require time and effort (Miller & Young, 1955; Spinrad, 1960). These are the members that are typically represented in unidimensional measures. The single-dimension approach to studying union participation may therefore reflect the activities of very few union members, perhaps misrepresenting the broader array of participation patterns. Second, even though high-involvement activities may be most essential to the union, union survival may well depend on the more passive efforts of a larger number of members. Thus, it is important to examine the aspects of participation reflecting both active and passive member behaviors that are supportive of the union (Cohen, 1994). Finally, a serious omission in the participation literature is an examination of behaviors that may undermine the union, reflecting more negative or potentially destructive aspects of participation.

One way of determining the value of Newton and Shore's (1992) conceptualization of union–member relations is to examine the potentially different links that instrumentality, loyalty, and alienation have with various facets of participation. Likewise, the appropriateness of a multidimensional approach to measuring union participation can be assessed by examining the degree to which differential linkages emerge between the attitudes and participation dimensions. To test these linkages, we developed participation items that were conceptually linked with the various forms of union–member relations (loyalty, instrumentality, alienation) proposed by Newton and Shore.

With the exception of Chacko (1985), who examined the effects of instrumentality on four specific behaviors, earlier research has focused on participation as a global measure instead of examining individual behaviors. Thus, there is little empirical guidance for making hypotheses about relationships between the various types of union–member relations and the participation behaviors. Instead, based on the underlying relationships with the union represented by the three attitudinal measures, as well as the basis for involvement in the union represented by these attitudes, below we describe logical linkages between the three attitudes and participation activities. This logic is then used to develop specific hypotheses.

Alienated members may be indifferent or hostile and would be expected to engage in behaviors that are potentially harmful to the union or that distance the member from union activities. Members who are high in loyalty would be expected to direct their efforts toward the welfare of the union and should also be quite willing to display their allegiance to the union publicly. It is more difficult to predict specific behaviors that would be associated with instrumentality, especially because positive instrumentality and loyalty are highly related (e.g., Fullagar & Barling, 1989; Kelloway & Barling, 1993; Shore, Tetrick, Sinclair, & Newton, 1994). Furthermore, Kelloway and Barling (1993) found that even though both instrumentality and loyalty were positively correlated with a global measure of participation across a number of samples, loyalty consistently showed the stronger correlations. This raises the question as to whether instrumentality would contribute to an explanation of participation beyond that provided by loyalty. Although we expected loyalty to provide the strongest explanation of participation behaviors among all the predictors (Fullagar & Barling, 1989; Kelloway & Barling, 1993), we still expected instrumentality to be associated with certain types of behaviors. For example, employees who are only moderately loyal but view the union as highly instrumental would still be likely to engage in behaviors that help maintain the union presence. In other words, because instrumentality reflects the member's recognition of the union's role in obtaining desired benefits, this construct would be likely to encourage monitoring activities so the member could stay informed about benefits as well as relatively low-effort member activities that would help ensure continuing union strength.

Building on the logic outlined above, participation items were generated to test these differential linkages as described. Some participation items were conceptually linked with alienation, including avoidance of participation in the union (e.g., avoiding meetings and preferring not to be a member), and undermining of support for the union (e.g., complaining). Items that were conceptually linked with instrumentality included self-serving and low-effort activities, such as staying informed about union activities (e.g., reading union communications) and voting. Given the strong affective and ideological basis for loyalty, we expected all previously discussed aspects of participation to be related to union loyalty. However, we included some additional activities that were most likely to be associated with loyalty in that they were for the betterment of the union (e.g., explaining benefits of being a member to others, volunteering time) and involved showing public support for the union (e.g., attending meetings and coming to social events sponsored by the local).

In summary, participation items can be described along several dimensions. One dimension is that of *union avoidance*, which should be strongly and positively related to alienation, strongly and negatively related to loyalty, and moderately and negatively related to instrumentality. A second dimension involves *complaining*, and should be strongly and positively related to alienation, strongly and negatively related to loyalty, and moderately and positively related to instrumentality. A third dimension is that of *union maintenance*, which involves fairly low-effort, self-serving behaviors. We expected that alienation would not be linked with these types of participation behaviors but that both loyalty and instrumentality would be positively related to maintenance behaviors. A final dimension is that of *sacrifice*, consisting of high-effort, self-sacrificing behaviors. We expected that alienation and instrumentality would not be as strongly linked as loyalty with these types of participation behaviors.

Correlations were used to examine the general pattern of associations that alienation, instrumentality, and loyalty had with the four categories of participation behaviors (i.e., union avoidance, complaining, union maintenance, and sacrifice). However, because we expected instrumentality, alienation, and loyalty to be related, we also compared their impact on participation behavior by using hierarchical regression to examine the unique variance accounted for by each of the union–member relations measures beyond that accounted for by the other two measures. The hypotheses tested in this study were thus as follows:

Hypothesis 1: Alienation would be positively correlated with participation behaviors in the union avoidance and complaining categories and negatively correlated with behaviors in the union maintenance and sacrifice categories. Instrumentality and loyalty would be negatively correlated with participation behaviors in the union avoidance and complaining categories and positively correlated with behaviors in the union maintenance and sacrifice categories.

Hypothesis 2: Alienation and loyalty would account for unique variance in avoidance activities and complaining behaviors, whereas instrumentality would not.

Hypothesis 3: Instrumentality and loyalty would account for unique variance in union maintenance behaviors, whereas alienation would not.

Hypothesis 4: Loyalty would account for unique variance in sacrificing behaviors, whereas instrumentality and alienation would not.

Hypothesis 5: Loyalty would account for the most unique variance in all of the participation behaviors.

METHOD

Sample

All 1,050 members of a large telecommunications local union in the Midwestern United States were sent an attitude survey. A total of 287 completed surveys were returned (27% return rate). Although relatively low, this response rate is not uncommon in union attitude studies (see, for example, Fullagar, 1986).

In addition, the gender composition of the sample (40% men and 60% women) was quite similar to that of the membership (44% men and 56% women), suggesting some support for the representativeness of the sample. The average age of the members responding to the survey was 42.5 years, with the youngest participant being 18 and the oldest 64. On average, the participants had worked for the company 18 years and in their present jobs 11.4 years. Forty-seven percent of the participants reported having had some college education, 35% indicated that they had completed high school, and 12% indicated that they had college degrees or some graduate work.

Measures and Procedure

A cover letter printed on union stationery and signed by the local president and the first author of this study, a survey questionnaire, and a computer-readable answer sheet were mailed to each participant. The cover letter stressed that participation was completely voluntary and that responses would be kept confidential. Two weeks after the survey administration, a reminder postcard was sent to all members who had not returned the survey. In addition, the union posted reminder notices at the work site.

Included in the survey were measures of a variety of union attitudes, including union loyalty, union alienation, and union instrumentality. A principal-components factor analysis showed that the items on these three scales loaded on separate factors. The 10-item Union Loyalty Scale (Gordon et al., 1980) had a coefficient alpha of .89 and used a 5-point response scale ranging from *strongly disagree* (1) to *strongly agree* (5). The 5-item Union Alienation Scale (available on request from the first author), which was adapted from a measure by Middleton (1963), had an alpha of .77 and also used a 5-point response scale ranging from *strongly disagree* (1) to *strongly agree* (5). Union instrumentality was measured by adapting existing measures (e.g., DeCotiis & LeLouarn, 1981; Fullagar & Barling, 1989) and by asking members to indicate the impact of the local union on 12 conditions of the employment relationship (e.g., wages, safety and health, company profitability, and job satisfaction). Consistent with the conceptual work of Newton and Shore (1992), who suggested that union instrumentality can be conceptualized as ranging from positive (the union improves benefits and working conditions) to negative (the union harms benefits and working conditions), the response scale ranged from 1 (*a very negative impact*) to 5 (*a very positive impact*). The coefficient alpha estimate of internal consistency across the 12 issues was .91.

A principal-components factor analysis of the union participation items with eight factors designated a priori was the basis for the development of the participation scales (shown in Table 1). Membership avoidance, which measures preferences rather than behavior, was not included in the factor analysis. Each of the scales was then categorized into one of the four dimensions discussed previously, including union avoidance, complaining, union maintenance, and sacrifice, as follows. Two scales were categorized into the union avoidance dimension. The Meeting Avoidance Scale consisted of 4 items ($\alpha = .79$) reflecting reasons for avoiding union meetings (e.g., "I don't like those who are active in the union"), and used a 5-point scale ranging from 1 (*almost never*) to 5 (*almost always*). The Membership Avoidance Scale consisted of 2 items ($\alpha = .87$) reflecting the member's preference not to belong to the union (Gallagher & Wetzel, 1990), using a 5-point scale (1 = *strongly disagree*, 5 = *strongly agree*). Only one scale reflected the complaining dimension of participation. Complaining comprised two items involving reports of complaining to coworkers, friends, and family ($\alpha = .86$) using a 5-point scale (1 = *never*, 5 = *frequently*). Two scales reflected the union maintenance dimension of participation. The 3-item Information Seeking Scale ($\alpha = .87$) involved reading union communications. The Voting Scale consisted of member reports of voting in union elections and contract ratification ($\alpha = .60$). Both scales used a 5-point scale ranging from *never* (1) to *frequently* (5). Four scales were categorized into the sacrifice dimension. The 3-item Communication Scale ($\alpha = .89$) reflected member attempts to disseminate positive information about the union to coworkers, family, and friends. The Self-Sacrifice Scale consisted of 8 items ($\alpha = .90$) reflecting volunteering time for activities that were beneficial to the union. The Social Activities Scale was composed of 3 items involving attendance at such union events as picnics, dances, and parties ($\alpha = .71$). These three measures used a 5-point scale ranging from 1 (*never*) to 5 (*frequently*). The Service Scale was a 3-item summative scale ($\alpha = .79$) asking how many times the member had served on a com-

Table 1

Factor Loadings of Participation Items

Item	Factor							
	1	2	3	4	5	6	7	8
Spoke up at a union meeting	.75	.20	.17	.10	.11.	.11	−.06	.06
Attended regularly scheduled union meetings	.74	.19	.36	−.05	.14	.09	−.05	.16
Recruited volunteers for union activities	.73	−.04	.11	.31	.23	.23	.01	.09
Campaigned for a candidate for union office	.72	.04	.01	.22	.15	.11	.06	.04
Attended information sharing meetings (e.g., during contract negotiations)	.72	.27	.27	−.22	.06	−.00	.01	.19
Volunteered time to help the union in administrative activities, such as stuffing envelopes or making phone calls	.71	.08	.03	.36	.11	.22	.03	−.07
Worked voluntarily on a union-sponsored charity project	.65	.09	−.13	.31	.10	.13	−.01	.21
Asked the steward for help on a work-related problem	.52	.21	.23	.37	.01	.14	−.12	−.04
Read memos and notices	.17	**.83**	.11	.20	.02	.07	.10	.10
Read the union bulletin board	.22	**.83**	.10	.19	.10	.08	.07	.06
Read the union newsletter	.09	**.78**	.12	.11	.08	.13	.09	.19
I don't know those who attend the meetings	−.13	−.09	**−.78**	−.01	−.06	−.10	.09	.04
My attendance is not important to the union	−.20	−.02	**−.68**	−.22	−.08	−.01	−.21	−.05
I don't like those who are active in the union	−.01	−.13	**−.62**	−.16	−.09	.02	−.34	.02

I am not interested in the union generally	−.17	−.24	**−.57**	−.42	−.07	−.12	−.17	−.12
Talked up the union to family and friends outside of work	.23	.24	.26	**.72**	.18	.10	.11	.11
Talked up the union to coworkers	.39	.34	.20	**.67**	.13	.10	.08	.05
Explained the benefits of being a union member to another member	.34	.19	.19	**.63**	.12	.13	−.03	.18
How many elected union offices have you held?	.01	.07	.13	.09	**.88**	.01	.04	.01
How many times have you run for office?	.23	.06	.10	.08	**.87**	.07	.02	−.05
How many times have you served on a committee?	.35	.08	−.00	.12	**.58**	−.06	−.01	.01
Attended the local union Christmas party	.07	.10	.04	.02	−.05	**.84**	−.02	.12
Attended the local union picnic	.23	.12	.09	.14	.07	**.75**	.02	.07
Attended local union sponsored dances	.44	.05	.02	.14	.02	**.59**	.09	−.00
Complained to coworkers about union activities	−.01	.06	.11	.04	.04	.05	**.91**	−.02
Complained to family and friends outside of work about union activities	−.04	.14	.16	.03	−.01	.00	**.90**	−.01
Voted for contract ratification	−.05	−.02	.00	.12	−.15	.02	−.05	**.77**
Voted for union officers	.15	.26	.16	.00	.11	.23	.01	**.65**
Read the union contract	.27	.17	−.11	.07	.05	.01	.02	**.59**
Eigenvalue	8.97	2.60	2.02	1.56	1.34	1.21	1.16	1.09
% variance explained	30.90	9.00	7.00	5.40	4.60	4.20	4.00	3.80
Cumulative % variance explained	30.90	39.90	46.90	52.30	56.90	61.10	65.10	68.80

NOTE: Factor 1 is the Self-Sacrifice Scale; Factor 2 is the Information Seeking Scale; Factor 3 is the Meeting Avoidance Scale; Factor 4 is the Communication Scale; Factor 5 is the Service Scale; Factor 6 is the Social Activates Scale; Factor 7 is the Complaining Scale; Factor 8 is the Voting Scale. Boldfaced values indicate factors with the strongest loadings.

mittee, how many elected union offices he or she had held, and how many times the member had run for office.

RESULTS

Means, standard deviations, and correlations are shown in Table 2. The pattern of correlations is consistent with Hypothesis 1. As expected, alienation was negatively related and instrumentality and loyalty positively related to participation behaviors in the union maintenance and sacrifice categories. Furthermore, alienation was positively related and instrumentality and loyalty negatively related to participation behaviors in the union avoidance and complaining categories. This pattern suggests that alienation is a negative type of union–member relationship, whereas instrumentality and loyalty represent positive union–member relations.

Hierarchical regression results are reported in Tables 3 and 4. Partial support was found for Hypothesis 2 because loyalty accounted for unique variance in the union-avoidance behaviors of meeting avoidance and membership avoidance. As expected, alienation accounted for incremental variance in membership avoidance. However, contrary to prediction, alienation did not account for unique variance in meeting avoidance, whereas union instrumentality did. This suggests that members do not avoid meetings because they are alienated. Rather, members appear to attend meetings due to positive union instrumentality perceptions and feelings of loyalty to the union. Finally, only loyalty explained incremental variance in complaining behavior, providing partial support for the hypothesis.

Hypothesis 3 predicted that only instrumentality and loyalty would explain additional variance in union maintenance behaviors. Interestingly, loyalty accounted for unique variance in information seeking and voting, whereas instrumentality did not account for incremental variance in either of the maintenance behaviors. Thus, mixed support was found for the pattern predicted in Hypothesis 3.

Hypothesis 4 was supported, because only loyalty explained incremental variance in the sacrifice category of behaviors, including commu-

Table 2

Means, Standard Deviations, and Correlations

Measure	M	SD	1	2	3	4	5	6	7	8	9	10	11
1. Alienation	2.61	0.71	—										
2. Instrumentality	3.58	0.66	-.61	—									
3. Loyalty	3.32	0.72	-.67	.67	—								
4. Meeting avoidance	2.26	0.92	.44	-.49	-.58	—							
5. Membership avoidance	2.40	1.03	.62	-.53	-.75	.61	—						
6. Information seeking	3.91	0.97	-.33	.34	.46	-.40	-.45	—					
7. Self-sacrifice	1.78	0.79	-.25	.26	.44	-.44	-.42	.46	—				
8. Social activities	2.02	1.01	-.24	.25	.35	-.26	-.27	.32	.49	—			
9. Communication	2.64	1.09	-.45	.47	.68	-.54	-.66	.53	.67	.41	—		
10. Service	1.53	3.80	-.13	.11	.27	-.25	-.27	.23	.47	.21	.36	—	
11. Complaining	1.94	0.90	.35	-.35	-.46	.33	.35	-.20	-.02	-.04	-.17	-.02	—
12. Voting	4.20	0.80	-.11	.16	.23	-.15	-.22	.39	.38	.30	.33	.11	-.02

NOTE: For correlations greater than .11, $p < .05$; for correlations greater than .15, $p < .01$.

Table 3

Change in R^2 for Alienation, Instrumentality, and Loyalty

Measure	Alienation		Instrumentality		Loyalty	
	$\Delta R2$	ΔF	ΔR^2	ΔF	ΔR^2	ΔF
Meeting avoidance	.00	0.10	.03	9.35**	.09	31.81**
Membership avoidance	.02	9.88**	.00	0.02	.17	86.76**
Information seeking	.00	0.30	.00	0.00	.08	20.90**
Self-sacrifice	.01	1.98	.00	0.00	.11	29.24**
Social activities	.00	0.05	.00	0.00	.04	10.91**
Communication	.00	0.99	.01	2.38	.20	83.18**
Service	.00	0.17	.00	0.47	.05	12.03**
Complaining	.00	0.22	.01	1.56	.07	22.27**
Voting	.00	0.03	.00	0.02	.02	4.64*

$^*p < .05.$ $^{**}p < .01.$

Table 4

Betas for Alienation, Instrumentality, and Loyalty

Participation measure	Alienation	Instrumentality	Loyalty	Total R^2	Overall F
Meeting avoidance	.03	−.22**	−.43**	.38	46.09**
Membership avoidance	.19**	−.01	−.60**	.55	93.02**
Information seeking	−.04	.02	.40**	.20	18.24**
Self-sacrifice	.11	.02	.47**	.18	16.49**
Social activities	−.02	.05	.30**	.12	10.14**
Communication	.07	.10	.65**	.46	64.81**
Service	.04	−.07	.33**	.07	5.67**
Complaining	−.04	.09	.40**	.24	23.89**
Voting	−.02	−.02	.20**	.04	3.22*

$^*p < .05.$ $^{**}p < .01.$

nication, self-sacrifice, social activities, and service. Hypothesis 5 was also supported, because loyalty consistently explained the greatest amount of variance in all of the participation behaviors.

DISCUSSION

The purpose of this study was to more fully explicate the union–member relationship by focusing on both positive and negative union attitudes and behaviors. The factor analysis results supported the distinctiveness of alienation, instrumentality, and loyalty, as well as the distinctiveness of several types of participation measures, including both positive and negative behaviors. However, when the attitudes and participation behaviors were linked, the value of examining the broad array of attitudes and behaviors appeared more doubtful. In particular, loyalty appeared to be the strongest and most consistent predictor of all of the varied forms of participation, raising questions as to the value of studying alienation and instrumentality, and also as to the need for multifaceted measures of participation. Below we first discuss issues pertaining to the union attitude measures and subsequently focus on participation.

The general pattern of correlational evidence provided support for our view that alienation was chiefly a negative type of union–member attitude, whereas both instrumentality and loyalty represented positive forms of union–member involvement. In particular, alienation was negatively related to participation behaviors that aided the union and positively related to behaviors that were detrimental to the union, consistent with the views of other researchers (Bigoness & Tosi, 1984; Klandermans, 1986; Miller & Young, 1955). The opposite pattern was found for instrumentality and loyalty.

The links between loyalty and member participation in union activities suggest, as with previous research (Fullagar & Barling, 1989; Kelloway & Barling, 1993), that loyal members are likely to engage in a variety of behaviors that contribute to the strength and viability of the union. The results for alienation and instrumentality, however, were much less compelling, with each of these measures explaining unique variance in only one participation behavior. This implies that at least for the participation behaviors included in the present study, loyalty, rather than alienation or instrumentality, is the chief contributor to most union-related behaviors.

Although the correlational results supported our conceptualization of alienation, the regression results for alienation were not as supportive. Consistent with predictions, alienation explained unique variance in membership avoidance, suggesting that those who are alienated would prefer not to be members. However, alienation did not account for incremental variance in either meeting avoidance or complaining. Nonetheless, we believe that further research on alienation is warranted for a number of reasons. First, the present sample had quite positive union attitudes in general (on a 5-point scale, $Ms = 3.58, 3.32,$ and $2.61,$ for instrumentality, loyalty, and alienation, respectively), which may have influenced the results. Perhaps in unions that are not viewed as favorably by members (i.e., where a greater number of members are alienated and view the union as hurting benefits), there may be more evidence of the impact of alienation on behavior. A union with higher rates of alienation may well be threatened by decertification (Newton & Shore, 1992). A second possibility, in light of the low response rate (27%), is that the more alienated members of the present local were unwilling to complete a survey sponsored by the union. Future research should attempt to gather information from a broad cross-section of unions so that greater variability in attitudes toward the union may be explored. Finally, our measure of alienation did not tap union opposition, a more negative form of the union–member relationship. Rather, alienation focused on indifference toward and disaffection from the union. A measure of opposition to the union might produce results more consistent with our expectations.

The regression results for instrumentality were also not consistent with predictions, in that instrumentality did not account for unique variance in either of the maintenance participation behaviors (information seeking and voting). Rather, loyalty alone appeared to explain these forms of participation. Furthermore, instrumentality explained incremental variance in meeting avoidance behavior beyond that provided by loyalty, which was not expected. This suggests that members who are high on either loyalty or instrumentality are less likely to avoid attending meetings due to a lack of interest in or a liking for the union and union members.

Given the similar pattern of correlations for instrumentality and loyalty and the limited role that instrumentality plays in explaining participation behaviors, it could be argued that instrumentality has limited value for understanding the dynamics of union–member relations. Perhaps, as suggested by Gordon et al. (1980), loyalty depends in part on the instrumentality of the union for obtaining desired benefits. In particular, instrumentality may be necessary for the development of loyalty among new members (Newton & Shore, 1992), but with greater tenure, these attitudes may become somewhat redundant in the prediction of member behavior. Another possibility is that instrumentality serves as a moderator between loyalty and member participation (Fullagar & Barling, 1989).

Our results were somewhat mixed in terms of supporting the value of a multidimensional approach to measuring participation. The factor analysis suggested the appropriateness of multiple participation scales. In addition, reliability results showed that almost all of the scales were internally consistent (except for the Union Voting Scale). Each of these participation scales consisted of items with an interpretable theme. Furthermore, correlations among the participation scales were not consistently high ($rs = -.02$ to $.67$), suggesting that at least some of the scales are tapping distinct constructs. Finally, each of the a priori categories of participation (avoidance, complaining, maintenance, and sacrifice) was represented by distinct scales. In contrast, evidence against the distinctiveness of the participation scales was shown by the regression results, in which loyalty was the only attitude contributing uniquely to seven of the nine participation scales. It is possible, however, that the unsupportive results were due to the nature of the predictors, rather than suggesting that a multidimensional approach does not accurately reflect the participation domain. Given that the majority of evidence supports the distinctiveness of the various forms of participation, the results overall appear to support the multidimensional approach to measuring participation. Nonetheless, additional research is needed that more explicitly tests the value of multi- versus unidimensional approaches to measuring participation before more conclusive statements can be made. In addition, research is needed to more fully explore potentially unique predictors of each form of participation, so that we can better understand the value of a multidimensional approach to assessing member behavior.

There were a number of limitations to our study that may have affected the results. First, both the union–member relations measures and the participation measures were obtained from union members. Thus, the pattern of results may well have been influenced by the exclusive use of self-report data. Future research should attempt to collect participation data through other sources as well, such as stewards, other members, and supervisors, and then examine the unique value of the union–member relations measures. Second, although fairly common in studies of unions, the response rate was somewhat low (27%), which may have affected the pattern of results. Third, responses were gathered from a single union local, perhaps contributing to a narrower range of results on the union–member relations measures (loyalty, alienation, and instrumentality) than might be found if multiple unions participated.

In conclusion, as the employment relationship between employees and employers changes, it is important to explore both the positive and negative consequences of these changes for unions. One way of understanding the potentially dynamic nature of the relationships between unions and members is to develop and evaluate a broader array of member attitudes and behaviors than has been studied in the past. This study contributed to the literature by showing that some union members view their relationship with the union as chiefly negative (i.e., alienation) and that members report preferences and behaviors that may undermine union support (i.e., membership avoidance and meeting avoidance). Future research should further develop the attitudinal and behavioral domains associated with union membership. Another contribution of this study was the evidence showing the importance of loyalty for predicting member participation along with the concomitant lack of impact that instrumentality had on participation. This suggests that as unions attempt to retain active participation among their members, union leaders need to explore

ways of enhancing loyalty rather than merely building member perceptions of union instrumentality.

REFERENCES

Anderson, J. C. (1979). Local union participation: A reexamination. *Industrial Relations, 18*, 18–31.

Belous, R. S. (1989, May). How human resource systems adjust to the shift toward
contingent workers. *Monthly Labor Review*, 7–12.

Bigoness, W. J., & Tosi, H. L. (1984). Correlates of voting behavior in a union decertification election. *Academy of Management Journal, 27*, 654–659.

Chacko, T. I. (1985). Member participation in union activities: Perceptions of union
priorities, performance, and satisfaction. *Journal of Labor Research, 4*, 363–373.

Cohen, A. (1994). An empirical assessment of the multidimensionality of union participation. *Journal of Management, 19*, 749–773.

DeCotiis, T. A., & LeLouarn, J. (1981). A predictive study of voting behavior in a
representation election using union instrumentality and work perceptions. *Organizational Behavior and Human Performance, 27*, 103–118.

Fullagar, C. (1986). A factor analytic study on the validity of a union commitment
scale. *Journal of Applied Psychology, 71*, 129–136.

Fullagar, C., & Barling, J. (1989). A longitudinal test of the antecedents and consequences of union loyalty. *Journal of Applied Psychology, 74*, 213–227.

Gallagher, D. G., & Strauss, G. (1991). Union membership attitudes and participation. In G. Strauss, D. B. Gallagher, & J. Fiorito (Eds.), *The state of unions*. Madison, WI: Industrial Relations Research Association.

Gallagher, D., & Wetzel, K. (1990, May). *The union membership roster as a source of
possible sample bias in the study of union commitment.* Paper presented at the
meeting of the Society for Industrial and Organizational Psychology, Miami,
FL.

Gordon, M. E., Philpot, J. W., Burt, R. E., Thompson, C. A., & Spiller, W. E. (1980).
Commitment to the union: Development of a measure and an examination of
its correlates. *Journal of Applied Psychology, 65*, 479–499.

Hagburg, E. C. (1966). Correlates of organizational participation: An examination
of factors affecting union membership activity. *Pacific Sociological Review, 9*,
15–21.

Hoyman, M. M., & Stallworth, L. (1987). Participation in local unions: A comparison of Black and White members. *Industrial and Labor Relations Review, 40,* 323–335.

Huszczo, G. E. (1983). Attitudinal and behavioral variables related to participation in union activities. *Journal of Labor Research, 4,* 289–297.

Kelloway, E. K., & Barling, J. (1993). Members' participation in local union activities: Measurement, prediction, and replication. *Journal of Applied Psychology, 78,* 262–279.

Klandermans, B. (1986). Psychology and trade union participation: Joining, acting, quitting. *Journal of Occupational Psychology, 59,* 189–204.

Kuruvilla, S., Gallagher, D. G., Fiorito, J., & Wakabayashi, M. (1990). Union participation in Japan: Do Western theories apply? *Industrial and Labor Relations Review, 43,* 374–389.

Leicht, K. T. (1989). Unions, plants, jobs, and workers: An analysis of union satisfaction and participation. *The Sociological Quarterly, 30,* 331–362.

McShane, S. L. (1986). A path analysis of participation in union administration. *Industrial Relations, 25,* 72–80.

Middleton, R. (1963). Alienation, race and education. *American Sociological Review, 28,* 937–977.

Miller, G. W., & Young, J. F. (1955). Membership participation in the trade union local. *American Journal of Economics and Sociology, 15,* 36–43.

Newton, L. A., & Shore, L. M. (1992). A model of union membership: Instrumentality, commitment, and opposition. *Academy of Management Review, 17,* 275–298.

Osterman, P. (1994). How common is workplace transformation and who adopts it? *Industrial and Labor Relations Review, 47,* 173–188.

Shore, L. M., Tetrick, L. E., Sinclair, R. R., & Newton, L. A. (1994). Validation of a measure of perceived union support. *Journal of Applied Psychology, 79,* 971–977.

Spinrad, W. (1960). Correlates of trade union participation: A summary of the literature. *American Sociological Review, 25,* 237–244.

Tetrick, L. E., Thacker, J. W., & Fields, M. W. (1989). Evidence for the stability of the four dimensions of the commitment to the union scale. *Journal of Applied Psychology, 74,* 819–822.

Thacker, J. W., Fields, M. W., & Tetrick, L. E. (1989). The dimensionality of the Union Commitment Scale: A confirmatory factor analysis. *Journal of Applied Psychology, 74,* 228–232.

10

Democratic Legitimacy in Swedish Labor Unions: The Role of Instrumentality in Forming Members' Perceptions

Kristina Ahlén

The purpose of this chapter is to examine the relationship between union members' political efficacy experiences and their perceptions of union legitimacy. *Political efficacy* in the union environment consists of the belief that individual action has, or can have, an influence on the union's decision-making process, and comprises perceptions of one's own competence, together with perceptions of the responsiveness of the union's officials (Petersson, Westholm, & Blomberg, 1989). It is thus related to the concept "instrumentality of participation," although the focus here is on a specific political efficacy experience rather than a general perception (cf. Barling, Fullagar, & Kelloway, 1992; Klandermans, 1984; Nicholson, Ursell, & Lubbock, 1981).

Legitimacy is defined as the gap between a person's norms about unions and the person's perceptions of reality. The particular focus here is on members' perceptions of their union's democratic legitimacy: the extent to which their democratic ambitions for their union's government are met by their personal experiences of how decisions are actually made in the union. Democratic legitimacy is an example of what I call *procedural legitimacy*, following the conceptual framework in Chaison, Bigelow, and

Ottensmeyer (1993). *Substantive legitimacy*, in contrast, concerns the goals and activities of a union, rather than the means by which these goals are determined. Although conceptually distinct, procedural and substantive legitimacy are likely to be interdependent to some extent.

In contrast to political efficacy, legitimacy perceptions are based in part on value-rationality, to use the Weberian term. In his book *The Theory of Social and Economic Organization* (1947), Max Weber argued that there are four bases of social action: *ends-rationality* or instrumentality, that is, expectations about the behavior of other individuals and, on the basis of these, rational calculations about "the successful attainment of the actor's own rationally chosen ends"; *value-rationality*, a "rational orientation to an absolute value. . . involving the conscious belief in the absolute value of some ethical, aesthetic, religious, or other form of behavior, entirely for its own sake and independently of any prospects of external success"; *affect*, which is "determined by the specific affects and states of feeling of the actor," especially the emotional; and *tradition*, the "habituation of long practice." Although Weber's theories of social action are no longer generally regarded as sound, his concepts continue to provide an important contribution to modern social science, as the various rational choice approaches (including the one taken here) testify.

The overall aim of the research project from which this chapter is drawn was to assess procedural legitimacy in Swedish unions generally and to begin identifying the effects that various internal political and organizational features of unions may have on that legitimacy. In addition to political efficacy, the other factors included in the broader study concern the members' socioeconomic and demographic characteristics (age, gender, family status, nationality, and language are examined in this chapter) and the organizational presence of the union at the workplace (i.e., a workplace club). In the following two sections, more detailed definitions of the main concepts are provided. This is followed by a section describing the theoretical and historical background to the issues addressed in the chapter. The succeeding two sections describe the research methods and research results, respectively. The chapter concludes with a discussion of the results and their implications for Swedish unions.

POLITICAL EFFICACY

The conceptualization of political efficacy used here follows Petersson et al. (1989). It begins with the individual's level of satisfaction with his or her situation and then assesses whether he or she made any efforts to change the situation, and if so, whether these efforts were successful. The political efficacy experience in a democracy may then take one of four possible forms: (a) A person is satisfied with his or her situation and consequently takes no initiatives; in this case the individual is *content*. (b) A person takes an initiative that is successful; in this case the individual has successfully *exercised power*. (c) A person takes an initiative, but is unsuccessful; in this case the individual experiences *powerlessness*. (d) A person is dissatisfied, but remains passive; in this case the individual experiences quiet impotence, or *resignation*. A graphical representation of these four possibilities is provided in Figure 1, which has been adapted from Petersson et al. (1989).

Part of the analysis reported below compares legitimacy perceptions across the four groups of union members defined by these political efficacy experiences. For that purpose, it is useful to note that two of these political efficacy experiences (exercise of power and powerlessness) involve the respondent's having taken an initiative; the other two (contentment and resignation) involved no initiative. Viewed from another perspective, we might also say that two of these experiences (contentment and exercise of power) are agreeable, whereas the other two (powerlessness and resignation) are disagreeable.

In this chapter I examine findings from a test of the hypothesis formulated by Petersson et al. (1989) regarding political efficacy and procedural legitimacy. They argued that there is a circular relationship between the specific political efficacy experience and more general estimations of one's ability to influence. Petersson et al. hypothesized that feelings of powerlessness can lead to more pessimistic judgments of one's own chances to exercise influence, which in turn reduce one's readiness to take future initiatives. These pessimistic judgments may thereby contribute to a widening of the gap between norms and reality, and thus a decline in le-

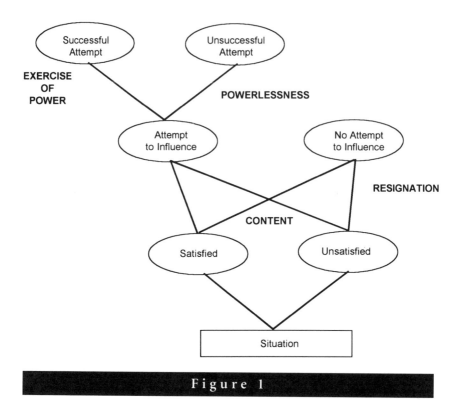

Figure 1

Political efficacy experiences. (From *Medborganas makt* by O. Petersson, A. Westholm, and
G. Blomberg, 1989, Stockholm : Carlsson. Copyright 1989 by Carlsson. Adapted with permission.)

gitimacy. The central hypothesis of this study is, therefore, that union
members who have made unsuccessful attempts to influence their union
will accord their union lower levels of legitimacy than either those who
have taken no initiative or those who have experienced successful exer-
cises of power.

DEMOCRATIC LEGITIMACY

Democratic legitimacy is treated as a concept having a number of dimensions. Here I examine two: the *legitimacy of participation* (which is the
extent to which and ways by which members participate in decisions that
affect them in order to influence their course); and the *legitimacy of responsiveness* (the extent to which the union leadership is perceived by the

members as responsive to their interests, that is, disposed to be influenced by the members and to seek input from them). Conceptually, participation encompasses two subdimensions: (a) expressing an opinion (which in turn includes several variables, such as voicing an opinion or introducing a topic at a union meeting, voting on a union issue, speaking informally to a union official about a union issue, writing a motion to the union congress, and writing a letter to the union newspaper or to a union official about a union issue) and (b) holding an elected position in the union. Note that this definition excludes some of the activities often associated with "participation," such as attendance at club meetings and study circles and reading the union newspaper. As I have argued (Ahlén, 1994), such activities are better placed in a dimension labeled *competence building*, defined as the extent to which union members make efforts to become sufficiently informed about how their union operates to be able to participate effectively, or at all. The responsiveness dimension may involve union officials' providing members with information, opportunities to express opinions, and opportunities to influence decisions.

THEORETICAL AND HISTORICAL BACKGROUND

The legitimacy of Swedish unions—both procedural and substantive—was seriously questioned in recent years by employers, the government, and even union members themselves. Both inside and outside of union circles, it became common to speak of a crisis of authority, and these perceptions were reinforced by more unstable membership levels. With the severe rise of unemployment in Sweden beginning in 1991, the return of the Social Democrats to office in 1994, and some recent internal changes in the Swedish unions, much of the public debate has subsided. But most observers are well aware that unions today are undergoing perhaps the most stringent test of their role in Swedish society since the early years of the Industrial Revolution.

This is a new situation for Swedish unions, which have been regarded by most scholars in recent decades as the most innovative and successful labor organizations in the world. They have also been the most powerful:

Union membership in Sweden, as a percentage of all employees, is the highest in the world, and union financial coffers are substantial. Swedish unions have also not been plagued by many of the problems other union movements have faced—internal strife, intransigent employers, a negative political climate, and so forth.

The challenge to substantive legitimacy has not been to the Swedish unions' right to exist, as it has been in many countries, but challenges to the right of central confederations to bargain collectively for their affiliates and to the right of national unions to provide collective services and benefits to their members. Beginning in the early 1950s, for example, collective bargaining in Sweden was highly centralized, with frame agreements between the employers' confederation, SAF, and the three central labor confederations (the blue-collar LO, the white-collar TCO, and the professional workers' SACO). During the 1980s, this system was broken down by the refusal of the employers to participate.

Reforms by the recent nonsocialist government have also aimed at weakening both the instrumental and value-rational bases of members' attachment to their unions. The elimination of adult education grants, which had helped finance union studies, dealt a serious blow to the strategy the union movement has used traditionally to maintain solidarity (cf. Offe & Wiesenthal, 1985). It was a direct attack on the means by which Swedish unions have built up workers' value-rational basis of commitment to their union. Increases in fees to the union-administered unemployment insurance funds, together with the sanctioning in 1994 of government-run alternatives to these funds, raised the apparent cost of union membership while offering an alternative to union membership to those who have believed that membership in the two is linked. This represented a direct attack on one of the foundations Swedish unions have traditionally had for creating the instrumental bases of workers' attachment to unions. Not surprisingly, this last reform was one of the first to be repealed by the new Social Democratic government, which has historical ties to the blue-collar unions.

As Swedish unions' roles are restricted and their ability to accomplish goals reduced by falling resources, members are likely to perceive their unions as less effective; that is, their perceptions of their union's instrumentality is likely to fall. Strikes at substantive legitimacy, moreover, may be an indirect strike at procedural legitimacy. Previous research suggests that perceptions of union instrumentality may affect members' union participation (Anderson, 1979; Fullagar & Barling, 1989; Kelloway, Barling, & Fullagar, 1990; Kolchin & Hyclak, 1984). Members are less likely to participate in union affairs if they perceive the union itself as an ineffective means of achieving their goals. To the extent that members believe they ought to participate in union affairs, then, a decline in participation could decrease their perceptions of the union's procedural legitimacy.

Swedish unions' democratic, procedural legitimacy is also being threatened more directly, from changes internal to the union movement. The most obvious of these are organizational merger and consolidation among the unions. The vast majority of workers in Sweden are organized in industrial unions, with one union per industry. The rest are organized in occupational unions. Altogether, Sweden today only has about 65 unions, which has been a reflection as well as a source of internal cohesion and strength for the union movement. But rational organizational boundaries may have their limits. Following a wave of mergers and the consequent centralization of union decision making in the 1960s and early 1970s, concerns surfaced about their effect on union democracy. The number of blue-collar unions was reduced through mergers from 44 in 1960 to 25 in 1973, whereas branch organizations were reduced from 8,000 to 2,000. These mergers mean that the size of the union organizational units increased, which altered traditional decision-making patterns and the union–member relation (Fiorito, Gramm, & Hendricks, 1991). A few years after the consolidation, Lewin (1977) found that three quarters of the union members in the blue-collar sector believed their influence within their union had weakened as a result.

Although concerns about the effects of this consolidation had yet to dissipate, unions in the late 1980s were forced to embark on a new round of consolidation. As a result of accumulated structural change in Swedish industry and in the public sector, some Swedish unions found themselves too small to be either self-sustaining or able to maintain their traditional high level of member services. Regional units were also required to consolidate in order to conserve resources.

One way union mergers will affect legitimacy perceptions, I hypothesize, is by diminishing members' perceptions of their own political efficacy. It is likely, for example, that as units within the union structure are enlarged, union officials will find it harder to be responsive to the same proportion of members as they have been accustomed. Political efficacy experiences may become less satisfactory; members may sense that there is less point in trying to influence officials in these larger units.

Changes in the employment relationship are also challenging Swedish unions' procedural legitimacy. Swedish employers are embracing a new management and production philosophy, termed "post-Fordist" production, which, in common with international trends, focuses responsibilities and increases labor–management interactions on the workplace level rather than the traditional national leadership levels. Wage negotiations are more decentralized and tied to productivity, autonomous work groups are taking over more decision making within the company, and employers are relinquishing many day-to-day decisions to lower levels in the organizational hierarchy. From the unions' point of view, the threat represented by these changes comes from the employers' simultaneous efforts to bypass workplace union organizations and to establish direct, close links of loyalty with the workers themselves. This increased workplace control over how work is carried out together with attempts to bypass union clubs means that unions' centralized decision structures are becoming out of sync with workplace realities. Union observers argue that union resources and decision-making authority ought to be redirected, away from the national level and toward the workplace level where decisions that affect their members increasingly are being made. Unfortunately, unions here have been slow to respond to the employers' decentralization, apparently hoping the power they had accumulated at the national level would somehow mitigate the adverse effects of these changes. In the following section, the methods used to study democratic legitimacy are described.

METHOD

Sample

This report is based on data from a large-scale survey recently carried out in Sweden. Two surveys were conducted among three blue-collar, private-sector unions, representing factory workers, food workers, and clothing workers. One of the surveys was addressed to rank-and-file members; the other was addressed to their local, elected representatives. The total rank-and-file sample numbers 1,343; the elected representatives' sample numbers 1,151. Our response rates were about 75% for both samples.

Measures

For each of the dimensions and subdimensions of democratic legitimacy, I constructed one normative question and one question regarding actual practice. For example, the respondents' perceptions of their actual opportunities to express opinions (in the responsiveness dimension) is captured by the question, "In general, do you feel that union members like you are given sufficient opportunities to express their opinions about what union goals ought to be?" Answers were along a 4-point scale ranging from *yes, definitely* to *no, definitely not*. The question about the respondent's normative position on opportunities to express opinions was "In general, should members have opportunities to express their opinions about what union goals ought to be?" Answers again could range along a 4-point scale from *yes, definitely* to *no, definitely not* (with a fifth alternative being *don't know*). Legitimacy scores were calculated for each subdimension by simple subtraction. Because the answers to both the normative and the practice questions were coded from 1 through 4, any given legitimacy score could have values ranging from -3 to 3. The lower the value, the less a person's perceptions of practice lived up to their norms about a particular issue. For the rank-and-file sample, the result was a set of five legitimacy scores, one each for the various subdimensions. For the elected representatives sample, four separate scores were calculated (office holding was excluded).

Procedure

The relationship between political efficacy experience and each of the sub-dimensions of legitimacy was tested using (hierarchical) analysis of variance techniques. Thus, the effect of the political efficacy experience is taken into account first among a number of additional antecedent variables. The latter were the existence of a union club or local ombudsman at the respondent's place of work (i.e., workplace contact) and the respondent's age, gender, cultural background (nationality and home language), education and skill level, family status, union affiliation, work schedule, and length of working week.

RESULTS

The political efficacy experience turns out to be significantly correlated with each of the subdimensions of democratic legitimacy. Thus, whether union members were satisfied with their union, whether they attempted to influence their union, and whether these attempts were successful appears to affect their general perceptions of union procedural legitimacy. Various aspects of the respondent's socioeconomic and demographic background occasionally played a role as well, as did the union's presence at the workplace, but there was no consistent pattern for any of these factors. Tables 1 and 2 summarize the results of the analyses of variance. The figures in parentheses in the body of the table indicate the variables that proved to be significant and the order in which they were entered into the analysis. Although the F values are significant in each case, the total amount of variation explained by these factors is actually quite modest. The highest multiple correlation squared is only .101.

The average legitimacy values among the four groups of members defined by political efficacy experience (i.e., the exercise of power, power-lessness, content, and resigned groups) provide clues to other factors that ought to be taken into account in subsequent research. By simple rank ordering of the four groups, distinct patterns emerge that may provide clues to future research. These are worth examining in some detail. In the following sections, the overall patterns are reported first, followed by the de-

Table 1

The Legitimacy of Participation: Rank-and-File Members and
Elected Representatives

	Rank-and-file members		Elected representatives
Variable	Express opinions	Office holding	Express opinions
Political efficacy	(1)	(1)	(1)
Age		(3)	
Gender		(4)	
Family status		(2)	
Analysis of variance			
F	10.91	7.60	3.26
P	.00	.00	.02
Adjusted R^2	.04	.08	.10
n	835	790	671
Missing cases	508	553	480

NOTE: The figures in parentheses indicate the variables that proved to be significant and the order in which they were entered into the analysis.

tails for each dimension (and subdimension). Finally, the components of the legitimacy scores are themselves examined.

There are two distinct patterns of relationships between political efficacy experience and average scores for democratic legitimacy. The patterns are defined by whether the political efficacy experience involved the taking of an initiative and whether the overall experience was agreeable or disagreeable (see above). The particular pattern depended on which aspect of union government was addressed. Political efficacy had one kind of effect with respect to participation in decision making (e.g., contributing to a discussion, voting on an issue). It had a completely different effect with respect to officials' responsiveness to members opinions. Below, the pattern for each of the legitimacy dimensions is examined in turn.

| | Table 2 | | |

The Legitimacy of Officials' Responsiveness: Rank-and-File Members

Variable	Given information	Given chances to participate	Have an influence
Political efficacy	(1)	(1)	(1)
Workplace club		(2)	
Cultural background	(2)	(3)	(2)
Analysis of variance			
F	13.86	15.00	14.72
P	.00	.00	.00
Adjusted R^2	.08	.10	.08
n	757	746	776
Missing cases	586	597	567

NOTE: The figures in parentheses indicate the variables that proved to be significant and the order in which they were entered into the analysis.

Participation

The pattern for the participation dimension is as follows: Those with the highest average legitimacy scores are those who took an initiative, regardless of the outcome of that initiative. Those with the lower scores are those who took no initiative. Within these two groups—the two with the higher scores (exercise of power and powerlessness) and the two with the lower scores (content and resigned)—there is also a pattern: The success of an initiative and an initial satisfaction with union affairs is often associated with significantly higher average legitimacy scores than failed initiative and initial dissatisfaction. Thus, the rank order of legitimacy scores is usually as follows: exercise of power, powerlessness, content, and resigned. This pattern holds for both of the subdimensions of participation and for both the rank-and-file and the elected representatives' samples. The differences among the four political efficacy groups are significant.

We can take a look at the norm and practice components of the legitimacy scores separately to see the source of these patterns better. As we recall, each subdimension of legitimacy is composed of the respondent's norms about that aspect of union government together with his or her perceptions about the actual practice of union government. The pattern of average values for one component can be entirely different from that of the second component. As it turns out, there is also a clear pattern of values for these two components of the legitimacy scores. To begin with, democratic norms as well as perceptions of reality vary greatly depending on whether the respondent took an initiative or not. Those who had taken an initiative tended to have more ambitious democratic norms; they agreed much more strongly than the noninitiators that union members ought to express their opinions in club meetings, introduce topics for consideration, vote on issues, write letters to union officials, and so forth. The initiators also tend to report higher actual levels of participation in decision making. Thus, those who had high legitimacy values both had more ambitious norms for their union and were more active democratically. Within the political efficacy pairs formed by whether an initiative was taken or not, the success of the initiative and the initial satisfaction with union affairs is often (but not always) associated with more ambitious norms and higher reported activity. Thus, there is a consistent pattern throughout this dimension of legitimacy; it pertains to the legitimacy score itself as well as to the components of the score. The following paragraphs report the way these patterns are manifested in each dimension.

For the rank-and-file union members, by far the highest average legitimacy score for the express opinions subdimension (-1.34) was among those who had exercised power; the lowest average value was among the group designated as resigned (-2.12). Those in the *powerless* group had an average score of -1.61, and in the *content* group, the average legitimacy score was -1.95. Whether one takes an initiative or not is the main factor explaining the rank ordering, and success and satisfaction are associated with higher average legitimacy scores.

Looking at the two sides of the legitimacy equation separately, those who had experienced powerlessness had more ambitious norms for expressing opinions than those who had exercised power, but the latter were much more likely to have actually participated than the former. Those who were content or resigned had almost identical norms: Neither group thought it was as important for members to express their opinions as the other two groups did. Those who were resigned, however, were somewhat less likely to have actually expressed an opinion than those who were content. Taking an initiative plays the expected role, but success and satisfaction have different effects for norms and practices.

Among the elected representatives, the differences in legitimacy scores for the express opinions subdimension are not quite as large, though they are statistically significant. For the four groups, the average scores were exercise of power, -1.89; powerlessness, -1.84; content, -2.09; and resigned, -1.89. Thus, the legitimacy assessments of both rank and file and their elected representatives for expressing opinions is to some extent, dependent on their personal experiences with trying to influence the union.

Political efficacy also plays a role in the office holding subdimension, but this time demographic and social factors are also important. The average values for the rank and file's four political efficacy groups do not follow the usual pattern. The rank ordering, in fact, is exactly the reverse of the usual pattern. Those who had exercised power have the lowest and only negative average legitimacy value (-0.62). Those who were resigned had the highest (0.93). Those who were content were next with an average of 0.78, and the score for the group who had experienced powerlessness (0.28) was higher than for those whose efforts had been successful.

The explanation for this odd rank ordering is related to the specific norms and practices. Those who were resigned were much less likely to believe one ought to serve as a representative at some time and were much less likely to have been a representative. Those who were most likely to have been a representative previously were those who had exercised power during the past year, and this group also had the highest percentage of members who believe that members ought to hold office. Thus, the group who had exercised power had higher ambitions than the other groups and had ambitions that outpaced their own activities in the union.

Responsiveness

The legitimacy of union officials' responsiveness follows a quite different pattern from the one just described. For both the rank and file and the elected representative samples, the political efficacy experience remains the most important of the factors for explaining the legitimacy perceptions. But the specific rank ordering among the four groups is completely different than it is for the participation dimension. Here, the highest average scores tended to be among those who had had agreeable political efficacy experiences: Those who exercised power had the highest, followed by those who were content. The lowest average scores tended to be among those who had had disagreeable experiences; those who had experienced powerlessness had the lowest.

A look at the individual norms and practices that make up these legitimacy scores also shows a different pattern from the one we saw in the participation dimension. Concerning their norms, or ambitions for union democracy, the four groups are rank ordered in much the same way as they were for participation: Those who took an initiative tended to have higher ambitions than those who did not. But concerning their actual experiences with officials' responsiveness, the rank ordering tends to be more like that for the legitimacy scores themselves: Those who had agreeable experiences (the exercise of power and content groups) reported having experienced officials' responsiveness significantly more than those who had disagreeable experiences (the powerless and resigned groups). Within these two groups, however, those who had taken an initiative had significantly higher average legitimacy scores than those who had not.

For the given information subdimension, for example, the question was whether union officials provided the members with as much information on which to form their opinions about union issues as they thought they ought to have. As before, political efficacy is the most significant of our factors for explaining differences in these legitimacy scores. The lowest average legitimacy scores among the rank and file are for those who have been categorized as having experienced powerlessness, followed by those who were resigned, then those who had exercised power. The highest average legitimacy values were among those described as content. Thus, those who had had agreeable efficacy experiences, regardless of whether they had taken an initiative, had higher average legitimacy scores and reported actually being given information to a greater extent than those who had had disagreeable efficacy experiences. A quarter or more of the powerless and the resigned groups said they had not received any information at all. Those who had exercised power had the highest estimates of having been given information, followed by those who were content. On the other hand, those who were most likely to think they *ought* to be given information were the ones who had taken an initiative. The rank order among the four groups on norms was the same found in the participation dimension.

For chances to participate, the lowest legitimacy assessments among the rank and file came from those who had experienced powerlessness, followed by those who were resigned. Higher scores were found for those who had exercised power and those who were content. Thus, the pattern is the general one for the responsiveness dimension. Those with agreeable efficacy experiences had higher legitimacy scores and reported greater opportunities to participate. Those who had taken an initiative had the highest ambitions. Those who were content were the least ambitious of the four groups. On the other hand, more of those who had exercised power reported having actually been given chances to participate. Those who were content had the second highest levels, followed by the powerless, and finally, the resigned.

The correlation between political efficacy and responsiveness is even more direct, of course, in the have influence subdimension, because this comes closest to the definition of political efficacy. But the pattern of scores is an exception to the general pattern for the responsiveness dimension. The rank and file's average legitimacy scores for have influence were exercise of power, -1.67; powerlessness, -1.74; content, -1.25; and resigned, -1.56. According to the data for the individual norms and practices, those who attempted to influence their union had somewhat stronger beliefs that members ought to have an influence (those who had been powerless had the strongest ambitions in this regard; those who were content had the weakest). Nevertheless, those who had exercised power reported more actual influence. Not surprisingly, half of those who had experienced powerlessness and half who were resigned reported having had no influence at all.

As expected, union affiliation was not related to any of the components of the responsiveness dimension for the rank-and-file sample. The existence of a workplace club, however, was correlated with given chances to participate. Those without a workplace club had lower legitimacy assessments than those with a club. The lower scores were related to the rank-and-file members' perceptions of actual responsiveness: Those with no access to a club reported lower levels than those with a club.

For the elected representative sample, political efficacy is again the main explanatory factor for assessments of responsiveness legitimacy, and the rank orders among the four groups follow the pattern found for the rank-and-file members. Those with agreeable efficacy experiences had higher legitimacy scores and reported more actual responsiveness, and those who took an initiative had greater democratic ambitions for their union.

The rank ordering among the groups on the extent to which they were actually given information is the same as the rank ordering for the legitimacy scores: Those who exercised power had the highest estimates, whereas those who were resigned had the lowest. Regarding their norms about being given information, those who took an initiative (the exercise of power and powerlessness groups) had similar, high ambition levels for their union; those who did not take an initiative during the past year had similar, and low, ambition levels.

The rank ordering for the have influence subdimension is due primarily to differences in perceived practices. The elected representatives' norms about whether they ought to have influence over union decisions are fairly consistent across the four groups. Those who had exercised power, however, tended to report more actual influence; the content group is next, followed by those who experienced powerlessness and those who were resigned.

The main factor that distinguishes the elected representatives' assessments of responsiveness legitimacy is the strong relationship found between these assessments and union affiliation. The union affiliation of the representatives seems to have significantly affected their assessments on given information. The study found that representatives in the clothing workers union (Bekladnäds) and the factory workers union (Fabriks) had higher average scores than those in the food workers union (Livs). Livs' representatives' norms were much stronger than Beklädnads' and slightly more ambitious than Fabriks', but their perceptions of whether they had actually received information was lower than that of the other representatives. They were more likely to say that they "definitely" ought to be given information and to have an influence on union issues. Beklädnads' representatives had somewhat less ambitious democratic norms for their union than those in the other unions: They were more likely to agree "somewhat" with this democratic ambition.

DISCUSSION

From the analyses of variance performed on these data, a set of factors emerged that are useful to begin building an explanation of legitimacy perceptions. What is especially significant about these results is that in each case, the political efficacy experience was a significant predictor of legitimacy perceptions. Thus, members' perceptions of the instrumentality of their participation appears to affect their value-based perceptions of union legitimacy. Political efficacy experiences reflect the instrumentality of participation. The findings reported above reinforce previous research that shows that participation in unions is affected by members' perceptions of the instrumentality of that participation.

The strong connection between legitimacy and political efficacy suggested a closer look at the actual values involved. Here there were clear patterns based on the rank ordering of the average scores as well as of the average values for the components of these scores. The low multiple correlation squared values in the analyses of variance show that much more is needed before we have a satisfactory model, and these rank orderings may provide clues for identifying the factors missing from this first effort at examining legitimacy perceptions. The next step is to formulate some hypotheses that may help explain these rank orderings. With this in mind, it ought to be useful to reflect on the results for the responsiveness dimension.

The lowest average legitimacy scores are, not surprisingly, among those who attempted to exercise influence and failed (i.e., the powerless group). What may be surprising is that the highest average legitimacy score is not among those who exercised influence, but among those who are content; that is, the ones who are satisfied and make no efforts to influence their union. Thus, the group of union members who did not make an attempt to influence the union had the more positive assessments of procedural legitimacy. Does this mean that the act of trying to influence the union itself implies a lower evaluation of union government? Or do those who have made an attempt develop a lower evaluation as a result of the attempt? Further research is needed to clarify these relationships. Certainly, time series data would seem to be imperative for testing alternative hypotheses, such as those proposed by Petersson et al. (1989).

The policy implications for unions will become clear with additional research. If it is true that those who make attempts to influence their unions develop lower evaluations of procedural legitimacy, for example, unions would do well to ensure that regardless of the outcome of the attempt, the political efficacy experience is handled carefully and that all due respect is given to members' right to express their opinions and influence their union.

As unions in Sweden grope for ways to reestablish their democratic legitimacy among their members, they may benefit by ensuring that their members' political efficacy experiences are "agreeable" and involve taking an initiative. In other words, I have found empirical grounds for arguing that unions need to find better ways of empowering their members by giving them real opportunities to influence their organizations and by ensuring that their efforts are acknowledged.

This argument is neither new nor especially radical. Swedish unions have formulated similar goals in recent policy statements. What is new is that in the context of the current antiunion movement, the stakes are much higher today. Also, this may be the first time that the effects of *not* fulfilling these official goals have been quantified.

REFERENCES

Ahlén, K. (1994). *Unfulfilled ambitions: Democratic legitimacy in Swedish labor unions* (Final report to Arbetsmiljöfonden). Stockholm: Arbetslivscentrum.

Anderson, J. (1979). A comparative analysis of local union democracy. *Industrial Relations, 17,* 278–295.

Barling, J., Fullagar, C., & Kelloway, E. K. (1992). *The union and its members: A psychological approach.* New York: Oxford University Press.

Chaison, G., Bigelow, B., & Ottensmeyer, E. (1993). Unions and legitimacy: A conceptual refinement. *Research in the Sociology of Organization [Special Issue on Labor Relations and Unions], 12,* 139–166.

Fiorito, J., Gramm, C., & Handricks, W. (1991). Union structural choices. In D. Gallagher & G. Strauss (Eds.), *The state of the unions: Industrial relations research association series* (pp. 103–137). Madison, WI: Industrial Relations Research Association..

Fullagar, C., & Barling, J. (1989). A longitudinal test of a model of the antecedents and consequences of union loyalty. *Journal of Applied Psychology, 74,* 213–227.

Kelloway, E. K., Barling, J., & Fullagar, C. (1990). *Extending a model of union commitment: The roles of union and work attitudes.* Unpublished manuscript.

Klandermans, P. G. (1984). Mobilization and participation in trade union action: An expectancy-value approach. *Journal of Occupational Psychology, 57,* 107–120.

Kolchin, M. G., & Hyclak, T. (1984). Participation in union activities: A multivariate analysis. *Journal of Labor Research, 5,* 255–261.

Lewin, L. (1977). *Hur styrs facket? Om demokratin inom fackföreningsrörelsen.* Stockholm: Rabén och Sjögren.

Nicholson, N., Ursell, G., & Lubbock, J. (1981). Membership participation in a white-collar union. *Industrial Relations, 20,* 162–178.

Offe, C., & Wiesenthal, H. (1985). Two logics of collective action. In C. Offe (Ed.), *Disorganized capitalism: Contemporary transformations of work and politics* (pp. 170–220). Cambridge, MA: MIT Press.

Petersson, O., Westholm, A., & Blomberg, G. (1989). *Medborgarnas makt.* Stockholm: Carlssons.

Weber, M. (1947). *The theory of social and economic action.* New York: Free Press.

11

Union Membership Behavior: The Influence of Instrumental and Value-Based Commitment

Magnus Sverke and Anders Sjöberg

S wedish unionism has many unique characteristics (Kjellberg, 1989), among them the high union density rate (around 84%), and the organization in just a few large unions in three national federations, one for blue-collar workers, one for white-collar workers, and one for professionals. Despite these specific attributes, there are important similarities between Sweden and most industrialized countries. Today, most unions, like Swedish unions, find themselves in a rapidly changing environment and are facing new challenges to the traditional ways of internal organization and task performance. The increase in alternative work arrangements (e.g., part-time employment), new information technology, globalization, and new management strategies to strengthen employees' commitment to the company (e.g., individual contracts) are all examples of factors that unions are confronting. One of the primary motives for the new managerialism is the recognition that the old control systems fail to develop the degree of employee involvement required in order to maximize efficiency in an increasingly competitive environment. The basis for organization is gradually shifting toward flexible specialization, market orientation, job-integrated structure, and coordinated independence of small semi-autonomous groups (Brulin & Nilsson, 1991; Heckscher, 1988).

The new managerial ideas have important consequences for unions. First, some modern enterprises seem to be able to make the union redundant, as the company becomes the object of collective identification (Boglind, 1989). Recent years have witnessed a development toward more direct participation for workers, partly at the expense of representative union participation (Abrahamsson, 1993a). Decentralization, corporate culture, and flattened hierarchies are some of the features characteristic of this development toward what Heckscher (1988) called high (company) commitment systems. A second consequence is that the decentralization of companies implies decision making at lower levels and, in turn, a decentralized bargaining structure. This represents a challenge to the internal organization and the centralized decision-making practices of many unions. In order to fulfill local level bargaining and to strengthen local union activity, unions have to rely on the allegiance and voluntary efforts of their members to an increasingly larger extent (Ahlén, 1992).

Although research in organizational psychology has traditionally focused on employees' work motivation and company attachment, psychologists have, after decades of neglecting labor unions, more and more turned their attention also to union-related attitudes and behaviors (Fullagar, 1986). In this respect, union commitment has become an important variable (Gordon & Nurick, 1981). However, although research on union commitment and union participation has burgeoned over the last few years, several questions remain unresolved. For example, although it has been recognized that unions, as voluntary organizations, require considerable membership participation to be effective, unions' needs for different membership behaviors in varying situations and under different circumstances have been less well addressed.

What is missing is a clear-cut theory describing the nature of union commitment and stating causal links between different types of commitment and different types of membership behavior (Sverke & Kuruvilla, in press). Furthermore, as noted by Gallagher and Strauss (1991), longitudinal research is required to widen the knowledge of commitment and participation and to test hypotheses about causality between the phenomena. Theory development and more longitudinal research would increase the knowledge about why members choose, or do not choose, to actively work for their unions. This is extremely important in times of changing employment relationships.

Different union purposes and actions require different kinds of union membership behavior, which, in turn, involve varying degrees of voluntary member efforts. Although for many of its members the union is merely a service agency, at critical moments the union is a social movement that must be able to mobilize its members into action, and even in its routine functioning the union needs voluntary activists to perform the daily tasks (Offe & Wiesenthal, 1980; Thompson, 1967). This implies that varying degrees of member effort are involved in membership behaviors. It also indicates not only that varying *degrees* of member commitment to the union are required for the fulfilling of different union activities, but also that different *types* of commitment, and possibly different combinations of commitment types, may have important consequences for individual members' decisions to perform or not perform various behaviors in favor of the union.

With the intent to extend the knowledge about the bases for member attachment to unions, Sverke and Abrahamsson (1993) and Sverke and Kuruvilla (in press) suggested a theoretical framework for union commitment based on a rationalistic assumption. The rationalistic approach addresses the nature of union commitment, suggests a typlogy of commitment patterns, and provides a model of commitment and membership behaviors. Two dimensions of commitment are identified, one of which is based on instrumentality (*instrumental rationality-based commitment to the union*) and the other based on value congruence between member and union (*value rationality-based commitment to the union*). These two dimensions are postulated to have different consequences for membership behavior. Moreover, different combinations of the commitment dimensions are proposed to relate differentially to various membership behaviors.

In the study reported here, several empirical examinations, based on longitudinal data from Swedish blue-collar unions, were conducted to establish the validity of the rationalistic approach. Our first purpose was to compare four groups, representing different combinations of instrumental and value rationality-based commitment, with respect to various membership behaviors. Our second was to conduct a formal test of a model of union commitment and membership behaviors. Although the first purpose focuses on a typology of commitment and the second purpose on a variable-based model, both examine the nature of commitment proposed by the rationalistic approach. Before we present the study methods and the results, we describe the rationalistic approach in more detail by focusing on the nature of union commitment, the commitment typology, and the proposed model of commitment and membership behavior.

THE RATIONALISTIC APPROACH TO COMMITMENT

The rationalistic assumption, which draws on the works of Abrahamsson (1993b), Ajzen and Fishbein (1980), Elster (1983), and Weber (1968), is a fundamental underpinning of our conceptualization of union commitment. First of all, it is assumed that before people act, they make systematic use of information available to them and then they decide either to engage or not to engage in a given behavior (Ajzen & Fishbein, 1980). Second, a certain degree of consistency is presupposed among an individual's beliefs as well as between these beliefs and the actions for which they are a cause (Elster, 1983). Furthermore, an action is to be viewed as rational if (a) it is oriented by a consciously, unambiguously formulated goal or value and (b) it uses the means that, according to available knowledge, best lead to the realization of the goal or value (Weber, 1968). This means that rationality is defined in terms of the actor and that an action can be rational even if the actor, because of a lack of knowledge, has not chosen the objectively most proper means to realize the goal or value. Finally, organizations are considered as instruments for realizing interests; individuals' rational strivings to realize their interests are assumed to lead to organized, collective action (Abrahamsson, 1993b). The rationalistic approach to union commitment identifies two forms in which such rational strivings may be expressed.

The Nature of Commitment

Sverke and Abrahamsson (1993) proposed two dimensions of union commitment that reflect Weber's (1968) rational foundations for social action: instrumental rationality and value-rationality. These two dimensions are proposed to be the key determinants for social action in organizations, such as labor unions, and to relate differentially to various membership behaviors. Both instrumental and ideological orientations have been recognized in earlier conceptualizations of union member attitudes and behaviors (Freeman & Medoff, 1984; Goldthorpe, Lockwood, Bechofer, & Platt, 1968; Newton & Shore, 1992), but the relative importance of instrumentality and ideology in the relationship between member and union is likely to vary between countries (Poole, 1981; Wheeler & McClendon, 1991). The rationalistic approach to union commitment embraces the possibilities and constraints that structure the relative importance of instrumental and ideological bases of social action.

Instrumental rationality-based commitment to the union reflects a utilitarian relationship between member and union. In Weberian (1968) terms, instrumental rationality involves rational considerations in which the end, the alternative means to the end, and the secondary results are all taken into account and weighed. Thus, the degree of instrumental rationality-based commitment to the union depends on conscious assessments of the costs and benefits associated with membership. This type of commitment is likely to develop if the individual member perceives the union as instrumental in satisfying certain salient goals defined by narrow self-interest.

Value rationality-based commitment to the union refers to the degree of value congruence between member and union. Value-rationality is denoted by "its clearly self-conscious formulation of the ultimate values governing the action and the consistently planned orientation of its detailed course to these values" (Weber, 1968, p. 25). This implies that union-related attitudes and behaviors may be determined by the belief in the value for its own sake of some cause, notwithstanding its prospects for success or satisfaction of self-interest needs. In referring to union ideology rather than to an exchange relationship with the union, value rationality-based commitment is assumed to be more long term and stable than instrumental rationality-based commitment.

Whereas members committed on an instrumental basis and members committed on a value-rational basis could both be expected to support certain union activities, the rationales underlying their support reflect varying degrees of responsibility associated with membership and, hence, will be markedly different. For example, although several of the members who express low degrees of commitment to the union in both dimensions could be expected to leave the union (in countries where that is an option), members with a unilateral commitment in either dimension are likely to remain as union members. They will, however, have different reasons for retaining membership. Instrumentally committed members stay because they evaluate the benefits associated with prolonged membership as exceeding the costs, whereas value-rationally committed members consider prolonged membership ideologically or morally right (Sverke & Abrahamsson, 1993).

Furthermore, value rationality-based commitment is proposed to be the key determinant of union activism. Because instrumental members will receive the same benefits whether they participate in union activities or not, instrumental rationality-based commitment is postulated to influence only such union activities that are aimed at satisfying goals defined by narrow self-interest and that involve little time and effort (cf. the logic of collective action advocated by Olson, 1971). However, unions require solidarity and an ideology, that is, a collective identity, to express the interests of their members; they "always find themselves forced to rely upon nonutilitarian forms of collective action" (Offe & Wiesenthal, 1980, pp. 78–79).

A Typology of Union Commitment

A schematic view of the present conceptualization is shown in Figure 1. The two axes in the figure represent the two commitment dimensions, which range from low (noncommitment) to high (commitment). Based on the combination of instrumental and value rationality-based commitment, the figure also presents a typology of patterns of union commitment.

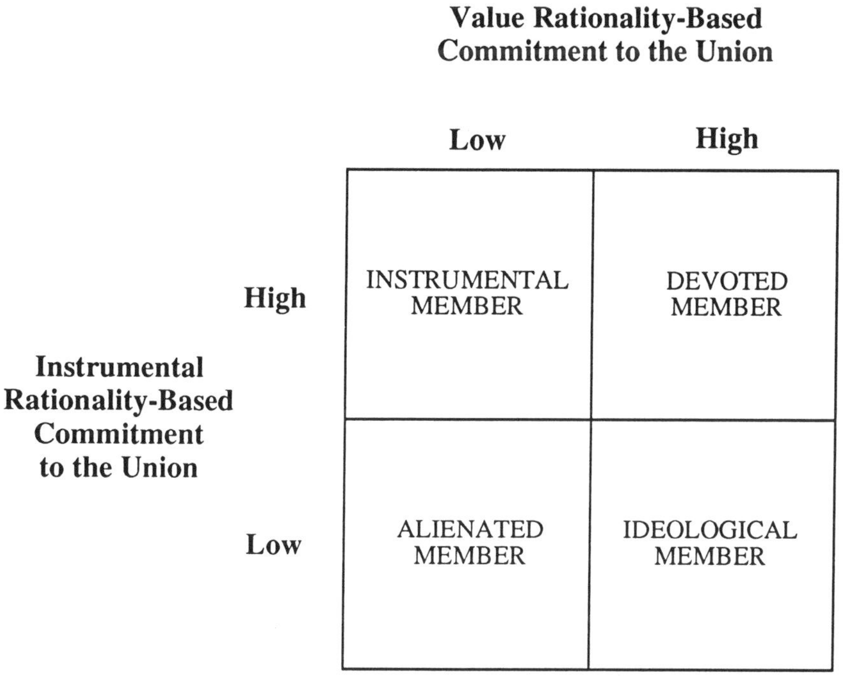

**Value Rationality-Based
Commitment to the Union**

		Low	High
High		INSTRUMENTAL MEMBER	DEVOTED MEMBER
Low		ALIENATED MEMBER	IDEOLOGICAL MEMBER

**Instrumental
Rationality-Based
Commitment
to the Union**

Figure 1

Patterns of instrumental and value rationality-based commitment to the union.

The term *alienated member* used in the figure refers to the category of noncommitted or alienated members who are likely to be nonpartic- ipative and who might intend to withdraw their membership. The mem- ber type characterized by a unilateral instrumental rationality-based commitment has been labeled *instrumental member* and reflects the "eco- nomic man" rationality suggested by Olson (1971). Instrumental mem- bers could be expected to retain membership and to support union ac- tivities directed at improving wages and working conditions. Members committed only on a value-rational basis (*ideological members*), due to their pro-union ideology, will support and take part in union activities. The *devoted member* category, representing members with high degrees of commitment in both dimensions, is postulated to contain the most active union members.

A Model of Commitment and Membership Behavior

Although instrumental and value rationality-based commitment are essential for the understanding of the various forms that member attachment to organizations can take, Sverke and Kuruvilla (in press) suggested an integration of the rationalistic approach with the theory of reasoned action (Ajzen & Fishbein, 1980; Fishbein & Ajzen; 1975) in order to develop a model of union commitment and membership behavior. The theory of reasoned action has gained increased interest among researchers studying union commitment (Kelloway & Barling, 1993; Kuruvilla & Sverke, 1993).

There are several advantages of the theory of reasoned action in comparison with traditional approaches to attitude–behavior research. First, it proposes a causal chain of variables that influence behavior. According to the theory, the immediate determinant of behavior is the prior intention to perform, or not perform, that behavior. The behavioral intention is, in turn, influenced by two prior factors: an expectancy-value attitude toward performing the behavior (i.e., beliefs about the consequences of a certain behavior weighted by evaluations of these expected outcomes) and a subjective norm (i.e., internalized perceived social pressures from important others regarding the performance of the actual behavior). Thus, a second advantage is that the theory takes into account perceptions of social pressures. Third, the theory of reasoned action explains how behavioral intentions are formed. Before formulating a behavioral intention, the individual is assumed to consciously consider the relative importance of the attitude and the subjective norm. Therefore, the theory of reasoned action is also consistent with the rationalistic approach, because it rests on the assumption that most actions are rational.

The primary feature distinguishing Sverke and Kuruvilla's (in press) integrated model from the traditional Fishbein and Ajzen (1975) model is that the behavioral intentions are seen not only as a function of subjective norms and an instrumental attitude (instrumental rationality-based commitment), but also of a second attitude of a different nature, that is, an attitude based on ideology and values (value rationality-based commitment). Sverke and Kuruvilla's model is also different from other commitment–participation models based on the theory of reasoned action. Kelloway and Barling (1993), for instance, who relied on a modified version of the theory, postulated subjective norms to have a direct influence on both attitudinal and intentional dimensions of commitment. The major difference between the two models is that they are based on differing conceptualizations and operationalizations of union commitment. Whereas Kelloway and Barling (1993) relied on an empirically derived conceptualization in which a general behavioral intention is seen as a commitment dimension, Sverke and Kuruvilla (in press) relied on a theoretically derived conceptualization in which the behavioral intentions are seen as outcomes of commitment.

The theory of reasoned action allows for studying specific as well as general behavioral intentions as long as the intentions correspond to the level of specificity or generality of the behavioral criterion (Ajzen & Fishbein, 1980). The study of specific intentions requires that the intentions be treated as outcomes of commitment. Therefore, the integration of the theory of reasoned action with the rationalistic approach to union commitment provides the researcher with flexibility to study either a general pro-union behavioral intention or a variety of intentions referring to specific behaviors relevant to the union (Sverke & Kuruvilla, in press).

More specifically, Sverke and Kuruvilla's (1993) integrated theory posits that value rationality-based commitment influences both members' willingness to retain membership and their intentions to participate in union activities, whereas instrumental rationality-based commitment is proposed to affect only the decision to remain a member. Subjective norms are suggested to affect both the participation and the membership retention intentions. Consistent with the Fishbein and Ajzen (1975) framework, the commitment dimensions are proposed to influence behavior only indirectly, that is, through the pro-union behavioral intentions.

METHOD

Participants and Procedure

The data for this study were collected in the first and second waves of a Swedish longitudinal research project on union member attitudes (Emerging Union Structures [the EMUS Project]). Two percent of the members (pensioners excluded) of three blue-collar unions (the Swedish Clothing Workers Union, the Swedish Food Workers Union, and the Swedish Factory Workers Union), all affiliated to the Swedish Trade Union Confederation (LO), were sampled in September 1991. Time 1 data were collected in the winter of 1991–1992; Time 2 data were collected approximately 18 months later (summer 1993). Although two of the unions (clothing and factory) were officially merged in 1993, results reported by Sverke, Kuruvilla, and Sjöberg (1994) reveal no differences in commitment, subjective norms, pro-union behavioral intentions, or union particpation between the merged and nonmerged unions at either of the time points.

Questionnaires were mailed to the home addresses of the participants, accompanied by cover letters explaining the purpose of the project and ensuring the confidentiality of the responses, and were returned to the research team in self-addressed, return-postage-paid envelopes. In Wave 1 a total of 2,831 questionnaires were distributed. Of these, 1,684 were returned (59.5%); the exclusion of blank and incomplete questionnaires resulted in 1,486 usable questionnaires (52.5%). Two analyses examining the representativeness of the sample were conducted. The first of these showed that the three union subsamples did not deviate significantly from their respective unions regarding mean age and gender distribution. The second, which was based on telephone interviews with 5% of the nonrespondents, revealed only minor differences between respondents and nonrespondents in terms of the variables used in the present study. Interestingly, nonrespondents had significantly ($p < .05$) higher means in value-based union commitment and membership intention items, and a larger percentage of the respondents attended union meetings regularly ($p < .05$).

Wave 2 questionnaires were distributed only to those 1,486 individuals who provided usable responses in the first wave. Of those, 1,170 (78.7%) respondents provided usable questionnaires in the second wave. Thus, the individuals used in the present study represent 41.3% of those initially selected for the survey. The average age, company tenure, and national union tenure were 41.36 ($SD = 12.91$), 11.78 ($SD = 9.20$), and

12.65 ($SD = 10.10$) years, respectively; 58% of the respondents were male. Using Time 1 data, comparisons of Time 2 respondents and nonrespondents did not suggest any significant differences in union commitment, subjective norms, behavioral intentions, or union participation measures (Sverke et al., 1994). However, the Wave 2 nonrespondents were significantly older ($p < .001$) and had spent a few more years in their unions ($p < .001$) as compared with the Wave 2 respondents.

Measures

Unless stated otherwise, responses on all items were made on Likert scales ranging from 1 (*strongly disagree*) to 5 (*strongly agree*). Indexes were constructed by summing the responses on items and then dividing by the number of items. Table 1 presents descriptive statistics, reliability estimates, and variable intercorrelations for both Time 1 and Time 2, as well as test–retest reliabilities for all variables measured at both time points.

Union commitment. Nine items from a scale developed by Sverke and Sjöberg (1994) were used to measure value rationality-based commitment (e.g., "My union and I have approximately the same basic values"; $\alpha = .91$ at both time points). A 7-item scale (Sverke & Kuruvilla, in press) developed in accordance with Ajzen and Fishbein's (1980) operationalization of instrumental attitudes was used to measure instrumental rationality-based commitment (αs $= .85$ at Time 1 and $.89$ at Time 2). Thus, each instrumental commitment item was assessed as the product of a behavioral belief (e.g., "My union's chances of improving my pay are great") and a corresponding outcome evaluation (e.g., "To get better paid is. . ."; rated on a scale ranging from *very unimportant* [1] to *very important* [5]). In order to equalize this scale with the other scales used (i.e., to achieve a final scale in which the values could range from 1 to 5), the square roots of the products were used for index construction. Results of confirmatory factor analysis studies (Sverke & Kuruvilla, in press) have demonstrated support for the hypothesized two-dimensional representation of union commitment.

To operationalize the typology of commitment patterns suggested by

Table 1

Descriptive Statistics and Variable Intercorrelations for Time 1 (Below the Diagonal) and Time 2 (Above the Diagonal)

Variable	Time 1 M	SD	α	1	2	3	4	5	6	7	8	9	10
1. Value rationality-based union commitment	2.48	0.94	.91	(.72)	.66	.45	.53	.57	.35	.26	.26	.32	−.01
2. Instrumental rationality-based union commitment	3.32	0.65	.85	.64	(.57)	.35	.42	.38	.24	.13	.10	.19	.02
3. Subjective norm	3.04	0.95	.80	.45	.37	(.51)	.27	.27	.14	.11	.12	.20	.02
4. Membership intention	3.96	1.21	.84	.57	.47	.31	(.59)	.24	.12	.14	.06	.11	.02
5. Activity intention	2.71	1.02	.58	.66	.43	.30	.35	(.55)	.41	.32	.37	.34	−.00
6. Union office intention	1.70	1.14	—	.42	.31	.19	.17	.49	(.51)	.22	.27	.23	−.01
7. Administrative participation	1.20	0.35	.74	.35	.16	.15	.15	.40	.29	(.61)	.50	.31	−.05
8. Occasional participation	1.26	0.28	.76	.37	.14	.17	.14	.43	.32	.55	(.63)	.54	−.07
9. Supportive participation	1.51	0.28	.62	.37	.18	.21	.15	.42	.33	.39	.57	(.55)	−.03
10. Membership turnover	—	—	—	—	—	—	—	—	—	—	—	—	(—)
M (Time 2)				2.68	3.38	3.06	4.17	2.89	1.74	1.17	1.24	1.50	1.09
SD (Time 2)				0.92	0.68	0.85	1.04	0.93	1.10	0.37	0.28	0.28	0.29
α (Time 2)				.91	.89	.75	.78	.42	—	—	.79	.60	—

NOTE: Test–retest reliabilities are given in the diagonal in parentheses. For $r \geq .06$, $p < 0.05$; $r \geq .08$, $p < .01$; $r \geq .10$, $p < .001$; scale ranges = 1–5 (Variables 1–6); 1–2 (Variables 7–10).

the rationalistic approach (see Figure 1), each Time 1 commitment dimension was also bifurcated at its mean value (Ms = 3.32 and 2.48 for instrumental and value rationality-based commitment, respectively). A combination of these dichotomized variables resulted in the four union commitment patterns, namely alienated member (values below the mean in both dimensions; n = 449), instrumental member (unilateral instrumental rationality-based commitment; n = 182), ideological member (unilateral value rationality-based commitment; n = 130), and devoted member (values greater than or equal to the mean in both dimensions; n = 367).

Subjective norms. To assess subjective norms, we followed Ajzen and Fishbein's (1980) definition of subjective norms (i.e., as the product of normative beliefs and motivations to comply), which has previously been used in studies of union commitment and participation (Kelloway & Barling, 1993). The scale included three normative belief items (e.g., "My co-workers think that I should be a union member") multiplied by their corresponding compliance items (e.g., "How much do you want to do what your co-workers think you should do?"; scale ranging from 1, *not at all*, to 5, *very much*). Also for this variable the square root of the products were used for index construction, and the resulting three-item scale demonstrated adequate internal consistency (αs = .80 at Time 1, .85 at Time 2).

Pro-union behavioral intentions. Three behavioral intention scales developed by Sverke and Kuruvilla (in press) were used in this study. Membership intention, that is, the intention to remain a union member, was measured by three items (αs = .84 and .78 at Time 1 and Time 2, respectively). A two-item scale was used to measure activity intention, that is, a general willingness to take active part in the daily union work (αs = .58 and .42 at the two time points, respectively). The intention to hold union office was measured by a single item.

Union participation. Three scales developed by Sverke and Kuruvilla (in press) and reflecting varying natures of participation (i.e., administrative, occasional, and supportive participation; McShane, 1986) were used in the study. Responses on items were coded 1 = *no* and 2 = *yes*, summed, and divided by the number of items to create participation sub-scales. Administrative participation, that is, whether or not the respondent had any representative position in the union, was measured by two items at Time 1 (α = .74) and a single item at Time 2. Occasional participation was measured by six items in which the respondents were asked to indicate whether they had, for instance, attended union meetings and taken part in bargaining during the past year (αs = .76 at Time 1 and .79 at Time 2). Supportive participation was assessed with five items; the respondents were asked to indicate whether they had been involved in any of the following activities during the past year: discussed union issues with colleagues, discussed union issues with union representatives, participated in a union study circle, read through the collective agreement, and read the union newsletter (αs = .62 for Time 1, .60 for Time 2).

Membership turnover. Union membership turnover, the only variable measured solely at Time 2, was assessed by two separate items asking the respondents about their current union affiliation. On the basis of these responses, a dichotomous variable was constructed (1 = *the respondent is no longer a member of the union he or she was affiliated with at Time 1; 2 = still a member of the same union*).

RESULTS

Commitment Groups and Membership Behaviors

To address the first purpose of the study, analyses of variance and multiple comparisons (Scheffé post hoc tests) were computed to examine whether the four commitment groups (Time 1) differed with respect to subsequent (Time 2) pro-union behavioral intentions, union participation, and membership turnover. These results are presented in Table 2.

As can be seen from Table 2, the *F* tests indicate that there were overall significant differences between the commitment patterns regarding all participation and intention variables. In general, these results indicate that the means were lowest for alienated and instrumental members and highest for ideological and devoted members. Members in commitment groups characterized by a high degree of value rationality-based commitment

Table 2

Tests for Mean Differences in Pro-Union Behavioral Intentions, Union Participation, and Membership Turnover (Time 2) for Groups with Different Combinations of Instrumental and Value Rationality-Based Commitment to the Union (Time 1)

	Commitment group (Time 1)					
	Alienated member	Instrumental member	Ideological member	Devoted member		Multiple
Variable (Time 2)	(1)	(2)	(3)	(4)	F	comparisons
Activity intention	2.50	2.74	3.02	3.39	72.75*	(1,2)(1,3)(1,4)(2,4)(3,4)
Membership intention	3.74	4.17	4.50	4.58	53.15*	(1,2)(1,3)(1,4)(2,3)(2,4)
Union office intention	1.49	1.57	1.92	2.08	22.12*	(1,3)(1,4)(2,4)
Administrative participation	1.11	1.11	1.20	1.26	12.86*	(1,4)(2,4)
Occasional participation	1.19	1.20	1.26	1.31	12.93*	(1,4)(2,4)
Supportive participation	1.44	1.47	1.54	1.57	17.67*	(1,3)(1,4)(2,4)
Membership turnover	1.11	1.08	1.08	1.09	0.64	—

NOTE: Degrees of freedom for the F tests are 3, 1082. For the multiple comparisons (Scheffé post hoc tests), the numbers in parantheses indicate that the difference between groups with corresponding numbers is significant at the .05 level.
*$p < .001$.

tended, as expected, to be more active and more willing to participate in union activities in comparison with members in commitment patterns defined by low levels of value-based commitment.

As to the intention to hold union office, the post hoc test implied that members in the devoted member quadrant were more willing to hold union office than are members in commitment quadrants represented by low degrees of value-based commitment. For the remaining two intention variables (activity intention and membership intention), the differences between commitment groups were more pronounced, and the post hoc tests identified significant differences between almost all groups. These results indicate that members with high levels of value rationality-based commitment had stronger pro-union behavioral intentions than their fellow members expressing low degrees of value-based commitment.

For the participation variables, the post hoc tests revealed significant differences between the two patterns representing low degrees of value rationality-based commitment (alienated members and instrumental members), on one hand, and the group with high degrees of commitment in both dimensions (devoted members), on the other. Consistent with our postulations, these tests also indicated that there were no significant differences between alienated members and instrumental members in terms of union participation. Thus, members with a low degree of value rationality-based commitment tended, regardless of their degree of instrumental commitment, to be less participative than members high in value-based commitment. However, the post hoc tests generally failed to support that ideological members were more participative than alienated members and instrumental members.

In terms of membership turnover, a total of 91 individuals had left their Time 1 union at Time 2. Of these, a majority reported that they left the union in connection with changes in terms of employment, such as switching occupation ($n = 36$), changing work tasks ($n = 5$), or changing employer ($n = 11$); others left due to unemployment ($n = 4$) or retirement ($n = 21$), or reported dissatisfaction with the union ($n = 3$) or other reasons ($n = 11$) as the motive. However, in Sweden a change of employer, occupational branch, or job may automatically imply a change of national union affiliation. Of the 91 individuals who had left their Time 1 unions, 60 had switched to other national unions for such reasons; only 31 individuals had left the union movement as a whole, 21 of these in connection with retirement. The low variation in membership turnover is reflected in the nonsignificant ($p > .05$) mean differences between the commitment groups.

The Commitment–Behavior Model

The second purpose of the study—to test a model of union commitment and membership behaviors—was addressed using a structural equation model. Structural equation modeling is delineated by (a) the estimation of multiple interrelated dependency relationships and (b) the ability to represent unobserved concepts (e.g., attitudes). Generally, structural equation modelling can be compared with regression analysis with less restrictive assumptions that allow measurement error in the independent as well as the dependent variables (Bollen, 1989).

The hypothesized model was tested using the maximum-likelihood estimation procedures of LISREL 8 (Jöreskog & Sörbom, 1993). The latent variable methods of LISREL involve a structural model (often referred to as the "causal" model; Bentler, 1980) and two measurement models (one for the exogenous [independent] variables and one for the endogenous [dependent] variables). The measurement models can be seen as confirmatory factor analyses of the hypothesized relationships between the latent (unobserved) factors, represented by circles, and the manifest (observed) variables, represented by rectangles, whereas the structural model represents the hypothesized causal relationships among the latent factors. We specified the measurement models such that the Time 1 measures were used for the commitment dimensions, subjective norms, and the intention variables and Time 2 measures were used for the membership behaviors. As to the structural model, the commitment dimensions and subjective norms were hypothesized to influence the behaviors only indirectly through behavioral intentions.

The matrix of observed covariances among model variables served as input for the structural equation analysis. On the basis of the specified, hypothesized relationships between these variables, LISREL produces an estimated matrix of covariances between the model variables. A hypothesized model is viewed as plausible, that is, to fit the data, if the difference between the estimated matrix and the matrix of observed covariances is small as signified through chi-square and several fit indexes.

Although the chi-square statistic for the hypothesized model, $\chi^2(395, N = 1,118) = 1,553.76$, $p < .001$, indicates a lack of fit of model to data, the comparison of the hypothesized model with a baseline model, in which no structural relationships between the variables were estimated, indicates that the hypothesized model provides a substantial and significant improvement in fit over the baseline model, $\Delta\chi^2(100, N = 1,118) = 15,252.41$, $p < .001$. However, the chi-square statistic, which is dependent on sample size, tends to be significant for large samples even if the fit of the model is only reasonable. Therefore, to assess the fit of the hypothesized model we also relied on several other fit indexes provided by LISREL, such as the goodness-of-fit index (GFI), the adjusted goodness-of-fit index (AGFI), the root mean square residual (RMSR), and the root mean square error of approximation (RMSEA). All these fit indexes for the hypothesized model are within acceptable standards and indicate good fit of the model to data (GFI = .90, AGFI = .89, RMSR = .06, RMSEA = .05), thus providing support for the model suggested by the rationalistic approach.

Figure 2 presents the LISREL estimates of the parameters in the hypothesized model. Standardized results are presented in order to facilitate comparisons of parameter estimates. We first turn our attention to the measurement models. The left side of the figure contains the relationships between the exogenous factors (value rationality-based commitment, instrumental rationality-based commitment, subjective norm) and the measures used to tap these factors; the right side shows the relationships between the endogenous factors (participation intention, membership intention, union participation, membership turnover) and their observed counterparts. As is apparent from the figure, all loadings of observed variables on latent factors are substantial and statistically significant, which supports the operationalization of the model variables.

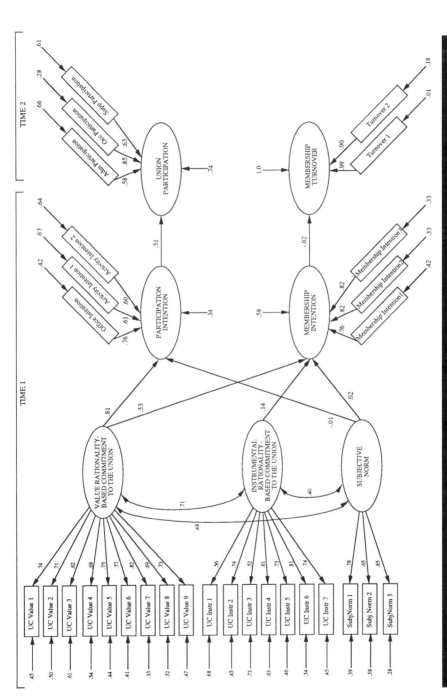

Figure 2

Standardized parameter estimates for the hypothesized model ($N = 1,118$).

In terms of the structural model, that is, the proposed relationships among the latent factors, consistent with the hypothesized model, value rationality-based commitment significantly predicts the participation and membership intentions in the model (in both cases, $p < .001$). The strong positive influence of this commitment dimension on the intention variables indicates that the more value-rationality committed members are, the more likely it is that they are willing to retain membership and to participate in union activities.

Also consistent with the predictions, instrumental rationality-based commitment significantly predicts membership intention ($p < .001$), indicating that willingness to remain a union member increases with higher levels of instrumental commitment. In accordance with the postulations of the rationalistic approach to commitment, the relationship between instrumental commitment and the intention to participate was not estimated in the hypothesized model. However, freeing the parameter for the effect of instrumental commitment on participation intention does not result in a significant parameter estimate ($p > .05$) or in a significant improvement in fit of the model to data, $\Delta\chi^2(1, N = 1,118) = 2.11, p > .05$. Unexpectedly, however, the subjective norm does not predict any of the pro-union behavioral intentions.

The relationships between the behavioral intentions and the actual behaviors are partly consistent with the hypothesized model because the participation intention significantly predicts union participation ($p < .001$); however, the membership intention does not predict membership turnover ($p > .05$). These results indicate a fair degree of intention–behavior consistency in terms of union particpation (the intention to participate has a strong positive influence on actual participation in the model), but not in terms of turnover (the intention to retain membership is unrelated to actual membership retention in the model possibly due to the distribution on actual turnover). In total, the model variables account for 66% of the variance in the participation intention, 42% in the membership intention, and 26% in union participation. The variance in membership turnover was not accounted for at all by the model.

DISCUSSION

The overall intent of this study was to address several implications of the rationalistic approach to union commitment by conducting empirical examinations of a typology of union commitment and testing a model of commitment and membership behavior. A central finding is that instrumental and value rationality-based commitment are dimensions of union commitment with different implications for union membership behavior.

The typological results clearly indicate that the four commitment patterns identified by the rationalistic approach represent members differentially involved in union activities with differing strengths in pro-union behavioral intentions. Members with high levels of value rationality-based commitment not only tend to participate in more union activities, but also are more willing to retain their memberships, in comparison with members expressing lower levels of value-based commitment. Moreover, members committed solely on an instrumental basis tend to be willing to participate only in union activities that involve little time and effort.

Although the fact that we artificially dichotomized the continuous commitment scales can be questioned from a statistical perspective (Maxwell & Delaney, 1993), we believe that the typology suggested by the rationalistic approach may be a useful tool for unions. It facilitates the ways of thinking about possible patterns of attachment to unions, provides a means for categorizing members, and can be used as a basis for discussions on how to change the patterns of commitment. The typology can be used to identify subgroups of members expressing a certain pattern of commitment and serve as a guide for focused campaigns aimed at, for instance, recruiting voluntary officials or increasing meeting attendance. However, future research is needed to establish more objective cut-off points to operationalize the typology (cf. Gordon & Ladd, 1990; Sverke & Sjöberg, 1994).

The test of the hypothesized model provides empirical support for several of the causal relationships suggested by the rationalistic approach to union commitment. Value rationality-based union commitment was found to be a strong predictor of intentions to participate and, in turn, of union participation. Furthermore, both commitment dimensions, as expected, predicted the membership retention intention. This is consistent with previous research (Klandermans, 1989), in which union commitment has been found to be negatively related to the intent to withdraw from membership.

Although our model variables accounted for a relatively large proportion of variance in membership intentions, we did not find a significant relationship between the membership intention and actual membership retention. However, only a very small percentage of the respondents had left their unions between Time 1 and Time 2; the majority of those had not left the union movement as a whole, but only switched union affiliations as a function of changed terms of employment. Future research efforts are needed to examine the intention–behavior consistency in terms of membership turnover decisions.

Contrary to the propositions of the theoretical framework, subjective norms, that is, the internalized social pressures, did not predict the intentions to retain membership and to participate. A plausible explanation for the nonsignificant effect of subjective norms is that the required levels of specificity were absent in our measures. Although the theory of reasoned action (Ajzen & Fishbein, 1980; Fishbein & Ajzen, 1975) requires the measurement of subjective norms that correspond to specific behaviors in order to find a predictive effect on the behavioral intentions, we used an operationalization of subjective norms that assessed the respondent's general perception that important others desire him or her to be a union member. Ajzen and Fishbein (1980, p. 58) noted that "variations in any of the four elements defining the behavior (i.e., action, target, context, and time) may influence the relative importance of the attitudinal and normative components." This points to a potential risk that the exogenous variables in our model (i.e., commitment dimensions and subjective norms) were not operationalized with equivalent care (Cooper & Richardson, 1986).

However, our findings are consistent with previous research in which the theory of reasoned action has been used to understand membership behaviors. Although Kelloway and Barling (1993) found support for a strong impact of a participation intention (willingness to work for the union) on union participation, they, too, reported a nonsignificant effect of subjective norms on the behavioral intention in one of their two samples. It is for future research to examine the relationships between subjective norms and behavioral intentions.

Although our findings suggest that both types of commitment may be sufficient for the willingness to retain membership, the results also indicate that members committed solely on an instrumental basis cannot be relied on to do voluntary work for the union. Although Kelloway and Barling (1993) found a commitment dimension partly based on instrumentality (union loyalty) to be predictive of the willingness to work for the union, our findings suggest that value rationality-based commitment is a central determinant of members' willingness to participate in union activities. However, the relative impacts of instrumental and value-based commitment on membership behavior may vary between cultural settings (Sverke & Kuruvilla, in press).

The implication for unions is quite significant, because our results suggest that members who are more ideologically committed to the union can be counted on to really work for the union, whereas members whose commitment is based on instrumental reasons are less likely to do so. It is the value-based type of commitment that unions should engender if increased activism is the goal. This implies that unions in many countries may have to revise their strategies for creating member attachment, that is, to more explicitly try to build a commitment based on union ideology (Goldthorpe et al., 1968; Offe & Wiesenthal, 1980).

Our findings raise questions about how value-based commitment can be developed. We believe that issues such as the union agenda and the union culture can have important consequences for the types and levels of members' attachment and involvement in the union. It is also possible that a number of structural characteristics, such as union size, the nature of the union's internal organization, and the degree of decentralization, can prove to be important in explaining the development of commitment.

In general, the results reported in this study provide empirical support for the theoretical framework suggested by Sverke and Abrahamsson (1993) and Sverke and Kuruvilla (in press). Although we claim that the rationalistic approach has a wide relevance, future research also should examine whether the results reported here generalize to white-collar unions and professional unions and to countries with other union traditions. The emphasis on both instrumental-rational and value-rational movers of orientation has wide implications. The rationalistic approach appears to provide a relevant theoretical framework for union commitment research in countries where both instrumental and noninstrumental attitudes are important aspects of the union movement.

REFERENCES

Abrahamsson, B. (1993a). Union structural change. *Economic and Industrial Democracy, 14,* 399–421.

Abrahamsson, B. (1993b). *Why organizations? How and why people organize.* Newbury Park, CA: Sage.

Ahlén, K. (1992, March). *Union legitimacy: Members perceptions of union government.* Paper presented at the Symposium on Emerging Union Structures: An International Comparison, Clark University Worcester, MA.

Ajzen, I., & Fishbein, M. (1980). *Understanding attitudes and predicting social behavior.* Englewood Cliffs, NJ: Prentice Hall.

Bentler, P. M. (1980). Multivariate analyses with latent variables: Causal modeling. *Annual Review of Psychology, 31,* 419–456.

Boglind, A. (1989). *Tjänstemännen, facket och företaget: En diskussion om förutsättningarna för facklig organisering i moderna företag.* Göteborg, Sweden: Prisma.

Bollen, K. A. (1989). *Structural equations with latent variables.* New York: Wiley.

Brulin, G., & Nilsson, T. (1991). From societal to managerial corporatism: New forms of work organization as a transformation vehicle. *Economic and Industrial Democracy, 12,* 327–347.

Cooper, W. H., & Richardson, A. J. (1986). Unfair comparisons. *Journal of Applied Psychology, 71,* 179–184.

Elster, J. (1983). *Sour grapes: Studies in the subversion of rationality.* Cambridge, England: Cambridge University Press.

Fishbein, M., & Ajzen, I. (1975). *Belief, attitude, intention and behavior: An introduction to theory and research.* Reading, MA: Addison-Wesley.

Freeman, R. B., & Medoff, J. L. (1984). *What do unions do?* New York: Basic Books.

Fullagar, C. (1986). A factor analytic study on the validity of a union commitment scale. *Journal of Applied Psychology, 71,* 129–136.

Gallagher, D. G., & Strauss, G. (1991). Union membership attitudes and participation. In G. Strauss, D. G. Gallagher, & J. Fiorito (Eds.), *The state of the unions* (pp. 139–174). Madison, WI: Industrial Relations Research Association.

Goldthorpe, J. H., Lockwood, D., Bechofer, F., & Platt, J. (1968). *The affluent worker: Industrial attitudes and behavior.* Cambridge, England: Cambridge University Press.

Gordon, M. E., & Ladd, R. T. (1990). Dual allegiance: Renewal, reconsideration and recantation. *Personnel Psychology, 43,* 37–64.

Gordon, M. E., & Nurick, A. J. (1981). Psychological approaches to the study of unions and union–management relations. *Psychological Bulletin, 90,* 292–307.

Heckscher, C. C. (1988). *The new unionism: Employee involvement in the changing corporation.* New York: Basic Books.

Jöreskog, K.-G., & Sörbom, D. (1993). *LISREL 8: Users guide.* Chicago: Scientific Software International.

Kelloway, E. K., & Barling, J. (1993). Members' participation in local union activities: Measurement, prediction, and replication. *Journal of Applied Psychology, 78,* 262–279.

Kjellberg, A. (1993). *Facklig organisering: tolv Länder* [Trade union organization in 12 countries]. Lund, Sweden: Arkiv.

Klandermans, B. (1989). Union commitment: Replications and tests in the Dutch context. *Journal of Applied Psychology, 74,* 869–875.

Kuruvilla, S., & Sverke, M. (1993). Two dimensions of union commitment based on the theory of reasoned action: Cross-cultural comparisons. *Research and Practice in Human Resource Management, 1,* 1–16.

Maxwell, S. E., & Delaney, H. D. (1993). Bivariate median splits and spurious statistical significance. *Psychological Bulletin, 113,* 181–190.

McShane, S. L. (1986). The multidimensionality of union participation. *Journal of Occupational Psychology, 59,* 177–187.

Newton, L. A., & Shore, L. M. (1992). A model of union membership: Instrumentality, commitment, and opposition. *Academy of Management Review, 17,* 275–298.

Offe, C., & Wiesenthal, H. (1980). Two logics of collective action: Theoretical notes on social class and organizational form. In M. Zeitlin (Ed.), *Political power and social theory* (pp. 67–115). Los Angeles: University of California.

Olson, M. (1971). *The logic of collective action: Public goods and the theory of groups.* Cambridge, MA: Harvard University Press.

Poole, M. (1981). *Theories of trade unionism: A sociology of industrial relations.* London: Routledge & Kegan Paul.

Sverke, M., & Abrahamsson, B. (1993). *Union commitment: A conceptualization based on instrumental and value rationality* (Research Report). Stockholm: Swedish Center for Working Life.

Sverke, M., & Kuruvilla, S. (in press). A new conceptualization of union commitment: Development and test of an integrated theory. *Journal of Organizational Behavior.*

Sverke, M., Kuruvilla, S., & Sjöberg, A. (1994). Union commitment, participation, and membership turnover in Sweden: A longitudinal study. In P. B. Voos (Ed.), *Proceedings of the Forty-Sixth Annual Meeting, Industrial Relations Research Association Series* (pp. 432–441). Madison, WI: Industrial Relations Research Association.

Sverke, M., & Sjöberg, A. (1994). Dual commitment to company and union in Sweden: An examination of predictors and taxonomic split methods. *Economic and Industrial Democracy, 15,* 531–564.

Thompson, J. (1967). *Organizations in action.* New York: McGraw-Hill.

Weber, M. (1968). *Economy and society.* Berkeley: University of California Press.

Wheeler, H. N., & McClendon, J. A. (1991). The individual decision to unionize. In G. Strauss, D. G. Gallagher, & J. Fiorito (Eds.), *The state of the unions* (pp. 47–83). Madison, WI: Industrial Relations Research Association.

12

Participation in Trade Unions in The Netherlands: Women and Part-Time Workers

Annelies Daalder

This chapter focuses on union participation rates of women and part-time workers in The Netherlands. As in many other countries, the composition of the labor force in The Netherlands has been changing rapidly, with increasing participation of women and part-time workers. At the same time, unemployment remains high and there has been a decline in union density. To set the backdrop for the present study, a brief description of employment relations in The Netherlands is provided. This is followed by a study of participation by women and part-time workers in unions in The Netherlands.

THE DUTCH EXPERIENCE

The Netherlands is a small country, with a population of more than 15 million. It has a relatively weak industrial base, less than 20% of the total labor force, and a small number of multinational firms employ half the industrial workforce (Visser, 1992). Compared with other countries, The Netherlands has a far more developed welfare state (e.g., we have Social Security and health care systems).

Since the end of the nineteenth century, social, cultural, and political activities and services have been organized by segments. Dutch society was "pillarized," and the four pillars, based on ideology and religion, were the Catholic, Protestant, socialist, and liberal segments of society (Lijphart, 1968). Within each of the segments, a high degree of elite control existed. A rigid separation at the lower level coexisted with cooperation of elites through interlocking directorates. Not until about 1970 did the pillarization start to decrease.

In the trade union movement this pillarization led to the creation of three separate central organizations: the social democratic Netherlands Federation of Trade Unions (NVV), the Netherlands Catholic Federation of Trade Unions (NKV), and the Netherlands Federation of Protestant Christian Trade Unions (CNV; Albeda, 1987). The social democratic NVV and the Catholic NKV worked together closely starting in 1976 and merged in 1982 to form the Dutch Federation of Trade Unions (FNV). The FNV unions together represent a majority of Dutch union members, about 60%. The Protestant CNV remained independent. In 1975, a new federation for clerical and managerial staff, the Federation of White-Collar Staff Organizations (MHP), was founded. A new federation of relatively small, mainly public and semi-public employee unions (AVC) was founded in 1990. Negotiations for a merger between the AVC and the FNV are currently at an advanced stage.

Trade unions vary greatly in size, from about 310,000 members in the union for civil servants to less than 1,000 members in the union for professional sportsmen. Also, the structure of unions in The Netherlands results in the fact that people working in the same company at the same level are often members of different unions. Although most of the time unions join each other in negotiations, sometimes the unions are not in agreement, and it is possible for employers to settle with only one of the unions involved. Trade unions within Dutch society also are strongly institutionalized, and for Dutch unions, "free riding" is a serious problem. Collective bargaining laws prevent discrimination between members and nonmembers, which intensifies the "public good" problem in union organizations, and there is no union-based system of grievance-handling in The Netherlands (see Olson, 1965). Union attempts to make nonmembers pay for their services have not been successful.

Between 1945 and 1979 unions organized a stable proportion of Dutch employees, around 35–40%. In the 1980s, the number of members of Dutch trade unions decreased tremendously, with the union density rate dropping to 24% of the labor force. These declines were experienced in all sectors and occupational groups, and all unions within all federations lost members. Several factors played a part in the trade union decline. There was a steep rise in unemployment in the early 1980s as well as a reduction of manual employment. Because unemployment insurance and labor exchange are state-administered activities in The Netherlands, Dutch unions had little to offer their members who became unemployed. Furthermore, econometric analysis of union growth shows a strong relationship with inflation (Visser, 1987), and inflation in The Netherlands fell sharply in the 1980s. Thus, the benefits for which workers tend to credit unions may have been reduced by the absence of wage increases in the 1980s. This econometric analysis also suggests that union growth in The Netherlands came to its saturation point relatively early. This might have been caused by a high degree of institutional security of Dutch unions in the past (Visser, 1990).

In 1987 the decline of trade union membership came to an end. After a year of small losses in 1986, all confederations made membership gains. However, because employment increased at a faster rate than union membership, union density continued to decline. A few years later membership gains exceeded employment growth and union density started to rise slightly, reaching 26% in 1994. At the moment union density seems to have stabilized.

Employers in The Netherlands also are well organized. Nearly all large firms (100 or more employees) are members of an association for employers. Like trade unions, employers also have been organized according to the pillarization described above. In 1970, the Catholic and Protestant federations merged into the Christian Employers' Federation (NCW), which forms the counterpart of the liberal Federation of Dutch Enterprises (VNO). Small firms are less organized, but some federations exist among them with strong ties to Christian and liberal political parties. Trade unions and employers' associations interact with each other and with the state in a number of national advisory boards.

The Netherlands has one of the lowest labor force participation rates in the Organization of Economic Cooperation and Development (OECD; Visser, 1992). Unemployment is high, rising from 4% in 1979 to 14% in 1984. After 1987 unemployment fell, but it is difficult to interpret the change in unemployment rates because the official definitions on which the Dutch statistics are based were changed a couple of times during this period. The current rate of 7.5% (1993) also is not comparable with other countries because about a third of the unemployed are removed from the official count on the grounds that they are not immediately available for work, often because they are classified as disabled.

The composition of the labor force in The Netherlands also has been changing rapidly. The number of women participating in the labor force has increased from 22% in 1960 to 38% in 1992. Labor force participation by women is low by international standards, but the number of women participating is still growing. Women's participation in the labor force is closely related to the increase in the number of people working part-time. In 1992, 34% of the labor force worked part-time, compared with about 14% in 1975, and almost 60% of the women in the labor force are working part-time.

The reasons for working part-time are numerous. It is recognized that many people want to work part-time; however, there are others who are forced to work part-time because they cannot find a full-time job. Also, many people who want to work part-time are not able to do so because their employer does not allow it. The employers argue that it is inefficient and they have to pay more social insurance contributions for two part-timers than for one person who works full-time. Now some unions are fighting for the right to work part-time for all employees. The combination of increasing numbers of women workers and part-time workers with low union density rates for these groups provides trade unions with a serious challenge. This is the focus of this chapter.

First, I briefly present the theoretical background for investigating the level of participation of women and part-time workers in trade unions. Then a description of membership rates for these two groups of workers is presented, as well as similar analyses for shop stewards. After this, exit rates of women and part-timers are examined. In the discussion at the end of the chapter, I offer some possible explanations for the level of union participation among women and part-time workers.

THEORETICAL BACKGROUND

There are several ways to participate in a trade union. People can, for example, be a member of a trade union, they can go on strike, or they can be a shop steward. Trade union participation is often argued to be multi-dimensional (Klandermans, 1986), and one way to order different forms of participation is to use intensity and time as two dimensions. If the intensity is low, the individual effort to participate is small. If the intensity is high, the individual effort to participate is high. *Time* refers to the amount of time an individual has to invest (van Rij, 1994). In this chapter I discuss only two forms of trade union participation: being a member and being a shop steward. Both forms are characterized by an indefinite length of time, but they differ in intensity. Being a shop steward requires more of a person in terms of intensity than being a trade union member.

There are many empirical studies about trade union membership and factors that influence membership rates and union density rates. In these studies, membership is often studied as a static concept. Whether someone is a member or not at a certain moment in time is, in fact, a result of two processes. First, there is the process of joining a union, and then there is the process of leaving a union. Reasons for joining and the moment of joining may be determined by different factors than reasons for leaving and the moment of leaving. Therefore, to be able to suggest possible explanations for under- and overrepresentation of certain groups of members requires knowledge of whether this under- or overrepresentation is caused by the number of people joining the union or by the number of people leaving the union.

van Rij (1994) recently studied the factors that influence the process of joining a trade union in The Netherlands and found that networks, contact with the union, and personal opinions were important factors.

Chances of joining a trade union increase if people have contacts with a trade union. Shop stewards have an important part in these contacts. A recent study in The Netherlands shows that members often become shop stewards out of collective and social motives (Klandermans & Visser, 1995), and many shop stewards are members of work councils (van Rij, 1994). A high level of unionization also increases the probability of joining a trade union, just as a positive attitude toward trade unions in one's working environment increases the probability of joining. Personal opinions encompass a general attitude toward trade union membership as well as costs–benefits considerations.

The process of leaving a trade union may be influenced by the same factors as the process of joining, but there are other factors as well. One important factor is commitment (Gordon, Philpot, Burt, Thompson, & Spiller, 1980). Another possible factor, according to Hirschman (1970), is the extent to which members think they can influence union policy. Here, factors related to union government can be important, but so is the support one thinks one can get.

METHOD

Sample

For practical reasons this chapter is limited to an analysis of data from unions that are associated with the FNV, which represent a majority of the Dutch union members, as mentioned before. For technical reasons it was not possible for some smaller unions to cooperate. Nevertheless, more than 97% of all FNV union members are included in this study. The union density and the position of women and part-time workers vary greatly across FNV unions; therefore, the rates for specific groups are presented separately for each union.

Measures

Union density rates given in this study refer to union density rates for FNV unions and were computed based on the number of FNV union members with a job divided by the number of employees, with the result multiplied by 100. Usually all union members are taken into account when computing union density rates. Because of the fact that in the denominator only people with jobs are taken into account, I do the same for the numerator. It should be noted that because only FNV union members are considered, union density rates in reality are higher than the ones presented in this chapter. For this reason it is not possible to compare them with union density rates in other countries. Here union density rates are used to compare membership rates between groups and several branches of industry, for which purpose the computed rates are well suited.

A shop steward is defined as a member of a trade union who fulfills some position for this union and has been registered as such in the administration of the union. Around 6.6% of all FNV trade union members are shop stewards according to this definition.

Exit rates are defined as the number of members who resigned in 1992 divided by the number of members as of January 1, 1992. The outcome is multiplied by 100.

Procedure

The data used in this study are from different sources. Data on characteristics of union members were supplied by the various unions associated with the FNV and reflect the total population of FNV—not just a sample. The data on the labor market, used for computing union densities, are official statistics supplied by the Netherlands Central Bureau of Statistics (CBS) and were collected by means of a national labor force survey that is conducted annually.

RESULTS

Membership

Table 1 shows union density rates for the different FNV unions. For all FNV unions together, the union density rate according to our definition was 14.6%. Union density rates appeared to vary greatly across FNV unions. The union for the construction industry had the highest rate. The union for the service sector (a very large sector) had by far the lowest rate.

Table 1

Union Density Rates by Union

Trade union	Union density rate (%)
Construction	28.0
Hairdressers	26.1
Transportation	22.9
Industrial	18.9
Civil servants	15.8
Teachers	13.8
Food industry	11.6
Catering	10.4
Service sector	5.3

In this sector, a relatively large part of the workforce was female. Because of the variety of density rates across unions and the possible influence of union government and union policy factors, I discuss the rates for specific groups separately for each union henceforth.

Women. The percentage of women among trade union members differed widely across unions. In most unions, women constituted a small minority. Exceptions were the union for hairdressers and the union for teachers. Of all FNV union members, about one fifth were female. This is in part a function of the fact that more than 60% of the labor force is male.

Table 2 shows union density rates for men and women by union. At a single glance one can see there is a big difference in density rates for men and women. On average, union density rates for men were twice as high as union density rates for women. But one can also see that the difference between men and women's density rates varies by union. In the union for the construction industry, the difference was very large. In this industry, most employees are male. Other unions where union density rates for women were relatively low were unions for industrial workers and the union for civil servants. In the union for the services sector and the union for teachers, women had approximately the same density levels as men.

However, it should be mentioned that union density rates for the services sector were very low overall.

When combined with age, the results (not mentioned in a table) show that for both men and women, union density rates increased with age. Overall, women's density rates increased from about 5% for women under 25 years of age to 12% for women between the ages of 45 and 64 years. Men's density rates increased from about 8% in the younger age group to 25% in the older group. The underrepresentation of women was found across all ages, but the difference between men and women was smaller among younger people. This may be due to growing participation among women. An alternative explanation is that there is a larger exit rate for women, which is discussed below.

Part-timers. It is difficult to analyze data on part-time workers because data on part-time workers are ambiguous and therefore difficult to compare. Unions use different definitions for part-time work, and their definitions differ from the definition used by the CBS for the labor market data. For the CBS, people are considered to work part-time if they

Table 2

Union Density Rates for Men and Women by Union

Trade union	Men (%)	Women (%)	Ratio
Construction	29.8	3.3	8.8:1
Hairdressers	—[a]	28.3	
Transportation	26.0	8.0	3.3:1
Industrial	21.6	8.8	2.5:1
Civil servants	21.8	11.0	2.0:1
Teachers	13.4	14.2	0.9:1
Food industry	15.6	5.9	2.6:1
Catering	14.7	6.8	2.2:1
Service sector	5.3	5.2	1.0:1

[a]For this cell The Netherlands Central Bureau of Statistics was not able to give a reliable estimate of the number of employees.

work less than 35 hours a week. Some unions use a definition for part-time workers as working less than 20 hours a week. It is not useful to compute union density rates with such diverse definitions. But because more than one third of Dutch employees work part-time and this group continues to grow, it is important to be able to say something about the participation in trade unions of this group. For that purpose I computed union density rates for part-timers for unions that used somewhat comparable definitions.

Table 3 shows the results. Most of these unions count a member as a part-timer when he or she works less than 100% of the time. In The Netherlands, 100% currently stands for 38 hours a week in most sectors. For the union for industrial workers, part-time means less than 32 hours. The union for employees in the food industry defines part-time as less than 30 hours. Despite the problems of comparability, Table 3 clearly indicates a low participation of part-timers in unions.

Shop Stewards

Women. Table 4 shows the percentage of women among shop stewards and among general members. We have seen already that women were underrepresented in trade unions. This table shows that the underrepresentation among shop stewards was even more sizable. The union for employees in the construction industry is an exception. In this union, the

Table 3

Union Density Rates by Hours of Work and Union

Trade union	Part-timers (%)	Full-timers (%)
Transportation	5.0	27.3
Industrial	4.3	22.6
Civil servants	5.3	24.4
Food industry	2.3	18.7
Service sector	3.2	6.2

Table 4

Percentage of Women Among Shop Stewards and General Members

Trade union	Shop stewards	General members
Construction	1.5	0.8
Hairdressers	84.1	93.8
Transportation	4.7	6.2
Industrial	5.5	10.2
Civil servants	29.4	39.0
Teachers	28.0	53.0
Food industry	13.3	21.8
Catering	26.8	36.2
Service sector	28.0	42.1

percentage of women among shop stewards was higher than the percentage among general members. However, the number of women in this union was very small overall. In all other unions, the number of women among shop stewards was smaller than would be expected from the membership rates.

Part-timers. Some union leaders discussed the possibilities of attracting part-timers as shop stewards. They suggested that a substantial number of the part-timers have some time left to spend as a shop steward. In Table 5 percentages of part-timers are shown for eight unions. This table includes data from three more unions than Table 3. This is possible because in this case the percentages do not have to be related to labor market data. The added unions define part-time as less than 20 hours of work per week. We have already seen that few part-timers participated in unions. Table 5 shows that relatively even fewer part-timers could be found among shop stewards. The unions for hairdressers and for catering employees were exceptions. These are both small unions.

Exit Rates

The results given above show that women and part-time workers were underrepresented in almost all unions. This may be caused by low intake

Table 5

Percentage of Part-Timers Among Shop Stewards and General Members

Trade union	Shop stewards	General members
Construction	0.0	0.1
Hairdressers	25.2	17.6
Transportation	3.9	4.3
Industrial	2.2	4.7
Civil servants	11.6	15.2
Food industry	5.0	8.7
Catering	9.9	8.4
Service sector	10.9	18.2

numbers or high exit numbers. Because of the limitations of my data and the fact that van Rij (van Rij, 1994) made an extensive study about joining trade unions, in this section I look only at exit rates.

Table 6 shows exit rates by union. Exit rates vary greatly by union, ranging from almost 6% up to almost 18%. On the level of trade unions

Table 6

Yearly Exit Rates by Union

Trade union	Exit rate (%)
Hairdressers	17.9
Catering	17.5
Service sector	14.8
Food industry	10.2
Teachers	8.9
Transportation	7.1
Industrial	7.1
Civil servants	6.5
Construction	5.9

as well as on the level of branches of industry, a negative correlation was found between exit rates and union density rates. In general, exit rates were higher in branches of industry and trade unions with lower union density rates. At this moment it is difficult to conclude which causes the other. Probably it is a matter of reciprocity.

Women. Exit rates for women and men are shown in Table 7. In almost all unions, exit rates for women were higher than exit rates for men. In some unions exit rates for women were more than twice as high. The only exception was the union for hairdressers, but this union formed an exception to almost every rule. Women do join unions, but they appear to leave sooner than men. Unions in which differences between men and women were large were unions with a low union density rate among women.

Combination of the data for different age groups (not shown) with data for different sexes leads to the conclusion that age and sex correlate separately with exit rates. Exit rates for women were higher in every age category. Accordingly, exit rates for young people were higher than for older people among women as well as among men. Overall, men's rates decreased from about 13% among men younger than 25 to 4% for men

Table 7

Exit Rates for Men and Women

Trade union	Men (%)	Women (%)
Hairdressers	19.8	17.8
Catering	15.0	22.1
Service sector	12.9	17.7
Food industry	8.8	15.9
Teachers	8.0	9.7
Transportation	6.9	10.2
Industrial	6.4	14.6
Civil servants	5.3	8.4
Construction	5.8	12.0

between the ages of 45 and 64. Overall women's rates decrease from 20% to 8% for the same age categories.

Part-timers. Exit rates for part-timers appear to be higher than exit rates for full-timers (see Table 8). These differences were smaller, however, than the differences between men and women. Combination of data for hours of work and sex leads to the interesting finding that it is not correct to conclude that exit rates are higher for people who work part-time. This was only the case for men. Since men working part-time are a relatively small minority in the labor force, it is more interesting to look at the exit rates of women. The opposite effect applies to female workers. Exit rates among female full-time workers were considerably higher than exit rates among female part-time workers. The relatively high exit rates for part-timers shown in Table 8 were due to the fact that a large majority of women are working part-time. It is because of the fact that exit rates for women were very high that one finds higher exit rates for part-timers.

DISCUSSION

This chapter focuses on participation in trade unions by two groups of employees who are becoming more numerous in the labor market. The

Table 8

Exit Rates by Hours of Work

Trade union	Full-timers (%)	Part-timers (%)
Hairdressers	16.5	18.5
Catering	18.2	19.7
Service sector	14.9	15.6
Food industry	10.3	11.8
Transportation	6.8	10.1
Industrial	6.9	11.4
Civil servants	5.7	7.8
Construction	6.3	6.8

extent to which women and part-timers participate in trade unions in The Netherlands was presented. The focus was on two forms of participation, namely being a member and being a shop steward. Women and part-timers have low participation rates. Union density rates reflecting membership for these groups were relatively low in almost all unions, and participation rates of women and part-timers in as shop stewards were even lower.

Given these results, a study of the reasons for the low participation of these groups is in order. As mentioned before, whether someone is a member or not at a certain moment in time is a result of two processes: the process of joining a trade union and the process of leaving a trade union. These processes can be influenced by different factors.

Theorizing about possible explanations for low participation rates of women and part-timers therefore requires knowledge of whether these low participation rates are caused by large exit rates or low intake rates. The data suggest that low union density rates for women and part-timers have been created by different processes. Low union density rates for women appear to result largely from high exit rates, whereas low union density rates for part-timers result mainly from low intake rates.

As mentioned above, van Rij (1994) suggested that contacts with a trade union, networks, and personal opinions influence the process of joining a trade union in The Netherlands. It seems likely that people who work part-time have fewer opportunities to contact a trade union or meet people from trade unions. In fact, a recent Dutch study shows that people who work part-time generally have fewer contacts with trade unions (van den Putte, van Rij, & Saris, 1992). Also, the balance of costs and benefits might be different for part-timers and full-timers. Part-timers might expect fewer benefits from trade union membership, and their costs are relatively high because their salary is typically much lower. Most unions have reduced contribution rates for part-timers, but the costs are still high. Further study is necessary to confirm these possible explanations.

The process of leaving a trade union may be influenced by these same factors, but there are other factors that also may have a significant effect. Empirical studies (e.g., Klandermans, 1989) show some effect of commitment on the likelihood that a person will consider resigning his or her membership. A recent study on membership turnover in The Netherlands also suggested that commitment is important in preventing people from withdrawing from the union (Daalder, 1994). The study of membership withdrawal shows that the probability of termination of membership is very large in the first few years and decreases sharply after that. It may be that members are leaving before commitment to the union is fully developed.

Hirschman (1970) indicated some other important factors. In his theory on exit, voice, and loyalty, next to commitment the choice between exit or voice is also affected by the possibilities one sees to influence union policy. These possibilities may be affected by union structure and union government, but also by the support one expects to get if one attempts to influence union policy. This may depend on the number of kindred spirits in one's branch.

This can play a part in the high exit rates for women. Maybe women in some unions feel isolated and therefore think they do not have much influence in changing union policy if they have intentions to do so. Next to this, women more often leave the labor market to raise children. We have to realize that there are relatively more young people among female union members. As the probability of terminating membership decreases with membership duration, exit rates are higher among young people. Other factors are likely to determine the high exit rates of young people and women, but with the present data, we are not able to confirm this.

The reasons for the underrepresentation of women and part-timers among shop stewards may be different. Many shop stewards became shop stewards after being asked by someone else to do so. Probably one of the reasons that not many young women are shop stewards is simply because they have not had enough time yet to get to know enough people and to be asked. Another reason is the unfamiliarity with the tasks of being a shop steward. Furthermore, a large majority of members think being a shop steward is very time-consuming (Klandermans & Visser, 1995). This may be why many women do not become shop stewards, because women often have to take care of children in addition to their jobs and do not have the time for such intense and time-consuming effort.

With the present data it is impossible to conclude which factors cause the low participation rates of women and part-timers. However, we know by now that the low participation rates of part-time workers mainly result from low intake rates, whereas the low participation rates of women result from high exit rates. As shown above, exit rates in The Netherlands are very high and vary greatly by union. Exit rates have been rising for several years and are especially high among women and young people. This is an alarming development for trade unions. We do not know yet what factors influence exit rates most. It may be union factors, labor market factors, network factors or personal factors. Currently, I am doing a study on the determinants of exit behavior, in which I am empirically testing a model for exit behavior.

Given the developments in the composition of the labor force, trade unions in The Netherlands cannot afford to wait for results of new research. They have to begin putting in extra effort toward unionizing these groups of employees, which are becoming more numerous in the labor market. Priority must be given to contacting part-time workers and trying to make unions more attractive for them. At the same time, unions must try to find out why exit rates for women are so high and what can be done to prevent women from leaving.

REFERENCES

Albeda, W. (1987). Recent trends in collective bargaining in The Netherlands. In J. P. Windmuller et al. (Eds.), *Collective bargaining in industrialised market economies: A reappraisal* (pp. 253–264). Geneva: International Labor Office.

Daalder, A. (1994). *Vrouwen en jongeren eerst, een statistische verkenning van het ledenverloop van de FNV in 1992* [Women and young people first, a statistical investigation of FNV membership turnover in 1992]. Amsterdam: University of Amsterdam.

Gordon, M. E., Philpot, J. W., Burt, R. E., Thompson, C. A., & Spiller, W. E. (1980). Commitment to the union: Development of a measure and an examination of its correlates. *Journal of Applied Psychology, 65*, 479–499.

Hirschman, A. O. (1970). *Exit, voice and loyalty: Responses to declines in firms, organisations and states.* Cambridge, England: Cambridge University Press.

Klandermans, P. G. (1986). Participatie in de Vakbond: Een overzicht van Theorie en Onderzoek [Participation in trade unions, an overview of theory and investigation]. *Tijdschrift voor Arbeidsvraagstukken, 2,* 14–29.

Klandermans, P. G. (1989). Commitment to the union: A replication and some tests in a Dutch context. *Journal of Applied Psychology, 6,* 869–875.

Klandermans, P. G., & Visser, J. (Eds.). (1995). *De vakbeweging na de welvaartsstaat* [Trade unions after the welfare state]. Assen, The Netherlands: van Gorcum.

Lijphart, A. (1968). *The politics of accommodation: Pluralism and democracy in The Netherlands.* Berkeley: University of California Press.

Olson, M. (1965). *The logic of collective action: Public goods and the theory of groups.* Cambridge, MA: Harvard University Press.

van den Putte, B., van Rij, C., & Saris, W. (1992). *De FNV Barometer 9: Uitsplitsing naar geslacht, werktijd en bedrijfssector* [FNV Barometer 9: An analysis of gender, working hours and branch of industry]. Amsterdam: University of Amsterdam, Netherlands Institute for Social and Marketing Research.

van Rij, C. (1994). *To join or not to join, an event-history analysis of trade-union membership in the Netherlands.* Amsterdam: University of Amsterdam, Netherlands Institute for Social and Marketing Research.

Visser, J. (1987). *In search of inclusive unionism: A comparative analysis.* Unpublished doctoral dissertation, University of Amsterdam.

Visser, J. (1990). Continuity and change in Dutch industrial relations. In G. Baglioni & C. Crouch (Eds.), *European industrial relations: The challenge of flexibility* (pp. 199–242). Newbury Park, CA: Sage.

Visser, J. (1992). The Netherlands: The end of an era and the end of a system. In A. Ferner & R. Hyman (Eds.), *Industrial relations in the New Europe* (pp. 323–356). Oxford, England: Basil Blackwell.

13

Taking Part in Industrial Action: General Versus Specific Readiness to Engage

Gerrita van der Veen and Sjoerd Goslinga

U sually a collective action, such as an action initiated by a labor union, is the result of a collective decision. After the decision has been made that a collective action will take place, the individual can choose either to join in the action or not. Research concerning the willingness to participate in collective action on the individual level is scarce. Those studies that have been conducted have all focused on the willingness to engage in action in a specific conflict situation. The willingness or readiness to participate is viewed, in these studies, as a function of the specific circumstances under which the action takes place. In the case of labor unions, these circumstances are typically discontent among employees and a labor union that mobilizes. The scope for mobilization, however, is not without its limits. Depending on their socioeconomic, cultural, or religious background and previous experiences with industrial action, union members may be reluctant to engage in action, and this sort of reserve can constrain mobilization.

To investigate the influence of these factors (i.e., factors unrelated to the specific circumstances of industrial action) on the willingness to participate, we make a distinction between general and specific readiness to

engage in action. Specific readiness is defined as the willingness to participate in action when a conflict is at hand. General readiness to engage in
action expresses the general tendency to support industrial action, whether
or not a conflict is at hand, and is viewed as the result of socialization
processes and experiences with collective action in the past. Compared
with specific readiness, general readiness is viewed as a stable individual
characteristic. We hypothesize that general readiness is a major determinant of specific readiness to participate and that employees with a high
general readiness to engage in action will, in case of a conflict, show a
higher *specific* readiness to participate. Specific action-readiness is proposed to be determined by the goals and circumstances of a specific industrial action.

The distinction between general and specific action-readiness can also
serve a practical purpose for labor unions. A strategy of action, which
means setting the goals and choosing the means or type of action, is based
at least in part on the estimated action-readiness of the rank and file. Recent economic and demographic changes in The Netherlands have
changed industrial action in such a way that it is very difficult, sometimes
even impossible, for union officials to determine action-readiness before
an action. The increase in unemployment since the 1980s and a population that is aging have led to growing numbers of social security beneficiaries, placing the Dutch social security system under a great deal of pressure. In addition, the integration of Europe is making extensive demands
on the economies of the countries involved. These developments have
forced the Dutch government to take a more dominant role in employment relations. This means that many union actions are directed against
governmental decisions and (European) legislation, and these actions go
beyond the level of a company or branch of industry and are of concern
to all employees. With so many people involved it is almost impossible for
union leaders to get a clear picture of the willingness to participate on
short notice. Still, in order to delineate the appropriate line of action, union
officials need this information in advance. It is therefore necessary to be
able to measure action-readiness at a general level. This general action-
readiness, then, should have predictive value in specific conflict situations.

In this chapter we take a closer look at the relationship between general and specific readiness to engage in action.

THEORETICAL ELABORATION

Klandermans's (1983) model of the willingness to participate in collective action is one of the few models concerning individual action-readiness amenable to empirical testing (Kelly & Kelly, 1992; Kryl, 1990). The willingness or readiness to participate, in this model, is viewed as an individual's intention to engage in collective action. Following Fishbein and Ajzen's (1975) theory of reasoned action, the intention is taken to be the best predictor of behavior in a given situation.

Apart from the intention or motivation ("willingness"), actual participation will only occur when the individual knows where and when the action is to take place ("awareness") and is also able to participate ("opportunity"). Illness, for example, can preclude participation. In Klandermans's (1983) willingness-to-participate model, the intention to participate is determined by the supposed instrumentality of actions. This supposed instrumentality is defined according to the "expectancy–value" approach to behavior (Feather, 1982; Fishbein & Ajzen, 1975; Vroom, 1964). In this approach, the motivation to participate in collective action is seen as a product of the expectation that participation has certain positive or negative consequences and the value of these consequences. The underlying assumption here is that participation in collective action is founded on the maximization of outcomes. In other words, participation is the result of weighing the perceived costs and benefits of participation. Before weighing the costs and benefits of participation, however, one has to be informed about the conflict and be supportive of the union's position in the matter (van der Veen, 1992). Klandermans's model has been tested in specific action circumstances: the collective bargaining of 1979 in The Netherlands in which a reduction of working hours was at stake. In that instance, the model did turn out to be useful in explaining *specific* action-readiness. However, the model cannot be used to determine *general* action-readiness. Research shows that a behavioral intention, measured separately from its specific circumstances, is not a good predictor of specific behavior (see Ajzen, 1988).

Because no model for general action-readiness was available in the literature on industrial action, we turned to the literature on political action, in which research has been done with the so-called "protest potential" (Barnes & Kaase, 1979; Marsh, 1974). Barnes and Kaase defined protest potential as the sum of the individual's various propensities to engage in unconventional forms of political behavior. Unconventional or unorthodox forms of political behavior are, for instance, petitioning authorities, organizing boycotts, obstructing traffic, and engaging in demonstrations or strikes. Examples of conventional forms of political behavior are voting, attending political meetings, and becoming a member of a political party. The unconventional forms of political behavior are comparable to collective actions organized by labor unions. Protest potential is understood as the sum of individual decisions, and thus is a concept at the group level, even though it is measured individually. For the purpose of our research, however, we use the concept of protest potential at the individual level, and therefore prefer the term *action-readiness*. On the basis of prior research, we also propose that the protest potential is a personal characteristic that is relatively stable in time (Elsinga, 1983; Prins, 1990).

In the concept of general action-readiness, generalized positive or negative attitudes toward collective action, the intention to participate, the expected effectiveness of action, and the perceived legitimacy of action are manifested. These aspects or dimensions are measured for different types of action and then combined in a composite scale. Although the concept of general action-readiness is taken from the political literature, it fits in well with social psychological attitude theory (Barnes & Kaase, 1979; Marsh, 1974). The dimensions of general action-readiness accord with the attitude–behavior model of Fishbein and Ajzen (1975). General positive or negative feelings toward action correspond with the attitude component in their model. Perceived legitimacy can be understood as a reflection of their social-norm component, and behavioral intention appears in both models. Only the effectiveness dimension cannot easily be placed in the Fishbein and Ajzen model, probably because of differences between collective and individual behavior. Taking part in a union action is collective behavior, whereas existing attitude–behavior models aim exclusively at explaining individual behavior (Kok & Damoiseaux ,1991). In collective behavior, expectations about the behavior of others play an important role. An employee can decide to go on strike, but a strike is usually effective only with unanimous participation of the employees in a company or department. In Klandermans's model, the expectation that participation will help realize the goals of action is viewed as a function of (a) the awareness that one's participation is needed for a good progression of action, (b) expectations about the number of participants, and (c) expectations about the chance of success of the action if enough people participate. We think these expectations about the participation of others are expressed in the effectiveness dimension of general action-readiness, that is, in people's opinions about the expected effectiveness of action. In this sense the effectiveness component is an important addition to the other three components.

General action-readiness is the weighted sum of the individual's general attitude toward action and the perceived legitimacy, the expected effectiveness, and the intention to participate for various types of action. According to attitude theory, a general behavioral intention can be measured best as the sum of specific intentions (Ajzen, 1988). The idea behind this is that specific intentions reflect a general disposition as well as the influence of the specific situation. By combining various specific situations, the influence of specific circumstances is eliminated. Research among labor union members has shown the existence of a general action-readiness that is related to (relatively) stable differences between individuals, such as age and political preference (van der Veen, 1992). We hypothesized that general action-readiness, together with the specific circumstances of a conflict, determines specific action-readiness. The real value of the concept of general action-readiness, therefore, can be determined only in a conflict situation. The focus of this chapter is thus, What meaning does general action-readiness have in the prediction of action-readiness in a conflict situation?

First of all, we examined whether general action-readiness has significance in a specific conflict situation. Second, we verified the explanatory value of the composite general action-readiness scale compared with general attitudes toward the separate types of action. Finally, we checked the assumption that specific action-readiness is a function of general action-readiness as well as of the specific circumstances of a conflict. We then addressed the question of whether specific action-readiness differs from general action-readiness.

METHOD

Sample

The study was conducted among members of the CNV (Dutch National Federation of Christian Trade Unions), the second largest trade federation in The Netherlands. The readiness of CNV members to participate in industrial action was assessed in response to a conflict about the Disability Insurance Act (Wet op de Arbeids-Ongeschiktheidsverzekering, or WAO). Under the WAO, all employees up to the age of 65 are insured against disability. Employees are entitled to benefits if they have been continuously incapable of working for 52 weeks and remain so at the end of this period. WAO benefits are 70% of the last earned income and are financed by employee contributions and administered by the industry boards.

From 1967 on (the year the WAO was implemented), work disability grew steadily. The number of people receiving WAO benefits rose from 160,000 in 1968 to 900,000 in 1990. In 1990, the Dutch government, employer organizations, and labor unions agreed that the growth in WAO beneficiaries had to stop. They disagreed about the way to achieve this, however. Government and employers wanted to change the allowance system itself in order to reduce costs and decrease its attractiveness (especially in comparison with unemployment benefits) for individual workers. The unions advocated regulations that would help people to continue or return to work. In July 1991 the Dutch government publicized its plans, announcing considerable limitations of WAO benefits. The three largest trade federations (FNV, CNV, and MHP) did not agree with the proposed plans, and together they decided to go into action. During September and the first week of October 1991, they organized an array of different collective actions (short work stoppages, protest demonstrations, meetings during working time, short strikes, and so on). The actions were the biggest in Dutch labor union history (after World War II). However, they were not very successful in influencing the proposed plans on WAO.

Measures and Procedure

We conducted two telephone surveys among CNV members. In the first one we measured general action-readiness; in the second we measured specific action-readiness. This was necessary because, otherwise, the debate on WAO would influence the answers on general action-readiness questions. The first survey was conducted in early 1991 and did not include questions on WAO. The second survey consisted of questions on WAO only and was conducted shortly after the organized actions in the fall of 1991. We gathered complete data for 157 CNV members.

General action-readiness. General action-readiness was measured by the general attitude, the legitimacy, the expected effectiveness, and the intention to participate with regard to five types of actions: strike, work-to-rule, demonstrative work stoppage, communicative work stoppage, and demonstration. By *communicative work stoppage*, we mean an action whereby employees stop working for discussion with other employees. In this study, of general action-readiness was based solely on the general attitude of union members toward the five types of action. The attitude dimension can be used as a shortened version of a general action-readiness scale (van der Veen, 1992). The question we asked was "What is in general your attitude toward [type of action]?" The answers varied from 1 (*very negative*) to 5 (*very positive*). To achieve a general action-readiness scale, we added the scores for the five types of action (Cronbach's alpha was .74).

Specific action-readiness. The second survey included the same kinds of questions on action-readiness, only this time we stated that the types of action named concerned WAO. The number of action types was limited to those likely to occur in this kind of conflict. We measured attitudes toward a demonstration, a work stoppage, and a strike concerning WAO.

Specific circumstances. By *specific circumstances of action*, we mean on the one hand agreement with the goals of action and on the other hand the cost–benefit nexus of participation. In our study we included only the degree to which one agreed with the goals of action. The diversity of the organized actions in the different companies made it impossible to include all possible costs and benefits. To determine the level of agreement with the goals of action we included questions on knowledge about the government's plans and opinions on these plans and the labor unions' position. We assumed that participation would occur only when one was familiar with the conflict and agreed with the unions on rejecting the proposed measures. The concept of knowledge was operationalized by the number of proposed measures in the government's plan that the respondents were able to name. The scale for knowledge ranged from 0 (*no measures named*) to 3 (*two or more measures named*).

In addition, an evaluation of the government's plans and the unions' position were obtained. The answers to both opinion questions were scored on a 5-point scale. A high score meant a positive attitude toward the unions' position or a positive attitude toward the government's plans.

RESULTS

On the basis of the composite scale of general action-readiness, we attributed a high general action-readiness (score 4 or 5) to 40% of the CNV members in our study and a low general action-readiness (score 1 or 2) to 20% of the respondents. As opposed to the attitude toward a strike, the average attitudes toward a work stoppage and toward a demonstration were positive. Of these two, the work stoppage was preferred. Concerning the WAO actions, the percentage of CNV members with a positive attitude toward action varied from 72% for a demonstration to 26% for a strike. A work stoppage was considered positive by 41% of the respondents.

General Action-Readiness and Specific Actions

To determine whether general action-readiness would have significance in a specific situation, Pearson product–moment correlation coefficients were calculated between the attitudes toward the three types of action (strike, work stoppage, and demonstration) concerning WAO and (a) the composite scale of general action-readiness and (b) the corresponding general attitudes toward the three types of action. This second point means that we examined the correlation between the attitude toward a strike concerning WAO and the general attitude toward a strike. We did the same for the other two types of action.

The correlations between the composite general action-readiness scale and the attitudes toward the three WAO actions were statistically significant, as shown in Table 1. The correlation coefficients varied from .44 for a demonstration to .52 for a strike. This indicates that respondents with a high general action-readiness were more positive about actions concerning WAO. We can conclude that general action-readiness had significance in this specific conflict situation. The correlation coefficients were, however, not high enough to conclude that the attitudes toward WAO actions were fully explained by general action-readiness. Thus, the attitudes toward WAO actions were partly determined by the conflict situation.

The correlation coefficients between the attitudes toward WAO actions and the corresponding general attitudes toward the three types of action were statistically significant as well, ranging from .33 for a work

Table 1

Pearson Product–Moment Correlation Coefficients Between General Action Readiness and Specific Attitudes ($N = 157$)

Attitude toward specific actions	Composite general action-readiness	General attitude toward the separate types of action
Strike	.52	.44
Work stoppage	.43	.33
Demonstration	.44	.35

NOTE: WAO = Disability Insurance Act. All correlations significant at the .01 level.

stoppage to .44 for a strike (see Table 1). However, all three of these correlation coefficients were lower than the correlation coefficients between the composite general action-readiness scale and the attitudes toward WAO actions ($p < .05$). This, together with the high reliability of the composite scale ($\alpha = .74$), indicates that the composite general action-readiness scale was a better predictor of the attitudes toward WAO actions than were general attitudes toward the three types of action.

Attitude Toward WAO Actions Further Explained

We made an inventory of the specific circumstances of action by asking the respondents what they knew about the government's plans and how they evaluated the plans and the union's position in the matter. Almost 90% of those interviewed knew one or more of the government's proposed measures on WAO. One third of the respondents could name only one of the proposed measures, another third was able to name two measures, and the remaining third could name more than two measures.

Three quarters of the respondents evaluated the union's position on WAO as "good" or "very good." A little more than 10% of those interviewed did not agree with the union's position, and 15% did not care either way. Of the respondents, 60% had a negative attitude about the government's plans ("bad" or "very bad"), and 15% agreed with the plans ("good" or "very good"). A little more than 20% did not care either way.

We hypothesized that specific action-readiness would be determined by general action-readiness as well as by the specific circumstances of conflict. Three regression analyses were performed to test this hypothesis. Each one of the three attitudes toward WAO actions (strike, work stoppage, and demonstration) served as the dependent variable. The results are displayed in Table 2.

The correlation coefficients between the attitude toward the WAO actions and the predictors were high. This means the more one knew about the government's plans on WAO, the more favorable one judged participation in action. The more an individual agreed with the union's position and the more negatively he or she judged the government's plans, the more positive his or her attitude toward WAO actions was.

Table 2

Results of Regression-Analyses With the Attitude Toward the Three Types of Specific Actions as Dependent Variables

Variable	Strike			Work stoppage			Demonstration		
	r	β	R^2	r	β	R^2	r	β	R^2
General action-readiness	.52**	.45**		.43**	.41**		.44**	.38**	
Unique variance			.18			.15			.13
Specific circumstances									
Knowledge of government's plans	.12	.16*		.19*	.22**		.25**	.26**	
Attitude toward labor union's standpoint	.31**	.10		.27**	.10		.38**	.20**	
Attitude toward government's plans	−.38**	−.26**		−.21**	−.11		−.25**	−.13	
Unique variance			.11			.08			.15
F		21.21**			12.68**			17.24**	
Total explained variance			.38			.27			.34

NOTE: WAO = Disability Insurance Act.
*$p < .05$. **$p < .01$.

The attitudes toward WAO actions turned out to be a function of general action-readiness as well as the specific circumstances. The amount of explained variance varied from 25% for a work stoppage to 36% for a strike. General action-readiness appeared in all three analyses as the best predictor of attitude toward a WAO action. In all three analyses the regression coefficient and the correlation coefficient of the general action-readiness scale did not differ substantially. We can conclude that general action-readiness offered an independent contribution to the predictions.

The knowledge of the plans, the evaluations of the plans, and the union's standpoint contribute significantly to the attitudes that were explained. The unique contribution of the specific circumstances in the explanation of the attitudes varied from 6% for work stoppage to 16% for demonstration. In addition to general action-readiness, the attitude toward a strike concerning WAO was mainly determined by the evaluation of the government's plans. The more the individual was opposed to the proposed measures, the more positive the attitude toward a strike was. Positive attitude toward a work stoppage concerning WAO was mainly determined by the knowledge of the government's plans, and positive attitude toward a demonstration concerning WAO was determined by knowledge of the government's plans as well as by the evaluation of the union's position in the matter.

DISCUSSION

Analyses of the data gave rise to the following conclusions. First of all, general readiness proved to be of importance in a specific conflict situation. This supports our hypothesis that a construct on a general level can be used to make predictions on a specific level. Second, the composite general action-readiness scale showed a stronger relation to specific action-readiness than did the more specific behavioral tendencies. This supports our contention that the composite scale represents the underlying disposition better than do the specific attitudes. Third, specific readiness can partly be explained by the specific circumstances of a conflict—in our case specific action-readiness was explained by the knowledge of the proposed governmental plans and the evaluation of government and labor union policy. Therefore, specific action-readiness is different from a general disposition measured in a specific situation. Based on these findings we conclude that a difference between general and specific action-readiness is confirmed on theoretical as well as empirical grounds.

We consider general readiness to engage in action to be an important addition to the theory on participation in industrial action. Previous theory lacked the distinction between general and specific action-readiness. The willingness or readiness to engage in action has (as far as we know) always been examined in specific conflict situations. Our concern here is whether the readiness to engage in action when a conflict is at hand can be predicted from general dispositional attitudes toward actions. By answering the question of how much readiness is determined beforehand, we also gain insight into the possibility that (for example) labor unions may have to influence the willingness to participate of their rank-and-file members. Prediction of the readiness of the constituency to engage in action and ways to influence this readiness are both of significance to a union. The ability to determine general action-readiness can be a useful tool for labor unions, especially when industrial action goes beyond the level of a single company or industry and it is harder for union officials to keep a finger on the pulse of the membership.

Earlier a scale for general action-readiness had been developed that is related to stable differences between individuals (van der Veen, 1992). The value of this scale, however, depends on its usefulness in practice. By means of a longitudinal study, we asked union members at different points in time about their attitudes toward actions. Thus, data on general action-readiness were gathered as well as attitudes toward actions in a specific conflict situation. A major advantage of this research method is that general action-readiness and specific action-readiness are measured separately in time. One comment, however, has to be made; at the time we measured general action-readiness, early 1991, the WAO already was of concern to the labor unions. Before a conflict gives rise to actions the tension and irritation has been building up for some time. Some influence of the debate about WAO on general action-readiness therefore cannot be ruled out completely. However, because general action-readiness was measured separately in a survey that did not include any questions on WAO, it would appear that general action-readiness was assessed without significant contamination.

A question that remains is in what way general action-readiness influences specific action-readiness. In the cost–benefit approach, the influence of other-than-expected outcomes of participation has never been denied. However, in this approach, participation is always the result of the cost–benefit nexus. This means that factors that are unrelated to the outcomes, such as personal background and previous experiences, also determine the costs and benefits of a certain action and how these costs and benefits are valued (Melucci, 1988). But is reality not forced into the straitjacket of the rational calculus? Kelly and Kelly (1992) found, for instance, that a consideration of costs and benefits seemed not always to precede the decision to participate. Another example of the limitations of the cost–benefit approach is the phenomenon of the free rider. A free rider is someone who profits from the outcomes of action without taking part. The free rider dilemma is connected to the cost–benefit approach to participation: Why would any union member engage in action if he or she expects to profit anyway? Klandermans (1985) found, however, that the number of free riders often falls short of expectations based on the cost–benefit approach. Moreover, Oliver, Marwell, and Texeira (1985) argued that no collective action will take place if no one is prepared to be the first to invest time, money, and other means even when there is no chance of success (when the number of participants has not yet reached the so-called "critical mass"). The distinction between general and specific action-readiness can help to explain these observations. If general action-readiness is a determinant of participation as well as the cost–benefit nexus, then participation is possible without a positive cost–benefit nexus. These approaches do not have to be mutually exclusive; general action-readiness could influence specific readiness not only through the perceived costs and benefits of participation, but also directly. In future research the way that general action-readiness influences the readiness to engage in a specific conflict situation should be examined.

REFERENCES

Ajzen, I. (1988). *Attitudes, personality, and behaviour.* Homewood, IL: Dorsey Press.

Barnes, S. H., & M Kaase, (1979). *Political action: Mass participation in five Western democracies.* Beverly Hills, CA: Sage.

Elsinga, E. (1983). Socio-political backgrounds of developments in political participation. In J. J. A. Thomassen, F. J. Heunks, J. W. van Deth, & E. Elsinga (Eds.), *Political opinion and behavior of Dutch citizens after the 1960's* (pp. 164–194). Alphen a/d Rijn, The Netherlands: Samson.

Feather, N. T. (1982). *Expectations and action: Expectancy value models in psychology.* Hillsdale, NJ: Erlbaum.

Fishbein, M., & Ajzen, I. (1975). *Belief, attitude, intention and behavior: An introduction to theory and research.* Reading, MA: Addison-Wesley.

Kelly, J., & Kelly, C. (1992). Industrial action. In J. F. Hartley & G. M. Stephenson (Eds.), *Employment relations.* Oxford, England: Basil Blackwell.

Klandermans, P. G. (1983). *Participation in a social movement: A mobilization campaign examined.* Amsterdam: Vrije Universiteit.

Klandermans, P. G. (1985). Vakbondsacties en het zwartrijdersgedrag [Labor union action and the problem of the free rider]. *Tijdschrift voor Arbeidsvraagstukken, 3,* 45–53.

Kok, G., & Damoiseaux, V. (1991). Influencing attitudes and behavior. In B. Klandermans & E. Seydel (Eds.), *To convince and to activate: Theory and practice of public communication.* Assen/Maastricht, The Netherlands: Van Gorcum.

Kryl, I. P. (1990). Union participation: A review of the literature. In P. J. D. Drenth, J. A. Sergeant, & R. J. Takens (Eds.), *European perspectives in psychology* (Vol. 3, pp. 147–166). New York: Wiley.

Marsh, A. (1974). Explorations in unorthodox political behaviour: A scale to measure "protest potential." *European Journal of Political Research, 2,* 107–129.

Melucci, A. (1988). Getting involved: Identity and mobilization in social movements. In B. Klandermans, H. Kriesi, & S. Tarrow (Eds.), *From structure to action: Comparing social movement research across cultures* (pp. 329–348). Greenwich, CT: JAI Press.

Oliver, P., Marwell, G., & Texeira, R. (1985). A theory of the critical mass: Interdependence, group heterogeneity and the production of collective goods. *American Journal of Sociology, 91,* 522–556.

Prins, P. M. (1990). *Actiepotentiaal: Ra, ra?! De constructie van een schaal voor actiebereidheid met behulp van het partial credit model* [The construction of a scale to measure action-readiness using the partial credit model]. Amsterdam: Vrije Universiteit.

Veen, G. van der (1992). *Principes in praktijk: CNV-leden over collectieve acties* [Principles in practice: CNV members and collective action]. Kampen, The Netherlands: Kok.

Vroom, V. H. (1964). *Work and motivation.* New York: Wiley.

14

Can Union Commitment Be Developed? A Quasi-Experimental Analysis

Victor M. Catano, Greg K. Cole, and Norman Hebert

The development of a criterion for union commitment by Gordon, Philpot, Burt, Thompson, and Spiller (1980) has generated renewed interest in the psychology of trade unions. Over the past 15 years, much research has been directed at investigating the psychometric properties of the Union Commitment Scale or the antecedents and consequences of the union commitment construct (Barling, Fullagar, & Kelloway, 1992; Gordon & Ladd, 1993). In discussing the future of union commitment research, Gordon and Ladd (1993) proposed an applied agenda that would have immediate, practical implications for organized labor, particularly at a time when trade unions are under increasing assault from both politicians and employers. Trade unions in Canada, the United Kingdom, and the United States have had to deal with legislation or judicial action that reduces the power and growth of trade unions; the selling off of unionized, public corporations to the private sector; and legislation abrogation of contracts with government employees. These changes appear to reflect

Part of this chapter is based on a thesis submitted by Greg K. Cole in partial fulfillment of the requirements for a master's degree in applied psychology. We wish to thank the members, executive, and staff of the Nova Scotia Government Employees Union for their support and cooperation.

a political ideology that values the private market above all other organizational relationships. Increasing union members' sense of commitment is seen as one way of bolstering unions against these threats. Greater involvement in union activities (i.e., serving in elected office, attending union meetings, voting in union elections), willingness to go on strike or take militant action, and support for a union's political agenda have been identified as consequences of increased levels of union commitment (Barling, Fullagar, & Kelloway, 1992). These commitment-related outcomes are fundamental to the immediate survival and future strength of unions and illustrate the importance of interventions designed to increase union commitment.

Longitudinal research has demonstrated that without any type of intervention, union commitment remains stable over time (Fullagar & Barling, 1991). Barling and Kelloway (1993) proposed that the development of an active intervention strategy to change rank-and-file members' union commitment is the next logical challenge in union commitment research. This study examined whether a planned intervention, a training workshop, would lead to increases in union commitment and other related variables.

DEVELOPING UNION COMMITMENT

Research on correlates and predictors of union commitment identifies two processes that are central to its development: (a) the exchange relationship between the union and its membership, that is, union instrumentality, and (b) the socialization process, that is, role and work experiences (Barling & Kelloway, 1993; Fullagar & Barling, 1989).

Union instrumentality. The perceived instrumentality of the union's effectiveness in improving working conditions or a member's general welfare is strongly related to an individual's level of union commitment (Barling, Fullagar, & Kelloway, 1992). Beliefs about union instrumentality predict commitment to the union (Catano, McDonald, & Hebert, 1994; Catano, Pretty, Southwell, & Cole, 1993; Fullagar & Barling, 1989). In North America, instrumentality, rather than ideology, appears to be one of the strongest influences on a worker's decision to vote for or against unionization (Barling, Fullagar, & Kelloway, 1992). Workers may even vote for a union they believe to be undemocratic and corrupt if they also believe it will be instrumental in gaining better wages and job security (Keaveny, Rose, & Fossum, 1988). This research clearly demonstrates that any intervention designed to improve union commitment must address the issues of how the union has improved working conditions and economic benefits in the past and how it will continue to do so in the future. In the absence of a planned intervention or training program, rank-and-file members' perception of the instrumentality of their union remains fairly stable over time (Fullagar & Barling, 1991). The instrumentality of the union cannot be taken for granted; rank-and-file members may not be aware of the role played by their union in achieving economic gains. Catano et al. (1994) found that workers who actually received a pay equity increase expressed less commitment to the union; only workers who believed their public service union was instrumental in implementing a pay equity program were more committed to the union. The benefits of a union-negotiated program may not necessarily be attributed to the efforts of the union. The rank-and-file must appreciate that their economic benefits and working conditions are derived through the direct efforts of their union.

Socialization. Organizational practices that communicate core values, norms, and roles have a positive impact on the organizational commitment of new members (Van Maanen & Schein, 1979). Tetrick (1993) held that in a union context, history, organizational goals and values, people, and politics are aspects of socialization that should have the most influence on union commitment. Relatively few studies have examined socialization within the union context. Those that have generally support a positive relationship between positive socialization experiences and increased levels of union commitment (Fullagar & Barling, 1989; Fullagar, Gallagher, Clark, & Gordon, 1992, 1993; Fullagar, McCoy, & Shull, 1992; Gordon et al., 1980). Recently, Fullagar et al. (1993) showed that institutional and individual socialization may have different outcomes on union commitment. Socialization that occurred in a collective and formal context was associated with affective attachment (loyalty) to a union and a sense of responsibility toward the routine requirements of union membership. Individual socialization practices, on the other hand, predicted loyalty and willingness to work for the union.

DESIGNING AN INTERVENTION TO INCREASE UNION COMMITMENT

The analysis given above identifies union instrumentality and socialization as the focus of any intervention to increase union commitment. Following Tetrick (1993) and Fullagar, McCoy, and Shull (1992), any formal training program should emphasize information about the union's goals, history, and climate; what is expected from union members; the formal and informal structure of the union; and the politics of the union. As well, information must be exchanged on the historic and current role played by the union in improving working conditions, economic benefits, and job security.

The union involved in this study has approximately 13,000 members. It supports both an education committee and paid staff who are responsible for carrying out the union's education program. On an annual basis courses are available both for the general membership and for members who hold positions within the union. The general course is designed to aid rank-and-file members in understanding the structure and purpose of the union. Specialized courses such as contract clause interpretation, leadership development, and occupational health and safety are offered to the more active members. Both the education committee and the union's education officer saw the need to develop a more specialized workshop for rank-and-file members that would, they hoped, lead to increases in member commitment and support for the union.

The new workshop, held over a 2-day period, was designed to help members review the history, goals, and values of the union. It included formal presentations and small-group discussions organized around four sessions. The first session focused on the structure of the union and explained how members' dues were used in implementing union services and benefits; it concluded with a review of current union policies. The second session dealt with union members' basic rights under their collective agreement; discussion centered on grievance procedures members could follow if they believed their employer had violated the collective agreement. The third session presented an overview of privatization of government services; this session was included because the union believed the employer (i.e., the government) was in the process of having private companies take over the provision of government services at the expense of its members' job security. The fourth session introduced occupational health and safety issues; workers' rights and responsibilities under relevant occupational health and safety legislation were reviewed. As with any workshop or training program, much informal socialization took place during and after the formal sessions through interaction between the participants and the workshop leader.

RESEARCH QUESTIONS

A longitudinal, quasi-experimental design was developed to determine whether the workshop led to an increase in union commitment and related constructs and to assess the stability of any changes over time. Previously, Kelloway, Catano, and Southwell (1992, Study 2) showed that significant correlations existed between union commitment and attitude toward the union, extrinsic priorities, responsiveness to members, union satisfaction, and propensity to strike, in a study of members of this same union. Therefore, the present study reexamined the relationships between these constructs, as well as that between union commitment and perception of both union power and union service. If the intervention was effective, participants should also show changes on the correlated measures. A consistent pattern of changes would strengthen the case that any changes were due to the intervention.

METHOD

Design

This study's quasi-experimental research design is presented in Exhibit 1. For a variety of reasons it was impossible to administer a pretest to workshop participants. Therefore, data that had been previously collected from a random sample of members of this union ($N = 925$) were used as a

Exhibit 1				
Study's Quasi-Experimental Research Design				

Time Increases →

Group				
Workshop A_1	XO			O
Workshop A_2		XO		O
....		—		—
....		—		—
Workshop A_n			XO	O
Workshop B_1	X			O
Workshop B_2		X		O
....		—		—
....		—		—
Workshop B_n			X	O
Baseline	O			
Control				O

NOTE: Xs indicate interventions; Os indicate observations.

baseline (Kelloway et al., 1992, Study 2). Members who participated in the workshops were not selected randomly. Rather, they were relatively nonactive members who had never held office in the union or served on a union committee. For this reason the overall baseline data were subdivided into *nonactive* and *active* groups. Nonactive baseline data were from respondents ($n = 754$) who were comparable to the workshop participants in not having held union office or served on a union committee; active baseline data were from members ($n = 152$) who had served in at least one of these capacities.

Workshops were held approximately every other week during an 18-month period, with between 10 and 25 members attending each workshop. The workshops were held throughout the province to make them geographically accessible to all members. All workshops were conducted by the same education officer. Some participants filled out a posttest questionnaire immediately following their workshop. Subsequently this group, Workshop A, received a second posttest administration of the questionnaire. Other participants, Workshop B, attended the workshop but completed a questionnaire only at the time of the second posttest. A control group did not attend the workshops but only received the second posttest questionnaire at the same time it was sent to workshop participants. Comparisons between control and overall baseline data allowed an examination of changes in union commitment and related constructs solely as a function of time. Comparisons between the control and workshop groups allowed an examination of differences on the study variables at the time of the second posttest. This design is a variation of an interrupted time-series design with switching replications, with the addition of a nonintervention control group. It controls for most threats to internal validity and has the potential for enhancing external validity, because an effect can be shown with two samples in at least two settings at different times (Cook, Campbell, & Peracchio, 1990). The inclusion of baseline and control data, both obtained from random samples, also allows simulation of the comparisons obtained from a Solomon four-group design.

Workshop Participants

Nonactive members of the union who had attended a general membership workshop within the previous year were invited to attend the training workshops. Generally, only newer members attend general membership workshops; however, any older members who had attended the general membership workshops were also invited, and all who had accepted the invitation were accommodated at a workshop. Members who chose to attend the workshops were paid a stipend to cover lost earnings and any expenses associated with the workshop. Payment of this stipend is a standard practice for any workshop the union sponsors.

Compared with the overall baseline, Workshop A participants were younger (54% less than 35 years old vs. 34%), $\chi^2(4, N = 1,081) = 10.78$, $p < .05$, and more likely to have been a union member for less than 5 years (63% vs. 30%), $\chi^2(3, N = 1,066) = 17.48$, $p < .001$. However, they differed from the nonactive baseline only in terms of length of membership; as expected, the workshop participants were newer members with less than 5 years of union tenure (63% vs. 32%), $\chi^2(3, N = 924) = 13.75$, $p < .01$. These demographics reflect the target audience for the training workshops. There is no reason to believe that Workshop B participants differed in any way from those in Workshop A.

Survey Respondents

About 1 year following the last workshop, the posttest questionnaire was mailed to all workshop participants and to a random sample drawn from the union membership list. Stamped, self-addressed envelopes were included along with a letter from the union president explaining the purpose of the study and urging the recipients to complete the survey. There were 141 questionnaires mailed to the Workshop A participants (response rate = 25.53%, $n = 36$); 378 to Workshop B participants (response rate = 31.75%, $n = 120$); and 400 to the control group (response rate = 24.75%, $n = 99$). Questionnaires could not be mailed to all workshop participants primarily because of job turnover. Because of other union activities, the survey had to be distributed during August, a time when many members were on vacation. A follow-up letter was sent 3 weeks after the first mailing. The response rates reported here are similar to those from other independent surveys conducted with this union (Catano et al., 1994, 30%; Kelloway et al., 1992, 34%).

Overall, 58% of the participants who responded to this second posttest were female, which is approximately the percentage of women, 60%, in the union. Respondents tended to be well educated, with 57% having continued their education to varying extents past high school. The majority (63%) were married, and 68% had children. The respondents were relatively younger (31% less than 35 years old) and newer (33% less than 5 years in seniority) members, reflecting the targeted audience for the workshops.

There were no differences between the demographic composition of the control group and the overall baseline. Control respondents differed from workshop respondents only in terms of education, $\chi^2(7, N = 1,002) = 19.64, p < .01$, and age, $\chi^2(4, N = 1,005) = 9.83, p < .05$; in general, the workshop respondents were younger (37% less than 35 years old vs. 21%) and less likely to have gone to college or university (49% vs. 70%). Wilcoxon signed-ranks tests were used to assess whether those workshop participants who responded to the second posttest differed demographically from those who responded to the first. There were no differences on any demographic variable that could be tested with this procedure.

Survey Instrument

The questionnaire included the 13-item Union Commitment Scale, which measures loyalty, responsibility to the union, and willingness to work for the union (αs = .94, .78, and .87, respectively; Kelloway et al., 1992). In addition, it contained 4 items that assessed the members' attitude toward the union to which they belonged ($\alpha = .83$; Martin, 1986); 7 items measuring satisfaction with the union ($\alpha = .87$; Glick, Mirvis, & Harder, 1977); and 10 items measuring propensity to undertake strike action ($\alpha = .89$; Barling, Fullagar, Kelloway, & McKelvie, 1992). The survey also included four 4-item scales developed by Chacko (1985): Extrinsic Priorities ($\alpha = .81$) measures union activity directed toward improving factors such as pay; Responsiveness to Members ($\alpha = .79$) assesses the degree to which members feel the union takes up the members' concerns and agenda; Perception of Union Power ($\alpha = .74$) assesses the perceived influence of the union; and Perception of Union Service ($\alpha = .76$) measures the extent to which members feel their union is improving job security, pay, and working conditions. The survey concluded with several demographic items. The questionnaire was developed in consultation with the union's education committee, executive committee, and staff to ensure the suitability of the questionnaire to the union members. The result of this process was, in some cases, a slight change in the wording or phrasing of existing items. No changes were made to the union commitment measure. All scale items were measured on a 5-point Likert scale with possible responses ranging from 1 (*strongly agree*) to 5 (*strongly disagree*). The internal consistencies for all these measures were well above accepted levels and in agreement with previously reported values.

RESULTS

Did the Workshop Produce Changes in Union Commitment?

This first research question was assessed through a series of *t* tests that compared changes on the first posttest after the workshop with baseline; differences on the second posttest between the workshop and both baseline and control groups; and differences between control and baseline groups. Stability of changes was examined by comparing the first with the second posttest for Workshop A. Because difference scores could not be calculated, this change was also evaluated by independent *t* tests. In cases like this, where a positive correlation is expected between the two posttests, the independent *t* test will underestimate the *t* value obtained from a dependent *t* test, providing a conservative estimate (Kenny & Judd, 1986). Using the Bonferroni procedure, the familywise error rate for these comparisons was set at .05, with the alpha for each pairwise comparison set at .002. All tests were one-tailed except those between baseline and control, where change in either direction was of importance.

Nonactive and active baseline members differed in loyalty, $t(880) = 5.93$, $p < .002$, responsibility, $t(891) = 5.07$, $p < .002$, and willingness to work for the union, $t(902) = 11.91$, $p < .002$. These results did not change when the baseline data were restricted to members ($n = 278$) with less than 5 years' tenure in the union, the status of most workshop participants. Additionally, the mean levels of commitment for these less experienced nonactive and active members were very similar to those for nonactive and active baselines. Therefore, the nonactive baseline was used to evaluate the changes on the posttests administered to workshop groups.

The overall baseline was used for comparisons with the control group, which was obtained through a random sample of the rank-and-file membership.

Table 1 contains the means and standard deviations for all study variables for the overall and nonactive baselines and the control group, Posttest 1 for Workshop A, and Posttest 2 for all workshops combined. All data were based on unit-weighted composites. Data were reverse coded to have higher scale values correspond to higher levels of a construct. Table 1 also contains comparisons of changes from the time of the pretest, nonactive baseline, to the time of the Workshop follow-up, Posttest 2, with an estimate of the effect size for the intervention, Cohen's d (Cohen, 1988). Following Cohen (1988), effect sizes of .20, .50, and .80 were used as standards for small, medium, and large effects, respectively.

Loyalty. Individuals who participated in the workshops reported higher levels of loyalty at Posttest 1 compared with nonactive baseline respondents, $t(912) = 17.84$, $p < .002$. There was no significant difference between overall baseline and control groups, $t(987) = 0.38$, *ns*. Loyalty decreased from the time of the workshop to the time of the second posttest 1 year later, $t(215) = -4.69$, $p < .002$. However, even with this decrease the new levels were still significantly higher than both nonactive baseline, $t(882) = 9.81$, $p < .002$, and control, $t(246) = 4.96$, $p < .002$, conditions, representing a large effect for the intervention ($d = 0.88$).

Responsibility. The results for responsibility were somewhat similar to those for loyalty. Like loyalty, responsibility increased above nonactive baseline immediately following the workshops, $t(921) = 11.74$, $p < .002$. Again, there was no significant difference between overall baseline and control groups, $t(1001) = 0.68$, *ns*, and workshop participants still reported higher levels of responsibility than either the nonactive baseline, $t(896) = 7.78$, $p < .002$, or control group, $t(252) = 4.21$, $p < .002$, at the second posttest. Unlike loyalty, responsibility did not decrease significantly over time, $t(214) = -2.03$, *ns*; the intervention had only a moderate effect ($d = 0.69$).

Willingness to work. Willingness to work was affected more like re-

Table 1

Comparison of Changes in Study Variables Over Time

Variable	Overall baseline	Nonactive baseline	Control	Posttest 1	Posttest 2	Posttest 2 vs. nonactive baseline t	df	Effect size (Cohen's d)
Sample size	925	758	99	184	156			
Loyalty								
M	18.78	18.34	18.99	24.94	22.56	9.81*	882	0.88
SD	5.01	4.77	6.23	3.17	4.97			
Responsibility								
M	14.16	13.93	14.39	16.77	15.99	7.78*	896	0.69
SD	3.12	3.07	3.18	2.17	2.68			
Willingness to work								
M	8.40	7.95	7.66	10.90	10.56	11.83*	903	1.05
SD	2.62	2.39	2.44	2.11	2.92			
Attitude toward the union								
M	13.80	13.70	13.37	15.77	14.77	4.12*	894	0.36
SD	2.96	2.94	3.49	1.90	3.03			

						F	n	
Extrinsic priorities						5.10*	898	0.45
M	16.93	16.80	17.00	17.89	17.82			
SD	2.31	2.30	2.41	1.87	1.91			
Responsiveness to members						6.23*	907	0.55
M	17.52	17.41	17.77	18.41	18.40			
SD	1.91	1.90	1.54	1.71	1.37			
Perception of union power						1.32	894	0.12
M	11.33	11.33	11.66	12.76	11.66			
SD	2.75	2.74	2.98	2.73	3.25			
Perception of union service						2.92	900	0.26
M	13.98	13.83	13.60	16.09	14.56			
SD	2.82	2.77	3.54	2.04	3.21			
Union satisfaction						3.32*	886	0.30
M	22.34	22.27	22.47	25.00	23.63			
SD	4.57	4.57	5.25	4.13	4.90			
Propensity to strike						3.99*	874	0.36
M	30.58	30.31	29.07	38.32	33.35			
SD	8.90	8.74	8.14	6.07	7.37			

*$p < .002$.

sponsibility than loyalty. It increased above the nonactive baseline following the workshops, $t(930) = 15.30, p < .002$. There was no significant difference between overall baseline and control groups, $t(1014) = -2.67, ns$. Workshop participants reported higher levels of willingness to work than either the control group, $t(249) = 8.18, p < .002$, or nonactive baseline, $t(903) = 11.83, p < .002$, at the second posttest. Similarly to responsibility, willingness to work did not decrease significantly over time, $t(217) = -2.28, ns$. However, as for loyalty, the effect of the intervention on willingness to work was large ($d = 1.05$).

Did the Workshop Produce Changes in Other Constructs?

Investigation of the second research question followed the procedure outlined for union commitment. All comparisons related to this question were considered a family for the purposes of the Bonferroni procedure, with the per comparison alpha again set at .002; one-tailed tests were used for all comparisons except those between overall baseline and control. The nonactive and active baselines differed for scores on Extrinsic Priorities, $t(898) = 4.00, p < .002$, Responsiveness to Members, $t(904) = 4.18, p < .002$, and Perception of Union Service, $t(900) = 3.92, p < .002$. There were no differences between these two baseline groups on attitude toward the union, $t(894) = 2.46, ns$, perception of union power, $t(894) = 0.44, ns$, union satisfaction, $t(886) = 1.27, ns$, and propensity to strike, $t(866) = 1.96, ns$. Once again, comparisons between data from nonactive and active members with less than 5 years' experience produced identical outcomes and very similar mean values to those for the unrestricted baselines. To maintain consistency, the nonactive baseline was used to evaluate changes on the posttests administered to workshop groups for all these measures, with the overall baseline used for comparisons with the control group.

Attitude toward union. Attitude toward union improved on nonactive baseline levels following the workshops, $t(922) = 9.00, p < .002$. There was no significant difference between overall baseline and control conditions, $t(1005) = -1.34$, *ns*. Attitude toward union decreased from administration of the first posttest to the second, $t(211) = -3.79, p < .002$, but still remained higher than that expressed by both the nonactive baseline, $t(898) = 4.12, p < .002$, and control, $t(252) = 3.04, p < .002$, groups, representing a relatively small effect ($d = 0.36$).

Extrinsic priorities. Scores on the Extrinsic Priorities scale improved on nonactive baseline following the workshops, $t(930) = 6.06, p < .002$. There was no significant difference between overall baseline and control conditions, $t(1010) = 0.28$, *ns*. Extrinsic Priorities scores did not change from the first to second posttest, $t(217) = 0.09$, *ns*, and remained above both nonactive baseline, $t(903) = 5.10, p < .002$, and the control group, $t(252) = 3.04, p < .002$. The workshop had a moderate effect ($d = 0.45$).

Responsiveness to members. Scores on the Responsiveness to Members scale also improved on nonactive baseline immediately following the workshops, $t(933) = 6.48, p < .002$. There was no significant difference between overall baseline and control conditions, $t(1016) = 1.26$, *ns*. Responsiveness to Members scores did not change substantially from administration of the first posttest to the second, $t(211) = -0.45$, *ns*. Responsiveness to Members scores remained above both the control, $t(251) = 3.45, p < .002$, and the nonactive baseline, $t(907) = 6.23, p < .002$, at the second posttest, representing a moderate effect due to the intervention ($d = 0.55$).

Perception of union power. Scores on the Perception of Union Power scale increased over nonactive baseline levels following the workshop, $t(921) = 6.22, p < .002$. There was no difference between overall baseline and control conditions, $t(1004) = 1.10$, *ns*. Perception of Union Power scores did not change from the first to second posttest, $t(212) = -2.21$, *ns;* neither did it differ from the nonactive baseline, $t(897) = 1.32$, *ns*, or the control group, $t(247) = 0.00$, *ns*. The effect of the intervention was negligible ($d = 0.12$).

Perception of union service. Scores on the Perception of Union Service scale also increased over nonactive baseline following the workshop, $t(930) = 10.27, p < .002$. Again, there was no difference between overall baseline and control conditions, $t(1010) = -1.23$, *ns*. Perception of Union Service scores decreased over time from the first to second posttest,

$t(214) = -4.43$, $p < .002$, to a level that did not differ from either non-active baseline, $t(901) = 2.92$, ns, or the control group, $t(249) = 2.30$, ns. The intervention had a small effect ($d = 0.26$).

Union satisfaction. Satisfaction with the union increased above non-active baseline levels following the intervention, $t(910) = 7.18$, $p < .002$. There was no difference between overall baseline and control conditions, $t(996) = 0.26$, ns. Union satisfaction did not change from the first to second posttest, $t(206) = -2.53$, ns. Although union satisfaction remained above the nonactive baseline at the second posttest, $t(888) = 3.32$, $p < .002$, it was similar to levels found in the control group, $t(246) = 1.76$, ns. The intervention had a small effect ($d = 0.30$).

Propensity to strike. Propensity to strike increased above nonactive baseline levels following the workshop, $t(899) = 11.53$, $p < .002$. Again, there was no significant difference between overall baseline and control conditions, $t(968) = 1.51$, ns. Propensity to strike decreased from the first to second posttest, $t(211) = -4.34$, $p < .002$. At the second posttest, propensity to strike remained higher for workshop participants compared with both the control, $t(242) = 4.43$, $p < .002$, and the nonactive baseline, $t(874) = 3.99$, $p < .002$, representing a small effect ($d = 0.36$).

DISCUSSION

The longitudinal study reported here strongly supports the view that relatively stable increases in union commitment can be developed in rank-and-file members through training workshops. The workshop intervention was based on known antecedents of union commitment, particularly union instrumentality and formal socialization components. As would be expected from such a formal intervention (Fullagar et al., 1993), the workshop led to increased loyalty and responsibility; however, it also had an effect on willingness to work. These points are discussed in greater detail.

Although the results from any quasi-experimental study are open to alternative interpretation, the consistent nature of the results and the pattern of changes that occurred not only over the three commitment dimensions, but also over associated constructs, argue quite strongly in support of the intervention as a causal factor. The quasi-experimental design used here is considered one of the strongest in protecting against threats to validity (Cook et al., 1990). Both the baseline and control data were obtained through random samples of rank-and-file members from the same union, taken approximately 3 years apart. There were no differences between baseline and control on any of the 10 measures. These results are quite consistent with those reported by Fullagar and Barling (1991) for loyalty, union instrumentality, and general union attitudes; these three measures, obtained from the same group of workers, remained stable for three measurements taken over 1 year. Considering the Fullagar and Barling data as a "proxy" control group lends further support to the efficacy of the intervention. In the absence of an intervention or a critical event, union commitment and other union-related attitudes remain stable over time.

Workshop participants improved on every one of the 10 measures taken immediately after the workshop, compared with a preworkshop baseline. All workshop participants reported higher levels of loyalty, responsibility, and willingness to work on the second posttest compared with the random control group, which had not attended workshops. Similar changes were found on the second posttest for four of the other seven measures: attitude toward the union, Extrinsic Priorities, Responsiveness to Members, and propensity to strike. Review of the changes in Workshop A from the first to second posttest show that there were decreases on 9 of the 10 measures during that period, with four of these significant. This pattern of results argues for the potency of the intervention. Attending the workshop led to an increase in loyalty, responsibility, willingness to work, and most of the related measures. These levels decreased as a function of time, but after a period of up to 30 months they were still significantly higher than levels found in randomly selected members. The pattern of results also supports the construct validity of the three commitment dimensions (Kelloway et al., 1992); constructs associated with union commitment dimensions exhibited consistent changes.

The results for Extrinsic Priorities and Perception of Union Service scales offer substantial support for the effectiveness of the workshop. The workshop emphasized the instrumentality of the union in achieving economic gains and improved working conditions (Barling, Fullagar, & Kelloway, 1992). Both of these measures assess union instrumentality. In both cases, workshop participants had more positive views following the workshops, although somewhat less so for Perception of Union Service.

Although the workshop was expected to have more of an impact on loyalty and responsibility than on willingness to work (Fullagar et al., 1993), improvements occurred on all three commitment variables, but to different degrees. Workshop groups showed significant increases compared with both the control group and baseline with no difference between these latter two conditions. For these three commitment variables, Cohen's d, the effect attributable to the workshop, ranged from moderate to large. The increases in responsibility and willingness to work remained relatively stable, whereas the increase in loyalty decreased over time. These differential results support the multidimensional nature of the union commitment construct (Kelloway et al., 1992). The improvement in willingness to work had not been expected from a workshop whose content was mainly based on instrumentality and formal socialization. However, the three commitment measures are not orthogonal (Kelloway et al., 1992); the unexpected increase in willingness to work, for the most part, may be a reflection of the workshop's effect on loyalty and responsibility.

Because this was a quasi-experimental design, it is possible that members who were more committed to the union chose to attend workshops. This is unlikely; the prospect of 2 paid days off work should have been an attractive incentive to attend the workshop regardless of commitment level. As noted, the workshop participants were mostly younger and newer members. Previously, Southwell (1990) reported a significant negative relationship between age and union commitment for this study's baseline data. Attitudes of members with less than 5 years' seniority were no different from the general membership for the baseline data; however, nonactive members in this subgroup were less committed to the union. If anything, workshop participants should have been less committed, as a group, to the union. Equally unlikely as an explanation for these results is a union commitment bias among survey respondents from the workshop groups.

Workshop respondents were similar to both the control and baseline groups on all demographic measures except those associated with the target audience. There is no reason to believe that the percentage of committed members returning surveys differed across the groups. More likely, the same percentage of committed members completed the questionnaire, but those in the workshop groups had higher levels of commitment. Not all workshop participants could be reached for the second posttest because of job turnover. Most of this attrition resulted from downsizing based on seniority; for any given level of experience, this situation should lead to the same proportionate loss of committed and uncommitted union members. Because seniority, in general, tends to be associated with commitment, differential attrition may be partially responsible for some of the changes that occurred here. Although plausible, this is not probable. There were no significant associations between seniority and any of the three commitment variables within the preworkshop baseline, the control, or the workshop groups; these correlations ranged from −.05 to .06. Nonetheless, because workshop participants were not selected randomly, these arguments cannot be ruled out entirely as alternative explanations.[1]

Although these results are persuasive in showing that the intervention was effective in improving union commitment, the increases were not permanent. They decreased over time. Although they were still above control and baseline levels at the second posttest, it is likely they will continue to erode unless additional efforts are taken to maintain the changes. Similarly, Stagner and Eflal (1982) found that increases in union-related attitudes that were caused by an unplanned intervention, a strike, dissipated over a 7-month period. This lack of permanency illustrates the need for the union to continue to offer training workshops on an ongoing basis for rank-and-file members or to put in place some other means of maintaining the increased levels of commitment that were developed through the workshops. Barling and Kelloway (1993) have proposed training shop

---

[1]The potential threats posed by differences in age and seniority were examined by reanalyzing the data using analyses of covariance with age and seniority as covariates. The results did not change; in most cases, the covariates themselves were not significant.

stewards in commitment-enhancing strategies. The stewards, as informal socialization agents and providers of information, would play a central role in influencing members' perception of the union. Ideally, the trained steward would reinforce the information, values, and goals presented to the rank-and-file member at a general training workshop of the type used in this study.

There is also a need in future applied research to establish programs that will specifically develop increased levels of willingness to work (Barling, Fullagar, & Kelloway, 1992; Fullagar et al., 1993; Kelloway & Barling, 1993; Kelloway et al., 1992). This dimension predicts active participation by members in the life of their union. Serving on committees, running for office, and acting as a steward are the lifeblood of unions. To survive, unions must continually find committed people who are willing to work on the union's behalf. Although willingness to work appears to have been affected by the intervention evaluated here, there were no theoretical reasons for it to have done so, given the nature of the intervention. As Fullagar et al. (1993) suggested, this dimension is likely to be influenced by individual socialization, which comes through one-on-one contact with shop stewards and other union leaders. This is another reason why using stewards to reinforce lessons from a more general workshop of the type presented here should be given consideration.

By showing that union commitment can be developed through a theoretically based intervention, this study helps remove union commitment research from the endangered species list (Gordon & Ladd, 1993). It sets the stage for future applied work and establishes that union commitment research is more than an academic exercise. It does offer promise for "keeping the union patient alive" (Gordon & Ladd, 1993, p. 24). This is particularly important in the current context of a global economy and the changing nature of employment relations. To compete globally, both public- and private-sector firms have increased their reliance on a contingent labor force made up of part-time and limited-contract workers, groups that have not been noted for their commitment to unions. Knowing that union commitment can be developed offers unions a degree of optimism for their survival in this new environment.

REFERENCES

Barling, J., Fullagar, C., & Kelloway, E. K. (1992). *The union and its members: A psychological approach.* Oxford, England: Oxford University Press.

Barling, J., Fullagar, C., Kelloway, E. K., & McKelvie, L. (1992). Union loyalty and strike propensity. *Journal of Social Psychology, 132,* 581–590.

Barling, J., & Kelloway, E. K. (1993, June). *Training shop stewards to enhance union commitment.* Paper presented at the invited International Workshop on Union Commitment, Amsterdam, The Netherlands.

Catano, V. M., McDonald, K. M., & Hebert, N. (1994, April). *Union commitment and pay equity: Linking feminist perspectives to unionization.* Paper presented at the Society for Industrial/Organizational Psychology, Nashville, TN.

Catano, V. M., Pretty, G. M. H., Southwell, R. E. S., & Cole, G. (1993, June). *Psychological sense of community as an antecedent of organizational and union commitment: Considering dual allegiance as an epiphenomenon.* Paper presented at the invited International Workshop on Union Commitment, Amsterdam, The Netherlands.

Chacko, T. I. (1985). Member participation in union activities: Perceptions of union priorities, performance, and satisfaction. *Journal of Labor Research, 6,* 363–373.

Cohen, J. (1988). *Statistical power analysis for the behavioral sciences* (2nd ed.). Hillsdale, NJ: Erlbaum.

Cook, T. D., Campbell, D. T., & Peracchio, L. (1990). Quasi-experimentation. In M. D. Dunnette & L. M. Hough (Eds.), *Handbook of industrial and organizational psychology* (2nd ed., Vol. 1, pp. 491–576). Palo Alto, CA: Consulting Psychologists Press.

Fullagar, C., & Barling, J. (1989). A longitudinal test of a model of the antecedents and consequences of union loyalty. *Journal of Applied Psychology, 74,* 213–227.

Fullagar, C., & Barling, J. (1991). Predictors and outcomes of different patterns of organizational and union loyalty. *Journal of Occupational Psychology, 64,* 129–143.

Fullagar, C., Gallagher, D. G., Clark, P. F., & Gordon, M. E. (1992, May). *A model of the antecedents of early union commitment: The role of socialization experiences and steward characteristics.* Paper presented at the Society for Industrial/Organizational Psychology, Montreal, Quebec, Canada.

Fullagar, C., Gallagher, D. G., Clark, P. F., & Gordon, M. E. (1993, June). *The impact of early socialization on union commitment and participation: A longitudinal study.* Paper presented at the invited International Workshop on Union Commitment, Amsterdam, The Netherlands.

Fullagar, C., McCoy, D., & Shull, C. (1992). The socialization of union loyalty. *Journal of Organizational Behavior, 13,* 13–26.

Glick, W., Mirvis, P., & Harder, D. (1977). Union satisfaction and participation. *Industrial Relations, 16,* 141–151.

Gordon, M. E., & Ladd, R. T. (1993, June). *Union commitment: An update.* Paper presented at the invited International Workshop on Union Commitment, Amsterdam, The Netherlands.

Gordon, M. E., Philpot, J. W., Burt, R. E., Thompson, C. A., & Spiller, W. E. (1980). Commitment to the union: Development of a measure and an examination of its correlates. *Journal of Applied Psychology, 65,* 474–499.

Keaveny, T. J., Rose, J., & Fossum, J. (1988, December). *Predicting support for unionization: Part-time versus full time workers and professional/technical blue collar workers.* Paper presented at the annual conference of the Industrial Relations Research Association, New York.

Kelloway, E. K., & Barling J. (1993). Members' participation in local union activities: Measurement, prediction, and replication. *Journal of Applied Psychology, 78,* 262–279.

Kelloway, E. K., Catano, V. M., & Southwell, R. R. (1992). The construct validity of union commitment: Development and dimensionality of a shorter scale. *Journal of Occupational and Organizational Psychology, 65,* 197–211.

Kenny, D. A., & Judd, C. M. (1986). Consequences of violating the independence assumption in analysis of variance. *Psychological Bulletin, 99,* 422–431.

Martin, J. E. (1986). Predictors of individual propensity to strike. *Industrial and Labor Relations Review, 39,* 214–227.

Southwell, R. R. (1990). *The dimensionality, antecedents and consequences of union commitment: A study of a civil service union.* Unpublished master's thesis, Saint Mary's University, San Antonio, TX.

Stagner, R., & Eflal, B. (1982). Internal union dynamics during a strike: A quasi-experimental study. *Journal of Applied Psychology, 67,* 37–44.

Tetrick, L. E. (1993, June). *Developing and maintaining union commitment: A theoretical framework.* Paper presented at the invited International Workshop on Union Commitment, Amsterdam, The Netherlands.

Van Maanen, J. V., & Schein, E. H. (1979). Toward a theory of organizational socialization. *Research in Organizational Behavior 1,* 209–264.

15

Organizational Citizenship and Union Participation: Measuring Discretionary Membership Behaviors

Clive J. A. Fullagar, Judi McLean Parks, Paul F. Clark, and Daniel G. Gallagher

In recent years there has been a resurgence of interest among industrial psychologists and organizational theorists in the study of unionization. Much of this research has been in response to the rapid decline in union membership over the last 40 years and the change in employment relations that this decline has brought about. Most of this research has been directed to cross-sectional studies of individual "attitudes" and "behavioral intentions" (Barling, Fullagar, & Kelloway, 1992; Gallagher & Strauss, 1991). The emphasis on attitudes is evidenced in the tremendous amount of research addressing such topics as union commitment; dual allegiance; the affective attachment of workers to their unions; belief in unionism; and individual responsibility to the union (e.g., Fukami & Larson, 1984, Fullagar & Barling, 1989; Gordon, Philpot, Burt, Thompson, & Spiller, 1980; Kelloway, Catano, & Southwell, 1992; Klandermans, 1989; Newton & McFarlane Shore, 1992). For many behavioral studies of unionization, the issue of behavior has actually focused on "behavioral intentions" rather than actual behaviors. This observation is most notable in the areas of union voting and union militancy, where the dependent variable has been operationalized in terms of anticipated behavior (i.e., how one is likely to vote, the likelihood of striking or picketing, and willingness to work for the union) rather than evidence of the actual behavior.

As suggested by Fullagar and Barling (1987), increased understanding of unions and union members requires that research shift from focusing on attitudes or intentions to an examination of the relevant behavioral outcomes. Such an orientation will require additional attention to the construct validity of the measures used to assess actual membership behaviors. The primary purpose of the current study was to establish the construct validity of a particular operationalization of union participation.

MEASURES OF UNION PARTICIPATION

We do not wish to imply that there have been no studies on union participation. To date, there exists a long history of research on the antecedents or correlates of union participation (Barling et al., 1992; Perline & Lorenz, 1970; Spinrad, 1960). However, the results of this research have tended to be inconclusive or contradictory. Furthermore, there are concerns about the measurement of the construct of union participation. Most research has measured union participation through one of the following approaches: (a) a single-item measure (e.g., Kolchin & Hyclak, 1984; Leicht, 1989); (b) multiple single-item measures (e.g., Blyton, Nicholson, & Ursell, 1981; Chacko, 1985; Hoyman & Stallworth, 1987); or (c) a single composite or additive scale of participatory behaviors (e.g., Cornfield, Filho, & Chun, 1990; Hammer & Wazeter, 1993; Huszczo, 1983; Kelloway & Barling, 1993). Although reliance on single-item measures of union participation raises general concerns of reliability, the use of single additive scales to measure membership participation in union activity may also be problematic.

First, close examination of most measures of union participation reveals a heavy reliance on "administrative" aspects of union involvement. Included within this administrative orientation to participation are items concerning local union office holding, steward duties, union committee work, or campaigning for union office. In addition to administrative aspects of participation, most measures of union participation also tend to emphasize other forms of formal or structured opportunities for membership participation such as voting in officers, contract ratification or strike authorization elections, and attending union meetings or grievance filing.

Second, it may also be argued that such an overreliance on "formal" forms of union participation, in particular the reliance on administrative participation, may artificially restrict the measurable opportunities for participation. For example, administrative forms of participation, such as office holding, are inherently likely to result in low levels of union participation among the membership for the simple reason that within any union only a small and finite number of administrative positions are available. Furthermore, the opportunities to participate in other democratic functions, such as voting on contract ratification or strike authorization, are likely to be infrequent.

Third, single additive measures of union participation, which tend to be composed of a checklist of participatory behaviors, fail to distinguish between measures on the "intensity" of participation. Most notably, voting in a contract ratification election would require substantially less personal investment in time or energy than seeking or holding union office.

Fourth, reliance on the use of a single-item measure of participation or single additive scale would appear to run counter to studies of participation that suggest that union participation may in fact be a multidimensional construct. Studies by Nicholson, Ursell, and Blyton (1981) and Klandermans (1986) have suggested that conflicting findings or inability to adequately explain union participation in prior research may reflect the fact that what predicts one type of participatory behavior might not predict another form of union participation. It has been further noted by Nicholson et al. (1981) that in the examination of correlates of individual participation items, certain items appeared to "group together" and share similar correlates, whereas other groups of items shared different correlates.

The multidimensionality of union participation has been empirically tested and supported by McShane (1986), who found many of the formal participatory items used in existing research (e.g., office holding, voting, meeting attendance) to constitute three different and conceptually distinct forms or dimensions of union participation. Subsequent studies by Gallagher, McLean Parks, and Wetzel (1987) and McLean Parks, Gallagher, and Fullagar (in press) have suggested that union participation is multidimensional and is reflective of behaviors centered around three forms of activity: "administrative" duties; participation in "intermittent" or scheduled activities (meetings and voting); and ongoing and unstructured "supportive" forms of behaviors (e.g., helping new members learn about the union, showing others how the union could be of help).

As suggested above, efforts to fully understand both the form and antecedents or correlates of union participation may be hampered by the overemphasis on more formal or structured forms of union participation (office holding, meeting attendance, and voting behavior). A broader and more informative measurement of union participation would involve an effort to incorporate more attention to those union activities that union members avail themselves of on a day-to-day or more unstructured basis. In the same way that Gordon et al. (1980) drew on the organizational commitment literature to enhance understanding of union commitment, we follow the suggestions of Tetrick (in press) and examine union participation from the perspective of organizational citizenship behaviors.

Organizational citizenship behavior and union participation share several defining characteristics: (a) Both types of behavior are discretionary; (b) both types of behavior are assumed to be beneficial for the organization; and (c) neither type of behavior can be specifically contracted, nor can organizational or union members be specifically penalized for *not* engaging in them.

It has long been recognized that organizations have a need for behaviors that go beyond strictly delineated role requirements (Katz & Kahn, 1978). Organizations not only need reliable role performance, but also spontaneous and innovative behaviors. Such extrarole behaviors are necessary in order to ensure the effective functioning, and perhaps even the survival, of the organization (Katz & Kahn, 1978).

Organ (1988) suggested that organizational citizenship behaviors went beyond job roles and were beneficial to the organization. This has resulted in a steady stream of research examining the construct of organizational citizenship behavior, which has been conceptualized as multidimensional in nature. One view of organizational citizenship behavior is that of Organ and his colleagues (Organ & Konovsky, 1989; Organ & Lingl, 1991), who have examined six distinct dimensions that incorporate both role-maintaining behaviors and extrarole behaviors: (a) *compliance*, which includes attendance and complying with minimal role expectations; (b) *conscientiousness*, conceptualized as overt diligence directed toward role behaviors; (c) *courtesy*, characterized by keeping coworkers informed; (d) *civic virtue*, which includes keeping informed about issues of interest to the organization; (e) *sportsmanship*, characterized by forbearance or restraint, such as avoiding complaints about trivial matters; and (f) *altruism*, which includes overtly helpful behaviors, such as helping a coworker catch up. In this conceptualization, the first two dimensions are oriented toward role maintenance, and the remaining dimensions are more proactive and role enhancing in nature.

In the context of unions, examples of in-role behaviors would include compliance with the union bylaws and union–management contract, regular attendance at union meetings, voting in union elections, and conscientiously carrying out the responsibilities of any union office that the member might hold. Each of these behaviors helps maintain the union and its democratic functioning, yet does little to *improve* the functioning of the union or to expand the roles of the members. It is important to note that it is these kinds of role-maintaining behaviors that have been the sole focus of previous conceptualizations of union participation.

Examples of role enhancing or expanding behaviors in the union context would include informing other union members of decisions that might affect the union and its membership, encouraging other members to vote, making suggestions to improve the union and its functioning, representing the union favorably to outsiders, and helping another union member with a union-related task. The opportunities for these types of activities are more frequent than the administrative behaviors studied in prior research, and they have been omitted from previous operationalizations of union participation.

The final purpose of this study was to establish the criterion-related validity of our conceptualization of union participation. In determining which criterion variables to measure, we again drew from the organizational citizenship behavior literature. Correlates of organizational citizenship behaviors include *satisfaction* (e.g., Karambayya, 1992; Moorman, Niehoff, & Organ, 1993; Organ & Konovsky, 1989; Organ & Lingl, 1991; Puffer, 1987; Smith, Organ, & Near, 1983; Williams & Anderson, 1991; Wolfe Morrison, 1992), *commitment* (e.g., Moorman et al., 1993; O'Reilly & Chatman, 1986; Wolfe Morrison, 1992), *positive attitudes* (e.g., George, 1991), and *performance* (e.g., George & Bettenhausen, 1990; Karambayya, 1992). Consequently, the current study measured union satisfaction, union commitment, attitudes toward unions in general, and traditional participation. To establish the predictive validity of our measure of union participation, we hypothesized that participation would be positively correlated with these criterion variables.

The study, therefore, had two main objectives: (a) to establish the construct validity of a particular measure of union participation in order to determine its dimensionality and (b) to ascertain the criterion-related validity of the dimensions of participation.

METHOD

Sample

The sample in the present study was part of larger study of members of the National Association of Letter Carriers (NALC). A total of 638 members were mailed questionnaires. Of these, there were 266 complete and usable responses, giving a response rate of 42%. The sample was 69% male, the average age was 36 years ($SD = 8$), and the mean tenure with the union 32 months ($SD = 23$). Union records were not detailed enough to ascertain whether the sample was representative of total membership.

Questionnaires

A questionnaire was constructed in consultation with the NALC and mailed to respondents who had responded to a previous survey. The questionnaires were accompanied by a cover letter from the researchers stating that the research was being conducted by a team of university researchers on behalf of the NALC. Participation was emphasized as being voluntary and confidentiality was guaranteed. Completed questionnaires were placed in stamped-addressed envelopes and returned directly to the researchers.

Union participation. Drawing from the organizational citizenship behavior literature and previous measures of union participation, an initial measure of 76 union participatory behaviors was developed. For practical purposes of operationalization and as a result of consultation with union officials, these behaviors were pared down to 36 items. Frequency of participation was measured by requesting respondents to indicate on a 6-point scale how frequently they engaged in each type of behavior, ranging from 0 (*never*) to 5 (*at every opportunity*) during the previous 18 months.

Criterion variables. Four criterion variables were selected to further establish the construct validity of union participation. Again, these were selected on the basis of research that has investigated the correlates of organizational citizenship behavior.

Satisfaction with the union was measured using a 12-item scale (Fiorito, Gallagher, & Fukami, 1988; Jarley, Kuruvilla, & Casteel, 1990). The scale used a 5-point response format (1 = *strongly disagree*, 3 = *neither agree nor disagree*, 5 = *strongly agree*). The internal consistency of this scale was found to be satisfactory (Cronbach's α = .92).

Kelloway et al.'s (1992) 13-item scale was used to measure union commitment. This scale was derived from Gordon et al.'s (1980) 48-item instrument and measures union loyalty, responsibility to the union, and willingness to participate in union activities. The reliabilities of each of these three scales was satisfactory (Cronbach's α > .75).

General attitudes toward unions were assessed using Deshpande and Fiorito's (1989) 10-item General Union Attitudes scale. Scale items had a 5-point response format (1 = *strongly disagree*, 3 = *unsure*, 5 = *strongly agree*). Again, the reliability of this scale was found to be satisfactory (α = .83).

Finally, three items were included to assess traditional forms of administrative union participation (e.g., frequency of attendance at union meetings, voting in elections, and whether respondent had ever held a union office, been a delegate to a convention, or ran for a union office). The first item assessed frequency of meeting attendance ("In the past 18 months how many branch meetings have you attended?" 0 = *none*, 5 = *all of them*). The second item asked whether or not members had voted in an election (0 = *no*, 1 = *yes*). The final item assessed whether members had ever held or ran for office (0 = *no*, 1 = *yes*).

Procedure

Because the behaviors assessed by the scale were not identical to organizational citizenship behaviors, but reflected the citizenship concept in a union context, it would not have been feasible to expect the dimensionality of the union participation instrument to mimic that of organizational citizenship scales. The kinds of "citizenship" behaviors engaged in by union members are very different from those of organizational employees. Also, given the fact that this type of operationalization of union participation is empirically relatively new, and also the diversity of views concerning the dimensionality of citizenship behaviors, a more exploratory approach was taken with the data by using a principal-components analysis on the 36 items and obliquely rotating the solution (the dimensions of union participation were expected to be correlated; Tabachnick & Fidell, 1989). The construct validity of the resulting operationalization of union participation was further assessed by correlating the resulting factors with the criterion variables described above.

RESULTS

Results of the principal-components analysis indicated that six factors should be extracted using Kaiser's criterion of a minimum eigenvalue of one. However, the scree plot indicated that only five factors should be interpreted. Together these five factors accounted for 59% of the variance. Furthermore, the factors were significantly correlated, justifying an oblique rotation. The results of the principal-components analysis are presented in Table 1.

Factor 1 accounted for 40% of the variance and consisted of 10 items that strongly resembled the civic virtue dimension of citizenship behavior described by Organ (1990). These items included such behaviors as keeping informed and participating in meetings and governance activities. However, this factor also consisted of instances in which members carried out certain extrarole behaviors well beyond the minimum required levels (such as participating in branch social, educational, and administrative activities, making innovative suggestions to improve the union, and speaking up at union meetings). This factor captured the essence of Graham and Dienesch's (1991) definitions of advocacy and social participation in that many of the behaviors involved innovation and proactively energizing other union members, and engaging in group meetings and activities. We labeled this factor Conscientious Activism, and it had a satisfactory internal consistency (Cronbach's $\alpha = .90$).

The second factor had eight items loading on it and explained 8% of the variance. This factor reflected (a) compliance with the minimal expectations associated with union membership (e.g., performing tasks expected of one as a union member and adhering to the constitution and by-laws of the union) and (b) focusing on what is right rather than what is wrong with the union (e.g., making the best of situations even when the union is the problem and protecting the image of the union). Consequently, we labeled this factor Compliant Sportsmanship, because it consisted of several basic maintenance, or in-role, behaviors that are oriented toward meeting role expectations and maintaining the role as it exists. The reliability of this factor was also satisfactory ($\alpha = .88$).

The third factor consisted of four items reflecting behaviors critical of the union (e.g., criticized what the NALC is doing, expressed opinions about what the union is doing and changes that might improve the NALC). We labeled this third factor Critical Involvement, because it also consisted of behaviors that indicated involvement in the union (e.g., making suggestions to help improve the union and consulting with other members about union actions and decisions). The internal consistency of this factor was .76.

Table 1

Factor Structure of Union Participation

| | Factor loadings | | | | |
Item	1	2	3	4	5
Factor 1					
7. Participated in branch social activities	.78				
21. Volunteered to be a member of branch committees	.73				
22. Gave advance notice when unable to attend a union function	.70				
34. Attended union meetings	.70				
20. Participated in a branch charity activity	.59				
3. Spoke up at a union meeting	.59				
23. Participated in a branch educational activity	.58				
13. Encouraged other members to speak up at meetings	.52				
30. Made innovative suggestions to improve the overall effectiveness of NALC	.39				
11. Actively looked for ways to help the union	.38				
Factor 2					
32. Tried to make the best of the situation even when there may be problems in the NALC		.91			
31. Tried to protect the positive image of the NALC		.80			
24. Made a conscious effort to meet expectations regarding my behavior as union member		.68			
17. Adhered to the constitution and by-laws of the union		.68			
12. Tried to avoid creating problems for other members		.66			
25. Focused on what is right with NALC instead of what is wrong		.64			
33. Encouraged other members to support the NALC on an issue		.57			
5. Performed the tasks that are expected of me as a union member		.38			

Factor 3

6. Criticized what the NALC is doing .87

15. Expressed my opinions about union issues even
    when other members think differently from me .52

10. Made suggestions to other members about
    changes that might improve the NALC .50

16. Consulted with other members who might be
    affected by my actions or decisions .42

Factor 4

36. Filed a grievance on your own behalf over
    an issue of concern to you −.71

2. Helped a fellow member prepare a grievance −.70

35. Contacted a branch official about an issue
    related to union representation −.51

28. Contacted branch to keep them informed
    on issues related to the NALC −.51

29. Discussed internal union business with a
    union official −.49

4. Shown another member how the NALC could
   help them with a problem −.48 −.37

27. Offered assistance to the NALC in solving a
    union related problem −.44

1. Discussed work related issues with a union
   official −.40

8. Helped another member campaign for a
   union office −.37

Factor 5

19. Read parts of the collective agreement
    between the NALC–USPS −.87

14. Read an NALC news publication on a
    regular basis −.83

18. Helped new members learn about the NALC −.45

Eigenvalue	14.30	2.86	1.60	1.32	1.20
% of variance	.40	.08	.04	.04	.03
Reliability (Cronbach's α)	.90	.88	.76	.89	.71

NOTE: NALC = National Association of Letter Carriers.

The fourth factor consisted of nine items that all loaded negatively and had a reliability of .89. It appeared to reflect a lack of involvement in union affairs in that it consisted of such behaviors as lack of contact and low interaction with other union members and officials, and lack of support for the union. We termed this factor Alienation, because it appeared to be the antithesis of union involvement. Kanungo (1982) argued that the opposite state of work involvement is work alienation, and we have extended this argument to unions in our interpretation of the fourth factor.

Finally, the fifth factor consisted of four items with negative loadings greater than .35. This factor was primarily defined by access to union information. The negative loadings may be indicative of lack of access of members to NALC news publications and the collective agreement between the NALC and the United States Postal Service. Furthermore, the factor only explained 3% of the variance and its internal consistency was not satisfactory (Cronbach's $\alpha = .52$). Because of the possible artifactual nature of the factor, its low reliability, and the low percentage of variance explained, this fifth factor was not interpreted.

Composite scores were computed for these four dimensions by simply adding the scores on those items that loaded on each factor. In the case of Alienation, because all items had negative loadings, items were reverse coded so that a higher score denoted more frequent engagement in alienating behaviors.

As further support for our notion that union participation is multidimensional, we undertook reliability analyses on the four dimensions defined above, as well as a reliability analysis of all 36 items. In each instance the internal consistency of the four factors exceeded the reliability coefficient of the overall scale (Cronbach's $\alpha = .67$).

The construct validity of our four-dimensional conceptualization of union participation was further established by ascertaining the correlations between the four factors and several criterion-related and concurrent variables (see Table 2).

First, we found Critical Involvement behaviors to be negatively associated with satisfaction with the union ($r = -.17, p < .05$), whereas Conscientious Activism and Compliant Sportsmanship were positively

Table 2

Correlations Between Union Participation Factors and Criterion-Related Variables

Variables	1	2	3	4	5	6	7	8	9	10
1. Conscientious Activism	.90[b]									
2. Compliant Sportsmanship	.60	.88								
3. Critical Involvement	.63	.50	.76							
4. Alienation	−.76	−.54	−.66	.89						
5. Union satisfaction	.12	.13	−.17	−.07	.92					
6. General union attitudes	.29	.33	.09	−.27	.36	.83				
7. Loyalty to the union	.29	.23	.00	−.24	.37	.75	.90			
8. Responsibility to the union	.23	.22	.07	−.26	.17	.49	.55	.75		
9. Willingness to work for the union	.42	.32	.19	−.39	.23	.64	.66	.47	.83	
10. Attendance at meetings	.50	.21	.23	−.33	.18	.29	.34	.23	.33	—

NOTE: $r > .13$, $p < .05$; $r > .18$, $p < .01$. Values in the diagonal are reliability coefficients (Cronbach's alpha).

correlated with union satisfaction ($rs = .12$ and .13, respectively; $p < .05$).

The first two participation factors encapsulate Graham's (1986) loyalty dimension of organizational citizenship behavior in that they include allegiance to and promotion of the union. This was supported by the significant positive correlations of these factors with union loyalty ($r = .29$, $p < .05$, Conscientious Activism; $r = .23$, $p < .05$, Compliant Sportsmanship). Alienation, on the other hand, was negatively associated with loyalty to the union ($r = -.24$, $p < .05$), whereas Critical Involvement had a zero correlation.

One would expect willingness to work with the union to be most strongly correlated with Conscientious Activism as well as positively correlated with Compliant Sportsmanship. These expectations were confirmed by our data ($r = .42$, $p < .05$, Conscientious Activism; $r = .32$, $p < .05$, Compliant Sportsmanship). In addition, Alienation was found to be strongly negatively correlated with willingness to work for the union ($r = -.39$, $p < .05$). Interestingly, Critical Involvement was also found to positively correlate with intention to work for the union ($r = .19$, $p < .05$), reinforcing the notion of constructive involvement in union activities.

Finally, we calculated correlations and t tests between the four dimensions of participation and more traditional measures of administrative participation, such as frequency of attendance at meetings and voting in elections, and serving as a union officer or delegate. The t tests showed that members who held office were more likely to be conscientiously active in the union, $t(268) = -10.69$, $p < .01$, more likely to engage in compliant sportsmanship behaviors, $t(264) = -9.51$, $p < .01$, more likely to voice criticism of the union, $t(264) = -8.82$, $p < .01$, and less likely to be alienated, $t(264) = 6.18$, $p < .01$. Looking at voting behavior, the first three participation dimensions were more likely to be associated with voting in elections, $t(194) = -5.55$, -3.79, -2.10, respectively, all $ps < .05$, whereas alienated members were less likely to vote, $t(194) = 3.56$, $p < .01$.

With regard to attendance at union meetings, the pattern of correlations with the four participation factors was similar. The strongest positive correlations were with Conscientious Activism ($r = .50$, $p < .05$), followed by Critical Involvement ($r = .23$, $p < .05$) and Compliant Sportsmanship ($r = .21$, $p < .05$). Alienation was significantly negatively correlated with meeting attendance ($r = -.33$, $p < .05$).

DISCUSSION

Despite the fact that all the data were collected using self-report measures and further research is needed to establish the reliability and external validity of our operationalization of union participation, the results of this study provide some corroborative evidence that union participation is a multidimensional construct. Each of the four dimensions consists of different subsets of behaviors. Although there was not a one-to-one correspondence between the dimensions of the current operationalization of union participation and organizational citizenship behavior, there are similarities. Conscientious Activism consisted of civic virtue behaviors (e.g., "participated in branch social activities"), conscientious behaviors (e.g., "gave advance notice when unable to attend a union function"), and altruistic behaviors (e.g., "actively looked for ways to help the union"). As the label suggests, Compliant Sportsmanship reflected both compliance (e.g., "adhered to the constitution and by-laws of the union") and sportsmanship (e.g., "tried to make the best of the situation even when there may be problems with the NALC"). Even Critical Involvement reflected Organ's notion of voice (e.g., "criticized what the NALC is doing"), but the nature of this criticism was constructive in that it was aimed at improving the union and reflected a sense of involvement in the policies adopted by the union (i.e., civic virtue). The exception to the analogy of union participation with organizational citizenship behaviors is Alienation. The behaviors that constitute this factor, although discretionary, are definitely not beneficial to the union. Kanungo (1982) has conceptualized alienation as being the opposite state of involvement. The strong negative correlations between Alienation and the other three factors and the criterion variables would appear to confirm our interpretation.

It appears that there are union participatory behaviors that are not identical to behaviors that have been described in previous, more traditional measures of union participation. Indeed, we would go further and suggest that focusing solely on administrative aspects of union involvement excludes a wide range of more frequently occurring behaviors. These behaviors, to a large extent, are similar to those that have been described in the organizational citizenship literature. They consist of role maintaining, or in-role, behaviors, as well as role expanding, or extrarole, behaviors. With the exception of Alienation, they are all supportive of the organization or union. Although members who are critically involved in the union are less satisfied with the union, they nevertheless also engage in Conscientious Activism and Compliant Sportsmanship, and they are likely to vote in elections, attend union meetings, and be willing to work for the union. Future research needs to investigate further the impact of these kinds of participatory behaviors on both union efficacy and union democracy.

The current findings tend to support the suggestions and empirical observations offered by Nicholson et al. (1991), McShane (1986), and Klandermans (1986) that union participation may be multidimensional in nature. From the perspective of union officials, such a finding may be of particular significance in the consideration of strategies to stimulate membership participation in their organizations. In particular, the types of strategies used by union officials to encourage formal office holding or voting participation may differ from strategies used to encourage more ongoing supportive citizenship behaviors. Of particular note may be the potential importance of new member socialization in both building membership commitment in terms of responsibility to the union and encouraging actual supportive behaviors outside of official union events (elections, committee work, office holding). Furthermore, it may be interesting to determine the extent to which particular citizenship behaviors are more reflective of individual characteristics or attitudes and are hence subject to limited union influence.

We do not wish to imply that prior and recent studies that have empirically supported the unidimensionality of participation are statistically or methodologically flawed. In contrast, this study suggests that the unidimensional operationalization of union participation may be an artifact of an extremely limited definition or range of behaviors that has been used to represent participation. When union participation is viewed as consisting of a broader range of behaviors, beyond the traditional forms of formal participation, then a multidimensional operationalization of participation appears to be a more inherently reasonable way to measure and understand the ways in which union members may, or may not, voluntarily participate in their union organizations.

In conclusion, we believe that union participation as traditionally conceptualized and examined is an oversimplification of a complex phenomenon. Resolving this oversimplification may provide a platform from which substantive research into the antecedents and consequences of union participation can yield consistent and meaningful results. Barling et al. (1992) have argued that there is a need to integrate theories of organizational behavior with the study of unions and unionization. We believe that the organizational citizenship literature and the union participation literature are two domains in which such an integration will be particularly fruitful. In the organizational domain, the importance of employees' (organizational members) going *beyond* delineated roles in order to ensure organizational health and survival has long been recognized. Organizational citizenship behaviors are a form of organizational participation and are one contribution that organizational members make to their organizations in exchange for organizational inducements. In unions, participation is largely voluntary and not directly remunerated. Consequently, understanding the nature of such participation and its antecedents may be particularly crucial. It is our intent to integrate the conceptual framework of organizational citizenship behavior into the domain of union participation in order to reach a richer understanding of union participation, its antecedents, and its outcomes.

As the nature of the global workforce changes in all aspects of diversity, it becomes increasingly important to understand the nature of individual attachment to workplace organizations. The current research has attempted to provide an alternative conceptualization of union participation that differs from traditional measures. We feel that this new definition may have important implications both in terms of union democracy and the efficiency of labor unions as representative and voluntary organizations. Furthermore, the definition of union participation provided here may also be applicable to other kinds of collective action organizations, such as professional, trade, and recreational associations, which are becoming more prevalent in the workplace and changing the nature of employment relations.

REFERENCES

Barling, J., Fullagar, C., & Kelloway E. K. (1992). *The union and its members: A psychological approach.* New York: Oxford University Press.

Blyton, P., Nicholson, N., & Ursell, G. (1981). Job status and white-collar members' union activity. *Journal of Occupational Psychology, 54,* 33–45.

Chacko, T. I. (1985). Member participation in union activities: Perceptions of union priorities, performance, and satisfaction. *Journal of Labor Research, 6,* 363–373.

Cornfield, D. B., Filho, H. B. C., & Chun, B. J. (1990). Household work and labor activism: Gender differences in the determinants of union membership participation. *Work and Occupations, 17,* 131–151.

Deshpande, S. P., & Fiorito, J. (1989). Specific and general beliefs in union voting models. *Academy of Management Journal, 32,* 883–897.

Fiorito, J., Gallagher, D. G., & Fukami, C. V. (1988). Satisfaction with union representation. *Industrial and Labor Relations Review, 41,* 294–307.

Fukami, C. V., & Larson, E. W. (1984). Commitment to company and union: Parallel models. *Journal of Applied Psychology, 69,* 367–371.

Fullagar, C., & Barling, J. (1987). Toward a model of union commitment. *Advances in Industrial and Labor Relations, 4,* 43–78.

Fullagar, C., & Barling, J. (1989). A longitudinal test of a model of the antecedents and consequences of union loyalty. *Journal of Applied Psychology, 74,* 213–227.

Gallagher, D. G., McLean Parks, J., & Wetzel, K. (1987). Methodological considerations in the measurement of union participation: The issue of a multidimensional construct. In R. A. Parsons & J. C. Saber (Eds.), *Proceedings of the Nineteenth Annual Meetings of the Decision Sciences Institute* (pp. 530–533). Boston: Decision Sciences Institute.

Gallagher, D. G., & Strauss, G. (1991). Union membership and participation. In G. Strauss, D. G. Gallagher, & J. Fiorito (Eds.), *The state of the unions* (pp. 139–174). Madison, WI: Industrial Relations Research Association.

George, J. (1991). State or trait: Effects of positive mood on prosocial behaviors at work. *Journal of Applied Psychology, 76,* 299–307.

George, J., & Bettenhausen, K. (1990). Understanding prosocial behavior, sales performance, and turnover: A group level analysis in a service context. *Journal of Applied Psychology, 75,* 698–709.

Gordon, M. E., Philpot, J. W., Burt, R. E., Thompson, C. A., & Spiller, W. E. (1980). Commitment to the union: Development of a measure and an examination of its correlates. *Journal of Applied Psychology, 65,* 479–499.

Graham, J. W. (1986, August). *Organizational citizenship informed by political theory.* Paper presented at the annual meeting of the Academy of Management, Chicago.

Graham, J. W., & Dienesch, R. M. (1991). *Organizational citizenship behavior: Con-*

struct redefinition, operationalization, and validation. Working paper, Loyola University of Chicago.

Hammer, T. H., & Wazeter, D. L. (1993). Dimensions of local union effectiveness. *Industrial and Labor Relations Review, 46,* 302–319.

Hoyman, M. M., & Stallworth, L. (1987). Participation in local unions: A comparison of Black and White members. *Industrial and Labor Relations Review, 40,* 323–335.

Huszczo, G. E. (1983). Attitudinal and behavioral variables related to participation in union activities. *Journal of Labor Research, 4,* 289–297.

Jarley, P., Kuruvilla, S., & Casteel, D. (1990). Member-union relations and union satisfaction. *Industrial Relations, 29,* 129–134.

Kanungo, R. (1982). *Work alienation: An integrative approach.* New York: Wiley.

Karambayya, R. (1992). *Do work unit differences in performance and satisfaction have implications for citizenship behavior?* Working paper, York University, Ontario, Canada.

Katz, D., & Kahn, R. L. (1978). *The social psychology of organizations* (2nd ed.). New York: Wiley.

Kelloway, E. K., & Barling, J. (1993). Members' participation in local union activities: Measurement, prediction and replication. *Journal of Applied Psychology, 78,* 262–279.

Kelloway, E. K., Catano, V., & Southwell, R. (1992). The construct validity of union commitment: Development and dimensionality of a shorter scale. *Journal of Occupational and Organizational Psychology, 65,* 197–212.

Klandermans, B. (1986). Psychology and trade union participation: Joining, acting, quitting. *Journal of Occupational Psychology, 59,* 189–204.

Klandermans, B. (1989). Union commitment: Replications and tests in the Dutch context. *Journal of Applied Psychology, 74,* 869–875.

Kolchin, M. G., & Hyclak, T. (1984). Participation in union activities: A multivariate analysis. *Journal of Labor Research, 5,* 255–262.

Leicht, K. (1991). Unions, plants, jobs and workers: An analysis of union satisfaction and participation. *The Sociological Quarterly, 30,* 331–362.

McLean Parks, J., Gallagher, D. G., & Fullagar, C. (in press). Operationalizing the outcomes of union commitment: The dimensionality of participation. *Journal of Organizational Behavior.*

McShane, S. L. (1986). The multidimensionality of union participation. *Journal of Occupational Psychology, 59,* 177–187.

Moorman, R., Niehoff, B., & Organ, D. (1993). Treating employees fairly and organizational citizenship behavior: Sorting the effects of job satisfaction, organizational commitment and procedural justice. *Employee Responsibilities and Rights Journal, 6,* 209–255.

Newton, L. A., & McFarlane Shore, L. (1992). A model of union membership: Instrumentality, commitment, and opposition. *Academy of Management Review, 17,* 275–298.

Nicholson, N., Ursell, G., & Blyton, P. (1981). *The dynamics of white collar unionism: A study of local union participation.* San Diego, CA: Academic Press.

O'Reilly, C., & Chatman, J. (1986). Organizational commitment and psychological attachment: The effects of compliance, identification, and internalization on prosocial behavior. *Journal of Applied Psychology, 71,* 492–499.

Organ, D. W. (1988). *Organizational citizenship behavior: The good soldier syndrome.* Lexington, MA: Lexington Books.

Organ, D. W. (1990). The motivational basis of organizational citizenship behavior. *Research in Organizational Behavior 12,* 43–72.

Organ, D., & Konovsky, M., (1989). Cognitive versus affective determinants of organizational citizenship behavior. *Journal of Applied Psychology, 74,* 157–164.

Organ, D. W., & Lingl, A. (1991). *Personality, satisfaction, and organizational citizenship behavior.* Unpublished manuscript, University of Indiana, Bloomington.

Perline, M. M., & Lorenz, V. R. (1970). Factors influencing membership participation in trade union activities. *American Journal of Economics and Sociology, 29,* 425–437.

Puffer, S. (1987). Prosocial behavior, noncompliant behavior, and work performance among commission salespeople. *Journal of Applied Psychology, 72,* 615–621.

Smith, C. A., Organ, D. W., & Near, J. P. (1983). Organizational citizenship behavior: Its nature and antecedents. *Journal of Applied Psychology, 68,* 653–663.

Spinrad, W. (1960). Correlates of trade union participation: A summary of the literature. *American Sociological Review, 25,* 237–244.

Tabachnick, B. G., & Fidell, L. S. (1989). *Using multivariate statistics* (2nd ed.). New York: Harper & Row.

Tetrick, L. E. (in press). Developing and maintaining union commitment: A theoretical framework. *Journal of Organizational Behavior.*

Williams, L. J., & Anderson, S. E. (1991). Job satisfaction and organizational commitment as predictors of organizational citizenship and in-role behavior. *Journal of Management, 17,* 601–617.

Wolfe Morrison, E. (1992). *Toward an employee-centered approach to organizational citizenship behavior.* Paper presented at the conference for the Society of Industrial and Organizational Psychology, Montreal, Quebec, Canada.

16

The Nature of Member Participation in Local Union Activities

E. Kevin Kelloway, Victor M. Catano, and
Anthony E. Carroll

I n a context of changing employment relations, the ability of the union to secure the active involvement of members is increasingly threatened. Members' participation in local union activities has been the focus of empirical inquiry for more than 40 years (for reviews, see Barling, Fullagar, & Kelloway, 1992; Perline & Lorenz, 1970; Spinrad, 1960; Strauss, 1977). Labor unions value and espouse democracy in decision making as an end in itself (Fullagar & Barling, 1987). Participation in union activities substantially increases members' involvement in union decision making (Anderson, 1979). In doing so, participation provides members with a "voice" (Hirschman, 1970) within the union and serves as a check on oligarchical tendencies within the organization (Barling et al., 1992; Nicholson, 1978). Not surprisingly, the widespread lack of involvement in union activities is a persistent concern for British (Sherman, 1986) and North American (Huszczo, 1983; R. W. Miller, Zeller, & Miller, 1965) labor leaders.

Members' participation also is plausibly related to the long-term via-

This research was supported by University of Guelph New Faculty Research Grant 896-17 and Social Sciences and Humanities Research Council of Canada Research Grant 41-92-0122. We appreciate the comments of Julian Barling and Lois E. Tetrick on a draft of this chapter.

bility of the union. In the absence of membership participation, the day-to-day responsibilities of running the union fall disproportionately to a small core group of members (R.W. Miller et al., 1965). These active members (often shop stewards and local leaders) devote large amounts of their time to the union (Clegg, Killick, & Adams, 1961; Kelloway, Catano, & Carroll, 1994; Partridge, 1977; Schuller & Robertson, 1983) and experience increased stress due to their involvement in the union and industrial relations (Kelloway & Barling, 1994; Kelloway et al., 1994) as well as the frustrations of dealing with an inactive membership (Winch, 1980, 1983).

Although members' participation has been identified as a predictor of union-relevant criteria such as democracy, more recent research has emphasized participation as an outcome of union attitudes. Specifically, members' participation has been seen as a behavioral outcome of union attitudes such as union commitment (Fullagar & Barling, 1989; Gordon, Philpot, Burt, Thompson, & Spiller, 1980; Kelloway & Barling, 1993; Kelloway, Catano, & Southwell, 1992) and psychological involvement in the union (Kelloway et al., 1994).

THE NATURE OF UNION PARTICIPATION

Participation in union activities has traditionally been defined as a behavioral construct; requiring the expenditure of time on union affairs (e.g., Sayles & Strauss, 1952). There are two distinct aspects to this definition. First, the Sayles and Strauss (1952) definition explicitly excludes measures of union attitudes or behavioral intentions to participate in the union. Although some researchers have used such measures of "willingness to participate" (e.g., Glick, Mirvis, & Harder, 1977), the magnitude of correlations between measures of behavioral intentions to participate and self-reported participation is sufficiently modest (Kelloway & Barling, 1993; Kelloway et al., 1992) to question this practice. Rather, Kelloway et al. (1992) have suggested that such measures are more appropriately viewed as behavioral intentions, rather than actual participation. To qualify as an act of participation, the member must actually *do* something. Although attitudes and intentions may precede or predict such action, they are not required for, nor should they be included in, the definition of participation in union activities.

Second, Sayles and Strauss (1952) suggested that participation requires members to do something that *supports* the union (i.e., the expenditure of time *on union affairs*). More recently, Barling et al. (1992) drew the analogy between members' participation in the union and individual productivity in business organizations. Much like productivity, participation in the union implies that members do things that are sanctioned, encouraged, or even required by the union. Activities such as campaigning *against* the union or disrupting union activities, for example, clearly require the expenditure of time and effort but are not measures of participation in the union per se. Just as organizational researchers have defined productive behavior as that which is relevant to the long-term survival of the company, participation measures must reflect those activities that support, and ensure the continuance of, the union.

To date, researchers have tended to define participation by relying on a small core group of activities such as meeting attendance, voting in union elections, holding union office, serving on union committees, and using the grievance procedure (Spinrad, 1960), with little consideration of how these behaviors might be conceptually related (Kryl, 1990). These behaviors represent "formal" (Fullagar & Barling, 1989; Kahn & Tannenbaum, 1954) participation in the union. They can be regulated or controlled to some extent by the structure or the constitution of the union (G.W. Miller & Young, 1955; Shepard, 1949; Steele, 1951), and they also represent visible forms of union activity.

By definition, these forms of formal participation occur in public and, in this sense, are visible manifestations of union support (Form & Dansereau, 1957). Moreover, formal involvement in the union contributes directly to union democracy. Most definitions of democracy are predicated on an actively involved membership (Kelloway & Barling, 1993). Although formal participation in the union does not guarantee democracy, democracy is unlikely to exist in the absence of such participation. Thus, formal participation in the union is a necessary, but not sufficient, condition for union democracy.

More recently, researchers have also recognized "informal" methods of participating in the union. Informal participation includes activities such as talking about union issues with other union members, campaigning in union elections, and speaking to union leaders about union issues (see, for example, Gordon et al., 1980). The focus on informal participatory behaviors comes about as a result of frequent calls to broaden the construct of participation (e.g., Nicholson, 1978) and to recognize other forms of participation (Barling et al., 1992). However, it is not at all clear that these activities reflect the same construct as measures of formal participation.

In contrast to measures of formal participation, informal participation is not regulated by the union, is not constrained to be a public activity, and is not necessarily supportive of union goals. To extend the Barling et al. (1992) analogy, informal participation in the union may be likened to organizational citizenship behaviors (Organ, 1988). As an organization, the union may rely on but does not encourage or mandate such behaviors. This is not to say that researchers should not be interested in informal participatory behavior. Rather, our suggestion is that such behaviors represent a fundamentally different interpretation of union participation and should be treated separately from formal participation in the union. For purposes of this discussion, we focus on indexes of formal participation in the union.

Given the list of participation measures cited above, it is clear that different forms of formal participation in the union require, or reflect, different levels of union involvement (Kahn & Tannenbaum, 1954; Kelloway & Barling, 1993; Nicholson, 1978). Moreover, some forms of participation, such as union leadership, are possible only for a limited number of individuals at any given time. Thus, in contrast to the "town meeting" model of union democracy described by Anderson (1978, 1979), in which each individual has an equal opportunity to influence union decision making, unions are more appropriately thought of as representational democracies (Kelloway & Barling, 1993). At any given point in time, some forms of participation such as leadership and committee service are available to a relatively small number of elected or appointed representatives. Other forms of participation (e.g., meeting attendance and voting) are open to all members in good standing, albeit at scheduled times.

THE DIMENSIONALITY OF UNION PARTICIPATION

Early research on members' participation in the union has been criticized for failing to recognize the differential involvement of the various forms of participation (McShane, 1986; Nicholson, 1978). Indeed, one early reviewer suggested that research findings were unaffected by the nature of the participation measure (Spinrad, 1960). More recently, researchers have argued for the multidimensional nature of union participation (e.g., Gallagher, McLean-Parks, & Wetzel, 1987; Klandermans, 1986; McShane, 1986).

The argument for the multidimensionality of participation is purely empirical. Both McShane (1986) and Gallagher et al. (1987) have demonstrated that factor analysis of measures of participation *may* result (for conflicting evidence, see Kuruvilla, Gallagher, Fiorito, Wakabayashi, 1990) in a solution containing more than one factor or component. In neither case was the factor structure postulated a priori on the basis of theory or observation. Rather, a set of measures was submitted to an optimizing technique and the results given a substantive interpretation. Therefore, the evidence presented thus far in support of a multidimensional interpretation of union participation is both conceptually and empirically flawed.

Perhaps most importantly, the use of factor analysis to discover the dimensionality of a construct is a fruitless endeavor. Factor analysis can be used to reveal the dimensionality of a given set of measures but not a construct. Indeed, the results of the factor solution may be "conditioned" by including multiple measures of one subdomain. Thus, by including two measures relating to meeting attendance and two relating to voting in addition to five other participation measures, McShane (1986) was able to produce a three-factor solution (Administrative Participation, Meeting Attendance, and Voting). In effect, McShane (1986) achieved a multidimensional solution by oversampling certain aspects of the construct domain. We suggest that this solution tells more about the selection of items than it does about the dimensionality of union participation.

Thus, the evidence for the multidimensional nature of participation is, at best, unconvincing. Analyses supporting a multidimensional interpretation have relied on empiricism rather than theory to specify appropriate measurement models, have failed to consider the nature of their data, and have produced solutions that fail to replicate across (e.g., Kuruvilla et al., 1990) or even within (Gallagher et al., 1987) samples.

Based on these considerations, Kelloway and Barling (1993) hypothesized that participation can be characterized as a unidimensional and cumulative construct. As such, participation measures were expected to be ordered along a continuum of involvement as specified by Nicholson (1978). Specifically, participation measures were expected to follow a Guttman (1947) scale model. In two studies, based on data from four separate unions (overall $N = 1,471$), strong support was found for this hypothesis. In each case, the Guttman scale model provided an excellent fit to the data. Moreover, consistent with the stability of participation (Klandermans, 1986), the scale showed substantial test–retest reliability and correlated in a predictable fashion with external criteria.

What is perhaps most important, the participation measures used by Kelloway and Barling (1993) were selected based on a review of the literature and the exact nature of the relationships between measures was specified a priori based on Nicholson's (1978) analysis. Thus, the analyses reported by Kelloway and Barling (1993) confirmed, rather than became the source for, hypotheses regarding the dimensionality of participation.

THE CURRENT STUDY

Although there has been some debate over the dimensionality of participation measures, to date researchers have not seriously tested their preferred model against the most plausible alternative. Indeed, there has yet to be a simultaneous consideration of more than one measurement model in any given analysis. Yet, without such a test, it is impossible to draw conclusions regarding the most appropriate measurement model for participation data. The purpose of this study was to provide such a comparison. Specifically, we tested three plausible measurement models: an empirically derived multidimensional factor model, a unidimensional confirmatory factor model, and a simplex model (Jöreskog, 1970, 1978; Jöreskog & Sörbom, 1989) as suggested by Kelloway and Barling (1993). Based on the foregoing discussion, we predicted that all three models would provide adequate fits to the data. Obtaining such results would lend support to our suggestion that the dimensionality of participation is not an empirically answerable question.

METHOD

Participants and Procedure

With the consent of the provincial executive, a survey instrument was mailed to 600 shop stewards of a provincial government employees' union. A total of 233 stewards (38.83%) returned completed surveys. The respondents were predominantly male ($n = 145$, 62%) and reported a median education of some university education (range = less than Grade 12 through postgraduate degree). The average age of respondents was 40.73 years ($SD = 7.96$ years). They reported a median union tenure of more than 10 years and had been stewards for an average of 5.83 years ($SD = 4.80$ years).

Measures

Respondents completed the 6-item measure of union participation described by Kelloway and Barling (1993). The respondents were asked to indicate whether, in the past year, they had held union office, served on a union committee, attended union meetings, voted in a union election, contacted the union for help with problems at work, or filed a grievance.

RESULTS

Confirmatory Factor Analysis

Two confirmatory factor analysis models were estimated. First, we estimated a unidimensional factor model hypothesizing one latent variable on which all six participation measures loaded. Second, on the basis of the pattern of loading suggested by an exploratory principal-components analysis, we estimated a two-factor confirmatory factor analysis model with oblique factors. Although we recognize that estimating both exploratory and confirmatory models based on the same data is inappropriate, the two-factor model was estimated to illustrate our contention that empirically derived solutions do not address the dimensionality of participation as a construct.

Both the one-factor model—$\chi^2(9, N = 233) = 12.30$, ns, goodness-of-fit index (GFI) = .98, adjusted goodness-of-fit index (AGFI) = .96, root mean squared residual (RMSR) = .04, normed fit index (NFI) = .96, parsimonious fit index (PFI) = .58—and the two-factor model—$\chi^2(8, N = 233) = 8.49$, ns, GFI = .99, AGFI = .97, RMSR = .03, NFI = .97, PFI = .52—provided acceptable fits to the data. Moreover the difference between the two models was not significant, $\chi^2_{\text{difference}}(1, N = 233) = 3.81$, ns. Standardized parameter estimates for both models are presented in Table 1.

Simplex Analysis

Following Kelloway and Barling (1993), we also examined a quasi-simplex model of participation. In brief, this model posited that holding executive

Table 1

Standardized Parameters for Both Confirmatory Factor Models

Item	One factor	Two factors	
		Factor 1	Factor 2
1. Hold office	.50	.50	
2. Serve on committees	.55	.55	
3. Attend meetings	.86	.86	
4. Vote in elections	.84	.84	
5. Contact union for help	.20		.50
6. File a grievance	.12		.53

NOTE: For the two-factor model the correlation between factors was .39.

office would predict serving on union committees. In turn, committee service would predict voting behavior, which would predict attending union meetings. Meeting attendance was held to predict approaching the union for help, which, in turn, predicted filing a grievance. Again, the resulting model provided an excellent fit to the data, $\chi^2(6, N = 233) = 7.64$, ns, GFI = .99, AGFI = .96, RMSR = .03, NFI = .98, PFI = .39. Serving on the union executive predicted committee service ($\beta = .91$, $p < .01$), which predicted voting in union elections ($\beta = .99$, $p < .01$). Voting predicted meeting attendance ($\beta = .88$, $p < .01$), which predicted contacting the union for help ($\beta = .37$, $p < .01$), which predicted filing grievances ($\beta = .48$, $p < .01$).

DISCUSSION

Empirically, the results of these analyses do not offer unequivocal support for either a multidimensional, unidimensional, or unidimensional and cumulative view of participation in local union activities. The one-factor, two-factor and simplex models each received substantial support, with all three models providing exceptional and essentially equivalent fits to the data. Both factor models were more empirically parsimonious than the simplex model. However, both the simplex model and the one-factor model were more conceptually parsimonious; postulating one rather than two underlying dimensions of participation. Moreover, there was no difference in the fit provided by the one-factor and the two-factor models.

Recognizing the empirical equivalence of the models, we suggest that the unidimensional and cumulative view of participation remains the most viable definition of the construct. There are three reasons for this assertion. First, the two-factor model examined in this study was derived from an exploratory components analysis. The exploratory and confirmatory analyses were based on the same data, thereby loading the dice in favor of the confirmatory factor model. Second, in contrast to both of the factor models presented here, the simplex structure emerges from a theoretical definition of participation in union activities along a single continuum of involvement (Kelloway & Barling, 1993; Nicholson, 1978). Finally, the simplex model tested here has now been replicated in five independent samples (Kelloway & Barling, 1993). The replicability of either the one-factor or the two-factor model remains in question.

We interpret these results to suggest that further (purely) empirical specification of the dimensionality of participation in union activities is unwarranted. Rather, we suggest that researchers would do well to develop and test theory-based models that specify the nature of participation. In brief, we argue that the dimensionality of participation is a theoretical rather than an empirical question. In the current study, the empirical evidence simply does not provide a basis for the rejection of either the multidimensional or the cumulative model of union participation. Our preference for the latter is based not on empirical superiority but on the fact that the model was specified a priori and has been replicated across multiple samples.

FUTURE DIRECTIONS

In the decade or so following the publication of Gordon et al.'s (1980) union commitment scale, researchers were drawn into a protracted debate regarding the dimensionality of the measure (e.g., Friedman & Harvey, 1986; Fullagar, 1986; Kelloway et al., 1992; Klandermans, 1989; Tetrick, Thacker, & Fields, 1989; Thacker, Fields, & Tetrick, 1989). Although there may have been some merit to the continual refinement of the scale, ultimately the debate detracted from more substantive issues relating to both the measurement (see Kelloway et al., 1992) and utility of the construct. As researchers turn their attention to the study of behavioral participation in the union, we run a similar risk. Beyond the dimensionality of the construct, there are more substantive and perhaps ultimately more useful questions to be asked regarding members' participation in union activities.

For example, to date researchers have focused primarily on a limited set of participation measures (Barling et al., 1992; Kelloway & Barling, 1993; Spinrad, 1960) primarily representing formal participation in local union activities. There is some evidence that this focus is changing with researchers now calling for a better, and presumably broader, operationalization of the construct. We endorse this call with several reservations.

Most important, we suggest that a broader sampling of behaviors will not necessarily result in better measurement. Adding items to participation measures on an ad hoc basis is more likely to result in replicating the errors of the past than on explicating the construct of participation. Thus, we condition the call for better operationalization with our call for better conceptual development and selection of the indicators of participation.

We suggest that as researchers move to consider alternate forms of participation they take care not to distort the definition of the construct. Consistent with the foregoing discussion measures of participation must be behavioral and support the goals of the union (Sayles & Strauss, 1952). Deviating from these guidelines distorts rather than operationalizes the construct.

It is also important that in the search for broader measures of participation, researchers ensure an adequate sampling of the construct domain. Failure to do so, for example, by including multiple measures of one form of participation, is likely to result in artifactual "dimensions" of participation. Dimensions produced by such means do not expand our knowledge of the construct. Rather, such measures detract from our knowledge by overemphasizing one aspect of participation at the expense of others. Again, and consistent with our current results, this caution suggests the need for an adequate and comprehensive definition of participation.

Rather than focus exclusively on measurement issues, perhaps a more important question for researchers is, Why study participation in the union? The current research interest in behavioral participation developed from a definition of participation as the criterion for studies of union attitudes (e.g., Kelloway & Barling, 1993). Before this, interest in participation had predicated on largely untested hypotheses relating participation to members' satisfaction with the union, members' support of the union, and union democracy. Implicit in these hypotheses is the notion that participation is directly related to the effectiveness of the union. In selecting measures of participation and more generally conducting research on participation, researchers would be well advised to consider the ultimate criteria of union effectiveness and how participation is related to effectiveness. As unions are faced with changing employment conditions (e.g., part-time work, contingent work) that are reflected in members' availability to become involved in union activities, it will become increasingly important to understand the nature and effects of members' active involvement in the union.

SUMMARY AND CONCLUSION

In summary, we have suggested and empirically demonstrated that the debate over the dimensionality of participation in union activities will not achieve resolution through primarily empirical means. However, we also believe that resolution of the debate has important practical consequences; addressing the question of whether interventions designed to increase participation can be targeted at specific behaviors or whether such interventions would have a more global effect on all forms of participation. In contrast to calls for an adequate operationalization of the construct, we call for rigorous definition and specification of the construct. Such definition should be tied closely to the ultimate criterion of union effectiveness and must be undertaken prior to the development of measures. In doing so we believe that researchers will move toward the production of research results that are both valid and useful to the labor movement.

REFERENCES

Anderson, J. C. (1978). A comparative analysis of local union democracy. *Industrial Relations, 17,* 278–295.

Anderson, J. C. (1979). Local union participation: A reexamination. *Industrial Relations, 18,* 18–31.

Barling, J., Fullagar, C., & Kelloway, E. K. (1992). *The union and its members: A psychological approach.* New York: Oxford University Press.

Clegg, H. A., Killick, A. J., & Adams, R. (1961). *Trade union officers: A study of full-time officers, branch secretaries, and shop stewards in British trade unions.* Oxford, England: Basil Blackwell.

Form, W. M., & Dansereau, H. K. (1957). Union member orientation and patterns of social integration. *Industrial and Labor Relations Review, 11,* 3–12.

Friedman, L., & Harvey, R. J. (1986). Factors of union commitment: The case for a lower dimensionality. *Journal of Applied Psychology, 71,* 371–376.

Fullagar, C. (1986). A factor analytic study on the validity of a union commitment scale. *Journal of Applied Psychology, 71,* 129–137.

Fullagar, C., & Barling, J. (1987). Toward a model of union commitment. *Advances in Industrial and Labor Relations, 4,* 43–78.

Fullagar, C., & Barling, J. (1989). A longitudinal test of a model of the antecedents and consequences of union loyalty. *Journal of Applied Psychology, 74,* 213–227.

Gallagher, D. G., McLean-Parks, J., & Wetzel, K. W. (1987). Methodological considerations in the measurement of union participation: The issue of a multidimensional construct. *Proceedings of the 19th Annual Meeting of the Decision Sciences Institute* (pp. 530–533). Boston, MA.

Glick, W., Mirvis, P., & Harder, D. (1977). Union satisfaction and participation. *Industrial Relations, 16,* 145–151.

Gordon, M. E., Philpot, J. W., Burt, R. E., Thompson, C. A., & Spiller, W. E. (1980). Commitment to the union: Development of a measure and an examination of its correlates. *Journal of Applied Psychology, 65,* 474–499.

Guttman, L. (1947). On Festinger's evaluation of scale analysis. *Psychological Bulletin, 44,* 451–465.

Hirschman, A. O. (1970). *Exit, voice, and loyalty: Responses to decline in firms, organizations, and states.* Cambridge, MA: Harvard University Press.

Huszczo, G. E. (1983). Attitudinal and behavioral variables related to participation in union activities. *Journal of Labor Research, 4,* 289–297.

Jöreskog, K. G. (1970). Estimation and testing of simplex models. *British Journal of Mathematical and Statistical Psychology, 23,* 121–145.

Jöreskog, K. G. (1978). Structural analysis of covariance and correlation matrices. *Psychometrika, 43,* 443–477.

Jöreskog, K. G., & Sörbom, D. (1989). *LISREL VII user's guide.* Mooresville, IN: Scientific Software.

Kahn, R. L., & Tannenbaum, A. S. (1954). Union leadership and member participation. *Personnel Psychology, 10,* 277–292.

Kelloway, E. K., & Barling, J. (1993). Members' participation in local union activities: Measurement, prediction, and replication. *Journal of Applied Psychology, 78,* 262–279.

Kelloway, E. K., & Barling, J. (1994). Industrial relations stress and union activism: Costs and benefits of participation. *Proceedings of the 46th Annual Meeting of the Industrial Relations Research Association* (pp. 442–451). Boston: IRRA.

Kelloway, E. K., Catano, V. M., & Carroll, A. E. (1994). *Psychological involvement in the union: Development of a measure.* Manuscript in preparation.

Kelloway, E. K., Catano, V. M., & Southwell, R. E. (1992). Construct validity of union commitment: Development of a shorter scale. *Journal of Occupational Psychology, 65,* 197–211.

Klandermans, B. (1986). Psychology and trade union participation: Joining, acting, quitting. *Journal of Occupational Psychology, 59,* 189–204.

Klandermans, B. (1989). Union commitment: Replications and tests in the Dutch context. *Journal of Applied Psychology, 72,* 319–332.

Kryl, I. P. (1990). *Causal modelling of predictors and outcomes of trade union participation.* Unpublished doctoral dissertation, Queen's University, Kingston, Ontario, Canada.

Kuruvilla, S., Gallagher, D. G., Fiorito, J., & Wakabayashi, M. (1990). Union participation in Japan: Do Western theories apply? *Industrial and Labor Relations Review, 43,* 374–389.

McShane, S. L. (1986). The multidimensionality of union participation. *Journal of Occupational Psychology, 59,* 177–187.

Miller, G. W., & Young, J. F. (1955). Membership participation in the trade union local. *American Journal of Economics and Sociology, 15,* 36–43.

Miller, R. W., Zeller, F. A., & Miller, G. W. (1965). *The practice of local union leadership: A study of five union locals.* Columbus: Ohio State University Press.

Nicholson, N. (1978). Mythology, theory and research on union democracy. *Industrial Relations Journal, 9,* 32–41.

Organ, D. W. (1988). *Organizational citizenship behavior.* Lexington, MA: Lexington Books.

Partridge, B. (1977). The activities of shop stewards. *Industrial Relations Journal, 8,* 28–42.

Perline, M. M., & Lorenz, V. R. (1970). Factors influencing member participation in trade union activities. *American Journal of Economics and Sociology, 29,* 425–437.

Sayles, L. R., & Strauss, G. (1952). Patterns of participation in local unions. *Industrial and Labor Relations Review, 6,* 221–231.

Schuller, T., & Robertson, D. (1983). How representatives allocate their time: Shop steward activity and membership contact. *British Journal of Industrial Relations, 21,* 330–342.

Shepard, H. A. (1949). Democratic control in a labor union. *American Journal of Sociology, 54,* 311–316.

Sherman, B. (1986). *The state of the unions.* New York: Wiley.

Spinrad, W. (1960). Correlates of trade union participation: A summary of the literature. *American Sociological Review, 25,* 237–244.

Steele, H. E. (1951). Membership participation in the Flint Glass Worker's Union. *Southern Economic Journal, 18,* 83–92.

Strauss, G. (1977). Union government in the U.S.: Research past and future. *Industrial Relations, 16,* 215–242.

Tetrick, L. E., Thacker, J. W., & Fields, M. W. (1989). Evidence for the stability of the four dimensions of the Commitment to the Union Scale. *Journal of Applied Psychology, 74,* 819–822.

Thacker, J. W., Fields, M. W., & Tetrick, L. E. (1989). The factor structure of union commitment: An application of confirmatory factor analysis. *Journal of Applied Psychology, 74,* 228–232.

Winch, G. (1980). Shop steward tenure and workplace organization. *Industrial Relations Journal, 11,* 50–62.

Winch, G. (1983). The turnover of shop stewards. *Industrial Relations Journal, 14,* 84–86.

17

Some Remaining Challenges

Michael E. Gordon, Julian Barling, and Lois E. Tetrick

The preceding chapters have made it clear that important changes are taking place in employment relationships throughout the industrial world. Employers have experienced increasing pressures to be competitive in the global environment and have responded to them by experimenting with new management and human resources' strategies. However, the effectiveness of the strategies that have been implemented has yet to be determined, and several of the chapters have presented theoretical and empirical evidence that suggests that the strategies may have negative effects on the employees and, in the long run, organizational effectiveness.

Organized labor has not been impervious to these changes. The increasingly competitive commercial environment has heightened the determination of managements worldwide to resist unionization. The prevalence of collective bargaining has declined in many industrial democracies (Chaison & Rose, 1991). In the United States, the proportion of private-sector, nonagricultural workers who were union members dropped from 35% in the 1950s to 11.2% in 1993. The severity and perplexity of this decline is more apparent when one considers that public opinion polls continue to show that most Americans express approval of unions and the right of workers to organize unions of their choice. E.E. Lawler and Mohrman (1987) pointed out that society should be very concerned about the weakening of organized labor, which has been an important voice for workers. The Dunlop Commission was similarly distressed by the apparent loss of an effective voice for workers, especially in its discussions of "contingent" worker–management relations and grievance arbitration in nonunion settings (Commission on the Future of Worker–Management Relations, 1994).

The purpose of this concluding chapter is to suggest how psychological research and theory can contribute to our understanding of these changes in employment relations. We focus here on three issues: who sets the research agenda; where behavioral research might usefully contribute to the effectiveness of organized labor in these changing times; and how we might usefully diversify the research methods used to study the problems confronting trade unions.

WHO SETS THE RESEARCH AGENDA?

With regard to the changing employment relationship, we must ask ourselves who sponsors and who receives the benefits of behavioral research on trade unions. In other words, why and for whom are we doing the research? In one sense, individuals do research in a particular arena because they choose to do so irrespective of its direct relevance in addressing organizational or social issues. As Hackman (1985) stated, "I strongly prefer to see a student do first-rate scholarship that has uncertain relevance for action than second-rate work that is immediately applicable to some organizational problem" (p .127). However, regardless of the impetus for the research or its immediate applicability, Pettigrew (1985) noted, "the activity of research is clearly a social process, not merely a rationally contrived act" (p. 222). Thus, it is important that researchers remain aware of the consequences and context of their research.

Within the context of research on unions, Gordon and Nurick (1981) noted that we have to consider whether our research is conducted on behalf of unions or management. We extend this argument here to ask whether the research we will conduct within the context of changing employment relations will serve our own academic interests, or will satisfy the needs of employers, their employees, or both. Campbell, Daft, and Hulin (1982) addressed this predicament by suggesting that significant research is most likely to occur when researchers are subjectively interested and involved in the topic and when they choose their research questions by asking their subjects, in this case employees, what the real issues are. We suggest that these two factors dictate how we should be setting our research agenda on changing employment conditions.

CHALLENGES TO ORGANIZED LABOR

These changing times have increased the salience of two issues to organized labor that were not considered in great detail in the preceding chapters: union organizing and leadership. Clearly, winning the right to represent employees must occur far more frequently than it does presently if the decline in union membership is to be reversed. At the same time, the challenge to union organizers has never been greater, given the hostility of employer campaigns to prevent certification and to provide tacit support for decertification efforts of unionized employees (J. J. Lawler, 1990).

Union leaders also have many new challenges. Increasingly, union officials are being asked to renounce traditional approaches to dealing with employment issues and instead embrace cooperative relations with management, including such programs as quality of work life or employee involvement. In helping to negotiate a meaningful role for unions in these new employment relationships, union leaders must be resourceful in helping employers deal with competitive pressures while remaining sensitive to the concerns of their union constituents about job security and justice in the workplace.

Whereas organizing has been the subject of numerous studies in the past, leadership has not received much attention from North American scholars (Barling, Fullagar, & Kelloway, 1992). It is our objective to raise questions about psychological and behavioral research on these matters.

Organizing

Psychologists seeking to apply behavioral science to the problems of organized labor have long recognized that organizing was among the most salient concerns of unions (Gordon & Nurick, 1981). Winning the support of workers to gain recognition for a union is the first step in creating union–management relations and gaining influence in the employment relationship. A great deal of research has been devoted to identifying the personal and organizational variables that are related to the willingness of workers to seek collective bargaining (Heneman & Sandver, 1983).

Despite the earlier popularity of this topic and its obvious importance to labor, organizing is, today, largely neglected by researchers. Several reasons may be cited for this current neglect. First, given the inclination of employers throughout the world to combat unionism, especially in the United States (Chaison & Rose, 1991), the goal of affecting the outcome of union organizing campaigns may be served better by legal initiatives than by additional behavioral studies. Second, research using actuarial methods of forecasting sentiment for union certification has already investigated many, if not most, salient predictors (Barling et al., 1992). Few stones appear to have been left unturned in the search for antecedents of support for unionization. Furthermore, there is substantial agreement across studies that job satisfaction and perceived union instrumentality consistently predict voting intentions and behavior in certification elections and that these two variables are central to models of the decision to join a union (e.g., Brett, 1980a; Premack & Hunter, 1988).

Research on organizing has reached a point of diminishing returns, and psychologists may have decided that the time is ripe to pursue new interests. If this is the case, it is relevant to ask what has been learned about the role of job satisfaction and perceived union instrumentality in organizing, that is, the process that *precedes* the union vote. Thus, we question whether the information collected about the unionization process by means of behavioral research has any potential application to union organizing campaigns.

Dissatisfaction with the employment relationship is the beginning of the union organizing process. Acting as individuals, most employees are not able to change the nature of the employment relationship so that it becomes more favorable to their interests. A coalition of similarly dissatisfied workers is required as a basis for a union organizing campaign. However, evidence about the role of job satisfaction is based on research in which the individual is the unit of analysis. The link between individual dissatisfaction and the outcome of the certification election is less direct because election-level research has not used job satisfaction as a predictor variable. Nonetheless, Heneman and Sandver (1983, footnote 4) indicated that the actual vote distribution in the certification election was found to be "very similar" to self-reported votes of the individual participants. Given the similarity between the distributions for job satisfaction and self-reported vote, it would not be unreasonable to expect that the extent of job dissatisfaction among a group of workers would predict the number of votes for the union and hence the election outcome.

The second central variable in models of unionization is perceived union instrumentality. Union instrumentality is defined as the perceived impact of the union on traditional work conditions (e.g., wages, benefits, job security, promotions, hours of work, and health and safety) and non-traditional work conditions (e.g., employee productivity, treatment of employees, employee–management relations, job satisfaction, and company profitability) that define the employment relationship (Shore, Tetrick, Sinclair, & Newton, 1994). Conceptually, instrumentality perceptions vary in direction (i.e., the impact of the union may be viewed as beneficial or harmful) and strength (i.e., the degree of confidence that the union will improve or harm the conditions). The intent to vote for union representation is related to the strength of expectations that collective bargaining will result in improved working conditions. "In the end, a decision to organize a union is instrumental. Do employees involved believe they will be better off with a union or not?" (Brett, 1980b, p. 49).

The major implications of these research findings on unionization are that unions might target organizing campaigns toward workplaces where there is substantial job dissatisfaction and there is some agreement among workers about the usefulness of unions in alleviating the unpleasant working conditions. Unfortunately, union officials are unlikely to consider these suggestions very enlightening. Indeed, organizers probably were well aware of the role of union instrumentality long before behavioral scientists discovered these phenomena. The importance of instrumentality is not lost on the present generation of union organizers, either. For example, in *Diary of an Organizer*, a conversation is described with a worker named Wendy in a suit manufacturing plant.

> Wendy, meanwhile, was willing to argue with me, although she didn't trust me. Her first words were the inevitable, "I need my job, you know." Then she questioned me about what the union could do for her. That's the best sign. (Windham, 1994, p. 38–39)

Research on organizing has stopped short of resolving a number of quite fundamental questions, the answers to which would be of substantial value to unions. For example, although perceived union instrumentality clearly is the "fulcrum" of the unionization process (Barling et al., 1992), little is known about how perceptions of union instrumentality develop. Union instrumentality has been treated as an exogenous variable in all recent research on predicting the intent to vote for a union; that is, the instrumentality variable is assumed to be determined by factors outside the causal model under consideration (e.g., Brief & Rude, 1981; Montgomery, 1989). Consequently, no attempt has been made to explain the variability in union instrumentality. It is unfortunate from the standpoint of unions that psychologists appear to have concluded their studies of organizing with a widely known pronouncement about the importance of union instrumentality. Far more useful in the future, in our opinion, would be work that results in a set of recommendations about organizing tactics grounded in behavioral science that are likely to influence the development of perceptions of unions being instrumental in the attainment of a variety of valued worker goals.

In addition, we suggest that a critical question is why some individuals choose not to vote in union certification elections. Roomkin and Block (1981) have shown that the margin of victory in certification elections is often so small that the abstainers could have changed the outcome. Initial analyses (Hepburn, Loughlin, & Barling, 1994) suggest that abstainers lie between pro-union and anti-union voters with respect to job satisfaction and union attitudes but that they also differ from both those groups with respect to how instrumental they believe their vote would be and their general interest in the election. This is an area for future research that could be central to union organizing.

In our view, psychologists should revive their interest in studying organizing. However, to do so may mean that traditional concepts and methodologies will have to be put aside in favor of less familiar epistemological approaches. In searching for a new epistemology, consider the comment of a union organizer from the Amalgamated Clothing and Textile Workers Union. When asked what he considered to be the most important determinant of the success of an organizing campaign, he answered that the outcome will be determined by who gets to describe the plant first to the workers, the union or management. This reply reflects an intuitive understanding of the principle of socially constructed environments (Berger & Luckman, 1966), that is, that the reality of a situation is determined in part by our interactions with significant others.

The reality of a "union" is dependent on social constructions that are shared among a number of people and that allow for coordinated action. However, unions and union representation are social constructions that are subject to wide differences in interpretation because they are imbued with meaning as a consequence of social processes. Given this conceptual starting point, the job of the union organizer may be described as assisting individual workers to construct a social reality of work with redefined notions of power sharing and worker rights. The organizer must help instill the belief that workers are entitled to due process in the workplace and that they can challenge certain management decisions. Furthermore, there must be consensus that these entitlements may be obtained only as a result of casting one's lot with fellow workers and facing the prospect of having to sacrifice personal goals, on occasion, for the good of others. Thus, the organizer's task is an imaginative one, providing a framework to account for the stream of events and actions that occur during the organizing campaign and supplying a social context within which organizational events and experiences take on meaning. The organizer is less a decision maker and more a creator of contexts in which decisions become meaningful. Organizers should recognize that they cannot control events, but they can influence the context against which events take on meaning through their use of stories, language, rituals, and symbols.

Leadership

It is no coincidence that we address the topic of leadership together with union organizing; indeed, the two topics go hand in hand. Although organizing constitutes one of the greatest challenges to present union officials, bold initiatives and inspirational leadership will be required to realize unions' organizing goals. For example, without becoming more inclusive through the effective representation of more minority and female workers, unions are unlikely to reverse the decline in membership levels in today's brutal industrial relations climate. Perhaps the goals of attaining greater inclusiveness and providing more effective representation would be more likely if, instead of being almost the exclusive province of White men, more top leadership positions were held by women and people of color, who constitute approximately 40% and 22%, respectively, of unionized workers (Bureau of Labor Statistics, 1992).

In terms of its salience for the problems of society as a whole, research on leadership always has been considered one of the most important undertakings of behavioral scientists (e.g., Rahim, 1981; Vroom, 1976). Literally thousands of studies of leadership were produced by social and industrial psychologists, although research by the former has decreased since the 1970s to a "quite modest" level (Meindl, 1993, p. 90). Although the popular appeal of this material is unquestioned, it may have little relevance for understanding union leadership. Indeed, it would be difficult to isolate any major leadership research within a psychological framework that has directly focused on union leaders.

However, the limited generalizability of current leadership literature is not simply a matter of its failure to study union officials directly. Rather, it is the assumptions that leadership is leader centered and that followers have unimportant roles to play in determining the behavior and organizational impact of leaders that limit the usefulness of leadership theory to unions. These assumptions are more apparent when one considers the agenda of leadership research over the past 40 years that was aimed at improving the application of leadership in business organizations. Study began with a search for various physical and dispositional characteristics that identified good leaders and then was dominated by inquiries about particular behaviors that constituted effective and ineffective leadership.

The current convention in leadership paints a portrait of leadership in terms of a process that the leader ultimately controls:

> Although mutual influence processes between leaders and followers are recognized, leadership is mostly conceptualized as something seized on, and exerted, by the leader. It is something to be performed by the leader; it is dispensed to, and used on, followers to influence and control them. (Meindl, 1993, p. 99)

This focus on the behavioral displays of leaders is consistent with the idea that they can wield considerable power. Managers, the subjects of most research on leadership, exercise control by virtue of their appointment to positions in a formal hierarchy that imbues them with legitimate power over subordinates. By contrast, union leaders have been empowered by their constituencies. Hence, union leaders are emergent leaders, and the legitimacy of their authority is derived from their election by constituents. This distinction is quite important because, if for no other reason, it offers clues as to where one is likely to find relevant literature that might provide theoretical and empirical foundations for informed study of leadership in unions.

Perhaps the research of greatest relevance to union leadership in this respect is the work of Hollander and his associates (e.g., Hollander, Fallon, & Edwards, 1977; Hollander & Julian, 1969). Appointed and emergent leaders were compared in a series of studies by examining the effects of the legitimacy of their authority. Basically, authority is a potential for action in social exchanges that occur within a social system. "Whether a leader's authority comes from appointment or election has been found to have distinct consequences for leader–follower relations" (Hollander, 1985, p. 507). These studies indicate that followers have greater personal investments in elected than appointed leaders. However, when things go wrong (i.e., the leader is perceived to lack competence or does not produce a favorable outcome), elected leaders are more susceptible to follower rejection. In negotiations experiments, elected representatives felt freer to yield on particular issues than appointed representatives, which was attributed to the elected representatives' lesser concern that taking liberties in reaching an agreement would compromise the loyalty of the group. Hollander (1985) suggested that these findings indicate that followers expect greater responsibility and success from leaders whom they elect.

Given the lack of substantial reward and coercive powers, Barling et al. (1992) pointed out that the traditional bases of influence for transactional leadership are not available to union leaders, who therefore cannot contrive effort exchanges (e.g., rewards in exchange for compliance). Consequently, influencing constituents is more reliant on transformational leadership, which is characterized by three factors:

> (1) charisma, whereby the union leader instills a sense of pride in the union and transmits the unions' mission, (2) individual consideration, which refers to the leaders' stimulation of learning experiences and individual involvement of rank-and-file members, and (3) intellectual stimulation, whereby the leader is intellectually innovative and stimulating, providing union members with new ways of looking at organizational issues. (Barling et al., 1992, p. 145)

Greater member identification with the goals of organized labor, and greater willingness to participate in voluntary union activities, presumably will be brought about by transformational leaders who cause members to behave in ways that transcend narrow self-interest.

The importance of transformational leadership is apparent in the writings of the few individuals who have investigated the effects of union leadership. Eaton (1992) linked the survival of organized labor to a stronger and more clearly articulated moral vision. Indeed, "union leadership is fundamentally moral leadership" (Eaton, 1992, p. 1). Given the aforementioned volatility of the international business environment, the viability of organized labor cannot be entirely based on economic self-interest. Rather, it is incumbent on union leaders to disseminate the fundamental message of organized labor's commitment to social and economic justice.

Lokar (1994) introduced some intriguing ideas about transformational leadership and union structure. His "falling dominoes" thesis states that transformational leadership at higher levels of a union will cascade downward within the union to produce a sense of empowerment among stewards. Stewards, in turn, are likely to increase their extrarole behaviors (e.g., exercising more initiative and persistence in the handling of grievances and promoting member participation) to produce a sense of empowerment among the rank and file. These ideas await empirical verification and further theoretical development. For example, like many of its conceptual predecessors, Lokar's characterization of transformational leadership is leader centered and overlooks the role of followers. Consequently, the notion of leadership "cascading down" may be misplaced in a union organization. Also, Hogan, Raskin, and Fazzini (1990) pointed out that there can be a "dark side" to charismatic leadership. Charismatic leaders with strong narcissistic needs and needs for personal power can have destructive effects on the organization and their followers.

In summary, there is a great deal of research that can provide inductive and deductive bases for future empirical study of leadership in unions. Given the complexity of the subject and the vastness of the relevant literature, we have not attempted to define a research agenda. However, we do note that the processes relevant to leadership at the national and local levels might well differ and require different research questions as well as strategies. Nonetheless, we are convinced that the study of leadership in unions promises benefits not just to officials of organized labor and their followers, but to the discipline of psychology as well. Perhaps a more complete picture of leadership will be developed if its emergence is examined in the context of unions. Such a program of research would unavoidably be drawn to the role of followers by the political nature of union office and, its focus, just as inevitably, would be linked to the essence of leadership per se: "Leadership is not something a leader possesses so much as a process involving followership" (Hollander, 1993, p. 29).

CHANGING TIMES CALL FOR COMPLEX
RESEARCH DESIGNS

Mitroff (1985) raised the question as to "why our old pictures of the world do not work anymore" (p. 18). In part, he suggested that we need to study the world as an organism. This suggestion implies that employment relationships can be understood only by examining all of the stakeholders within the employing organization (e.g., management, the employees and unions) as well as the larger social, political, and economic milieus in which the organizations (both the employing organization and the union) and individuals are embedded. In order to conduct research within these multiple levels of analysis, one must first understand the phenomenon. Understanding at the more basic level may require descriptive research or more sophisticated methods underlying the analysis of dynamic systems (e.g., Levine & Fitzgerald, 1992) before we can embark on research that has implications for practice.

For example, we earlier cast union organizing into the conceptual framework of socially constructed environments. This presents both new problems and opportunities for psychologists and behavioral researchers to develop more meaningful insights into the organizing process. Among the more obvious problems is the fact that the study of how we attach meaning to things, events, and people has not been a traditional area of study for industrial and organizational psychologists. Rather, the fields of interpretative sociology, the sociology of knowledge, and cognitive social psychology have focused on the processes by which humans come to share particular visions of the world and organizations within it.

Following these theoretical guidelines also recommends reliance on a variety of unfamiliar research methodologies. As opposed to the quantitative, actuarial approach used by many behavioral scientists in studying union organizing, social scientists who have conducted research on socially constructed environments have relied on qualitative methodologies. For example, in one study of union organizing derived from the social constructionist perspective, Prasad (1991) used document analysis and in-depth interviews to reconstruct the successful organizing campaign of Local 34 of the Hotel Employees and Restaurant Employees among clerical and technical workers at Yale University. Another qualitative approach, ethnography, entails getting to know an organization "from the native's point of view" (Schwartzman, 1993, p. 1). This may entail researchers' becoming participants in organizing campaigns as a way of deriving meaning from the events and activities.

Psychologists interested in the study of unions can expect several types of returns from their investments in new theory and methods that may guide future research along salient paths and broaden our insights into the organizing process. For example, from a vantage point on the ground, it may become more obvious how union instrumentality is developed. This information would appear to be useful to union organizers who might prepare more effective tactics for persuading workers to vote for unions. Also, behavioral scientists might embellish models of the unionization process that, as indicated above, have not thoroughly examined union instrumentality. Finally, research using the social constructionist metaphor has rarely been used to study organization creation (Prasad, 1991). Rather, biological metaphors, such as the population ecology model, have been used to examine organization building (e.g., Hanan & Freeman, 1987). Unfortunately, these organismic perspectives are not particularly informative as to what brings people together and how they identify emerging social relations as the foundation for an organization. The social construction metaphor directs one to examine the subjective meanings of actions for various members of the emerging organization, and unions would be studied as constructions and destructions of meaning.

There is a second institutional benefit to be derived from the suggested approach. The collection and analysis of data in an ethnographic study probably will require researchers to become more aware of day-to-day activities in a union. As a consequence, the psychologist is likely to gain a far more intimate and detailed understanding of unions and union leaders. In addition, union members are likely to gain a better appreciation of who psychologists are and what they try to accomplish with their science. Developing a better, more productive relationship between psychologists and unions has been a long-standing challenge (Gordon & Nurick, 1981;

Shostak, 1964). Perhaps this research approach will accomplish what conferences and research bulletins intended to build bridges between academicians and organized labor have failed to achieve in the past.

The ultimate, practical question is whether a meaningful course of action or intervention can be developed based on our research. Organizations, whether corporations or unions, are unlikely to let us intervene without some assurance that the intended consequences have value to the enterprise and are likely to occur given proper implementation of the intervention. To provide such assurance, researchers need to have the richer understanding of the environment that can be derived from qualitative research and an established working relationship with the organization. Therefore, the coupling of qualitative research with more traditional methodologies (such as creative quasi-experimental designs like that used by Catano, Cole, & Hebert, 1994) promises to advance our understanding of the challenges of changing employment relations and strategies for meeting these challenges.

CONCLUSION

Throughout this book, the focus has been on changing employment relations. Specifically, the nature and extent of changing employment relations have been examined as have some of the consequences for organizations and their members. The similarities across national boundaries are striking. Employers are reducing their commitment to individuals by providing less long-term, full-time employment. Employees are experiencing increased stress because they must work harder in the short term with less job security for the long term. At the same time, declining union representation removes protection of the workers from arbitrary actions on the part of the employer. Similarly, diversification of the workforce in many countries has made the task of satisfying workers' needs and expectations more complicated for both employers and union.

Fundamental changes have occurred in employment relations, and most of our contributors expect change to be a hallmark of organizations in the future. Some of these changes will be the result of internal processes in the organizations themselves (e.g., new forms of union representation, mandated works councils in Europe, and the acceptance of social clauses by transnational firms that guarantee minimum workers' rights). Other changes will occur as a consequence of volatility in the economic, political, and social environments. Recognizing this, it is apparent that future research on unions should be informed by both the concepts and methods of other disciplines, such as social psychology and social cognition theory, and should recognize the insights and units of provided by other epistemologies, such as the social construction of reality. This is especially important in understanding employment relations that are changing and that are defined by multiple actors and groups with common as well as conflicting interests.

REFERENCES

Barling, J., Fullagar, C., & Kelloway, E. K. (1992). *The union and its members: A psychological approach.* New York: Oxford University Press.

Berger, P. L., & Luckman, T. (1966). *The social construction of reality: A treatise in the sociology of knowledge.* New York: Doubleday.

Brett, J. M. (1980a). Behavioral research on unions and union management systems. In B. M. Staw & L. L. Cummings (Eds.), *Research in organizational behavior* (Vol. 2, pp. 177–213). Greenwich, CT: JAI Press.

Brett, J. M. (1980b). Why employees want unions. *Organizational Dynamics, 8,* 47–59.

Brief, A. P., & Rude, D. E. (1981). Voting in union certification elections: A conceptual analysis. *Academy of Management Review, 6,* 261–267.

Bureau of Labor Statistics. (1992). *Union members in 1991* (U.S. Department of Labor Publication No. 92–61). Washington, DC: U.S. Government Printing Office.

Campbell, J. P., Daft, R. L., & Hulin, C. L. (1982). *What to study: Generating and developing research questions.* Beverly Hills, CA: Sage.

Catano, V. M., Cole, G. K., & Hebert, N. (1994, May). *Can union commitment be developed? An exploratory analysis.* Paper presented at the Conference on the Psychology of Industrial Relations Under Changing Employment Relationships: An International Perspective, Detroit, MI.

Chaison, G. N., & Rose, J. B. (1991). The macrodeterminants of union growth and decline. In G. Strauss, D. G. Gallagher, & J. Fiorito (Eds.), *The state of the unions* (pp. 3–45). Madison, WI: Industrial Relations Research Association.

Eaton, S. C. (1992). *Union leadership development in the 1990s and beyond* (Center for Science and International Affairs Discussion Paper No. 92-05). Cambridge, MA: Kennedy School of Government, Harvard University.

Commission on the Future of Worker–Management Relations. (1994). *Fact finding report.* Washington, DC: U.S. Department of Labor.

Gordon, M. E., & Nurick, A. J. (1981). Psychological approaches to the study of unions and union-management relations. *Psychological Bulletin, 90,* 293–306.

Hackman, J. R. (1985). Doing research that makes a difference. In E. E. Lawler, A. M. Mohrman, S. A. Mohrman, G. E. Ledford, T. G. Cummings, & Associates (Eds.), *Doing research that is useful for theory and practice* (pp. 126–148). San Francisco: Jossey-Bass.

Hanan, M. T., & Freeman, J. (1987). The ecology of organizational founding: American labor unions, 1836–1985. *American Journal of Sociology, 92,* 910–943.

Heneman, H. G., & Sandver, M. H. (1983). Predicting the outcome of union certification elections: A review of the literature. *Industrial and Labor Relations Review, 36,* 537–559.

Hepburn, C. G., Loughlin, C., & Barling, J. (1994). *To vote or not to vote in a union representation election: That is the research question.* Manuscript in preparation.

Hogan, R., Raskin, R., & Fazzini, D. (1990). The dark side of charisma. In K. E. Clark & M. B. Clark (Eds.), *Measures of leadership* (pp. 343–354). West Orange, NJ: Leadership Library of America.

Hollander, E. P. (1985). Leadership and power. In G. Lindzey & E. Aronson (Eds.), *The handbook of social psychology* (3rd ed., pp. 485–537). New York: Random House.

Hollander, E. P. (1993). Legitimacy, power, and influence: A perspective on relational features of leadership. In M. M. Chemers & R. Ayman (Eds.), *Leadership theory and research: Perspectives and directions* (pp. 29–47). San Diego, CA: Academic Press.

Hollander, E. P., Fallon, B. J., & Edwards, M. T. (1977). Some aspects of influence and acceptability for appointed and elected group leaders. *Journal of Psychology, 95,* 289–296.

Hollander, E. P., & Julian, J. W. (1969). Contemporary trends in the analysis of leadership processes. *Psychological Bulletin, 71,* 387–397.

Lawler, E. E., & Mohrman, S. A. (1987). Unions and the new management. *The Academy of Management Executive, 1*, 293–300.

Lawler, J. J. (1990). *Unionization and deunionization: Strategy, tactics and outcomes.* Columbia: University of South Carolina Press.

Levine, R. L., & Fitzgerald, H. E. (Eds.). (1992). *Analysis of dynamic psychological systems: Methods and applications.* New York: Plenum.

Lokar, T. G. (1994, May). *A social–cognitive approach to the empowerment of shop stewards: The role of transformational leadership at upper-levels of union leadership.* Paper presented to the Conference on the Psychology of Industrial Relations Under Changing Employment Relationships: An International Perspective, Detroit, MI.

Meindl, J. R. (1993). Reinventing leadership: A radical, social psychological approach. In J. K. Murnighan (Ed.), *Social psychology in organizations: Advances in theory and research* (pp. 89–118). Englewood Cliffs, NJ: Prentice Hall.

Mitroff, I. I. (1985). Why our old pictures of the world do not work anymore. In E. E. Lawler, A. M. Mohrman, S. A. Mohrman, G. E. Ledford, T. G. Cummings, & Associates (Eds.), *Doing research that is useful for theory and practice* (pp. 18–35). San Francisco: Jossey-Bass.

Montgomery, B. R. (1989). The influence of attitudes and normative pressures on voting decisions in a union certification election. *Industrial and Labor Relations Review, 42*, 262–279.

Pettigrew, A. M. (1985). Contextualist research: A natural way to link theory and practice. In E. E. Lawler, A. M. Mohrman, S. A. Mohrman, G. E. Ledford, T. G. Cummings, & Associates (Eds.), *Doing research that is useful for theory and practice* (pp. 222–248). San Francisco: Jossey-Bass.

Prasad, P. (1991). Organization building at Yale. *Journal of Applied Behavioral Science, 27*, 337–355.

Premack, S. L., & Hunter, J. E. (1988). Individual unionization decisions. *Psychological Bulletin, 103*, 223–234.

Rahim, A. (1981). Organizational behavior course for graduate students in business administration: Views from the tower and battlefield. *Psychological Reports, 49*, 583–592.

Roomkin, M., & Block, R. (1981). Case processing time and the outcome of representative elections: Some empirical evidence. *University of Illinois Law Review, 1*, 75–97.

Schwartzman, H. B. (1993). *Ethnography in organizations.* Newbury Park, CA: Sage.

Shore, L. M., Tetrick, L. E., Sinclair, R. R., & Newton, L. A. (1994). Validation of a measure of perceived union support. *Journal of Applied Psychology, 79,* 971–977.

Shostak, A. B. (1964). Industrial psychology and the trade unions: A matter of mutual indifference. In G. Fisk (Ed.), *The frontiers of management psychology* (pp. 144–155). New York: Harper.

Vroom, V. (1976). Leadership. In M. D. Dunnette (Ed.), *Handbook of industrial/ organizational psychology* (pp. 1527–1551). Chicago: Rand McNally.

Windham, L. (1994, Spring). Diary of an organizer. *Southern Exposure,* pp. 36–41.

Author Index

Numbers in italics refer to listings in the reference sections.

Subject Index

About the Editors

Lois E. Tetrick is professor of psychology at the University of Houston. She received her doctorate in industrial/organizational psychology from the Georgia Institute of Technology and was a member of the psychology faculty at Wayne State University in Detroit before moving to Houston. She is the author of numerous journal articles and serves on the editorial boards of the *Journal of Applied Psychology*, the *Journal of Organizational Behavior*, the *Journal of Occupational Health Psychology*, and *Advanced Topics in Organizational Behavior*.

Julian Barling is professor of organizational behavior in the School of Business, Queen's University, Kingston, Ontario, Canada. He received his doctorate in psychology from the University of the Witwatersrand, South Africa. He is the author of *Employment, Stress, and Family Functioning; The Union and Its Members: A Psychological Approach* (with Clive J. A. Fullagar and E. Kevin Kelloway); and numerous journal articles. He is currently coeditor of the Sage series *Advanced Topics in Organizational Behavior*, consulting editor of the *Journal of Organizational Behavior*, and on the editorial boards of the *Journal of Occupational Health Psychology* and *Stress Medicine*. He served previously as the chair of the Advisory Council on Occupational Health and Safety to the Minister of Labour in Ontario.